W9-DBE-715

HABITS OF THOUGHT
IN THE ENGLISH RENAISSANCE

The New Historicism: Studies in Cultural Poetics
Stephen Greenblatt, General Editor

1. *Holy Feast and Holy Fast: The Religious Significance of Food to Medieval Women,* by Caroline Walker Bynum
2. *The Gold Standard and the Logic of Naturalism: American Literature at the Turn of the Century,* by Walter Benn Michaels
3. *Nationalism and Minor Literature: James Clarence Mangan and the Emergence of Irish Cultural Nationalism,* by David Lloyd
4. *Shakespearean Negotiations: The Circulation of Social Energy in Renaissance England,* by Stephen Greenblatt
5. *The Mirror of Herodotus: The Representation of the Other in the Writing of History,* by François Hartog, translated by Janet Lloyd
6. *Puzzling Shakespeare: Local Reading and Its Discontents,* by Leah S. Marcus
7. *The Rites of Knighthood: The Literature and Politics of Elizabethan Chivalry,* by Richard C. McCoy
8. *Literary Practice and Social Change in Britain, 1380–1530,* edited by Lee Patterson
9. *Trials of Authorship: Anterior Forms and Poetic Reconstruction from Wyatt to Shakespeare,* by Jonathan Crewe
10. *Rabelais's Carnival: Text, Context, Metatext,* by Samuel Kinser
11. *Behind the Scenes: Yeats, Horniman, and the Struggle for the Abbey Theatre,* by Adrian Frazier
12. *Literature, Politics, and Culture in Postwar Britain,* by Alan Sinfield
13. *Habits of Thought in the English Renaissance: Religion, Politics, and the Dominant Culture,* by Debora Kuller Shuger

HABITS OF THOUGHT IN THE ENGLISH RENAISSANCE

Religion, Politics, and the Dominant Culture

DEBORA KULLER SHUGER

University of California Press
Berkeley · Los Angeles · Oxford

University of California Press
Berkeley and Los Angeles, California

University of California Press, Ltd.
Oxford, England

Library of Congress Cataloging-in-Publication Data

Shuger, Debora K., 1953–
Habits of thought in the English Renaissance: religion, politics, and the dominant culture/Debora Kuller Shuger.
p. cm.—(The New historicism; 13)
Includes bibliographical references.
ISBN 0-520-06715-0 (alk. paper)
1. Religious thought—England—History—17th century. 2. Philosophy, English—17th century. 3. Renaissance—England. 4. Political science—England—History—17th century. 5. England—Intellectual life—17th century.
I. Title. II. Series.
BR756.S48 1990
942.06′1—dc20 89-5192

Printed in the United States of America CIP
1 2 3 4 5 6 7 8 9

The paper used in this publication meets the minimum requirements of American National Standard for Information Sciences—Permanence of Paper for Printed Library Materials, ANSI Z39.48-1984. ∞

To my friends and colleagues
at the University of Arkansas

Contents

Preface

My deepest thanks are due to the National Humanities Center, which gave me a quiet place to work, all the books I needed, and an endless supply of coffee. And I would also thank the Rockefeller Foundation for underwriting my year there with a generous fellowship. Various people read drafts and helped immeasurably by their comments and suggestions, especially Anne Hall, John Headley, Lorraine Helms, Peter Kaufmann, David Kramer, Michael Schoenfeldt, and William Sessions. I owe particular gratitude to John Knott of the University of Michigan, who, from beginning to end, has been an encouraging and valuable critic.

This book could not have been written without the kindness and support of friends who saw me through a difficult and perplexing year: Ann, Bill, Carol, Donna, Doug, Geoffrey, Helen, Pamela, Preston, Sue. And yet once more I am grateful to my family for their patience and trust.

For the sake of uniformity and intelligibility, I have modernized the orthography and translated the Latin (except in brief tag phrases) throughout the text. I have not, however, translated material appearing in the footnotes.

Introduction

The new historicist critique of traditional formulations of English Renaissance thought—what used to be called the "Elizabethan World Picture"—rests on two principal objections. First, such formulations are oversimplified, or, in Stephen Greenblatt's words, "monological"; that is, earlier studies assumed that the same beliefs were shared by "the entire literate class or indeed the entire population."[1] Second, this assumption of shared belief conceals the role of "orthodoxy" in the processes of social repression and control.[2] These objections do not deny the existence of a body of ideas roughly identical to those of the "Elizabethan World Picture" but claim that they do not articulate a communal consciousness, having been instead produced by power for its own interests. The critics of traditional historicism thus distinguish a dominant ideology or orthodoxy from a host of subversive, marginalized voices, whether those of the oppressed or the skeptical.

The trouble with this division of beliefs into the orthodox and subversive is that so-called subversive ideas keep surfacing, however contained, within the confines of orthodoxy. In "Invisible Bullets" Greenblatt observes that the Machiavellian implications of Harriot's *A Brief and True Report of the New Found Land of Virginia* did not prevent it from being "published by the great Elizabethan exponent of missionary colonialism, the Reverend Richard Hakluyt."[3] Jonathan Dollimore's *Radical Tragedy,* which centers on the opposition between or-

1. Stephen Greenblatt, "Introduction," in *The Forms of Power and the Power of Forms in the Renaissance,* ed. Stephen Greenblatt, Genre Special Topics 7 (Norman, Okla., 1982), p. 5.

2. Jonathan Dollimore, "Introduction: Shakespeare, Cultural Materialism, and the New Historicism," in *Political Shakespeare: New Essays in Cultural Materialism,* ed. Jonathan Dollimore and Alan Sinfield (Ithaca, 1985), pp. 6–7; Jonathan Dollimore, *Radical Tragedy: Religion, Ideology, and Power in the Drama of Shakespeare and His Contemporaries* (Chicago, 1984), p. 90.

3. Stephen Greenblatt, "Invisible Bullets: Renaissance Authority and Its Subversion, *Henry IV* and *Henry V,*" in Dollimore, ed., *Political Shakespeare,* p. 25.

thodoxy and subversion, consistently runs up against the fact that radical questioning, alternate voices, and perception of contradiction manifest themselves *within* supposedly orthodox texts. He thus admits that Luther and Calvin have no illusions about the absence of order and justice in history; rather, "for Calvin faith was generated on the axis of paradox and from within experienced contradiction," and Luther confesses with "dangerous clarity" that "God governs the external affairs of the world in such a way that, if you regard and follow the judgement of human reason, you are forced to say, either that there is no God, or that God is unjust."[4] Dollimore likewise observes that the Reformation itself raises basic epistemological questions, making faith problematic not only for Montaigne but for the conservative Anglican Richard Hooker.[5] But here Dollimore's somewhat perplexed recognition of subversive messages within orthodox religious works runs into further problems, for the passage he cites from Hooker to indicate this skeptical crisis of the Renaissance is, in fact, virtually a translation from Aquinas's commentaries on the *Sentences* of Peter Lombard.[6] A similar difficulty with sorting out orthodox from subversive shows up in the introduction to a recent collection of essays on women in the Renaissance. The authors claim that the official "hierarchical social theories" of the period "proclaimed 'as the first law of women . . . submission and obedience. . . . Theory said that all women must be ruled.' "[7] One notes with some surprise, therefore, that Sir Thomas Smith—Cambridge professor of civil law, Principal Secretary to Edward VI, and French ambassador under Queen Elizabeth—holds that husband and wife "ech obeyeth and commaundeth other, and they two togeather rule the house."[8] Not only is the global division of ideas into "subversive" and "orthodox" problematic, a matter we will discuss later, but it is not always clear what precisely is subversive with respect to the dominant ideology,[9] nor does orthodox ideology seem

4. Dollimore, *Radical Tragedy*, pp. 105–6.

5. Dollimore, *Radical Tragedy*, pp. 70–71.

6. See chapter 1, pp. 42–43.

7. Margaret W. Ferguson, with Maureen Quilligan and Nancy J. Vickers, "Introduction," in *Rewriting the Renaissance: The Discourses of Sexual Difference in Early Modern Europe*, ed. Margaret W. Ferguson, Maureen Quilligan, and Nancy J. Vickers (Chicago, 1986), p. xx.

8. Sir Thomas Smith, *De republica Anglorum* (c. 1562–65), ed. Mary Dewar, Cambridge Studies in the History and Theory of Politics (Cambridge, 1982), p. 59.

9. For the difficulty of discriminating orthodoxy from subversion, one might consider the following descriptive phrases: "obscure," "ambiguous," "self-conscious,"

quite as monolithic and hegemonic as either Tillyard or his critics seem to have supposed.[10]

The confusion over what counts as orthodoxy stems in part from the contemporary lack of interest in the subject. Recent scholarship has focused on heterodoxy, whether sexual, political, literary, or religious, often remaining content to presuppose the contents of "official" belief. Far more work has been done on Puritans and radicals than on the principal defenders of the Elizabethan Settlement and royal supremacy. Even the enthusiasm for James I and courtly politics has not trickled over to courtly theology and erudition. Indeed, it could be argued that modern Renaissance scholars know less about the intellectual culture of their period, especially after 1520, than scholars working on any other epoch.[11] But the result of the contemporary interest

"playful," "melancholy," "habitual subjectivity," "amused even by his own fascination with himself," "turns himself into art," "allows reader to follow the course of his mind as he contemplates his subject." This sounds like Montaigne, although actually Joan Webber's characterization of conservative Anglican prose, in *The Eloquent "I": Style and Self in Seventeenth-Century Prose* (Madison, 1968), pp. 8–13.

10. On the centrifugal diversity of late Renaissance thought and the ferment and confusion of its intellectual life, see Christopher Hill, *Intellectual Origins of the English Revolution* (Oxford, 1965), p. 7; Brian Vickers, "Introduction," in *Occult and Scientific Mentalities in the Renaissance,* ed. Brian Vickers (Cambridge, 1984), p. 29; Patrick Collinson, *The Religion of Protestants: The Church in English Society, 1559–1625* (Oxford, 1982), p. 282; Peter G. Lake, "Calvinism and the English Church, 1570–1635," *Past and Present* 114 (1987): 68; Michel Foucault, *The Order of Things: An Archaeology of the Human Sciences* (New York, 1970), p. 32. For an opposing view that sees all the participants in the theopolitical debates of the seventeenth century as sharing basically the same premises about reason and value, see Lotte Mulligan, " 'Reason,' 'Right Reason,' and 'Revelation' in Mid-Seventeenth-Century England," in Vickers, ed., *Occult and Scientific,* pp. 375–401.

11. Part of this problem is obviously due to the fact that almost all scholarly books—almost everything of interest on law, medicine, history, rhetoric, philology—were written in Latin. A rough estimate suggests that of the books listed in the original 1605 Bodleian catalogue less than 2½ percent were in English. A random sampling of some pages in the catalogue indicates the extent to which the intellectual world of the period remains obscure to us. Thus, one page in the *Libri theologici* yields the names Conr. Keollin, David Kimhi, Michlol Kimhi, Joseph Kalon, R. Kylwarby, Martinus Kemnitius, Timothius Kirchnerus, and Ant. Konigstein. The entries under the *Liber artium* are not much more familiar; again, a random page lists Barocius, Barozzio, Bocadus, Beroaldus, Bonacursius, Bombelli, Beza, Blanchini, Barros, Blasius, Beurheusius, Bullengerus, Beda, and Botero. This obscurity is a qualitative as well as a simple quantitative matter; my research in Renaissance rhetoric suggests that Latin texts were generally more sophisticated and theoretical than their vernacular counterparts. (The results of this study were published under the title Debora Shuger, *Sacred Rhetoric: The Christian Grand Style in the English Renaissance* [Princeton, 1988].) Because of their polemic immediacy, however, theological works were more likely to be written in English than other species of scholarship.

in Renaissance ideology combined with limited concern for its actual articulations is that more familiar modern issues and terms of analysis quietly (or not so quietly) displace historical ones. But if no unchanging human nature exists, and what "man" is cannot be separated from his culture, then we cannot approach a given period or its texts by disregarding the self-interpretation of that period. Which is not to say that one ought never interpret an earlier work or era in light of subsequent theoretical assumptions. As Plato includes (and rejects) Hobbism in his system, so Hobbes includes (and rejects) Platonism. It is just that a student of Plato should not confuse the two and must start with the first, even if ultimately deciding the second is correct. This study is an attempt to fill such an academic *aporeia,* to reconstruct not a monologic yet nonexistent "world picture" shared by all literate persons but the dominant culture of the period between the Elizabethan Settlement and the Civil War, between, that is, the consolidation of this dominant culture and its dissolution. In fact, I will focus on the center of this era, the years between 1580 and 1630, but with occasional digressions, where warranted, back to Henrician times and forward to the Restoration.

But one must locate this dominant culture before studying it. As a minimal definition one might say that its members are those who preferred the status quo in church and state over the Genevan or Roman—or Paduan—alternatives. But both "culture" and "dominant" require further explication. Culture, one might say, consists of both a subject and a predicate, a content and a function. That is, following Clifford Geertz, we can define "culture" as "a multiplicity of complex conceptual structures" that operate as "control mechanisms . . . for the governing of behavior."[12] In this study, however, I am primarily interested in the conceptual structures—the content of culture rather than its operations—and hence with how a given community *constructs* meaning and thereby constitutes its world rather than how such constructions enable it to function in the world. The division may be artificial but seems justified by the specific difference between a Renaissance literary scholar and an anthropologist, namely, that the former studies dead people—or, rather, the textual traces of dead people. The books remain with their constructions of meaning; the

12. Clifford Geertz, *The Interpretation of Cultures* (New York, 1973), pp. 10, 44.

rest of the cultural evidence has, for the most part, like an "insubstantial pageant faded."[13] The notion of a *dominant* culture does, however, relate conceptual structures to their social matrix, since a culture is dominant in relation to a society's centers of power. For Renaissance England these comprise the principal political, religious, and academic institutions of the period: the court, Parliament, the church, the Inns of Court, and the universities. I have therefore chosen to concentrate on a few figures who both left behind a considerable body of textual traces and had significant connections to these centers, principally Lancelot Andrewes, Richard Hooker, George Herbert, and John Donne, but also William Perkins, Fulke Greville, King James, and various other churchmen, humanists, and political figures.

The large number of ecclesiastics in this list should not be disconcerting. As Fredric Jameson has remarked, religion "is the master-code of pre-capitalist society," the discourse through which it interprets its own existence.[14] The almost total neglect of society's religious aspects in favor of political ones—a reaction against the theological bias of earlier Renaissance criticism—has produced in recent literary scholarship a curiously distorted picture of the period.[15] But while no one would deny that the dominant culture of the Renaissance was (in some sense) religious, the relation between religion and culture needs careful

13. Obviously we do have all sorts of records that throw light on the activities of Renaissance people, but since deviant behavior and opining are far more likely to be recorded than their uncontroversial counterparts, these records can often be misleading. We know very little about what Hooker's, Herbert's, and Donne's parishioners thought of their erudite ministers or, more generally, how the conceptual structures visible in texts diffused into social behavior. Chapter 6 attempts to establish some connection between conceptual models and social behavior, but the longer I worked, the more conscious I became of how hypothetical and a posteriori such connections are—a difficulty in no small part owing to the fact that social historians often sharply disagree with one another, so that one does not even know *what* behaviors should be connected with a given conceptual structure.

14. Fredric Jameson, "Religion and Ideology: A Political Reading of *Paradise Lost*," in *Literature, Politics, and Theory*, ed. Francis Barker et al., New Accents (London, 1986), p. 39. Compare Boyd M. Berry, *Process of Speech: Puritan Religious Writing and "Paradise Lost"* (Baltimore, 1976), pp. 4–5. The sociologist Edward Shils makes the important general point that "sensitivity to the sacred" remains the distinguishing feature of the intellectual in all periods (*The Intellectuals and the Powers and Other Essays* [Chicago, 1972], p. 3).

15. There are, however, important exceptions, especially the chapters on More, Tyndale, and Wyatt in Stephen Greenblatt's *Renaissance Self-Fashioning from More to Shakespeare* (Chicago, 1980) and Richard Strier's *Love Known: Theology and Experience in George Herbert's Poetry* (Chicago, 1983).

explication if religion is not to be confused with society itself or narrowed into theology. Religion is, first of all, not *simply* politics in disguise, a set of beliefs that represent and legitimate the social order by grounding it in the Absolute. Such an assumption would lead straight to Jameson's view that one analyzes theological discourse in order to find the "materialist and political kernel" within, I suppose, the religious nut.[16] Religious belief is "about" God and the soul as much as it is "about" the sociopolitical order. Whether or not one believes in the former two entities, one gains very little by assuming that the culture under investigation did not itself comprehend the essential nature of its preoccupations. But it is equally true that in the Renaissance religious discourse enfolds more than such specifically theological concerns as the manner of eucharistic presence, the necessity of church elders, or the fourfold senses of Scripture. Religion during this period supplies the primary language of analysis. It is the cultural matrix for explorations of virtually every topic: kingship, selfhood, rationality, language, marriage, ethics, and so forth. Such subjects are, again, not masked by religious discourse but articulated in it; they are considered *in relation to* God and the human soul. That is what it means to say that the English Renaissance was a religious culture, not simply a culture whose members generally were religious.

Moreover, although all the persons discussed here belonged to the Church of England, this is not a study of "Anglican" as opposed to "Puritan" (nor "Arminian" as opposed to "Calvinist") belief. Although still useful, these dichotomies create as many problems as they resolve, in part because they preselect the issues by focusing on points of disagreement, whereas even the proto-Laudian Andrewes still argues as late as 1610 that all Reformed churches "hold a single faith."[17] In addition, the meaning of these terms can be extremely difficult to specify.[18] This difficulty has several causes. Sometimes it is not clear

16. Jameson, "Religion and Ideology," pp. 38–39.

17. Lancelot Andrewes, *Responsio ad Bellarminum,* in *The Works of Lancelot Andrewes,* 11 vols., Library of Anglo-Catholic Theology (Oxford, 1854), 8:36.

18. The difficulty of fixing firm dividing lines between theological camps is exacerbated by the fact that they all used the same patristic sources. Roman Catholics, Lutherans, Calvinists, and Conformists not infrequently sound a good deal alike because each sounds like Augustine and Chrysostom. For a bibliographic summary of some of the problems involved in distinguishing Anglicans from Calvinists see Borden W. Painter, "Anglican Terminology in Recent Tudor and Stuart Historiography," *Anglican and Episcopal History* 56 (1987): 237–49; Gene Edward Veith, Jr., *Reformation Spirituality: The Religion of George Herbert* (London, 1985), pp. 28–32.

on which side of the fence a doctrine should be placed. Thus, as Patrick Collinson notes, Calvinists as well as Laudians lined up behind *divino iure* episcopacy.[19] Or, while Strier uses Herbert's rejection of decorum to indicate his affinity with radical Protestantism, the same rejection of the analogy "between earthly and heavenly glory" informs the works of the conservative Bishop Andrewes, who defends the lowliness of Christ's birth by denying any "natural conveniency" between sign and signified, that is, by inverting the principle of classical decorum: "the less glorious, the more glorious; the less glorious His sign, the more glorious He."[20]

Sometimes also a doctrine jumps from one side of the fence to the other. Both Strier and Veith make inner assurance of salvation a touchstone of Calvinist spirituality,[21] but English Calvinism at least is hopelessly contradictory on the matter. William Perkins, for instance, affirms that one can discern one's own predestination according to the following rules: the elect have a "full persuasion" [that is, assurance] that "they are children of God"; however, people may lack such certainty and nevertheless be sure of their election by the testimony of their sanctification; yet if such testimony proves "very feeble," they must not "be dismayed, because it is most sure that if they have faith but as much as a grain of mustard seed . . . it is sufficient to ingraft them into Christ"; but even if a person cannot find one such grain in himself, he may not "set down that himself or any other is a reprobate, for God doth oftentimes prefer those which did seem to be most of all estranged from his favour to be in his kingdom above those who in man's judgment were the children of the kingdom."[22] There is thus for Perkins *no* necessary relation between assurance and election. In fact, assurance may be a sign of reprobation, since "many professors of Christ . . . persuade themselves that they are in the estate of grace. . . . Yet when the day of grace is past, they shall contrariwise

19. Collinson, *Religion of Protestants,* p. 19.

20. Strier, *Love Known,* pp. 183ff.; Andrewes, *Works,* 1:202; compare 3:268, 368. Thus Joan Webber comments that the "indecorous blending" of the lowly and majestic is not only characteristic of Andrewes but that "the closest poetic parallel, I believe, is Herbert" ("Celebration of Word and World in Lancelot Andrewes's Style," in *Seventeenth-Century Prose: Modern Essays in Criticism,* ed. Stanley Fish [New York, 1971], pp. 344–45).

21. Strier, *Love Known,* p. 114; Veith, *Reformation Spirituality,* p. 96.

22. William Perkins, *A Golden Chain,* in *The Work of William Perkins,* ed. Ian Breward, The Courtenay Library of Reformation Classics (Appleford, Eng., 1970), pp. 257–58.

find themselves to be in the estate of damnation, remediless."[23] So whereas "Arminians" held that a person may fall from grace while "Calvinists" claimed that the gift of grace included perseverance, the experiential difference between the two positions seems negligible, since the "Calvinist" could never be sure that he was actually in "the estate of grace." Furthermore, sometimes doctrines disguised their position with respect to fences. Peter Lake thus notes that while men like Whitaker, Chaderton, and Ashton, whom he calls "moderate Puritans," were strict predestinarians in their theological works, in their sermons and pastoral writings "they seldom referred to the elect and hardly ever to the reprobate," but spoke as if individuals could choose or reject a salvation offered to all.[24] Sometimes, finally, the fences are mislabeled. It has become fashionable, following Nicholas Tyacke, to refer to the High Churchmen of the Laudian variety as "Arminians," after the Dutch theologian Jacobus Arminius. But Arminianism, properly so-called, is a liberal and rationalist variant of Calvinism, fundamentally distinct from the patristic and liturgical emphases of men such as Andrewes and Laud.[25]

The difficulties associated with terms like Anglican and Puritan suggest that they are of limited use as analytic categories. They are not, obviously, of no use at all, especially with respect to questions of church polity where the difference between Presbyterian Puritanism, Roman Catholicism, and the Church of England are clear and straightforward—but the first two categories by definition fall outside the dominant culture. For exploring that culture itself, it seems better not to put too much weight on theological labeling but instead to view religious discourse as a language of analysis or "ideology," although not in the Marxist sense of false consciousness. As Dollimore observes, in recent theory "ideology" is not confined to the production and maintenance of power but signifies "the very terms in which we

23. Perkins, "A Treatise Tending unto a Declaration Whether a Man Be in the Estate of Damnation or the Estate of Grace," in *Work*, p. 357. These contradictions provide the starting point for R. T. Kendall's *Calvin and English Calvinism to 1649*, Oxford Theological Monographs (Oxford, 1979), see esp. pp. 61–75.

24. Peter, G. Lake, *Moderate Puritans and the Elizabethan Church* (Cambridge, 1982), pp. 151–52.

25. Professor Lake has redenominated the "Laudian" or "Arminian" position as "avant-garde Conformity"—a splendid paradox, which I will not steal but hope catches on (Folger Library Conference, "The Mental World of the Jacobean Court," Spring 1988).

perceive the world, almost—and the Kantian emphasis is important here—the condition and grounds of consciousness itself."[26] In Bacon's words, "methods of procedure are potentially things themselves."[27] Since people receive such methods from their culture, ideology inevitably centers on "that pivotal and almost inaccessible juncture between society and consciousness."[28] It gives the terms and models—the "methods of procedure"—by which the world is perceived, by which existence is made intelligible. Therefore ideology is not a dispensable, oppressive fiction, the need for intelligibility and meaning being as real and pressing as libidinal drives or the will to power.[29] Furthermore, while part of that "making intelligible" concerns naturalizing the structures of power and allocation, it also concerns numerous other issues: what counts as a reason; what counts as evidence; what is the relation of language, thought, and desire to "reality," whether natural or supernatural, and so forth. Ideology thus signifies what I will call "habits of thought," a culture's interpretive categories and their internal relations, which underlie specific beliefs, ideas, and values. And Renaissance habits of thought were by and large religious.

Investigation of these habits of thought in the dominant culture of the English Renaissance yields surprising results. Despite their general agreement on doctrinal matters, the figures studied present an unexpected and at times drastic ideological pluralism. Instead of a monologic world picture, one uncovers complex and divergent assumptions (at which point this study seemed fated to share the incoherence of its chosen subject). The focus that emerged followed the realization that the divergences were structured by a central problematic: the placement of boundaries. I defined "habits of thought" above as a culture's interpretive categories and their relations, and the question of boundaries is precisely that of the relation between categories. For various reasons, which will be detailed in subsequent chapters, in the Renaissance these relations were in a state of flux, a negative measure of which appears in the obsessive desire for systematic order evident in

26. Dollimore, *Radical Tragedy*, p. 9. The usage is Althusserian.

27. Francis Bacon, *The Refutation of Philosophies*, in *The Philosophy of Francis Bacon*, ed. and trans. Benjamin Farrington (Chicago, 1964), p. 128.

28. Donald R. Kelley, *The Beginning of Ideology: Consciousness and Society in the French Reformation* (Cambridge, 1981), p. 4.

29. Geertz, *Interpretation*, p. 140.

the compulsive symmetries of Ramist dichotomizing,[30] in the visceral hatred of "mixture" that pervades Calvinism,[31] and in the radical dualism of Descartes. The impulse to define and distinguish, whether logic from rhetoric, elder from doctor, soul from body, words from things, state from church, mind from nature, results from a prior sense of confusion and lack of demarcation.

The problem in the Renaissance concerns not only where boundaries should be placed but also their "thickness"; Descartes, for example, differs from earlier thinkers not by distinguishing soul from body but by insisting on an absolute distinction, whereas his predecessors generally made a more fluid and partial separation between the corporeal and incorporeal. Melanchthon, for example, argues that the organic animal spirits ascend to the brain, where in a rarified state they "mix" with the Holy Spirit.[32] Bacon's Idols are radical in the same sense of "thickening" the partition between mind and the world. Previously, thinkers as diverse as Ficino and Hooker could argue from mental events to objective truths, from the ingrained human desire for happiness to the existence of heaven, because the "natural" desires of the mind were felt to participate in the order of things, the same God

30. For example, the fascination with establishing the precise boundaries between the various arts and sciences, which reaches its apogee in Ramism but is characteristic of the systematic temper of late medieval and Renaissance thought in general. See, for example, Bernard Weinberg, *A History of Literary Criticism in the Italian Renaissance,* 2 vols. (Chicago, 1963), 1:1.

31. William J. Bouwsma, *John Calvin: A Sixteenth-Century Portrait* (Oxford, 1988), p. 34. This fear of mixture suffuses Cartwright's endless polemic with Whitgift; for example, he complains that in the Church of England, "the pastor's office is confounded with the deacon's; whilst women do minister the sacraments, which is lawful only for men; whilst private men do that which belongeth unto public persons; whilst public actions are done in private places; whilst the church is shuffled with the commonwealth; whilst civil matters are handled by ecclesiastical persons, and ecclesiastical by those which be civil; and, to be short, whilst no officer of the church keepeth his standing, and one member doth take upon it the office of another: which things as they hazard the army, and destroy the body, so they do presently hinder, and will shortly (if remedy be not provided) utterly overthrow the church" (cited in John Whitgift, *Works,* 3 vols., ed. Rev. John Ayre, The Parker Society [Cambridge, 1852], 1:18).

32. Philip Melanchthon, *Liber de anima,* vol. 13 of *Opera quae supersunt omnia,* 28 vols., ed. Carolus Gottlieb Bretschneider, Corpus reformatorum (Brunswick and Halle, 1834–60), 89–90: "Iam cogitent studiosi hoc mirandum Dei opus in homine. Spiritu vitali et animali actiones praecipuae efficiuntur, vitae conservatio, nutritio, generatio, deinde sensus, motus, cogitatio, adfectus in corde. Ideo aliqui dixerunt, animam esse hos spiritus seu flammulas vitales et animales. . . . Et, quod mirabilius est, his ipsis spiritibus in hominibus piis miscetur ipse divinus spiritus, et efficit magis fulgentes divina luce, ut agnitio Dei sit illustrior, et adsensio firmior, et motus sint ardentiores erga Deum."

being the creator of both. For Bacon, the mind "naturally" distorts its objects, its desires (for example, the desire for symmetry) having no corollary in "nature," now defined so as to exclude thought. Generally speaking, the sacramental/analogical character of premodern thought tends to deny rigid boundaries; nothing is simply itself, but things are signs of other things and one thing may be inside another, as Christ is *in* the heart, or turn into something else, as the substance of the eucharistic bread turns into the body of Christ. With the advent of modernity the borders between both conceptual and national territories were redrawn as solid rather than dotted lines.

In the long run, the movement from premodern to modern thought describes a thickening of boundaries, but the period between 1559 and 1630 is not the long run. Rather, these years exhibit conflicting and contradictory tendencies just as the rationally organized, "bounded," spaces of High Renaissance painting give way to the incoherent perspectives and spatial distortions of mannerists such as Pontormo and Il Rosso. The Renaissance may differ from all previous renascences by the achievement of perspective, but it was an achievement quickly modified, abandoned, regained, rejected. Renaissance habits of thought did not move in a steady, unilinear direction from interpenetrating boundaries to compartmentalized space. Nevertheless, these polarities seem to govern the ideological "shape" of the dominant culture, stiffening, relaxing, and reconfiguring the lines between categories. For instance, on the one hand, all Reformed theories of the Eucharist presuppose a sort of rationally organized space, since they begin from the claim that because Christ is "in heaven" He cannot be "in" the Host. On the other hand, they also constantly speak of Christ (or the Spirit) as being "in" the soul, as the radical center of personality and Holy Ghost in the machine, a notion that both defies spatial location and disclaims the sense of individual autonomy traditionally ascribed to the Renaissance.

The problem of boundaries touches almost every area of Renaissance culture, from the organization of the arts curriculum to the respective limits of Crown and Parliament, but particularly the relations among the sociopolitical order, the self, and God. Although subsequent discussion will complicate all generalities, the following points may serve to suggest the intertwinings and untwinings of these relations:

1. The private recesses of the individual anima replace the medieval church as the primary point of contact between God and persons.
2. This internalization of presence secularizes the sociopolitical, emptying it of ultimate meaning and thus enabling a "realistic" appraisal of such things as institutional behavior, hierarchy, power, coercion, and so forth.
3. This split between the sociopolitical and the divine is simultaneously inscribed and erased. That is, secularization and cosmology coexist within the dominant culture, the latter reinventing the divinity of the king and the supernatural ground of the social order.
4. The sacralization of the political arena tends to correspond to a politicization of the sacred. The analogy between kings and God thus works both ways.
5. The retreat of presence inward creates history (or historical consciousness), that is, the arena of specifically human action over time, while "cosmological" habits of thought, whether of a medieval or Calvinist variety, transform events and institutions into expressions of the divine will.
6. Both sides of any given contradiction may be held by a single individual, sometimes in a single work.
7. Both ethical and theoretical concerns are subordinate to the need for intimate contact with God. There is thus little emphasis on morality or natural theology.[33]

These differences with respect to the relations among the self, God, and the sociopolitical order are best considered as differences not of propositional content—the traditional "history of ideas" approach—but of ideology; that is, they do not manifest doctrinal disagreement but exist in that more obscure and nebulous realm of assumptions, desires, and senses of the real, which determines both the kind of questions asked and the kind of answers acceptable—both logically and psychologically. The fundamental *beliefs* held by the dominant culture are by and large invariable—the royal supremacy, the Nicene Creed, the value of order—while differentiation occurs at the more

33. C. F. Allison, *The Rise of Moralism: The Proclamation of the Gospel from Hooker to Baxter* (New York, 1966).

fundamental level of how the mind interprets the world.[34] Therefore, we should add to the list of intertwining relations the one between mind and not-mind. To the extent that boundaries were felt as "thick," the relation between the perceiver and the perceived became problematic. Thus, if, as in Calvin, the Holy Spirit "penetrate[s] into our hearts" and provides "inward testimony" to the truth of Holy Scripture, then there is no real hermeneutic problem, the same Spirit being both interpreter and interpretandum. Hence Calvin can conclude, "Scripture exhibits fully as clear evidence of its own truth as white and black things do of their color, or sweet and bitter things do of their taste."[35] Questions of interpretive method arise and intensify as the perceiving self separates from its divine ground.[36]

Therefore, I want to begin the investigation of the dominant culture in Renaissance England with this problem of the boundaries between mind and not-mind, focusing on Richard Hooker and Lancelot Andrewes, since they present the sharpest contrast between a habit of mind that tends toward differentiation and one in which distinctions remain blurred and permeable. This contrast suggests the copresence in the late Renaissance of radically different ways of understanding language, textuality, tradition, analogy, and historical change, and therefore the peculiar configuration of this culture that in its most orthodox center exhibits both a troubled modernity and a drastic archaism. The second chapter moves from contrast to identity, to the one area where Andrewes and Hooker operate with largely the same assumptions. This area is spiritual psychology, the inner life of faith.

34. For example, while Hobbes and Andrewes both support absolute monarchy, they interpret the world from nearly opposite standpoints. Thus Hobbes grounds absolutism on the need to prevent the perpetual warfare of the state of nature, Andrewes, on the divinity of kings.

35. John Calvin, *Institutes of the Christian Religion,* 2 vols., ed. John T. McNeill, trans. Ford Lewis Battles, The Library of Christian Classics (Philadelphia, 1960), 1.7.2–4.

36. Calvin and his followers did not, of course, deny the need for scriptural interpretation. However, as Peter Lake remarks, "for those English protestants most committed to a view of scripture as a self-validating and self-interpreting source of religious authority, the reliance of scripture on the autonomous decoding powers of human reason had always been a source of ideological embarrassment. They had circumvented the difficulties which this involved for them in the struggle against Rome by reducing the autonomous role of reason to the automatic, and therefore impersonal, application of certain linguistic and syllogistic procedures to the sacred text [that is, Ramism]" (*Anglicans and Puritans? Presbyterianism and English Conformist Thought from Whitgift to Hooker* [London, 1988], p. 153).

The third chapter, which focuses on George Herbert, continues examining spiritual psychology, but now in relation to society and history, and thus the emergence of an inwardness or subjectivity sharply distinguished from social roles and historical process. The final three chapters concern the relation between religion and politics and, in particular, the analogies of God, king, and father: chapter 4 exploring the king as God and father; chapter 5, God as king; chapter 6, God and king as father. In addition, each of these final chapters approaches the relation between religion and politics from a different perspective. Chapter 4 thus concerns institutional issues, especially the institutional locus of the holy and the revival of sacred kingship. Chapter 5, which treats Donne and Greville, deals with the theological implications of sacred kingship, that is, how the absolutist metaphor of the king as God is played out in reverse in the image of God as an absolute monarch. Chapter 6 investigates patriarchy as a political and religious theory and its apparently contradictory role in assimilating temporal power to sacred order and in asserting their distinction. As this summary indicates, each chapter deals with a specific issue and can therefore be read in isolation; nevertheless, the individual discussions repeatedly show traces of a common problematic, so that, for instance, Hooker's twofold epistemology described in chapter 1 is connected to the notion of the *duplex persona* in chapter 3, and this in turn to the double headship of the church discussed in chapter 4 and the contrast between father and king in chapter 6. In the conclusion, I will draw together some of these strands.

This book began as a search for orthodoxy, for the beliefs and values held by members of the dominant culture in the middle years of the English Renaissance, the "Golden Age" of Spenser, Shakespeare, Donne, and Jonson. What it stumbled into was not mere pluralism of the "*x* is a Calvinist, but *y* is an Arminian" variety but conflicts as much within individuals as between sects or parties,[37] conflicts that seemed to have less to do with formulated doctrines (for example, "*x* believes in the real presence, but *y* is a memorialist") than with barely articulated assumptions and feelings about how the pieces of the world fit together, about what counts as fitting. In some respects, the dominant culture was more radical, probing, and self-critical than has often

37. See Bouwsma, *Calvin,* p. 4.

been assumed, in others it seems more primitive, more alien from our own habits of thought, closer perhaps to those of traditional societies.[38] Such failures of coherent systematization derive from the contradictions of history, for insofar as thought is public, rhetorical, and historical, it remains responsive to the variable molding of circumstance, although not simply material circumstance. We can see this in Andrewes. In a Latin sermon preached at the departure of James's daughter and her new husband, Frederick, the Count Palatine (soon to be the "emergent occasion" of the Thirty Years' War), to the Palatinate in 1613,[39] Andrewes makes his famous assertion of the normative value of tradition. The rule of faith in the Church of England rests on Christian antiquity, with its "one *canon* given by God in Scripture, *two Testaments, three Creeds, four general Councils, five centuries, and the succession of Fathers* during that period."[40] But four years earlier, the controversy with Cardinal Bellarmine forces him to deny tradition any independent value whatsoever. If the English church has broken with its Catholic "fathers," it is because paternity is irrelevant to truth: "we know that for many centuries our *forefathers* and yours were pagans; nevertheless (I am sure) you will not council *your forefathers* to follow in their footsteps. Therefore, howevermuch you frame a rule about following one's forefathers, it cannot be trusted; it will deceive its follower." At this point, the historical relativism latent in Europe's colonial adventure enters; Andrewes remarks to Bellarmine, "even today, let some Indian say this to the Jesuits there (if indeed they are there): *allow me to enjoy my old religion, that practiced for many centuries by my fathers, grandfathers, great-grandfathers.* I scarcely think they will willingly listen to this talk."[41] If tradition supplies a valid norm, then

38. Several recent studies have emphasized the survival of beliefs and habits of thought generally associated with primitive or traditional cultures into both the high and popular culture of the seventeenth century. See Timothy J. Reiss, *The Discourse of Modernism* (Ithaca, 1982), pp. 30–31, 43–44, 51–54; Brian Vickers, "Analogy versus Identity: The Rejection of Occult Symbolism, 1580–1680," in Vickers, ed., *Occult and Scientific,* pp. 95–163; Keith Thomas, *Religion and the Decline of Magic: Studies in Popular Beliefs in Sixteenth- and Seventeenth-Century England* (London, 1971); Jean Delumeau, *Catholicism between Luther and Voltaire: A New View of the Counter-Reformation,* trans. Jeremy Moiser (London, 1977), p. 163; Lucien Febvre, *The Problem of Unbelief in the Sixteenth Century: The Religion of Rabelais,* trans. Beatrice Gottlieb (Cambridge, Mass., 1982), pp. 380–464.

39. The sermon, however, was not printed until 1629, when the English/Protestant cause was in shambles.

40. Andrewes, *Works,* 9:91.

41. Andrewes, *Works,* 7:95–96.

Hindus should resist conversion. Andrewes's deep and nostalgic conservatism, his sense that the outpouring of grace that descended from Christ to the Apostles has shrunk to "but some small stream," becoming "the further, the thinner, as the nature of things liquid is,"[42] exists uneasily side by side with his awareness that the past really authorizes nothing. His desire to defend the established church both in its break from Rome and in its basically traditional character produces not the Official Dogma that we have come to associate with orthodoxy but the internal contradictions and subversions that make this culture, to continue our former metaphor, perhaps more of a gerund than a noun, more a thinking than a thought. Renaissance works noticeably lack a systematic coherence, their discontinuities instead exposing the struggle for meaning that fissures the last premodern generation.

42. Andrewes, *Works,* 3:287.

1

Richard Hooker, Lancelot Andrewes, and the Boundaries of Reason

To reconstruct the habits of thought (or ideologies) available within the dominant culture of the English Renaissance I want to begin with two clergymen, Richard Hooker and Lancelot Andrewes.[1] They were almost exact contemporaries (although Andrewes outlived Hooker by a quarter century), both among the most eminent scholars of their time, both devoted defenders of church, Crown, and "the order of things established." The establishment repaid the compliment. Andrewes was court preacher to both Elizabeth and James, as well as being on the latter's Privy Council. According to Walton, when James came to England he immediately asked Whitgift about Hooker (already dead) and expressed his deep admiration for *The Laws*. Charles I's *Eikon Basilike* recommends the works of Hooker and Andrewes to his daughter, the Lady Elizabeth.[2] Both Hooker and Andrewes not

1. For Hooker's biography and role in theological controversies, see Izaak Walton's *Life of Hooker*, reprinted in the first volume of *The Works of that Learned and Judicious Divine, Mr. Richard Hooker*, 3 vols., ed. Rev. John Keble (Oxford, 1888; reprint, New York, 1970), 1:1–87; Peter G. Lake, *Anglicans and Puritans? Presbyterianism and English Conformist Thought from Whitgift to Hooker* (London, 1988), pp. 145–238; Richard Bauckham, "Hooker, Travers, and the Church of Rome in the 1580s," *Journal of Ecclesiastical History* 29 (1978): 37–50; John E. Booty, "Hooker and Anglicanism," in *Studies in Richard Hooker: Essays Preliminary to an Edition of His Works*, ed. W. Speed Hill (Cleveland, 1972), pp. 207–39; C. J. Sisson, *The Judicious Marriage of Mr. Hooker and the Birth of "The Laws of Ecclesiastical Polity"* (Cambridge, 1940; reprint, New York, 1974); W. Speed Hill, "The Evolution of Hooker's *Laws of Ecclesiastical Polity*," in Hill, ed., *Studies in Hooker*, pp. 117–58; Willem Nijenhuis, *Adrianus Saravia (c. 1532–1613)*, Studies in the History of Christian Thought (Leiden, 1980), esp. pp. 145–46; Stanley Archer, *Richard Hooker* (Boston, 1983). For Andrewes, see Douglas Macleane, *Lancelot Andrewes and the Reaction* (London, 1910); Paul A. Welsby, *Lancelot Andrewes, 1555–1626* (London, 1958); Maurice F. Reidy, S.J., *Bishop Lancelot Andrewes, Jacobean Court Preacher: A Study in Early-Seventeenth-Century Religious Thought* (Chicago, 1955); Mark Pattison, *Isaac Casaubon, 1559–1614* (London, 1875), pp. 328–32, 347, 374–75, 389–96; Trevor A. Owen, *Lancelot Andrewes* (Boston, 1981).

2. Hooker, *Works*, 1:171–73. Until the notes to the new Folger text are available, Keble's edition remains the most useful and accessible. (*Eikon Basilike* was actually in large part ghostwritten by Bishop Gauden, but this is not important for our purposes.)

only won royal approbation but were variously connected to many of the most important courtly, clerical, and scholarly figures of their day. Because of his premature death, Hooker never attained Andrewes's public eminence, but his friends and associates included Andrewes himself, who preserved Hooker's manuscripts after his death,[3] as well as John Rainolds, the great Puritan Hebraist; Adrianus Saravia, the expatriate Dutch theologian and political theorist; Edwin Sandys, son of the archbishop of York; and the archbishops Jewel and Whitgift, who were his patrons.[4] Even during his lifetime, Hooker achieved an international reputation. Walton recounts a delightful story of how Dr. Stapleton came to Italy around 1594 and boasted of Hooker's excellence to Pope Clement VIII. The pope hereupon requested that Stapleton translate at sight the first book to him in Latin, which Stapleton did. The pope's response to this performance is reported to have concluded: "this man indeed deserves the name of an author; his books will get reverence by age, for there is in them such seeds of eternity, that if the rest be like this, they shall last till the last fire shall consume all learning."[5]

Andrewes's scholarly, political, and literary acquaintances included half the important men in Jacobean England. Fulke Greville proffered him the deanery of Westminster; Walsingham, the vicarage of Saint Giles and other ecclesiastical posts. He was a friend of George Herbert, who dedicated *Musae responsoriae* to him, as well as of Camden, Selden, Bacon, Harington, Laud, Donne, and the great continental

3. Andrewes apparently willed the manuscripts to Bishop Usher, who finally had them published. See Sisson, *Judicious Marriage,* p. 104.

4. There is some debate as to whether Hooker began *The Laws* under Whitgift's encouragement/patronage or whether at least the first draft was written privately. For a summary of this debate, see Hill, "The Evolution," in Hill, ed., *Studies in Hooker.* Hooker's relation to both popular opinion and political power is more problematic than one would suspect from his frequent citation as spokesman for official Tudor beliefs. When Hooker brought the manuscript of *The Laws* to publishers in 1592, he was uniformly told that there was no market for such a work. In a letter written by Andrewes to Dr. Parry immediately after Hooker's death, Andrewes hints that the three books remaining in manuscript might be destroyed or altered by powerful persons as being unorthodox or controversial. And, as is well known, those three books did not appear until over a half century later, for reasons not quite clear but apparently related to a disagreement between Andrewes and Sandys over Hooker's discussion of penance in book 6. Although *The Laws* are explicitly an attempt to defend Tudor orthodoxy and the status quo, in some respects it is more helpful to view Hooker as a fairly independent thinker rather than as simply a mouthpiece for a preexistent World Picture. For a recent assessment of Hooker's relation to sixteenth-century conformist thought, see Lake, *Anglicans and Puritans?,* pp. 225–30.

5. Hooker, *Works,* 1:71.

philologists, Isaac Casaubon, Daniel Heinsius, and Gerhard Vossius.[6] Milton and Crashaw mourned his death in poems.

Both Andrewes and Hooker were, in the broadest sense, representatives of Renaissance orthodoxy.[7] Yet their works reveal considerable differences not only of opinion (Hooker was a contractualist, Andrewes an absolutist)[8] but of habits of thought. Their presuppositions and methods appear fundamentally different, whether the issue is how language operates, the way the mind apprehends truth, or the status of history: the various relations, that is, between mind, sign, and signified. In Hooker the fissures separating things—mind from world, word from thing, sign from signified, God from nature, institutions from presence—are clearly visible, while in Andrewes they are not. Hooker characteristically draws distinctions, historicizes, analyzes; Andrewes constructs a discourse that seems indifferent to ontological barriers: words, things, thought, history, myth, nature, supernature appear only semidetached, each permeable to the other. To put it another way, Hooker's thought is "rational," that is, it produces a gap between mind and not-mind and then endeavors to negotiate that space by rational method. In Andrewes's thought such a gap does not exist; the mind instead participates in not-mind, apprehends meaning as directly given with the object rather than something to be reached by rational processes.[9] His thought, in fact, resembles both the primi-

6. Welsby, *Andrewes*, pp. 161–62, 225ff. On the friendship between Donne and Andrewes, see Augustus Jessopp, *John Donne, Sometime Dean of St. Paul's, A.D. 1621–1631* (New York, 1972), pp. 51–52.

7. Not of Calvinist orthodoxy, however, since both men explicitly denied double predestination (see chapter 2). Lake pinpoints Hooker as the originator of English Arminianism—where "Arminianism" has less to do with Arminius than with the church fathers and medieval schoolmen—which then flows from Hooker to Andrewes to the Laudians ("Calvinism and the English Church, 1570–1635," *Past and Present* 114 [1987]: 42–45). For the debate over whether English orthodoxy was explicitly Calvinist before the 1620s or a more inclusive and tentative Anglicanism, see Lake, "Calvinism"; Nicholas Tyacke, "The Rise of Arminianism Reconsidered," *Past and Present* 115 (1987): 201–16; Peter White, "A Rejoinder," *Past and Present* 115 (1987): 217–29.

8. J. P. Sommerville, *Politics and Ideology in England, 1603–1640* (London, 1986), pp. 11, 47.

9. For the notion that a dramatic increase in felt distance between knower, sign, and signified differentiates modern from premodern thought, see Timothy J. Reiss, *The Discourse of Modernism* (Ithaca, 1982), p. 59; Brian Vickers, "Introduction," in *Occult and Scientific Mentalities in the Renaissance*, ed. Brian Vickers (Cambridge, 1984), p. 26; Ian Maclean, "The Interpretation of Natural Signs: Cardano's *De subtilitate* versus Scaliger's *Exercitationes*," in Vickers, ed., *Occult and Scientific*, p. 244; Bruno Snell, *The Discovery of the Mind in Greek Philosophy and Literature*, trans. T. G. Rosenmeyer (New York, 1982), pp. 60–61, 231; Michel Foucault, *The Order of Things: An Archaeology of the Human*

tive *mentalité* described by anthropologists such as Durkheim and Levy-Bruhl and the cognitive habits frequently ascribed to prescientific or occult figures in the Renaissance.[10] The ensuing discussion will, one hopes, clarify these distinctions. Even in this compact form, they suggest that the dominant culture of the period was more multiform, more fissured and internally divided than its traditional depictions—whether old or new historicist—often suggest.

This multiformity should not, I think, be understood according to Raymond Williams's generally useful categories of residual, dominant, and emergent culture. The claim that the complexity of Renaissance culture arises from the unstable copresence of earlier (residual), dominant, and modern (emergent) elements seems to imply the existence of a mythical moment, generally identified with the residual culture, of hegemonic orthodoxy, of secure faith and stable, pastoral order.[11] Williams thus describes the residual elements in contemporary English society as "absolute brotherhood, service to others without

---

Sciences (New York, 1970), pp. 49–56, 61; Zevedei Barbu, *Problems of Historical Psychology,* International Library of Sociology and Social Reconstruction (London, 1960), p. 158. On the concept of participation, see Lucien Levy-Bruhl, *How Natives Think,* trans. Lilian A. Clare (New York, 1979), pp. 76ff., and his *The "Soul" of the Primitive,* trans. Lilian A. Clare (New York, 1966), pp. 15–19, 144; Emile Durkheim, *The Elementary Forms of the Religious Life,* trans. Joseph Swain (New York, 1915); Owen Barfield, *Saving the Appearances: A Study in Idolatry* (New York, n.d.), pp. 28–52 and passim; Barbu, *Historical Psychology,* pp. 23–30, 74. The terminology for this distinction has not yet been standardized. Hence, the contrast between participatory and rational parallels Reiss's distinction between the discourse of patterning and analyticoreferential discourse or that of Foucault between resemblance and the analysis based on identity and difference (*The Order of Things,* pp. 17–58).

10. Durkheim and Levy-Bruhl scarcely constitute the most up-to-date stratum of anthropological thought. I have used them because the phenomena they describe seem to "fit" Renaissance texts; whether they "fit" current data concerning primitive cultures makes very little difference for my purposes. In part, their works have slipped into desuetude not because they have been disproved but because recent anthropologists are wary of the notion of "primitive mentality" as being implicitly racist. This objection is not relevant for a study of English theologians. The fact that Levy-Bruhl's work in particular seems so applicable to Andrewes is curious. The resemblance may derive from the fact that early anthropologists unconsciously drew from their own cultural past to understand the "primitive" in other societies—a possibility supported by the fact that the term "participation" is a central category in medieval thought. See Charles H. Long, *Significations: Signs, Symbols, and Images in the Interpretation of Religion* (Philadelphia, 1986), pp. 79–84.

11. See also John Bossy, "Blood and Baptism: Kinship, Community, and Christianity in Western Europe from the Fourteenth to the Seventeenth Centuries," in *Sanctity and Secularity: The Church and the World,* ed. Derek Baker, Studies in Church History (Oxford, 1973), p. 130.

reward . . . [and] rural community."[12] Everything, then, that challenges religious faith, epistemic certainty, and traditional practice falls under the aegis of subversion and emergent modernity, like a cancer eating away at a body already weakened by contradictions. The problem with this view is that no such moment exists, neither in the Renaissance nor, more generally, in Western culture, at least after the sixth century B.C. In the Renaissance, the central tendencies within the dominant culture—humanism, the Reformation—contribute both to the revival of patristic, Neoplatonic, occult, and various forms of traditional or "magical" thought and to the radical questioning of tradition and the development of historical, empirical, and rationalist inquiry. The dominant culture itself is complex and diverse. Obviously some elements of this culture seem more modern or more archaic to us, but that is not the issue.

Furthermore, this copresence of rational/empirical and traditional elements is not a Renaissance phenomenon but characterizes Western culture from very early on—and perhaps, to some extent, all cultures, if we accept Evans-Prichard's claim, based on his studies of witch doctoring in Azande tribes, that "faith and scepticism are alike traditional."[13] But to confine our attention to the West, it seems evident that "irrational" beliefs and practices, whether magical or religious—the line is sometimes very hard to draw—existed alongside and often mingled with skeptical, scientific, and rationalized attitudes from the pre-Socratic period through the Renaissance.[14] This copresence is not merely a function of class or indoctrination—the educated being more "rational/skeptical," the ignorant more credulous. In fact, a case could

12. Raymond Williams, *Marxism and Literature,* Marxist Introductions (Oxford, 1977), pp. 121–27. Compare Jonathan Dollimore, *Radical Tragedy: Religion, Ideology, and Power in the Drama of Shakespeare and His Contemporaries* (Chicago, 1984), pp. 7–8. In *The Secularization of the European Mind in the Nineteenth Century* (Cambridge, 1975), Owen Chadwick describes this "historiographical sin": the historian imagines "an age of faith, where bishops were prime ministers, religion the only source of physics or astronomy or morality, kings deposable by popes, all art inspired by gospel narratives, and theology queen of sciences. From this paradise or this hell, according to the point of view, all that followed was decline or progress. Then any change in constitutions or in society since the thirteenth century can be labelled secularization" (p. 3).

13. Quoted in G. E. R. Lloyd, *Magic, Reason, and Experience: Studies in the Origin and Development of Greek Science* (Cambridge, 1979), p. 18.

14. Lloyd, *Magic,* p. 4; Vickers, "Introduction," and Brian Vickers, "Analogy versus Identity: The Rejection of Occult Symbolism, 1580–1680," in Vickers, ed., *Occult and Scientific.* This coexistence entails that Reiss's rather convoluted attempt to prove that analyticoreferential discourse only emerged in the Renaissance, allowing him to

be made that the reverse is true, that before the Enlightenment the social role of intellectual culture (at least in the Christian era) was not to demystify ideological constraints but to sustain transcendental imperatives in the face of popular empiricism. It is the Clerk who tells the story of patient Griselda in response to the Wife of Bath's pragmatic sensuality. It is the "country people," Herbert remarks, who "think that all things come by a kind of natural course," while their aristocratic and learned parson "labours to reduce them to see God's hand in all things."[15] There are obviously exceptions all along the line. From Protagoras to Machiavelli, genuinely subversive thinkers challenged the religious and metaphysical assumptions of their culture; Gorgias, Pyrrho, Lucian, Frederick Barbarossa, Pietro Pomponazzi come to mind. Even among those who generally accepted such assumptions, questioning, conflict, and diversity nevertheless existed, as witnessed, for example, in Bernard of Clairvaux's attack on Abelard, in the 1277 condemnations by Etienne Tempier, in the Nominalist controversies, even in such popular texts as the *Romance of the Rose* and *The Decameron*. The observation of the legal historian Harold Berman that "perhaps the most distinctive characteristic of the Western legal tradition is the coexistence and competition within the same community of diverse jurisdictions and diverse legal systems" has relevance for the broader intellectual culture as well.[16] It is not a question of earlier (residual) and later (emergent) beliefs but of a persistent and unsettling pluralism within the high official culture.

In addition, one should be wary of assuming that all the unsettling came from rationalist-skeptical attitudes which subverted "infantile fairy-tale worlds" of belief. Geertz forcefully argues that even "primitive" religion must cope with "bafflement, suffering, and a sense of intractable ethical paradox," that religion characteristically does not provide an idealized escape from the material conditions of existence but "has probably disturbed men as much as it has cheered them;

posit the existence of another sort of discourse prior to that period, is unnecessary (*Modernism*, pp. 55–107). What Reiss calls the "discourse of patterning" may have flourished in antiquity and the Middle Ages without requiring the nonexistence of other discursive modes.

15. George Herbert, *A Priest to the Temple, or the Country Parson*, in *George Herbert and Henry Vaughan*, ed. Louis L. Martz (Oxford, 1986), 228.

16. Harold J. Berman, *Law and Revolution: The Formation of the Western Legal Tradition* (Cambridge, Mass., 1983), p. 10.

forced them into a head-on, unblinking confrontation of the fact that they are born to trouble."[17] In other words, awareness of paradox, problematics, and dissonance do not belong solely to the disenchanted, nor can we equate traditional faith (orthodoxy) with the attempt to conceal "actual" social contradictions by an unproblematized optimism. The question is not one of "foreign subversives" but of a complexity and tension within the dominant culture.

Such pluralism is therefore not best understood in terms of orthodoxy and subversion, since these tend to reify a cultural center (orthodoxy) which is, in fact, both Janus-like and protean.[18] Beliefs, in any case, cannot be analyzed exclusively in terms of their legitimation or subversion of the dominant social order. First of all, as Edward Pechter has noted, it is not clear that the "will to power . . . [is] the defining human essence";[19] indeed, if "human nature" is a function of culture, there can be no such essence, and it follows that post-Enlightenment politicized categories may not be applicable to pre-Enlightenment history.[20] Second, as Greenblatt himself acknowledges, the use of terms like "subversion" in recent criticism is an unhistorical retrojection of modern classification: we select as subversive those tendencies in the Renaissance that "now conform to our own sense of truth and reality. That is, we locate as 'subversive' in the past precisely those

17. Clifford Geertz, *The Interpretation of Cultures* (New York, 1973), pp. 100–103.

18. On Hooker's own difficulties in remaining free of a politicized polemical debate that would cast him in the role of official spokesman for the anti-Puritan party in Parliament, forcing him to attempt to legitimate the status quo rather than appeal to the Puritan "as a man who appreciated the essential inwardness of his religious experience," see Hill, "The Evolution," pp. 149–52. According to Hill, Hooker had finished *The Laws* to his satisfaction in 1592, when, unable to find a publisher, he was compelled not only to rely on Sandys's financial support but to modify the work to conform to Cramner's and Sandys's political goals.

19. Edward Pechter, "The New Historicism and Its Discontents: Politicizing Renaissance Drama," *Publications of the Modern Language Association* 102 (1987): 301.

20. This is the basic problem with Jean Howard's generally excellent review article, "The New Historicism in Renaissance Studies," *English Literary Renaissance* 16 (1986): 13–43. Howard both wants to argue that the "nature of man" is the variable product of "specific discourses and social processes" (p. 20) and that critics would benefit from employing Marxist analysis in their studies of Renaissance literature (p. 27)—despite the fact that retrojecting the "nature of man" presupposed in all Marxist analysis onto this earlier period implies that such "nature" is a constant. The effort to hold together these incompatible positions can lead to some odd assertions, for example, Dollimore's claim that Machiavelli and Hobbes do *not* posit an unchanging human nature (which seems clearly false) but grasp the unchanging truths about human nature disclosed by Marxist demystification (*Radical Tragedy*, pp. 153–54, 170–72).

things that are *not* subversive to ourselves."[21] No doubt most Renaissance rulers found Machiavelli threatening, but there is also Lancelot Andrewes's observation that "all other laws teach us to enlarge kingdoms and to be in favour with princes; but this our religion supernaturally teacheth us that live, to hate life. And so the prophets did not seek the favour of princes, but reproved them to their faces"—a subversiveness Sir Thomas More and Bishop Fisher, or Latimer, Cramner, and Ridley, for that matter, could not have failed to appreciate.[22]

But, as long as neither term is taken pejoratively, it does seem useful to describe this pluralism along the polarities of mystical and demystifying, where "mystical" signifies a habit of thought based on the participation of the knower in the known and of the sign in the signified, and "demystifying" the habit of thought that perceives the connection between knower, sign, and signified in terms of logical or empirical (including historical) relations. By extension, "mystical" (or "mystifying") habits of thought see social practices and institutions as participating in the sacred—whether the "divine order" or the "nature of things"—while "demystification" strips off this veil of sanctity to expose the contingencies of the world's body. Again, despite the recent preference for the latter procedure, neither seems to have any essential superiority. For various reasons, the Renaissance was probably the last era in the West where mystical and demystifying habits of thought obtained relative parity within the central discourse; by the end of the seventeenth century, Newton is still writing allegorical commentaries on Daniel, but he does not publish them.[23] Those reasons include most of the major events of the period: the invention of

21. Stephen Greenblatt, "Invisible Bullets: Renaissance Authority and Its Subversion, *Henry IV* and *Henry V*," in *Political Shakespeare: New Essays in Cultural Materialism*, ed. Jonathan Dollimore and Alan Sinfield (Ithaca, 1985), p. 29. This is particularly true in the case of religion. The challenge to authority and the status quo in the Renaissance so often passionately affirms religious priorities that the attempt of some new historicists to equate subversion with the secular and skeptical penetration of ideology (including religious belief) makes one wonder to what extent the Marxist critique of classical idealism is interfering with a historical grasp of the issues at stake in Renaissance discourse. In the early seventeenth century, Jesuits seemed considerably more subversive than Baconians. For the radical political implications of Jansenism in France see Jean Delumeau, *Catholicism between Luther and Voltaire: A New View of the Counter-Reformation*, trans. Jeremy Moiser (London, 1977), pp. 116–17.

22. Lancelot Andrewes, *The Works of Lancelot Andrewes*, 11 vols., Library of Anglo-Catholic Theology (Oxford, 1854), 6:51.

23. Vickers, "Introduction," in Vickers, ed., *Occult and Scientific*, p. 15.

movable type, the collapse of a spiritually united Christendom, the rise of science, the development of humanist philology, the recovery of ancient texts, the voyages of discovery. All these encouraged an examination of the grounds of knowledge and belief that had the effect of permanently distancing the mind from its objects, thereby privileging "rational" and empirical methods as the sole means of bridging that distance.

Religious thinkers, from Erasmus on, were caught in a peculiar paradox. The desire to find a rational ground for belief in order to solve religious conflict by something other than a sword problematized belief itself; it threw into question the authority of tradition, custom, subjective certainty, ritual, spiritual exegesis. But this statement needs careful hedging. Most religious thinkers were not aware of being caught in any such paradox. In the mid-1570s the Puritan Thomas Cartwright could still write to Whitgift with an unproblematic epistemic assurance that those who wished further reform "profess nothing of themselves, but only a bare and naked knowledge of the truth," and the archbishop's reply gives no indication that he thought his adversary was talking nonsense.[24] Indeed, the reason most of the religious controversy of this period is so dull is that very few of the combatants were apparently willing or able to address the fundamental issues involved—or apparently aware that such issues were involved. Nor was this just a matter of spiritual pusillanimity. The contrast between Hooker and Andrewes suggests that while demystification was an option, it was by no means the only option. Instead, traditional habits of thought continued to be accessible and culturally "central." The late Renaissance, after all, witnessed the flowering of Protestant (and Catholic) scholasticism, the patristic revival, Spanish mysticism, devotional meditation, and other largely traditional religious expressions. This copresence of rationalized and traditional habits of thought is, as I have argued, characteristic of the dominant culture in the West. But in the Renaissance the contradiction between these modes of representing experience becomes more evident, more acute. To perceive this is to see that the dominant culture was not an obscurantist monolith of ideological (in the Marxist sense)

24. John Whitgift, *Works,* 3 vols., ed. Rev. John Ayre, The Parker Society (Cambridge, 1852), 1:144.

commonplaces nor were questioning and doubt invariably subversive attacks on a monological orthodoxy. Even in such conservative establishment figures as Hooker and Andrewes one discerns a groping to hold together the disparate elements of a changing culture, seemingly archaic mystical representations, a problematic historicism, epistemic contradictions.

But these claims must be demonstrated from the texts themselves. I want therefore to turn to the works of Hooker and Andrewes, focusing on what I have called their "habits of thought," that is, the interpretative categories and relations by which they order and analyze experience. In both cases, it seems best to begin with questions of *biblical* interpretation (since that is what their works are primarily about).[25] These hermeneutic considerations lead into a variety of other issues concerning history, language, the sacraments, and epistemology, all of which relate in one way or another to the relationship between the mind, signs, and the signified. I will treat each author separately, beginning with Hooker, as he was the elder by two years.

POLEMICAL CONTEXT AND THE DISCOVERY OF IDEOLOGY

In Hooker's *Laws of Ecclesiastical Polity* and minor works one perceives the emergence of a modern hermeneutic with its appeal to reason, evidence, historical context, and linguistic change. It is a theory not only about how texts should be interpreted but implies and is implied by premises concerning history, the sacraments, and knowledge. In Hooker this modern hermeneutic and its premises explicitly function to defend catholic tradition and orthodoxy. In fact, however, the method and premises can only partially sustain their predetermined conclusions. Certain disturbing divergences from traditional Christian thought appear, and at the same time an alternative and discontinuous epistemology slips back in.

25. There exists very little valuable work on exegetic or hermeneutic principles in Andrewes and Hooker. The best study is perhaps Egil Grislis's "The Hermeneutical Problem of Richard Hooker," in Hill, ed., *Studies in Hooker*, pp. 159–206. See also Erwin R. Gane, "The Exegetical Methods of Some Sixteenth-Century Anglican Preachers: Latimer, Jewel, Hooker, and Andrewes," *Andrews University Seminary Studies* 17 (1979): 23–38, 169–88; Victor Harris, "Allegory to Analogy in the Interpretation of Scriptures," *Philological Quarterly* 45 (1966): 1–23.

The Laws derives from a polemical context. Hooker defends a hermeneutic based on reason and evidence in order to counter the Puritan claim that correct interpretation is a matter of divine inspiration.[26] The reforming preachers, according to Hooker, persuade their auditors "that it is the special illumination of the Holy Ghost, whereby they discern those things in the word, which others reading yet discern them not."[27] Once persuaded, "let any man of contrary opinion open his mouth to persuade them, they close up their ears, his reasons they weigh not, all is answered with rehearsal of the words of John, 'We are of God; he that knoweth God heareth us.'"[28] Unable to argue from ecclesiastical authority or normative tradition, Hooker erects reason as the interpretive standard:

> forasmuch as persuasions grounded upon reason are either weaker or stronger according to the force of those reasons whereupon the same are grounded, they must every of them from the greatest to the least be able for every several article to shew some special reason as strong as their persuasion therein is earnest. Otherwise how can it be but that some other sinews there are from which that overplus of strength in persuasion doth arise? Most sure it is, that when men's affections do frame their opinions, they are in defence of error more earnest a great deal, than (for the most part) sound believers in the maintenance of truth apprehended according to the nature of that evidence which scripture yieldeth. . . . It is not therefore the fervent earnestness of their persuasion, but the soundness of those reasons whereupon the same is built, which must declare their opinions in these things to have been wrought by the Holy Ghost, and not by the fraud of that evil spirit, which is even in his illusions strong.[29]

Here we have the basic hermeneutic polarities governing Hooker's thought: reason and evidence versus emotional delusion, objective

26. Like so many other historical labels, both the precise extension and intention of "Puritan" remain controversial. How are what we retrospectively identify as "Puritans" different from (or not different from) Calvinists? To what extent were the religious views of men like Cartwright and Travers representative of a large and influential segment of the population, to what extent were they marginal, subversive, or radical? By "Puritan" here I mean those whom Hooker identified as trying to introduce a presbyterian form of church government into England.

27. Hooker, *Works,* 1:150.

28. Hooker, *Works,* 1:153.

29. Hooker, *Works,* 1:150–51; compare 1:323; 2:41.

truth versus subjective projection.[30] Unlike Calvin, he disallows the suprarational, internal testimony of the Spirit as a warrant for both the truth and meaning of Scripture.[31] Similarly, he rejects spiritual exegesis as arbitrary and therefore unable to disengage the exegete's preconceits from the actual sense of the text: "I hold it for a most infallible rule in expositions of sacred Scripture, that where a literal construction will stand, the farthest from the letter is commonly the worst. There is nothing more dangerous than this licentious and deluding art, which changeth the meaning of words . . . maketh of any thing what it listeth, and bringeth in the end all truth to nothing."[32]

One result of Hooker's rational hermeneutic is the discovery of ideology (again in the Marxist sense). Once correct interpretation becomes a matter of reason rather than illumination,[33] the causes of misinterpretation can likewise be demystified to reveal their socioeconomic roots. Thus Hooker argues that Puritanism does not attract converts on theological grounds, these being too abstruse for mass consumption, but by holding out promises of power and ecclesiastical spoils.[34] Its preachers have learned to play on social discontent, attacking the vices of those in authority, imputing "all faults and corruptions" to the "ecclesiastical government established," and proposing their own platform "as the only sovereign remedy of all evils." So they appeal to "minds possessed with dislike and discontentment at things present."[35] Such minds conceal from themselves the motives behind their conversion to reformed ecclesiology, instead imagining "herein they do unto God a part of most faithful service."[36] Puritanism suc-

30. On the rational basis of Hooker's hermeneutics, see Lake, *Anglicans and Puritans?*, pp. 152–53. In addition, Hooker endeavors to establish a distance between the will of God and human opinion (*Works*, 1:130, 182, 189–90); he pleads for an arena of secular rationality and debate as an alternative to the prevalent bipolarism where all was couched in the stark oppositions of divine versus demonic, allowing no compromise. See Barbu, *Historical Psychology*, p. 54; Stephen Greenblatt, *Renaissance Self-Fashioning from More to Shakespeare* (Chicago, 1980).

31. Lake, *Anglicans and Puritans?* p. 154.

32. Hooker, *Works*, 2:263.

33. On the relation between exegesis and divine illumination in the Middle Ages, see Henri de Lubac, S.J., *Exégèse médiévale: les quatre sens de l'écriture*, 4 vols. (n.p., 1964), 1:128, 305–8, 355–63.

34. Hooker, *Works*, 1:146, 157; 3:2–3.

35. Hooker, *Works*, 1:146–47.

36. Hooker, *Works*, 3:143

ceeds not as a religious doctrine but as a utopian ideology, an occluded expression of political frustration.[37]

Furthermore, Hooker's analysis draws the connection between ideology and hermeneutics, in this case biblical hermeneutics. An ideology, he observes, must create an interpretive method to remove possible contradiction and create, in a circular fashion, its own evidence. What one perceives depends on one's "preconceit."[38] This the reforming preachers fashion by their ideologically based reading strategies, which preassign meaning and reference. "Assuredly," Hooker argues,

> the very cause which maketh the simple and ignorant to think they even see how the word of God runneth currently on your side, is, that their minds are forestalled and their conceits perverted beforehand, by being taught, that an "elder" doth signify a layman admitted only to the office or rule of government in the Church; a "doctor," one which may only teach . . . a "deacon," one which hath charge of the alms-box, and of nothing else: that the "sceptre," the "rod," the "throne" and "kingdom" of Christ, are a form of regiment, only by pastors, elders, doctors, and deacons.[39]

To control naming is to construct reality, to "naturalize" ideology. For similar ends, Hooker notes, the Puritans set up a new typology, whereby the prophets and apostles signify themselves, their enemies prefiguring the Church of England; Ezra and Nehemiah are thus read "as if purposely the Holy Ghost had therein meant to foresignify, what the authors of Admonitions to the Parliament, of Supplications to the Council, of Petitions to her Majesty, and of such other like writs, should either do or suffer in behalf of this their cause."[40] Puritan

37. For Hooker's understanding of Puritanism as an ideology in the Marxist sense (or an Idol in the Baconian sense), see Grislis, "The Hermeneutical Problem," pp. 171–73; Arthur B. Ferguson, *Clio Unbound: Perception of the Social and Cultural Past in Renaissance England,* Duke Monographs in Medieval and Renaissance Studies (Durham, N.C., 1979), pp. 218–19. Other Renaissance theologians tend to talk as if all error and misbelief (from their perspective) were either the work of the devil or conscious hypocrisy—whether as a mask for gaining power or due to some perverse resistence to truth. See Hill, "The Evolution," p. 139; John Jewel, *An Apology of the Church of England,* ed. John E. Booty, Folger Documents of Tudor and Stuart Civilization (Charlottesville, Va., 1963), pp. 7–8, 101, 112, 119, 137; J. W. Allen, *A History of Political Thought in the Sixteenth Century* (London, 1928), pp. 70–71.

38. Hooker, *Works,* 1:148.

39. Hooker, *Works,* 1:148–50.

40. Hooker, *Works,* 1:150; compare 1:189.

exegesis thus reads itself back into the text. In this sense, it is not markedly different from medieval exegesis,[41] and Hooker does not try to pit one ahistorical, spiritualized hermeneutic against another. Instead he turns to the most potent polemical tool of the sixteenth century, grounding his refutation on the historical, philological methods of humanist scholarship. The escape from ideological hermeneutics lies on the road of reason, history, and the literal sense. However, this escape, while refuting the Puritan manipulation of terms and analogies, dislodges, however slightly, the normative claims of tradition and Scripture.

ANALOGY OR HISTORY?

Again and again Hooker dismisses the putative isomorphism of past and present, his grave irony mocking arguments based on historical analogy. So he wonders "by what rule the legal hallowing of besoms and flesh-hooks [in the Old Testament] must needs exclude all other readings in the church save Scripture."[42] Or to the claim that Anglican ceremonies are like "the scandalous meats, from which the Gentiles are exhorted to abstain in the presence of Jews,"[43] he replies flatly, "neither are our weak brethren as the Jews, nor the ceremonies which we use as the meats which the Gentiles used."[44] Again, to the Puritan argument that if God had wished the church to have bishops, the New Testament would have given as explicit instructions for their functioning as the Old gave for priests and Levites, Hooker responds that the same supposed analogy would deny the lawfulness of churches, since the Old Testament gives rules for the construction of the Temple, while the New keeps silence on ecclesiastical architecture.[45]

41. Compare de Lubac on Joachimite exegesis in the commentaries of Nicholas of Lyre and his imitators (*Exégèse médiévale,* 4:326–65). Earlier Reformers similarly see themselves as types of biblical figures, especially the despised and outcast prophet or the early Christian martyr. The ubiquity of this model suggests that even during the heyday of the Tudor myth, Tudor theologians recognized political power as always potentially Other—the City of Man. See chapter 4.

42. Hooker, *Works,* 2:72.

43. Like "Puritan," "Anglican" is an anachronism which nevertheless serves as a convenient and easily understood shorthand for talking about those members of the Church of England who preferred episcopal to presbyterian government and were, in general, reasonably satisfied with the Elizabethan Settlement.

44. Hooker, *Works,* 1:468–69.

45. Hooker, *Works,* 3:219–20.

In like fashion, Hooker deconstructs the very Elizabethan analogies drawn from natural history and social practice. Countering the Puritan assertion that since God is a great king, Christian worship should "respect what precepts art delivereth touching the method of persuasive utterance in the presence of great men," he wittily fantasizes how typical Puritan services would stand up as courtly ceremony:

> Suppose that the people of a whole town with some chosen man before them did continually twice or thrice in a week resort to their king, and every time they come first acknowledge themselves guilty of rebellions and treasons, then sing a song, after that explain some statute of the land to the standers-by, and therein spend at the least an hour, this done, turn themselves again to the king, and for every sort of his subjects crave somewhat of him, at the length sing him another song, and so take their leave. Might not the king well think that either they knew not what they would have, or else that they were distracted in mind, or some other such like cause of the disorder of their supplication? . . . Should we hereupon frame a rule that what form of speech or behaviour soever is fit for suitors in a prince's court, the same and no other beseemeth us in our prayers to Almighty God?[46]

Hooker similarly rejects Cartwright's parallel between baptism by a woman and stealing the king's seal; against another of Cartwright's arguments he again replies by dismissing analogical reasoning: "The softness of wax may induce a wise man to set his stamp or image therein; it persuadeth no man that because wool hath the like quality it may therefore receive the like impression."[47]

In fact, throughout *The Laws,* Hooker carefully restricts the scope of analogical argument. Scriptural examples are normative only insofar as present circumstances are identical to the earlier ones, an isomorphism he apparently considers rare.[48] Arguments based on precedent work only if the historically specific reasons justifying the prior act continue to support its subsequent application.[49] Finally, typological

46. Hooker, *Works,* 2:150–52.

47. Hooker, *Works,* 2:299, 365.

48. Hooker, *Works,* 1:401; 2:60. Guicciardini and Montaigne make the same argument for the disanalogy of the past—although in these instances, the classical past. See *The Complete Essays of Montaigne,* trans. Donald M. Frame (Stanford, 1965), p. 819; and Frank Whigham, *Ambition and Privilege: The Social Tropes of Elizabethan Courtesy Theory* (Berkeley, 1984), p. 86.

49. Hooker, *Works,* 2:334.

reasoning assumes the essential changelessness of sacred history, having validity only if the church actually recapitulates the structural and temporal patterns recorded in the Old Testament. This sense of unvarying pattern unites Puritan and medieval exegesis and is precisely what Hooker renounces. When the Jews needed a new law to deal with emergent occasions, they had "the Oracle of God, they had the Prophets: and by such means God himself instructed them from heaven what to do, in all things that did greatly concern their state and were not already set down in the Law."[50] These laws are not applicable to the church, for "laws positive are not framed without regard had to the place and persons for which they are made"; hence the laws of Israel do not bind a church composed of all nations. Moreover, although God legislated for the Jews in detail and almost in person, He does not do so for the church; it is not "with us as it was with them."[51] Sacred history unfolds not as the repetition of timeless patterns but as the linear evolution of particular and culturally specific moments.[52] Hooker concludes, "a more dutiful and religious way for us were to admire the wisdom of God, which shineth in the beautiful variety of all things, but most in the manifold and yet harmonious dissimilitude of those ways, whereby his Church upon earth is guided from age to age, throughout all generations of men."[53] Insofar as sacred history reveals diversity rather than pattern, the typological inference from the old to the new dispensation, based as it is on an *analogia temporum,* cannot hold.

In place of the Puritans' analogical ground, Hooker's arguments stress historical context; in place of the normative example, they emphasize circumstantial particularity.[54] It is absolutely characteristic of

50. Hooker, *Works,* 1:397.

51. Hooker, *Works,* 1:395–97.

52. For Hooker's suspicion of contemporary applications of typology, see Ferguson, *Clio Unbound,* pp. 202, 211; Lake, *Anglicans and Puritans?,* p. 209. In the next century, the Frenchman Jean Daillé (1594–1670) similarly argues that patristic texts cannot be referring to contemporary conditions, and therefore their conclusions are not necessarily relevant. See his *Traicté de l'employ des saincts peres* (Geneva, 1631), Englished during the Interregnum as *The Right Use of the Fathers* (London, 1651).

53. Hooker, *Works,* 1:398.

54. On Hooker's historicism, see John K. Luoma, "Who Owns the Fathers? Hooker and Cartwright on the Authority of the Primitive Church," *Sixteenth Century Journal* 8 (1977): 53, 58; Ferguson, *Clio Unbound,* pp. 75–76, 207–22. For general discussions of Renaissance historicism, see also F. Smith Fussner, *The Historical Revolution: English Historical Writing and Thought* (New York, 1962); Donald R. Kelley, *Foundations of Modern Historical Scholarship: Language, Law, and History in the French Renaissance* (New

Hooker's mode of analysis to trace a historical narrative to demystify the text or practice in question by exposing its circumscribed and contingent origins. The purpose of such demystification, however, is *not* to discredit the rule or practice but to legitimate it. Hooker is properly a historical thinker because he does *not* oppose mutability to truth. Law and rite are rooted in history, capable of change, contingent on circumstances; yet, if rightly ordered, they articulate the eternal divine will. Hence, his accounts of the gradual development of litanies, fasting, the diaconate, the parochial clergy, and penance, for example, demonstrate both the contextual evolution of practice and the divine authority inherent in the church to evolve practices suitable to specific contexts.[55]

Hooker's acceptance of change is of a piece with his defense of reason and with his general teleological outlook. The view that the goodness of an action derives from its end undermines the myth of sacred origins, with its confusion of chronological and ontological priority.[56] For Hooker neither the practice of the Old Testament nor of the primitive church is strictly normative.[57] The Puritans, he observes, claim it is "out of doubt that the first state of things was best, that in the prime of Christian religion faith was soundest . . . and therefore it must needs follow, that customs, laws, and ordinances devised since are not so good for the Church of Christ." He then responds: "Which rule or canon we hold to be either uncertain or at leastwise unsufficient, if not both. . . . Our end ought always to be the same; our ways and means thereunto not so."[58] This combination of histori-

York, 1970); J. G. A. Pocock, "The Origins of Study of the Past: A Comparative Approach," *Comparative Studies in Society and History* 4 (1961–62): 224–34; Christopher Hill, *Intellectual Origins of the English Revolution* (Oxford, 1965), pp. 173–92. The fact that Raleigh's treatment of history closely resembles Hooker's suggests the extent to which such basically secular views belonged not to a radical fringe but within a dominant religious culture. At least the differences between a purportedly modernist thinker (Raleigh) and a traditional one (Hooker) seem difficult to discern.

55. Hooker, *Works,* 2:174, 415–16, 476, 500; 3:15.

56. Earlier Protestant writers seem more ambivalent. For example, at times Jewel seems to hold that the early church does not represent an ideal past, that it too was rent by conflict, heresy, and pride; however, elsewhere he claims it as a normative ideal (*Apology,* pp.44, 121–23).

57. On the political implications of Hooker's rejection of analogy in favor of a pragmatic teleology, see W. D. J. Cargill Thompson, "The Philosopher of the 'Politic Society': Richard Hooker as a Political Thinker," in Hill, ed., *Studies in Hooker,* p. 60.

58. Hooker, *Works,* 1:421–22; compare 2:73, 442, 504.

cism and teleology wedges apart the unchanging goal of the church from any set of specific rites or institutions. Within the overarching teleological scheme, the emphasis falls on the particular. In fact, for Hooker, the aim of all serious theology is to negotiate that space between the infinitely various historical particulars and the general ends of all religion and virtue, not to collapse the two poles by insisting that the rules established in one context are themselves these ends. If Puritan thought is based on the notion of law, Hooker's rests on that of equity, the flexible adjustment of specific circumstances to general principles.[59]

As often in the Renaissance, hermeneutic and historical considerations are inseparable. Hooker rejects typological and analogical interpretation of Holy Scripture because he perceives history in terms of culturally specific change rather than patterned repetition. He rejects a reading that infers rules from primitive examples because he likewise rejects a view of history as devolution from sacred origins: "Ye think that he which will perfectly reform must bring the form of church-discipline unto the state which then it was at. A thing neither possible, nor certain, nor absolutely convenient."[60]

Yet both the hermeneutic and the historicism seem at odds with Hooker's defense of tradition. That is, in order to authorize tradition he must appeal to principles elsewhere put in question: the "mystical communion" between different ages, the identification of temporal and ontological priority, and the normative status of primitive practice.[61] In addition, the argument for tradition rests precisely on the *failure* of reason to deliver certainty.[62] Although men possess "that light of Reason, whereby good may be known from evil," very few things exist "the goodness whereof Reason in such sort doth or easily can discover."[63] In almost every specific controversy neither side possesses "reasons demonstrative" and "what thing was there ever set down so agreeable with sound reason, but some probable shew against it might be made?"[64] For error can generally "allege in defense of itself

59. Hooker, *Works,* 2:38–39, 514.
60. Hooker, *Works,* 1:158.
61. Hooker, *Works,* 1:159; 2:170, 381; 3:23.
62. Grislis, "The Hermeneutical Problem," in Hill, ed., *Studies in Hooker,* p. 179.
63. Hooker, *Works,* 1:222–23.
64. Hooker, *Works,* 1:170–71; compare 1:477.

many fair probabilities." In this absence of certainty, probable reasoning must yield "general obedience" to authority and to tradition.[65] In the first case, the attempt to ground Christian faith and practice in reason and history shifts uneasily between its relativizing and secularizing results and the return to supposedly excluded subjective principles. In the second, the attempt itself discloses the inability of rational method to provide an epistemic ground; instead it opens onto the rhetorical arena of competing probabilities, which can only be stabilized by supposedly excluded authoritarian principles. These implicit tensions (if not contradictions) will be discussed in more detail later on. In the meanwhile, I want to pursue some additional implications of Hooker's rationalized and historicized approach.[66]

RES AND *VERBA*

Hooker's essentially historical perspective governs his treatment of language and thus has further implications for his hermeneutic. In the discussions of language scattered through *The Laws,* Hooker consistently distinguishes words from things. He thus denies any substantial connection between the two, such as was posited in almost all Neoplatonic, occult, or medieval accounts. He expresses considerable doubt whether words were originally "correctly" imposed on things by a wise legislator and, therefore, whether the etymology of a word picks out the true meaning of its referent.[67] Instead he tends to see the meaning of a term as its meaning in current ordinary usage. At least "concerning popular use of words that which the wisdom of their inventors did intend thereby is not commonly thought of, but by the name the thing altogether conceived in gross." Thus "priest" no longer means sacrificer any more than "senator" an old man.[68] Meaning is conventional and cultural, not inherent in language. Therefore when interpreting texts from earlier cultures, one cannot argue naively from words to things. Language reflects culture, but cultural shifts usually precede linguistic ones, so that episcopal orders could have

65. Hooker, *Works,* 1:171, 2:291; see also 2:32–34.

66. For a somewhat exaggerated appreciation of Hooker's rationalism, see Peter Munz, *The Place of Hooker in the History of Thought* (London, 1952), p. 62.

67. Hooker, *Works,* 2:470–71.

68. Hooker, *Works,* 2:471–72.

existed before the use of specific terms to designate them.[69] From this Hooker infers a fundamental principle of semantic change from the general to the specific: whereas "apostle" and "bishop" originally referred to all messengers or overseers, after the emergence of distinctively Christian cultural roles, the terms were restricted to their ecclesiological meanings.

However, language does not only reflect culture and cultural concepts but plays a constitutive function. Although a title in itself is "a matter of nothing," Hooker observes, if that of the lord mayor were abolished "suppose we that it would be a small maim unto the credit, force, and countenance of his office?"[70] As language sustains cultural representations, so it is also "the mother of all error," what Bacon came to call the Idol of the Market Place. For if words fail to distinguish between things in fact distinct from one another (or vice versa), they deceive thought and so divorce the conceits of the mind from "the nature of things conceived."[71]

Hooker's awareness of the interrelation between culture and language and the concomitant separation between words and things underlies his two essential hermeneutic principles. The first is simply the general rule of humanist exegesis: passages must be taken in context. One cannot legitimately isolate a sentence embedded in some specific discussion and propound it as a universal law but must consider both authorial intention and historical setting.[72] The second principle is more radical. Like medieval Catholic exegesis, the Protestant tradition from Luther on linked the hearing of Scripture with the experience of the Spirit. Although sympathetic to humanist scholarship, it simultaneously insisted that to read aright is to experience a "supernatural force acting through Scripture."[73] Thus for Tyndale the exegete must "'feel the power of faith, and the working of the Spirit in the heart' and not trust to 'blind reason and foolish fantasies.'"[74] Calvin makes the same point: in reading the Bible one experiences direct illumination from the Spirit, whereby "we feel that the undoubted power of his

69. Hooker, *Works,* 3:146–48.
70. Hooker, *Works,* 3:263; compare 2:66.
71. Hooker, *Works,* 1:355.
72. Hooker, *Works,* 1:302–4, 325–26, 360; 3:253–56.
73. John R. Knott, Jr., *The Sword of the Spirit: Puritan Responses to the Bible* (Chicago, 1980), p. 32.
74. Quoted in Knott, *The Sword,* p. 20.

divine majesty lives and breathes there. . . . Such, then, is a conviction that requires no reasons . . . such, finally, a feeling that can be born only of heavenly revelation."[75] The act of reading is the experience of divinity. Hooker, however, denies this. The Holy Scriptures do not mediate presence but, like any other text, require interpretation, and interpretation is a matter of human judgment: "between true and false construction, the difference reason must shew."[76] Reason becomes a "necessary instrument" in scriptural exegesis because

> the operations of the Spirit . . . are as we know things secret and undiscernible even to the very soul where they are. . . . Wherefore albeit the Spirit lead us into all truth and direct us in all goodness, yet . . . we therefore stand on a plainer ground, when we gather by reason from the quality of things believed or done, that the Spirit of God hath directed us in both, than if we settle ourselves to believe or to do any certain particular thing, as being moved thereto by the Spirit.[77]

The reader cannot passively receive meaning and presence but must reconstruct the intention, scope, and application of the text, and "all this must be by reason found out."[78] Presence is thus deferred, a space set up between divine meaning and human reading—a space mediated by reason but therefore almost always productive of probabilities and conjectural inferences rather than certain knowledge. Like the emphasis on history, that on reason distances and objectifies the text, disallowing an experiential participation of the Spirit by interposing the interpretative act between object and subjectivity.

REAL PRESENCE

The split between *res* and *verba* distancing text from reader parallels a separation of sign from signified dividing visible form from spiritual substance. This separation appears both in Hooker's sacramental the-

75. John Calvin, *Institutes of the Christian Religion,* 2 vols., ed. John T. McNeill, trans. Ford Lewis Battles, The Library of Christian Classics (Philadelphia, 1960), 1.7.5.

76. Hooker, *Works,* 1:378.

77. Hooker, *Works,* 1:371, 378.

78. Hooker, *Works,* 1:381; compare 1:328–29. This was probably the single most controversial assertion in *The Laws.* For the subsequent debate over Hooker's claim that reason must determine what is Scripture and how it is to be interpreted see Cargill Thompson, "The Philosopher," in Hill, ed., *Studies in Hooker,* p. 31; Grislis, "The Hermeneutical Problem," in Hill, ed., *Studies in Hooker,* pp. 192–93; Booty, "Hooker and Anglicanism," pp. 222–28.

ology and his ecclesiology. In the former, Hooker draws on both the Reformed tradition of Calvin, Bullinger, and Bucer and the fourteenth-century nominalists to argue that sacramental signs do not contain or cause grace but instead signify God's concomitant yet independent bestowal of it.

> Scotus, Occam, Petrus Alliacensis, with sundry others [show] . . . very good reason, wherefore no sacrament of the new law can either by virtue which itself hath, or by force supernaturally given it, be properly a cause to work grace; but sacraments are therefore said to work or confer grace, because the will of Almighty God is, although not to give them such efficacy, yet himself to be present in the ministry of the working that effect, which proceedeth wholly from him without any real operation of theirs, such as can enter into men's souls.[79]

The sacraments are infallible but empty signs[80]—not empty in the Zwinglian sense of being simply memorials of Christ's sacrifice, but empty insofar as the signs themselves neither contain nor effect anything, although they really signify and "exhibit" the recipient's "*participation* of his body and blood."[81] They are not "magical signs."[82] Similarly, ceremonies and ritual have no intrinsic efficacy, although they are justified on the grounds of decorum or psychological function.[83]

The separation between sign and substance in Hooker's ecclesiology seems more ambivalent, for Hooker struggles to hold together the national church and the channels of grace, defending the role of that church in the political and spiritual well-being of the community.[84] Nevertheless, especially in his treatment of penance and the royal

79. Hooker, *Works,* 3:88.

80. On sacramental theology during the Reformation, see Delumeau, *Catholicism,* pp. 13–15; B. A. Gerrish, "The Lord's Supper in the Reformed Confessions," *Theology Today* 23 (1966): 224–43; Nijenhuis, *Saravia,* pp. 193–205.

81. Hooker, *Works,* 2:352. For the medieval and Roman Catholic understanding of the sacrament as *containing* grace, see Hugh of Saint Victor, *On the Sacraments of the Christian Faith (De sacramentis),* trans. Roy Deferrari (Cambridge, Mass., 1951), pp. 155–57.

82. Hooker, *Works,* 3:95.

83. Hooker, *Works,* 2:29, 53–57. However, as Lake notes, by giving ritual a genuine psychological function and thereby giving it real spiritual value, Hooker attributed far more significance to liturgy, ceremony, and gesture than earlier Anglican writers (*Anglicans and Puritans?,* pp. 164–69).

84. Hooker, *Works,* 2:13–19.

headship, the visible and mystical bodies of Christ divide.[85] The national church performs an administrative function, calling and dissolving assemblies, legislating "orders concerning religion," appointing bishops, punishing offenders in church courts. This "power external and visible in the Church" is sharply distinguished from "that spiritual power of Christ's own regiment, which power is termed spiritual, because it worketh secretly, inwardly, and invisibly."[86] Like the sacraments, institutions too are empty signs, or, more properly, the power that informs them is political rather than transcendent. We will return to this topic in chapter 4.

This dedivinization of the sign is characteristic of Calvinism as well as of Hooker's thought, but whereas in Calvin and the English Puritans the locus of presence transfers to the faithful community, in Hooker it transfers to the individual.[87] The relation between God and the soul becomes privatized, loosened from institutional and ecclesiastical moorings. Thus, for example, while the Reformed tradition insisted on public confession, not for remission of sins but to strengthen and satisfy the community, Hooker argues that penance does not require confession to either priest or congregation but instead only inward contrition.[88] The clearest instance of this privatization comes

85. A similar split appears in the ecclesiology of both Luther and Whitgift. In part, it was the legacy of Marsilius of Padua. See Munz, *The Place of Hooker,* pp.96–111; Cargill Thompson, "The Philosopher," in Hill, ed., *Studies in Hooker,* pp. 34–35, 51, 55–57; Hill, "The Evolution," in Hill, ed., *Studies in Hooker,* pp. 148–49; Ferguson, *Clio Unbound,* pp. 198–99; Lake, *Anglicans and Puritans?,* p. 126.

86. Hooker, *Works,* 3:341, 390; compare 1:338–42; 3:374.

87. John Bossy, *Christianity in the West, 1400–1700* (Oxford, 1985), pp. 132, 140–42; Nijenhuis, *Saravia,* p. 201; Lake, "Calvinism," pp. 39–40 and *Anglicans and Puritans?,* pp. 29–34, 47, 65, 177; John S. Coolidge, *The Pauline Renaissance in England: Puritanism and the Bible* (Oxford, 1970), pp. 51, 75, 147; David Little, *Religion, Order, and Law: A Study in Pre-Revolutionary England* (Oxford, 1970), pp. 54, 74, 89. The Anglican view of a broad church membership, basically coextensive with the entire population of the nation and including both godly and ungodly, seems to have encouraged a split between institutional membership and private spirituality. In Puritan thought, the visible church is (ideally) identical to the community of the godly, thus minimizing any distance between institutional and spiritual life. Barbu notes similar features during the decline of the polis: on the one hand, a tendency toward privatized spirituality, on the other, a groupism expressing a preindividualist communal solidarity (*Historical Psychology,* pp. 52–54).

88. Hooker, *Works,* 3:48, 54, 62, 100. In *The Reason of Church Government,* John Milton advocates the Presbyterian discipline precisely because it effectively manipulates shame as an instrument of social control: "For where shame is, there is fear, but where fear is, there is not presently shame. And if anything may be done to inbreed in us this generous and Christian reverence one of another, the very nurse and guardian of piety

in Hooker's treatment of the Eucharist.[89] Again, the Reformed tradition tended to view the sacrament in terms of the godly community. There is no trace of this in Hooker. Instead, here the traditional language of mystical participation, indwelling, and real presence suddenly reemerges—yet not with reference to mediated sacramental action but to God's direct contact with the individual soul. Hooker thus apparently retains mystical participation but, by a slight shift, interiorizes it. The contact is signified but not effected through the visible sign. The passages on Holy Communion thus speak of the "mystical conjunction" between Christ's flesh and the communicant, a "participation of the grace, efficacy, merit or virtue of his body and blood"; he "inhabits" and "dwells" in the recipient. A "divine and mystical kind of union . . . maketh us one with him"; this "mystical participation giveth life," for Christ assists "this heavenly banquet with his personal and true presence," and we have "participation also in the fruit, grace and efficacy of his body and blood, whereupon there ensueth a kind of transubstantiation in us."[90] It is now the recipient and not the sign that transubstantiates. "The real presence of Christ's most blessed body and blood is not therefore to be sought for in the sacrament, but in the worthy receiver of the sacrament."[91]

As sign, institution, and history are drained of essential presence, the point of contact, of transubstantiation, becomes internalized in the

---

and virtue, it cannot sooner be than by such a discipline in the church as may use us to have in awe the assemblies of the faithful, and to count it a thing most grievous, next to the grieving of God's Spirit, to offend those whom he hath put in authority as a healing superintendence over our lives and behaviours, both to our own happiness and that we may not give offence to good men." (*Prose Selections,* ed. Merritt Y. Hughes [New York, 1947], pp. 127–28).

89. Hooker's relation to the Reformation eucharistic controversies is complex. Doctrinally he is close to Calvin, Jewel, and especially Bullinger (compare Gerrish, "The Lord's Supper," pp. 226, 242). Like them he tends to combine the traditional realist language of participation with a denial of the real presence of the signified in the sign. However, as Lake notes, the importance Hooker assigns to the sacrament both associates him with earlier Catholic piety and points ahead to Andrewes and Laud ("Calvinism," p. 75). His stress on the transformation within the recipient rather than in the sign is echoed in Saravia's early-seventeenth-century *De eucharista* (Nijenhuis, *Saravia,* pp. 193–94, 201). See also John Booty, "Hooker's Understanding of the Presence of Christ in the Eucharist," in *The Divine Drama in History and Liturgy,* ed. John Booty, Pittsburgh Theological Monographs (Allison Park, Penn., 1984), pp. 131–48; Lake, *Anglicans and Puritans?,* pp. 173ff.

90. Hooker, *Works,* 2:252–53, 352, 356–58; compare 2:238, 249ff.

91. Hooker, *Works,* 2:352.

individual soul and conscience. In a way that anticipates Descartes's radical distinction between mind and body, Hooker splits subject from object, spiritual from visible, inwardness from institution. This split creates two distinct discourses: one of reason and evidence, the other of mystical participation. In the latter, knowledge results from indwelling presence;[92] in the former, knowledge by assimilation gives way to knowledge by objectification—by historical and philological analysis of the evidence.

THE PROBLEMATICS OF REASON

The two discourses resemble the terms of the dichotomy established at the outset of *The Laws* between rational and subjective/affective grounds. At that point, the dichotomy served to distinguish Hooker's hermeneutic from that of the Puritans. We have already seen that the legitimation of tradition, insofar as it rests on subjective and authoritarian grounds, threatened this dichotomy.[93] But now the possibility appears that Hooker himself deploys both discourses (or epistemologies). Hooker's incipient rationalism and historicism do not press to their logical—and radical—conclusions because they are "supplemented" by an incompatible secondary epistemology.

That this is the case can be seen by beginning with an observation made several times in *The Laws:* that, contra Calvin, Holy Scripture cannot prove itself to be the word of God. The text is not self-authenticating but demands assent only if reason can demonstrate its divine origin, for "it is not required or can be exacted at our hands, that

92. Hooker, *Works,* 2:361. At one point, Hooker's struggle to preserve the discourse of mystical participation within a largely rationalized epistemology surfaces vividly. In his third sermon, he tries to explain what the Bible means when it speaks of Christ as dwelling within people, observing that "somewhat strange it seemeth, that a thing in Scripture so often inculcated should be so hardly understood." What he argues is that to expound this "conjunction with Christ to be a mutual participation whereby each is blended with other . . . doth fight openly against reason." There cannot be any *material* penetration, since Christ is "locally divided and severed." Instead, "Christ is in us . . . according to that intellectual comprehension which the mind is capable of." Christ, that is, is "in" us in the same way that any idea is "in" our minds; He is in us "as things which we know and delight in are said to dwell in our minds and possess our hearts." But this drastic reduction of participation to conceptualization disappears within a paragraph, as Hooker calmly returns to speak of Christ "dwelling" in the faithful as "the soul of their souls moving them" (*Works,* 3:611–13).

93. Ferguson, *Clio Unbound,* pp. 216–18.

we should yield unto any thing other assent, than such as doth answer the evidence which is to be had of that we assent unto."[94] While Hooker stoutly affirms that "we have necessary reason" for holding the Bible to have been divinely inspired, he in fact never offers any reasons or evidence at all for this affirmation.[95] Indeed, as Augustine, Aquinas, and Calvin recognized, no such objectively necessary reasons exist, only probabilities.[96] If, therefore, assent should be proportioned to evidence, Christianity dwindles to a hypothesis.

Hooker never directly faces this dilemma. But he does explicitly treat the grounds of faith in his first extant sermon, "Of the Certainty and Perpetuity of Faith in the Elect," preached at the Temple in 1586 and a source of considerable controversy. In this, Hooker clearly lays out a dual epistemology. Drawing on Aquinas's early commentary on the *Sentences* of Peter Lombard, he distinguishes the grounds of rational belief from those of religious faith. Aquinas had argued that what we believe is less certain to us than what we know, because in knowledge (*scientia*) the intellect can *see* its grounds, while in faith the will (*voluntas*) commands the intellect to believe what it cannot see. Therefore "the certainty which is in knowledge and the intellect derives from the evidence itself [*ex ipsa evidentia*] of those things which are said to be certain; but the certitude of faith derives from a firm adherence [*adhaesio*] to that which is believed." But because faith rests not on seeing (*visio*) but the command of the will, the believer experiences "some motion of doubt."[97]

The corresponding passage in Hooker's sermon is basically an expanded translation of this distinction. We are, he argues, certain of some things because their truth is evident to us. Things evident to us are either logically demonstrable or available to sense perception. In neither sense, however, is there much evidence for the existence of God: "we have less certainty of evidence concerning things believed,

94. Hooker, *Works,* 1:323; compare 1:267–69, 375–77.

95. Hooker, *Works,* 1:322.

96. St. Augustine, *Contra epistolam Manichaei quam vocant fundamenti* (cited in Calvin, *Institutes,* 1:76n); Calvin, *Institutes,* 1.8.1; St. Thomas Aquinas, *Summa contra gentiles,* 1.2.3. See Gunnar Hillerdal, *Reason and Revelation in Richard Hooker,* Acta Universitatis Lundensis, new series, 54 (1959–61): 79, 114.

97. St. Thomas Aquinas, *Commentum in quatour libros sententiarum Magistri Petri Lombardi,* 3.23.2.2, in vol. 7 of *Opera omnia* (Parma, 1852–73; reprint, New York, 1948). See also his *De veritate* q. 14, a.1.

than concerning sensible or naturally perceived." The ground of faith is not what Hooker calls the "Certainty of Evidence" but, following Aquinas, the "Certainty of Adherence." Unlike Thomas, however, Hooker does not speak of the will commanding the intellect to believe; rather he alters "will" to "heart," giving the process of adherence an emotional and also sensuous dimension absent in his source. The certainty of adherence is engendered "when the heart doth cleave and stick unto that which it doth believe." A person believes in God because "his spirit having once truly tasted the heavenly sweetness thereof, all the world is not able quite and clean to remove him from it; but he striveth with himself to hope against all reason of believing." Abandoning Aquinas's abstractly epistemic focus, Hooker traces the subjective contradiction, the simultaneous experience of doubt and intense, illogical desire, characterizing religious belief. One clings with "a sure adherence unto that which he doth but faintly and fearfully believe." He trusts in God *despite* the evidence and believes "against all reason," because he "tastes" God's goodness and falls in love.[98]

While *The Laws* avoids explicit treatment of the issue, reference to the same dual epistemology comes up in passing. Hooker thus will talk about a "habit of faith in us," derived not so much from rational conviction as from baptismal grace, which is "the first and most effectual cause out of which our belief groweth."[99] Or, again, he speaks of an "affection of faith," itself a gift creating "love to Godward above the comprehension which she [reason] hath of God."[100] This is faith formed by love, the old *fides caritate formata* of the Middle Ages.[101] Correspondingly, as in his first sermon, "reason" in *The Laws* often slips over to being an empirical faculty, bounded by sense perception and therefore intrinsically secular, while a necessarily subjective love or desire becomes the ground of faith.

A traditional mystic epistemology thus partially displaces the po-

98. Hooker, *Works,* 3:470–71. The passage resembles Herbert's "The Glance," where the original moment of "sugared strange delight" disappears, yet the memory of that taste/glance overcomes subsequent grief and anguish.

99. Hooker, *Works,* 2:305, 310–311.

100. Hooker, *Works,* 2:305.

101. Steven Ozment, "Luther and the Late Middle Ages: The Formation of Reformation Thought," in *Transition and Revolution: Problems and Issues of European Renaissance and Reformation History,* ed. Robert M. Kingdon (Minneapolis, 1974).

lemical hermeneutic based on reason and historical evidence.[102] For this connection between desire and assent, like Hooker's eucharistic theology, presupposes a participatory rather than a rational and objectifying link between the self and reality, a link implicit in the medieval axiom he accepts "that natural desire cannot utterly be frustrate." The fact that all men desire infinite happiness, a happiness not given in this world, itself guarantees the existence of something "above the capacity of reason," something "divine and heavenly" capable of satisfying that desire.[103] The psyche participates in reality so that its subjective needs correspond to actual possibilities. Hooker's spiritual psychology consistently makes desire rather than reason the epistemic ground.[104] Nevertheless, his understanding of self-deception and ideological hermeneutics problematizes this optimism of self-warranting desire: one can feel very strongly and still be very wrong.

HABITS OF THOUGHT

Two epistemologies or discourses thus coexist in Hooker, one underlying his treatment of signs, language, and history, the other, his spiritual and sacramental psychology. Because the former is both more explicit and more modern, it has received the most attention from Hooker scholars. But, in fact, it is the simultaneous existence of both that discloses what I take to be a central tension in Renaissance habits of thought. This tension plays itself out between the polarities of participatory and rational consciousness—where by "consciousness" I mean simply habits of thought, that is, the culturally based ways the mind categorizes and structures the world, which in turn determine its representations.

Rational consciousness sees reason as the primary connection between self and reality. The function of reason is to distinguish, and rational consciousness therefore individuates and maintains clear

102. As before, "mystic" does not refer to any form of mysticism per se but to a nonempirical participation, as in the phrase "mystical body of Christ." Coming at this question from a discussion of reason and revelation in Hooker, Hillerdal reaches a similar conclusion that Hooker's ostensibly rationalizing epistemology in the end takes "an astonishing turn to a kind of irrationalism" (*Reason and Revelation,* p. 135; compare pp. 58, 79, 86, 94–95, 117–19, 134, 147).

103. Hooker, *Works,* 1:257.

104. Hooker, *Works,* 1:254–61.

boundaries between individual entities. It is thus sensitive to the gap between subject and object, as well as to that between words and things. It tends to empty cosmos, state, and history of their sacramental numinosity, perceiving them as neutral objects of investigation—valued or rejected in terms of their function rather than because of any intrinsic or supernatural quality. Participatory consciousness, on the other hand, assumes the primacy of desire in the act of knowing. It therefore does not oppose psyche and world, since the desires of the mind assure the reality of the desired object. Rather than opposing or distinguishing entities, participatory consciousness perceives relatedness; its categories are indistinct and permeable. It thus tends not to separate words from things, instead treating both as signs, each linked to the other. Because things are also signs, the natural and social worlds have a significance independent of function; they reflect the supernatural order and symbolize transcendence.[105]

For the late Renaissance this distinction should not be drawn too sharply. Hooker exhibits both habits of thought, as do many of his contemporaries—the mystical excursions of scientists from Kepler to Newton come to mind at once. Studies of Renaissance magic, occult, witchcraft, and related practices indicate the persistence of prescientific mental habits through the seventeenth century.[106] Our understanding of corresponding structures in aspects of intellectual culture not related to science is less clear, partly because we tend to be preoccupied with doctrines rather than representations. Nevertheless, it is arguable that genuine participatory consciousness continues into the late Renaissance, not only on its magical or folk margins but within the dominant

105. Barbu thus observes, "The development of rational thinking is closely associated with what . . . is called reality testing function, a term which often can be rendered as rational consciousness. The formation in the mind of the individual of such a function presupposes in the first place a shift in the orientation of his consciousness . . . from inner-emotional to external factors. As a result of this, things and events are no longer, or are to a lesser degree, perceived as symbols or functions of obscure magic or mythical forces lying beyond them: things and events become reality itself" (*Historical Psychology,* p. 115).

106. Hill, *Intellectual Origins,* pp. 148–49; Vickers "Introduction," in Vickers, ed., *Occult and Scientific,* pp. 27–32; Lotte Mulligan, "'Reason,' 'Right Reason,' and 'Revelation' in Mid-Seventeenth-Century England," in Vickers, ed., *Occult and Scientific,* pp. 382–83, 391–92; Foucault, *The Order of Things,* pp. 32–34; Keith Thomas, *Religion and the Decline of Magic: Studies in Popular Beliefs in Sixteenth- and Seventeenth-Century England* (London, 1971); Frances A. Yates, *The Rosicrucian Enlightenment* (London, 1972).

culture.[107] Furthermore, viewed in this light, the fine-spun theological debates of the period gain intelligibility. They reflect not merely dogmatic differences (why was the Real Presence such a vital and divisive issue?) but also the rather surprising longevity of traditional habits of thought contemporaneous with the growing hegemony of rational consciousness. The theological struggles may have been tempests in teapots, but they were heated by an epochal flame.

This coexistence of contradictory habits of thought might be shown from any number of texts. At present, however, I want to focus on Lancelot Andrewes, both because his works exemplify participatory consciousness almost untouched by rational differentiation and because, as I mentioned before, he is so closely connected not only to Hooker but to the entire dominant intellectual culture of the time.[108] But if Andrewes differs significantly from Hooker, then the picture of a homogenous Anglican rationalism, reaching back to Aquinas and forward to Tillotson, cannot be sustained.[109] Given the notorious difficulty of defining "Anglican" in any case, recent church historians like Nicholas Tyacke have almost abandoned the endeavor, writing about religious debates as if the *contents* of the positions were irrelevant—just labels around which to gather a faction.[110] One alternative to such desperate trivializing—the one attempted here—is to explore whether some sort of massive, but very gradual and complex, paradigm shift did not leave multiple fissures throughout the cultural land-

107. Anthropologists like Levy-Bruhl and Durkheim studiously avoid remarking on similarities between this primitive religious consciousness and Christianity, a reticence E. E. Evans-Pritchard attributes either to ignorance or to a deliberate half-concealment of the subversive implications of their conclusions (*Theories of Primitive Religion* [Oxford, 1965], pp. 17–19).

108. The fact that Andrewes seems "archaic" does not mean that he was not also, in another sense, avant-garde—a sympathizer with the Remonstrants, a friend of Casaubon, a leader of the reaction against Calvinism. Arminianism, particularly the British variety, often displayed a confusing mixture of patristic conservatism and rationalism. Men like Casaubon were at once drawn to the Church of England because it was closest to the thought and practice of the early church and yet they themselves were some of the most influential critics of the myths on which the normative authority of the early church rested—witness Casaubon's attack on the antiquity of the Hermetic corpus and Dionysius the Areopagite. See Pattison, *Casaubon*.

109. Samuel L. Bethell, *The Cultural Revolution of the Seventeenth Century* (London, 1951), pp. 13–37.

110. Nicholas Tyacke, "Puritanism, Arminianism, and Counter-Revolution," in *The Origins of the English Civil War*, ed. Conrad Russell (New York, 1973), and Nicholas Tyacke, *Anti-Calvinists: The Rise of English Arminianism, c. 1590–1640*, Oxford Historical Monographs (Oxford, 1987).

scape. Andrewes is a highly suggestive figure for this purpose since he seems to be writing out of a deeply unfamiliar mode of thought, whose only obvious affinities are to anthropological descriptions of primitive mentality and studies of hermeticism and the occult. The difference between his thought and Hooker's seems to follow the principal fault line where the fissuring occurs and thus to indicate the nature of the underlying tension within the central discourse. As before, we will concentrate on hermeneutics, history, and epistemology.

THE WORD OF GOD

The most noticeable feature of Andrewes's works is his use of language: his puns, quibbles, near-rhymes, parallelisms, sound play, and loving attention to the precise connotations of each word in his chosen text. The playfulness, the lack of transparent referentiality, is almost Derridean; the ontology is the exact opposite. If, as Stanley Fish notes (quoting Ricoeur), "'Structuralism is Kantianism without a transcendental subject,' then Christianity is structuralism *with* a transcendental subject," both opposing, however, the "ideology of the referent."[111] The relation between word and transcendental subject is made explicit in Andrewes's conception of biblical language. While he acknowledges that all discourse about God remains inadequate, broken human speech, yet "since the Holy Ghost hath made choice of these terms, they are no idle speculations that are drawn from them."[112] The words are quite literally transcendent signifiers—chosen by the Spirit and "containing" something capable of being "drawn" out—for "the Holy Ghost useth no waste words," no "idle tautologies"; "every one of them is *verbum vigilans,* as St. Augustine speaks, 'awake all;' never an one asleep among them."[113]

It is the word that is awake, not simply its referent. Andrewes does not, in fact, think in terms of reference. The meaning or nature of the object is contained in the word, or at least essentially bound to it, for God's "nominals be reals"; the word is the thing, and "the name is that

111. Stanley E. Fish, "Sequence and Meaning in Seventeenth-Century Narrative," in *To Tell a Story: Narrative Theory and Practice* (Los Angeles, 1973), p. 59.

112. Andrewes, *Works,* 1:108.

113. Andrewes, *Works,* 3:84, 336; 1:420. See Boyd M. Berry, *Process of Speech: Puritan Religious Writing and "Paradise Lost"* (Baltimore, 1976), p. 48.

whereby we know a man or a thing."[114] The term in its etymological depths corresponds to and discloses the true nature of its *res*. This sense of a radical connection between language and being shapes Andrewes's famous dissection of the name "Immanuel" in his ninth Nativity sermon. (Because Andrewes is less well known even than Hooker and takes longer to make his point, quotations will suffer from being both annoyingly long and annoyingly fragmentary.) Andrewes begins:

> And now, to look into the name, It is compounded, and to be taken in pieces. First, into *Immanu* and *El;* of which, *El* the latter is the more principal by far; for *El* is God. . . . For the other, *Immanu;* though *El* be the more principal, yet I cannot tell whether it or *Immanu* do more concern us. For as in *El* is might, so in *Immanu* is our right to His might, and to all He hath or is worth. . . . This *Immanu* is a compound again; we may take it in sunder into *nobis* and *cum;* and so then have we three pieces. 1. *El,* the mighty God; 2. and *anu,* we, poor we,—poor indeed if we have all the world beside if we have not Him to be with us; 3. and *Im,* which is *cum,* and that *cum* in the midst between *nobis* and *Deus,* God and us—to couple God and us; thereby to convey the things of the one to the other.[115]

The etymology of the word reveals the nature of salvation, for the thing is implicit in the name. Andrewes's punning resembles the etymological word play of the Bible itself, for both rest on the traditional view of language as significant rather than merely signifying, a view reflected in Andrewes's own primary aesthetic categories of full and forcible.[116]

Words are full or pregnant because they contain a richness of meaning that discloses the complex theological structure of reality. The first Nativity sermon thus exfoliates the word *apprehendit* as if the term held in its core the whole nature of divine love shown in the Incarnation. Characteristically, Andrewes approaches the spiritual implications of the word by etymologizing to its physical basis:

114. Andrewes, *Works,* 1:142; 6:144. For the inherence of the thing in the word (and vice versa) in premodern thought, see Reiss, *Modernism,* pp. 31–32, 76–77; Foucault, *The Order of Things,* pp. 26–38; Vickers, "Analogy," in Vickers, ed., *Occult and Scientific,* pp. 95–163; Maclean, "Natural Signs," in Vickers, ed., *Occult and Scientific,* p. 245; Levy-Bruhl, *How Natives Think,* p. 50; John Chamberlin, *Increase and Multiply: Arts-of-Discourse Procedure in the Preaching of Donne* (Chapel Hill, 1976), pp. 8–18.

115. Andrewes, *Works,* 1:144.

116. Andrewes, *Works,* 1:2, 340; 2:315; 3:140, 202; 4:35, 278, 305.

> Of *apprehendit,* first. Many words were more obvious, and offered themselves to the Apostle, no doubt; *suscepit,* or *assumpsit,* or other such like. "This word was sought for . . ." saith the Greek Scholiast; and he can best . . . tell us also what it weigheth. . . . "this word supposeth a flight of the one party, and a pursuit of the other—a pursuit eager, and so long till he overtake;" and when he hath overtaken . . . *apprehendens,* "laying fast hold, and seizing surely on him."[117]

The etymological image of flight and pursuit then discloses the mystery latent in the word, beginning with original sin when "man fell, and fled too, and 'hid himself in the thick trees' from the presence of God." Our flight spurred Christ's pursuit: "to come Himself after us; to say, *Corpus apta Mihi, Ecce venio*; 'Get Me a body, I will Myself after Him';—this was exceeding much, that we fled and He followed us flying." The metaphor of exhausting pursuit then modulates into history, as the sweat of the chase becomes the bloody sweat of Christ's agony: "And He gave not over His pursuit, though it were long and laborious, and He full weary; though it cast Him into a 'sweat,' a 'sweat of blood.'"[118] The word continues to unfold, pointing now to the intensity of Christ's love, for *apprehendit* "is not every 'taking' . . . [but] 'to seize upon it with great vehemency, to lay hold on it with both hands as upon a thing we are glad we have got, and will be loath to let go again.'" The word next suggests the manner of the Incarnation; Christ "*apprehendit semen.* He took not the person, but 'He took the seed,' that is, the nature of man."[119] In the course of the sermon, *apprehendit* comes to include man's apprehension by the devil and Christ's seizing us from his jaws, Christ's apprehension of our hand "to lead us even by the way of truth to the path of life," our "double 'apprehension'" of Christ by faith and works, and finally our "mutual and reciprocal 'apprehension'" of Him in the Eucharist.[120] Indeed, a full, waking, and forcible word, one that compacts the actual relations of man and God, whose signification is not conventional and external but like the organs of a body covered and held in by a verbal integument. The deep structure of the word is the world. One can see why the later seventeenth century with its referential semantics found this intolerable.

117. Andrewes, *Works,* 1:6
118. Andrewes, *Works,* 1:6–7.
119. Andrewes, *Works,* 1:8–9.
120. Andrewes, *Works,* 1:10–16.

Typically, Andrewes's etymologies push behind the abstract signification of a term to its primitive unity of concrete and spiritual meaning. As Owen Barfield points out, the evolution of language from this unity to the separation of abstract and concrete meanings parallels the evolution of consciousness from participation to subject-object dualism. Before "the exclusive disjunction between outer and inner," the same word signified both a physical and spiritual or mental state (for example, melancholy, spirit, blood) precisely because these were either undifferentiated or only partly so.[121] As anyone who has glanced at its scientific works will recognize, the absence of clear boundaries between the corporeal and incorporeal persists through the Renaissance. This absence informs Andrewes's usual manner of interpretation. Rather than moving from word pointing to concept pointing to thing, he reads, as it were, downward and inward: from concrete etymology contained in the word to the spiritual understanding "drawn" from this root physicality.

To take only one example, in his second Passion sermon, based on Lamentations 1:12,[122] Andrewes begins with the Hebrew etymologies of the central terms:

> The first is מכאוב, *Mac-ob,* which we read "sorrow," taken 1. from a wound or stripe, as all do agree.
>
> The second is עולל, *Gholel;* we read "Done to me," taken 2. from a word that signifieth melting in a furnace, as St. Hierome noteth out of the Chaldee, who so translateth it.
>
> The third is הוגה, *Hoga,* where we read afflicted, from a word which importeth renting off, or bereaving. The old Latin turneth it *Vindemiavit me,* as a vine whose fruit is all plucked off. The Greek, with Theodoret, *ἀπεφύλλισέ με*, as a vine or tree whose leaves are all beaten off, and is left naked and bare.[123]

The wounding, melting, and stripping uncovered here then become not simply metaphors for Christ's suffering but clues to its hidden

121. Barfield, *Saving the Appearances,* pp. 116–19.

122. The pericope (according to the Genevan translation) reads: "Have ye no regard, O all ye that pass by the Way? consider, and behold, if ever there were sorrow like My sorrow, which was done unto Me, wherewith the Lord did afflict Me in the day of the fierceness of His wrath." Where helpful, I will include the pericope in the notes for the sake of readers who may not be able to conjure up the passage if given only chapter and verse.

123. Andrewes, *Works,* 2:143.

nature and meaning. As before, the historical event resides in the etymological ground of the word. Thus Andrewes explores the implications of Christ's being "afflicted" (*hoga*):

> what is left the meanest of the sons of men, was not left Him, not a leaf. Not a leaf! Leaves I may well call all human comforts and regards, whereof He was then left clean desolate. 1. "His own," they among whom He had gone about all His life long, healing them, teaching them, feeding them, doing them all the good He could, it is they that cry, "Not Him, no, but Barabbas rather." . . . But these were but withered leaves. They then that on earth were nearest Him of all, the greenest leaves and likest to hang on, and to give Him some shade; even of them some bought and sold Him, others denied and forswore Him, but all fell away, and forsook Him. Ἀπεφύλλισέ με, saith Theodoret, not a leaf left.
>
> But leaves are but leaves, and so are all earthly stays. The fruit then, the true fruit of the Vine indeed, the true comfort in all heaviness, is *desuper,* "from above," is divine consolation. But *Vindemiavit Me,* saith the Latin text;—even that was, in this His sorrow, this day bereft Him too. . . . and He left in the state of a weather-beaten tree, all desolate and forlorn. . . . His soul was even as a scorched heath-ground, without so much as any drop of dew of divine comfort; as a naked tree—no fruit to refresh Him within, no leaf to give Him shadow without.[124]

The word "afflicted" holds the image of the barren tree that interprets Christ's suffering. We thus come back to the inseparability of words and things, although the manner of that inseparability is never elucidated, for like most premodern thinkers Andrewes lacks a metatheoretical vocabulary. The analysis of the word is simply enmeshed with the analysis of the event, without clarification of the precise relationship. Even when Renaissance writers do attempt to label this sort of relation with a word like "metaphor," it remains uncertain whether such a relation picks out only the *perceived* similarities between entities or some essential resemblance.[125]

Participatory consciousness glosses over the distinction between words and things; it also, as Levy-Bruhl notes, remains relatively indifferent to the law of noncontradiction itself. According to the

124. Andrewes, *Works,* 2:145–47.

125. Debora Shuger, *Sacred Rhetoric: The Christian Grand Style in the English Renaissance* (Princeton, 1988), pp. 167–68, 213–14.

"savage mind," for example, a creature can be both a man and a tiger.[126] Conjunctive ("both-and") relations thus tend to predominate over disjunctive ("either-or") ones. Andrewes's hermeneutic seems to exhibit this "savage" inclusivity. He apparently feels little pressure to ascertain the single "right" meaning of a word or passage but will admit several incompatible versions as the literal sense. Hence, concerning the angels' greeting to the shepherds at Christ's birth, he remarks, "εὐδοκία, or εὐδοκίας, nominative or genitive, let it not trouble you. 'To men a good-will;' or 'to men of good-will'—no great matter whether."[127] Similarly he observes that *sine timore* in Luke 1:74 may modify either *liberati* or *serviamus* and concludes, "but we may well reconcile them both, if we say, which truly we may say, 'that without fear we were delivered, to serve Him in a state without, or void of, fear.'"[128] Almost always he prefers to accept all the alternatives as equally correct. At times he accepts without visible embarrassment a philologically unsupported reading alongside what he knows to be the only historically possible one. The tenth Pentecost sermon notes that "this word 'broken-hearted' the Hebrews take not as we do: we, broken for sin; they, broken off, or from sin. . . . Both senses: either of them doth well, but both together best of all."[129]

This inclusive hermeneutic differs from the medieval notion of multiple exegetic levels because Andrewes speaks here only of the literal, historical sense, yet the two procedures are similar. It is as though the training of humanist philologists were placed in the service of a medieval sensibility. As Henri de Lubac points out, medieval exegetes accepted that there could be plural interpretations of the same passage because no single human explanation could exhaust the richness of Holy Scripture. One never discovered the sense of the text but only *a* sense, always more or less superficial and incomplete—the only restriction being that all exegesis must accord with the Catholic faith.[130] Andrewes provides a similar justification for inclusivity. Having given three meanings for ἀνακεφαιώσασθαι, he concludes, "which of the three you take, nay take them all three, you cannot do

126. Levy-Bruhl, *How Natives Think*, pp. 76–78, 91–92.
127. Andrewes, *Works*, 1:218.
128. Andrewes, *Works*, 4:369.
129. Andrewes, *Works*, 3:295.
130. De Lubac, *Exégèse médiévale*, 4:86–87.

amiss. They be all true, all tend to edify."[131] Truth is edification, is the expression of the true faith and not a matter of historical accuracy. Elsewhere he comments that the reader may "'embrace both senses;' both be good and profitable to men. Take whether you will, or both if you will, you shall not take amiss; and if both, you shall be sure to take right."[132] Here again rightness or truth concerns spiritual profit—an utterly ahistorical principle. The text is not perceived as a document lodged in a context but as the sum of its (orthodox) interpretations. Exegesis then is not a question of finding the meaning but the fullness of meaning; "the holy word is best expounded when it is most enlarged."[133] The hermeneutic presupposes and explicates the full and forcible word. It rests on nonanalytic habits of thought. Instead of operating by division and disjunctive exclusion, it perceives a mystical density of signification and so proceeds conjunctively.

SIGNS

Andrewes's tendency not to separate words from things rests on a semiotic view of reality. All things are also signs, thus erasing any real distinction between language and the external world of objects and events. At times, Andrewes conceives of the relation between sign and signified as one of resemblance; for example, the "nature and properties of the Holy Ghost" resemble those of "His sign or symbol, the dove."[134] This is basically the Augustinian notion of things signifying other things based on similar properties.[135] More often, however, Andrewes pictures signification as a movement in depth, a "seeing into" the sign, rather than as juxtaposition or "placing next to" of similar entities. The sign is viewed as a window or book, as a transparent or legible surface disclosing the signified beneath. The crucified body of Christ is thus the "*liber charitatis,* 'the very book of love' laid open before us."[136] Alternatively, his wounds are "as lattices . . . as windows, through which we may well see all that is within Him."[137]

131. Andrewes, *Works,* 1:266.
132. Andrewes, *Works,* 1:353.
133. Andrewes, *Works,* 5:451.
134. Andrewes, *Works,* 3:251–52.
135. Augustine, *On Christian Doctrine,* trans. D. W. Robertson (Indianapolis, 1958), 2.14–16, 23–26.
136. Andrewes, *Works,* 2:132; compare 2:180.
137. Andrewes, *Works,* 2:178.

The spear that pierced Christ's side is "'a key, letting us through His wounds see His very bowels,' the bowels of tender love and most kind compassion."[138] The wounded body is the sign, allowing us to read and behold within the love it signifies. One interprets such signs as one interprets words: by penetrating to the etymological or semiotic center where meaning and sign connect in the entymon which is also the thing, the bowels which are also the love. Not surprisingly, Andrewes will speak of signs as sacraments and vice versa;[139] the visible sign quite literally contains the invisible reality, for Andrewes, I think unequivocally, accepts the doctrine of the real presence of Christ in the Eucharist, of the "hypostatical union of the [sacramental] sign and the thing signified."[140] It is equally not surprising that Andrewes defends a theory of divine right or sacred kingship. Neither sign, sacrament, nor institution is distanced from presence.

Because Andrewes does not sharply distinguish words from things but treats both as signs, the distinction between the metaphoric and the literal blurs. Thus, like most traditional thinkers, he tends to see metaphoric resemblances as indicating objective analogies and thus to slip from trope to fact as if they occupied the same discursive plane.[141] For instance, at one point he infers that the Holy Spirit is a person from the fact that the Spirit is said to "seal" the faithful, and "to 'seal' is ever an act personal."[142] (We, of course, would say the term is being used metaphorically and admit no such conclusion.)

The coexistence of literal and metaphoric in the same discourse—as if they were the same sorts of things—suffuses Andrewes's prose. In his eleventh Nativity sermon, the famous allegory of the four daughters of God based on Psalm 85, Andrewes writes:

1. With Righteousness it works two ways; first, "down she looks."
2. Whether it was that she missed Truth, to see what was become of her, and not finding her in Heaven cast her eye to the earth.

138. Andrewes, *Works,* 2:132.
139. Andrewes, *Works,* 1:281; 2:394.
140. Andrewes, *Works,* 1:281.
141. Vickers, "Analogy," in Vickers, ed., *Occult and Scientific,* pp. 95–98. Conversely, "modernist" and "rationalist" thinkers like Sebastian Castellio tend to stress the distinction between metaphoric and true. If something is a metaphor, then it is eo ipso not true. See his *De arte dubitandi et confidendi, ignorandi et sciendi (1563),* ed. Elisabeth Feist Hirsch, Studies in Medieval and Reformation Thought (Leiden, 1981), pp. 170–73.
142. Andrewes, *Works,* 3:206.

3. But there, when she beheld *Verbum caro factum,* "the Word flesh," the truth freshly sprung there where it had been a strange plant long time before, *aspexit* and *respexit,* she looked and looked again at it.
4. For a sight it was to move, to draw the eye; yea a sight for Heaven to be a spectator of, for the Angels to come down and look at, for Righteousness itself to do so too.
5. *Παρακύψαι* is the Angels' word in St. Peter; *διακύψαι* is the Septuagint's word here.
6. Both mean one thing.
7. The Greek word is to "look," as we say, "wishly" at it, as if we would look *διὰ*, even "through it."
8. The Hebrew word,—that is as if "Righteousness did beat out a window," so desirous was she to behold this sight.[143]

The first two sentences clearly belong to the allegory, and Truth is female. But in the third, Truth changes gender and becomes the infant Jesus, although Righteousness remains allegorical. Likewise in the fourth sentence, personification and actual angels move in the same syntactic space. The next three sentences shift to a philological examination of the Greek text, but in the last, that philology provides an analysis of the psyche of the personification. This syntactic intermingling of allegory, history, and scholarship obscures the ontological status of the narrative: did this really happen? if so, in what sense?

This sermon, although Andrewes's only sustained allegory, is not atypical, especially of the festal sermons based on an Old Testament lection. For another example, we may look at his seventeenth Easter sermon, which treats Isaiah 63:1–3.[144] Andrewes describes the passage as a dialogue between Christ and the prophet, Isaiah having been "taken up in the Spirit" to behold a vision. From the outset, it is not wholly clear whether this vision is symbolic, that is, like the visions in Daniel and Revelations, or a literal "time-travel" seeing of future historical events. It is evidently, however, a vision of Christ's trium-

143. Andrewes, *Works,* 1:187.

144. "Who is this That cometh from Edom, with red garments from Bosrah? He is glorious in His apparel and walketh in great strength; I speak in righteousness, and am mighty to save. Wherefore is Thine apparel red, and Thy garments like him that treadeth in the winepress? I have trodden the winepress alone, and of all the people there was none with Me; for I will tread them in Mine anger, and tread them under foot in My wrath, and their blood shall be sprinkled upon My garments, and I will stain all My raiment."

phant return from the dead on Easter Sunday. Andrewes proceeds to describe this triumph:

> "He loosed the pains of hell," trod upon the serpent's head, and all to bruised it, took from death his "sting," from hell his "victory," that is his standard, alluding to the Roman standard that had in it the image of the goddess Victory. Seized upon the *chirographum contra nos,* the ragman roll that made so strong against us . . . made His banner of it, of the law cancelled, hanging at it banner-wise. And having thus "spoiled principalities and powers, He made an open show of them, triumphed over them" in *Semetipso,* "in His own person" . . . and triumphantly came thence with the keys of Edom and Bozrah both, "of hell and of death" both, at His girdle, as He shews Himself. And when was this? if ever, on this very day.[145]

The description derives from the ancient *Christus Victor* theology, which enters the West through the Harrowing of Hell episode in the apocryphal Gospel of Nicodemus. Its apocryphal origins are crucial here. For it is not only a question of whether the heroic, military images, based as they are on canonical Scripture, are to be taken metaphorically but the historical status of the whole event. In what sense did Christ descend into hell and do battle with the devil? Are we meant to demythologize the passage? The descent into hell (although not the harrowing) is an article of the Creed, and presumably the devil is real enough. Yet since the *Christus Victor* narrative is apocryphal it is hard to imagine that Andrewes took it as history rather than a theological allegory.[146] The compactness of the mythic narrative here does not permit a firm differentiation of its contents into the historical and metaphoric. Nevertheless, in the paragraph that follows, we are clearly back among actual events: "And coming back thus, from the debellation of the spiritual Edom . . . it is wondered who it should be. Note this; that nobody knew Christ at His rising, neither Mary Magdalene, nor they that went to Emmaus. No more doth the Prophet here."[147] Even in this passage, one is not certain whether the

145. Andrewes, *Works,* 3:66.

146. Reginald Pecock, the fifteenth-century Catholic bishop and humanist, is already aware that the medieval incorporation of the descent into hell into the Creed and symbolism of the church has no biblical foundation. See Ferguson, *Clio Unbound,* p. 139; Munz, *The Place of Hooker,* pp. 41ff.

147. Andrewes, *Works,* 3:66.

Christ of the prophet's vision is identical to the figure encountered by Mary Magdalene.

The fusion of discourses grows more complex as the sermon progresses. Andrewes begins to explain the second verse as a mistake on the prophet's part; he sees the garments of the approaching figure are red and wrongly guesses that they have been stained in a winepress: "He calls it wine, but the truth is it was no wine, it was very blood." The next paragraph makes the error a "simile." Both the Cross and the descent into hell may be likened to a winepress. But in what immediately follows, the rhetorical comparison approaches an identification of wine and blood.

> The press, the treading in it, is to make wine; *calcatus sum* is properly of grapes, the fruit of the vine. Christ is the "true Vine," He saith it Himself. To make wine of Him, He and the clusters He bare must be pressed. So He was. Three shrewd strains they gave Him. One, in Gethsemane, that made Him sweat blood; the wine or blood,—all is one, came forth at all parts of Him. . . . The last strain at Golgotha, where He was so pressed that they pressed the very soul out of His body, and out ran blood and water both. *Haec sunt Ecclesiae gemina Sacramenta,* saith St. Augustine, out came both Sacraments, "the twin Sacraments of the Church."[148]

"Wine or blood—all is one"; although no one would suppose that Christ was a grapevine in the same sense that He is man, the final sacramental allusion fixes what the whole passage implies—that there exists a real, if mysterious, connection between wine and blood. The triple repetition of "is" as the main verb at the beginning of the passage immediately obscures the boundary between literal and figurative predication. Similarly, the simple "so He was" identifies the crushed grapes with the bleeding body, as does the pun on "strain," which can mean both torture and squeezing. Thus, to insist that the winepress is merely a metaphor is to miss the whole linguistic pressure of the passage to confuse the distinction, to replace the "is" of logical predication with that of mystical participation.[149] To put it another way, to categorize the language here as either metaphoric or literal lacks relevance because the underlying division between symbolic and historical

148. Andrewes, *Works,* 3:69–70.
149. Levy-Bruhl, *How Natives Think,* pp. 91, 125.

events remains peripheral to Andrewes's thought. I certainly would not wish to assert that Andrewes does not know the difference between a fact and a simile, but to the extent that either can be a sacred sign, it participates in a reality that includes both empirical phenomena and symbolic representations, both the truth of the Cross and the truth of the winepress.

PATTERN

The merging of words and things that informs Andrewes's etymologizing and figuration likewise governs the larger structures of his hermeneutic. Andrewes's characteristic exegetical method involves selecting one or two words, usually concrete nouns or verbs, from his lection and then connecting them with related terms or images, generally from other portions of the Bible. The result of this procedure is not, as might be expected, a concordance masquerading as a sermon, but a theology of history. The verbal patterning running through the biblical text corresponds to the pattern of history. The connection between images in Holy Scripture reveals the connection between events, for history becomes not a matter of linear, causal sequence but is the temporal unfolding of meaning through signs, and the pattern formed by the temporal signs is that formed by the textual ones. We have already seen this in the first Nativity sermon, where the term *apprehendit* comes finally to describe and link man's flight from God in the Fall, Christ's pursuit in the Incarnation, His assumption of human nature, our apprehension of Him by faith and works, and the mutual partaking that occurs in the Eucharist. The structure created by the recurrence of the same word in different contexts discloses the relationship between those contexts, discloses the underlying rhythm in sacred history of pursuit and flight, seizing and being seized.

In his sixth Easter sermon, Andrewes gathers up the stones from both Old and New Testament in a typological pattern focused on Christ.

> 1. In His Birth: Daniel's "Stone, cut forth without hands." 2. In His Passion: Zachary's Stone, graven and cut full of eyes, all over. 3. In His Resurrection: Esay's Stone, laid in Sion . . . "he that believeth in Him then, shall not be confounded," saith St. Peter, *Hic est Lapis*. He is the Stone of our faith, saith St. Peter, *Lapis erat Christus*. And *Petra erat*

> *Christus,* saith St. Paul. He is "the Stone" of our Sacraments; the Water of our baptism, and of our spiritual drink, both issue from Him.[150]

The sermon then describes the multiple ways Christ is like a stone: He is a stone in His firmness and suffering; a building stone that gathers men "into one frame of building"; a cornerstone uniting them; the headstone of the cosmos; a living stone in His Passion; a headstone again in His Resurrection, and so forth.[151] The word "stone" scattered throughout the Scriptures forms a pattern that both interprets the life of Christ and is interpreted by it. The repetition of the word constitutes the deep structure of history. But the king is a stone as well, for "*lapis erat David,* is likewise true," and the image proceeds to unfold the nature of King James's authority over church and state.[152] In the end, the Eucharist is also "the corner-stone of the Law and the Gospel"; it may "serve us for a corner-stone" by uniting us to Christ and to each other "as living stones."[153] The image thus displays the connection between the Testaments, between the events of Christ's life, between the divine and political order, between Christ and the sacraments. The textual, verbal patterning turns out to be the pattern of history, the key to the mystic connections that structure discreet events into a providential narrative.

Dozens of Andrewes's sermons, in toto or in part, express the same homologies of text and time. This patterning also appears in Andrewes's handling of tropology or the "moral sense." He has very little interest in ethics, at least in the modern sense of rules for behavior. Instead he explores the personal application of the text (*quid agas*) in terms of the inwardness of faith—its desires, fears, longings—by transforming the historical signs of Scripture into allegories of spirituality. Historical pattern is at the same time psychological pattern. Occasionally the allegorization is explicit. In the seventh Easter sermon, the Passover narrative becomes a (wholly traditional) metaphor for the individual's passage through life and through the Red Sea of death: the first-born of the Egyptians become souls; Egypt, the world; and so on.[154] More often, the tropological and literal senses are woven together without such precise allegorizing of detail. A single narrative

150. Andrewes, *Works,* 2:274–75.
151. Andrewes, *Works,* 2:275–78.
152. Andrewes, *Works,* 2:282–87.
153. Andrewes, *Works,* 2:288–89.
154. Andrewes, *Works,* 2:293.

line swings easily between history and inwardness, Andrewes from time to time briefly signaling the parallels. Thus the splendid Easter sermons on Mary Magdalene at the empty tomb are a careful, close reading of specific incident and character while simultaneously an analysis of religious experience in general.[155] The transition sentences bring to the surface the consistently felt duality:

> And this case of Mary Magdalene's is our case oftentimes. In the error of our conceit to weep, where we have no cause; to joy, where we have as little. . . . Why, He is found of them that seek Him not; but of them that seek Him, never but found. . . . So find Him they shall, but happily not all so fully at first, no more than she did. . . . Whom she sought, He asks her "Whom she sought.". . . If she seek Him, why knows she Him not? If she know Him, why seeks she Him still? A common thing with us, this also; to seek a thing, and when we have found it, not to know we have so, but even . . . "to ask Christ for Christ."[156]

Mary Magdalene thus represents "unto us the state of all mankind." Her grief and love are not simply exemplary (indeed they are not exemplary at all, since her grief proceeded from lack of faith), but, to use Andrewes's term, "analogic."[157] Her actions and feelings inscribe a pattern repeated in the inner life of faith, so that the rhythms of individual experience recapitulate those of sacred history. The fourteenth Nativity sermon thus connects the time of Christ's birth with the eternal pattern of God entering history in moments of communal and private affliction: "The days of Herod the King. . . . Dismal days certainly. Why, then comes Shiloh; when man's help farthest off, then God's nearest. When it is dark, then rises the star. . . . The time and place fit well. For the time of affliction makes the place—makes humility. Which place Christ is born in."[158]

Like Interpreter's House in Bunyan's *Pilgrim's Progress,* the biblical text makes existence intelligible by offering paradigms. The scriptural paradigm differs from ordinary experience in that the divine meaning is, so to speak, on the narrative surface. Christ's baptism differs from our own not because the Spirit was present in the former but because it was visibly present. The dove "shews what was done in us. . . . In-

155. Berry, *Process of Speech,* p. 45.
156. Andrewes, *Works,* 3:11–17.
157. Andrewes, *Works,* 2:272.
158. Andrewes, *Works,* 1:238.

deed, his whole baptism is not so much His as ours."[159] That the Magdalene's hopeless grief allowed her to meet Christ in the flesh enables us to know His hidden presence in apparent absence. Such a view depends on a sense of history as repeated pattern that largely excludes change, secondary causality, and contextualization. Inner life participates in the paradigmatic event, as events—both inner and outer—participate each other through mystical connections that also bind together text and history. The duty of the exegete is not to distance the text by historicizing it but to "take off the 'veil of Moses' face,'"[160] that is, to discover the typological web of relatedness that is the meaning of history.[161]

The same habit of thought persists in Andrewes's physics and politics. As before, this habit represents entities and categories as participating each other, so that (from our perspective) firm boundaries and distinctions consistently blur into a semidifferentiated connectedness. The strict dichotomization of word and thing, text and history, subject and object, nature and supernature, knower and known seems relatively absent; instead everything seems capable of fusing or merging with everything else.

Obviously Andrewes has no physics in either the Aristotelian or modern sense. His few scattered remarks on natural processes do

159. Andrewes, *Works,* 3:256–57.

160. Andrewes, *Works,* 3:312.

161. Andrewes's explicit hermeneutic sometimes rests on the classic spiritual senses, sometimes on their late medieval variants. In one place he thus lists three senses: the prophetic, which refers to Christ; the historical; and the analogic, which points ahead to the present (*Works,* 2:272). Alternatively he lists four senses: the literal; the analogical, which here signifies the patterning within the Old Testament, so that David parallels Moses; the moral, which offers the paradigmatic rhythms of divine action in history; and the prophetic or Christological (*Works,* 3:222–23). Elsewhere he seems to be using the late medieval figural/typological exegesis of the double literal sense, where the Old Testament text can have both a historical and a Christological literal meaning since all redemptions are types of Christ's (*Works,* 1:103–4, 175–76; 2:139–40, 300; 3:61–64; 4:362). The feeling for synchronic patterning excludes a sense of historical context. Thus Andrewes treats Persian law as if relevant to England (*Works,* 4:132) and speaks of all Holy Scripture as written by the Wisdom of God (that is, Christ; *Works,* 4:277). History repeats the same play, only with new actors (*Works,* 1:308). For the history of medieval exegesis, see de Lubac, *Exégèse médiévale;* James Samuel Preus, *From Shadow to Promise: Old Testament Interpretation from Augustine to the Young Luther* (Cambridge, Mass., 1969); William G. Madsen, *From Shadowy Types to Truth: Studies in Milton's Symbolism* (New Haven, 1968); Harris, "Allegory to Analogy"; Harry A. Wolfson, *The Philosophy of the Church Fathers,* vol. 1, *Faith, Trinity, Incarnation* (Cambridge, Mass., 1970), pp. 24–61; Beryl Smalley, *The Study of the Bible in the Middle Ages* (Oxford, 1941); T. H. L. Parker, *Calvin's New Testament Commentaries* (Grand Rapids, Mich. 1971).

confirm, however, the tendencies evident in his treatment of words, signs, and history. In general, he does not distinguish either nature from supernature or the corporeal from the incorporeal or spiritual. He thus often uses the term "natural" to describe the direct activity of God. In contrast, physical processes may be "spiritual." Thus the creation of the world "by the Spirit moving upon the waters of the deep" is "natural," as opposed to the "same Spirit moving on the waters of baptism," which is "spiritual."[162] Likewise, the activity of the Spirit within the human soul is a "natural motion" because the moving force is internal to the creature.[163] Yet light, sounds, and smells are "spiritual things" because they can be participated in without diminution.[164]

All this may be just a question of terminology, but it seems to rest on a strictly sacramental view of the physical world that erases any merely "natural" space, any arena for natural law or secondary causation. This sacramentalism appears most vividly in Andrewes's *Pattern of Catechistical Doctrine* and the early sermons on the Temptation of Christ and the Lord's Prayer.[165] These all bring up the nature of bread, in each instance affirming that "it is not the bread (considered barely in itself) that nourisheth us, but the virtue and grace of the word infused into it," for "outward means [that is, secondary causes] . . . of themselves are of no more efficacy without the operation and grace of the word, than a hammer and a saw without a hand able to employ them."[166] Bread cannot nourish without a direct infusion of the divine word; like the sacraments, natural objects are visible signs into which spiritual efficacy must be poured.[167] On this model there can be no firm separation between nature and supernature. Even the wild birds and beasts are not merely natural creatures. So the catechism argues for the existence of providence by claiming that, if orphaned, "young

162. Andrewes, *Works,* 3:191.

163. Andrewes, *Works,* 3:194, 274, 393.

164. Andrewes, *Works,* 2:377.

165. For the dating and publication history of these works, see Welsby, *Andrewes,* pp. 22–23, 36–37.

166. Andrewes, *Works,* 5:506–8; compare 5:417, 423; 6:35–36.

167. See Augustine's remarks on medicine in *Christian Doctrine,* 4.33; see also William Perkins, *The Foundation of Christian Religion,* in *The Work of William Perkins,* ed. Ian Breward, The Courtenay Library of Reformation Classics (Appleford, Eng., 1970), p. 150; Calvin, *Institutes,* 1.16.2; 1.16.7.

ravens are fed of God" and frightened beasts cry out to Him for help.[168]

As no merely natural arena exists, so the political arena is also sacred space, its events being inspired and directed by God and the devil.[169] Political power not only derives from God but is actively maintained by Him. In fact, the general tenor of Andrewes's political sermons lies in their somewhat strained insistence that the events of James's reign are miracles, that God immediately sustains and defends the Stuarts as He did the Israelite kings.[170] The insistence seems strained because Andrewes elsewhere sees history as a movement away from presence.[171] But, at least in the political sermons, he refuses to allow any gap between biblical sacred history and modern politics or between presence and institutions. In this, Andrewes resembles the Puritans, a similarity strengthened by his attempt to ground the episcopal hierarchy on the Levitical priesthood,[172] much like the Puritan endeavor to derive the presbyterian ministry from apostolic orders or to read their history according to biblical typologies—both efforts resting on ahistorical analogies and the fusion of secular and sacred.

Andrewes's uncongenial politics merits independent consideration. I will return to the subject in chapter 4 and mention it here in passing only to indicate its connection to the larger body of his thought. At least in Andrewes, the defense of divine right belongs to a habitual sacramentalism that sees nature as infused with divinity and therefore explicitly rejects any secular grounding of power in a communal will or compact.

THE TESTIMONY OF THE INNER LIGHT

Inevitably, participatory consciousness represents the mind differently from rational consciousness. The latter, as previously noted, distances subject from object, bridging the space thus newly created by the twin concepts of reason and evidence. Subjective desire becomes the mech-

168. Andrewes, *Works*, 6:35; compare 5:413.
169. Andrewes, *Works*, 4:96, 133, 212, 269, 280, 292, 350.
170. Andrewes, *Works*, 2:271; 4:22, 39, 94, 154, 237–38, 329, 366, 387, 395.
171. Andrewes, *Works*, 3:287.
172. Andrewes, *Works*, 6:339–62.

anism of ideological distortion, that which makes us close our eyes to the evidence. In contrast, Andrewes virtually never uses "reason" in this sense. It becomes rather a neutral, almost negative, term, generally contrasted to the truth grasped only by faith.[173] Andrewes's catechism thus begins with the claim that "we cannot come to God by reason" since "the principles of reason are from the sense, but God is above sense and reason, and beyond both."[174] For Andrewes, knowledge becomes possible only when subject participates in its object, eradicating the distance between them. Thus, concerning the gifts of the Holy Spirit, he writes, "and God grant we may know it, that is, that we may receive it, for then we shall, but otherwise we shall never know it."[175] For, he notes, "take this for a rule; no knowing of *Ejus absque Eo,* 'of His without Him,' Whose it is."[176] God cannot be known as an object external to the knower; only when He is inwardly present can He be perceived without.

Knowing is thus not a matter of evidence but the penetration of the knower by the known, a penetration Andrewes alternatively refers to as signing, inspiration, and enlightening.[177] It is not that evidence is irrelevant—the star led the Wise Men to the manger—but without God's "sending the light of His Spirit within into their minds" they could not have *understood* the star. Reason, in Andrewes, never interprets the evidence; instead, interpretation of the star requires an indwelling of its consubstantial light.[178] Andrewes's understanding of "knowledge" (that is, faith) here resembles Hooker's certainty of adherence and is utterly traditional. Both ground belief in an inward "something": taste, light, presence. So Hooker writes that in "life spiritual," Christ and his spirit dwell within men "as the soul of their souls moving them."[179] For both, furthermore, faith presupposes love, grasps its object by loving it. Andrewes thus insists, "if we love Him not, we know Him not."[180] And the converse also holds, both accepting the axiom of self-warranting desire. The soul's love for Christ (a love possible because of His prior love for us) guarantees its

173. Andrewes, *Works,* 1:5, 138, 253–54; 3:21.
174. Andrewes, *Works,* 6:20.
175. Andrewes, *Works,* 3:232.
176. Andrewes, *Works,* 1:256.
177. Andrewes, *Works,* 1:205, 256; 6:22.
178. Andrewes, *Works,* 1:255–56.
179. Hooker, *Works,* 3:613.
180. Andrewes, *Works,* 3:149.

fulfillment—in Andrewes's elliptical phrase: "of them that seek Him, never but found."[181] Rather than distorting thought, desire here forms the precondition of knowledge. But in Hooker such views occupy the margins of a generally rationalized epistemology, while in Andrewes they are *almost* unopposed.

THE PROBLEMATICS OF PARTICIPATION

The bulk of Andrewes's work belongs to the discourse of participation. Even the endless Latin controversial works share, at least negatively, in this mode, being almost devoid of theoretical analysis. That is, unlike Hooker, Andrewes appears innocent of second-order reasoning. He offers no general theory about sovereignty, law, or the state but argues almost exclusively from analogy or biblical and patristic authority, with a deep disregard for history, change, or context. Some of the minor polemical works therefore come as a shock. The *Two Answers to Cardinall Perron* and *A Discourse of Ceremonies,* neither published in Andrewes's lifetime and both probably late works, are experiments in humanist demystification. Both insist on the conventional, positive nature of ritual, emptying ceremony of intrinsic (sacramental) meaning. Both treat ritual in terms of the historical evolution of custom. He thus notes how originally pragmatic uses, such as having candles on the altar in the dark catacomb churches, subsequently gave rise to a posteriori mystical interpretations and how pagan practice gradually transmuted into Christian ritual.[182] Indeed the whole point of *A Discourse* is to prove that the ceremonies of the Church of England derive from "british and english ancient pagans," whose customs were retained in order to preserve political stability.[183] Both treatises therefore split form from significance, arguing that the former rests on political utility rather than on sacramental mystery. Both likewise employ humanist philology. The *Two Answers* uses Valla-style source criticism to distinguish genuine from spurious texts, to clear up ambiguities of reference, and to establish historical proba-

181. Andrewes, *Works,* 3:14; compare 3:20–21.
182. Andrewes, *Works,* 11:33–34.
183. Andrewes, *Works,* 6:365.

bility. *A Discourse* cites Hooker to the effect that names and ceremonies have no necessary etymological tie to their original signification.[184]

A Discourse is the more disturbing piece. Its apparent intention is to refute the papal claim that the Church of England borrows all its ceremonial from Rome, by asserting a native British origin for Anglican custom and then, more generally, a pagan origin for virtually all Christian custom.[185] The piece may also be related to contemporary interest in the pre-Norman roots of the common law. Andrewes was himself a member, probably the only clerical member, of the Antiquarian Society that included Spelman, Cotton, and Camden.[186] Be that as it may, in the treatise Andrewes seems to have ended up showing more than he bargained for. Among the items mentioned as having been borrowed from the pagans he lists the forms and places of divine worship, the consecration of churches and churchyards, sprinkling holy water, monasticism, fasts and feasts, the "whole corps of the canon law," church buildings, bishops and priests, saints' days, ordination by imposition of hands, surplices, excommunication, preaching, perambulation, general confession, thanksgiving and intercession, the royal supremacy, and tithing.[187] The forms of Christian life and worship turn out to be purely conventional traces of earlier cultures, the deposit of historical processes. Since Andrewes, unlike Hooker, never appeals to divinely grounded natural law, similarity between pagan and Christian practice resolves into mere borrowing, legitimated exclusively by the need for social order. Ceremony and church polity become, in the Varronian (and Hobbist) sense, matters of civil religion, while Christianity shrinks to doctrine, leaving empty these now secularized spaces. History is resolutely demystified. Not surprisingly, the piece has no conclusion. The participatory links be-

184. Andrewes, *Works,* 11:40–41; 6:367.

185. The same idea appears briefly in Richard Bancroft, *Tracts Ascribed to Richard Bancroft,* ed. Albert Peel (Cambridge, 1953), pp. 115–16, 158–59. This notion that Christian practices derive from pagan ceremony is obviously different from the polemical commonplace that Roman Catholic practices derive from pagan ceremony. Jewel, for example, notes parallels between Roman Catholic and pagan ritual in order to prove that the former's rituals are inherently corrupt. Therefore, unlike Andrewes, he never proposes such origins for Christian practice in general. See his *Apology,* p. 35.

186. Welsby, *Andrewes,* p. 85.

187. Andrewes, *Works,* 6:370–90.

tween sign and signified are simply replaced by temporal, contingent ones.[188]

Hence in Andrewes, as in Hooker, the minor works show the beginnings of fragmentation. The danger to participatory modes of thought implicit in historicism is more apparent in Andrewes than Hooker because no effort is made to conceal the discontinuity within a teleological natural-law framework. Instead the awareness of historical context and change leads to drastic secularization or politicization of practice. Thus both the differences between Hooker and Andrewes and the internal contradictions in the works of each manifest the same fissuring of the central discourse into two opposed hermeneutics. The tension lies between these, it would seem, rather than between a hypothetical discourse designed to naturalize the political and the real mechanisms of control and repression. The problem for the Renaissance is not that rationality is mystification but that rationality (associated with rather than opposed to historicism) snips apart the mystic bonds of participatory consciousness. Or, to put it in the terms of Richard Waswo's recent *Language and Meaning in the Renaissance,* the problem is not referentiality itself—that is a later problem—but the emergence of a referential semantics, with its associated distinction between words and things, from a conceptualization prior to the clear separation of sign from signified.

The dominant intellectual culture in the sixteenth and early seventeenth centuries seems a deeply pluralist one rather than a monolithic hegemony. That is, two opposite things seem true. First, that a good deal of serious thought decidedly resembles anthropological descriptions of primitive mentality, or, at the very least, late-antique supernaturalism. Second, that the cat has nevertheless been let out of the bag: that historicism, secularism, and Weberian rationalism are easily discernible not only in some avant-garde theorists, like Castellio or

188. Welsby raises the possibility that Andrewes did not write *A Discourse*. There is no external evidence for this: the first edition (1653) claims that the text was set from Andrewes's own autograph copy, and there is no other evidence as to authorship. Those who have doubted that Andrewes wrote the treatise argue that it is unlike the rest of his works. To this two replies can be made. First, the thesis of *A Discourse* has clear affinities with the defense of custom in Andrewes's 1618 Easter sermon. Second, by the same sort of reasoning one would have to deny that Hooker wrote his first sermon, since its epistemology appears nowhere in *The Laws*.

Montaigne, but in the center of the Church of England and the order of things established. Furthermore, the (re)emergence of rational consciousness seems only indirectly related to socioeconomic changes. Instead, the breakdown of Catholic Christendom (for whatever reasons) led to over a century of fierce polemical debates. The internal dynamic of these controversies then encouraged the radical questioning of theological and traditional grounds and, in turn, the need to find solid philological and evidentiary bases for one's beliefs, thus insinuating that only such evidence counted as a reason. At least for a while, controversial rationalism could be compartmentalized from habits of thought traditionally connected with the practice of faith rather than its defense.[189] Thus the spirituality of both Andrewes and Hooker is basically participatory, historicism being largely restricted to their polemical works.

The unstable discontinuities of Renaissance culture are not altogether different from the situation in modern developing nations. Geertz remarks that the "social changing of the mind" in those countries seems "so hesitant, shot through with uncertainty and contradiction. . . . There is, in such matters, no simple progression from 'traditional' to 'modern,' but a twisting, spasmodic, unmethodical movement which turns as often toward repossessing the emotions of the past as disowning them. . . . In Java, Anderson finds 'archaic-magical' and 'developed-rational' theories of power existing side by side."[190] This complex "changing of the mind" belongs to the infrastructure of Renaissance discourse as much as do changes in social, economic, and political arrangements, and while the two may be related, that relation is not greatly illuminated by assuming that discourses are primarily about social, economic, and political matters. It seems at least plausible that they are about meaning, about, that is, the relation between subjectivity and God and history and language and the Bible and reason. They are therefore also about increasingly opposed impulses to blow open these relations—to distinguish and distance categories—and to preserve their undifferentiated compactness.

189. The Middle Ages likewise distinguishes the literal exegesis suitable for argument from the spiritual one allowable only for edification.

190. Geertz, *Interpretation*, pp. 319–20.

2

The Hungering Dark

Spiritual Psychology and the Failure of Participation

Why art Thou as a foreigner in the land?
Or as a native, that comes but to his inn?
As one that is fallen into a sleep?
As a man that is not able to save?
Andrewes, *Devotions*

There is always a temptation to transform a complex copresence of ideas into a linear evolution, in this case to view the relation between Andrewes and Hooker in terms of the development of historicism and a rational approach to Christian evidence. Instead, however, I want to take the opposite course and look more carefully at the connection between participatory habits of thought and the spiritual psychology common to both Hooker and Andrewes. As we have already noted, their spiritual psychology seems largely the same. Here they share the traditional language of participation with its understanding of the nonrational, nonevidentiary basis of faith. In a few sections of *The Laws* and in the sermons of both, a focus on inner spiritual experience is expressed in terms of adherence, desire, sacramental union, and incorporation into the mystical body of Christ. These texts likewise share a common epistemology based on the presence of the known in the knower and the axiom of self-warranting desire. Finally, in both Hooker and Andrewes this spiritual psychology is rendered problematic by the fact that they elsewhere employ a far more secular, historicized approach, although the balance of these contradictory elements is different, since Hooker's main work is primarily in the latter mode, while historicism surfaces only in Andrewes's minor treatises.

Andrewes knew Hooker's sermons because after the latter's death they were entrusted to him. The similarities therefore may be more than accidental. The most striking of these is that while both analyze spiritual experience in the language of participation and thus seem to affirm the presence of God to the soul, in fact, that analysis and that affirmation take place only within a larger context that represents religious existence as suffused with doubt, fear of rejection, a sense of the absence of God that verges on despair. They struggle with the apparent lack of justice in history, with the failure of faith, with the fear that God is indifferent or hostile. Hooker's sermons in particular are marked with a sense of desolation. Thus after describing the promises of God to reward the righteous, he comments:

> These being the words of God's own mouth, how are they performed when the righteous are hourly led as sheep to the slaughter, their goods taken from them by extortion, their persons subject unto violence, nothing about them but that which they cannot look or think upon without tears: impious despisers of God in the meanwhile rejoicing pleasantly upon their beds, living long, waxing old, increasing in honour, authority, and wealth, their houses peaceable without fear, the rod of God not upon them nor near them. Can these things cleave together, God true in his word, and we such in our estate?[1]

Hooker's first sermon, arguably the greatest sermon of the period, depicts the doubt and terror occasioned by the experience of suffering: the fear that one is "clean crost out of God's book, that he regards us not," and the additional dread that such feelings themselves confirm their own truth. That is, how, in a theology based on justification by faith, can such loss of faith signify anything besides condemnation. Temporal suffering is excruciating not primarily because of the material or social loss involved but because it means that one is not loved, that one has been abandoned by God. Thus, suffering causes doubt, and doubt intensifies the suffering into despair. Toward the end, the prose moves into a prosopopoeia of agonized consciousness:[2]

> Then we think, looking upon others, and comparing them with ourselves, Their tables are furnished day by day; earth and ashes are our

1. Richard Hooker, *The Works of that Learned and Judicious Divine, Mr. Richard Hooker,* 3 vols., ed. Rev. John Keble, 7th ed. (Oxford, 1888; reprint, New York, 1970), 3:631.

2. "Prosopopoeia," a rhetorical term, signifies the representation of an imaginary or absent person as speaking.

> bread: they sing to the lute, and they see their children dance before them; our hearts are heavy in our bodies as lead, our sighs beat as thick as a swift pulse, our tears do wash the beds wherein we lie: the sun shineth fair upon their foreheads; we are hanged up like bottles in the smoke, cast into corners like the sherds of a broken pot: tell not us of the promises of God's favour, tell such as do reap the fruit of them; they belong not to us, they are made to others. The Lord be merciful to our weakness, but thus it is.[3]

The passage contrasts the solitary desolation occasioned by loss and failure with a natural, almost pastoral, fulfillment; the broken and useless pot, the bottle hidden and fouled by smoke, the lonely bed all image the isolation of inwardness from the innocent social life of food, children, dance, and sunshine. The images of desolation come from the Psalms, especially the penitential Psalms: from Psalm 102, "For I have eaten ashes like bread"; Psalm 31, "I am forgotten as a dead man out of mind: I am like a broken vessel"; Psalm 6, "all the night make I my bed to swim; I water my couch with my tears"; and Psalm 119, "for I am become like a bottle in the smoke." These echoes, coupled with the plural pronoun, associate individual suffering with communal experience of longing for an absent God. They connect the inner voice of pain with the public, ecclesiastical representation of holiness, thus implicitly transferring the question of abandonment from the peculiarities of an individual consciousness to the historic crisis of religious existence: the disturbing lack of empirical evidence for God's love. Moreover, Hooker carefully avoids the conventional suggestion, visible in Wyatt's rendition of the penitential Psalms, that such suffering results from sin. The sermon does not concern questions of guilt and punishment but rather locates the central problem of faith in the agony of an *incomprehensible* forsakenness.[4] In his sermons, Hooker is constantly aware that history seems empty of either justice or love, that we can only "hope against all reason of believing," that "we must learn to suffer with patience even that which seemeth almost impossible to be suffered."[5]

3. Hooker, *Works,* 3:479.

4. In *The Rise of Moralism,* C. F. Allison observes that the notion of sin as transgression, as breaking rules, only began to dominate Anglican theology after 1640; earlier Anglicanism instead emphasizes separation and alienation (*The Rise of Moralism: The Proclamation of the Gospel from Hooker to Baxter* [New York, 1966], p. 202).

5. Hooker, *Works,* 3:471, 647.

The same anguish is visible in Andrewes. The Easter sermons on the visit of the Marys to Christ's tomb center on the problem of love without faith. Mary Magdalene weeps at the grave because she believes Christ is dead, yet she loves and finally her love brings her to the vision of the Resurrected Christ. As in Hooker, adherence rather than evidence becomes the ground of faith, but it is the adherence of a hopeless adoration weeping in despair. Even after Christ has shown Himself to her, the fact that He forbids her to touch Him leads Andrewes again to contemplate how God seems to be insensitive to human need. Andrewes is deeply interested in Mary's feelings of hurt, betrayal, and frustrated desire. She reaches out for Him in love: "it was for pure love, and nothing else, she desired it. To love, it is not enough to hear or see; it is carried farther, to touch and take hold." She has suffered so much that "one poor touch had been but an easy recompence." But He rebuffs her—and here Andrewes brings up the possibility that perhaps the risen Christ is like a king or great prince—"not familiarly to be dealt with."[6] But this picture of a distant, regal Lord cannot mitigate Mary's hurt, and so in the following sermon Andrewes returns to the problem of Christ's prohibition: "But what, shall she be quite cast off in the mean time? Denied touching; denied it, granted nothing for it?"[7] Passionate human love is met by what feels like divine indifference and remoteness.

Similarly, several Easter and Pentecost sermons focus on the disciples' terror at the thought of Christ's departure: "For Him no sooner to come, but gone again, and leave them to the wide world."[8] In another sermon Andrewes imagines their response to Christ's announcement that unless He leaves them the Holy Spirit will not come. They plead with Him almost like children begging their parents to stay home: "Be it so; let Him not come, stay you. *In Te satis nobis,* we are well enough, we desire no other Comforter."[9] At times the Apostles express something close to anger in their uncomprehending disappointment at Christ's willingness to depart: "Why not Christ stay, and yet He [the Holy Spirit] come? Why may not Christ send for Him, as well as send Him? . . . Why not? Are they like two buckets? one

6. Lancelot Andrewes, *The Works of Lancelot Andrewes,* 11 vols., Library of Anglo-Catholic Theology (Oxford, 1854), 3:25–26, 32.

7. Andrewes, *Works,* 3:40.

8. Andrewes, *Works,* 3:50.

9. Andrewes, *Works,* 3:168.

cannot go down, unless the other go up?"[10] Like Hooker, Andrewes uses prosopopoeia to convey the inward experience of childlike fear and resentment at being abandoned. Like Mary, the disciples can see no reason for Christ's actions; they are only conscious that His actions are not what they want or need.

Andrewes's early sermons on the temptation of Christ and on the Lord's Prayer further explore these failures of participation and presence. On earth "we are as men shut out of the presence of God," for "though He be our Father, yet so long as we be on earth we are strangers and exiles from Him."[11] Distance engenders doubt, especially the fear that "God is either a poor God, not able sufficiently to reward those that serve Him; or else an unkind God That will not reward the duties that are performed by those that serve Him."[12] They deal with the terror of being unloved, alone in a hostile world governed by an indifferent God. It is the devil who promises us good things "as though he were very liberal in rewards, and as though God were unkind or ungrateful, not once regarding us for all our service, but suffers us even to starve." The devil exposes the contradiction between the promises of Scripture and material actuality, laboring "to persuade us that God is an unkind God, that so we may burst forth into those terms, This good did I get at God's hand, to wit, hunger."[13] So too he tempts us with a nightmare image of an evil deceiver: "In Adam the devil first brought him into a conceit that God envied his good, and of purpose kept him hoodwinked lest he should see his good, as we see falconers put hoods over hawks' eyes to make them more quiet and ruly"—a Machiavellian deity.[14]

For both Hooker and Andrewes the central problem of faith is not sin but absence. This understanding of spiritual psychology differs radically from that found in most Puritan sermons and, interestingly, Donne's. In these, the problem is sensuality and religious indifference. In Hooker and Andrewes we are dealing not with moral culpability but with the sufferings of an utterly theocentric psyche. Whereas Donne assumes a largely secularized audience, Hooker and Andrewes speak to souls longing for God and shattered by their own failure to believe or feel His presence and often haunted by a suspicion that they

10. Andrewes, *Works,* 3:170–71.
11. Andrewes, *Works,* 5:324, 374.
12. Andrewes, *Works,* 5:546–47.
13. Andrewes, *Works,* 5:482–83.
14. Andrewes, *Works,* 5:496–97.

are unloveable or God is unloving. Their sense of the sheer difficulty of belief lowers the moral stakes considerably. Hence in Andrewes the "heroical and 'free spirit' " of the Christian is defined not in terms of active accomplishments but simply as sorrow over inevitable failure and a frustrated "wish that we could do more than we can" that makes us "grieve that we cannot do so much as we ought."[15]

The theological positions of Andrewes and Hooker separating them from the Calvinism of *The Institutes* as well as from the "Calvinist orthodoxy" of English Puritanism seem a response to this understanding of spiritual life as marked by doubt, grief, and longing. The distance separating Hooker and Andrewes from the Calvinist consensus of the period appears greatest over the issue of predestination. Both unequivocally reject double predestination, the doctrine that God eternally elects some to salvation, some to reprobation, without respect to either their virtues or sins.[16] Consequently, they both virtually ignore the catastrophic, right-angle dynamics of Reformed spirituality: the horrifying realization of one's utter sinfulness precipitating first hellish despair in the contemplation of God's wrath and then the pivotal act of faith that apprehends God's promise of mercy.[17] They stress neither human sin nor divine anger. Both additionally draw back from Calvinist notions of providence that make God responsible for all events, both good and bad (a subject we shall return to in chapter 5). Hooker thus argues that God does not cause temporal evils, that "those things which here we suffer are not still inflicted by the hand of God's revengeful justice." He therefore readmits the distinction between God's permissive and active will, which Calvin had denied in favor of attributing all to God's direct volition.[18] Andrewes's tendency to treat

15. Andrewes, *Works,* 5:410–11.

16. On Calvinist predestination, see Jaroslav Pelikan, *The Christian Tradition: A History of the Development of Doctrine,* 5 vols., Vol. 4, *Reformation of Church and Dogma, 1300–1700* (Chicago, 1984), pp. 217–32. For the influence of Beza in giving rise to the stress on predestination in the Calvinist orthodoxy of the later sixteenth and seventeenth century, see R. T. Kendall, *Calvin and English Calvinism to 1649,* Oxford Theological Monographs (Oxford, 1979), pp. 29–31; Brian G. Armstrong, *Calvinism and the Amyraut Heresy: Protestant Scholasticism and Humanism in Seventeenth-Century France* (Madison, 1969).

17. See, for example, William Perkins, *A Treatise Tending unto a Declaration,* in *The Work of William Perkins,* ed. Ian Breward, The Courtenay Library of Reformation Classics (Appleford, Eng., 1970), pp. 362–68.

18. Hooker, *Works,* 2:571; compare 2:564; Pelikan, *Reformation,* p. 224.

redemption along the lines of Greek *Christus Victor* theology, rather than the Latin Anselmian tradition, seems to function in a similar manner. By making salvation hinge on the contest between Christ and Satan—instead of Christ's satisfaction of the Father's demand for penal justice—responsibility is, so to speak, transferred from God's shoulders to the devil's.[19] The latter becomes the "enemy" in the story, although at the price of an unbiblical dualism. The transfer seems to derive from Andrewes's worry that the Calvinist stress on the absolute sovereignty of the divine will leads to hatred of God: "We cannot love him well, whom we think not well of. We cannot think well of him, whom we think evil comes from. . . . Men, when their brains are turned with diving into God's secrets, may conceit as they please; but when all is said that can be, no man can ever entirely love Him Whom he thinks so evil of as to be the Author of evil."[20] Like Hooker, Andrewes prefers to limit God's immediate and active control of the world in order to guarantee His goodness. That evil exists is a given; either God does it or He does not—if He does, then His love becomes problematic, if not, His presence. Hooker and Andrewes create the crisis of desolation to protect the love of God.

Both Hooker and Andrewes preferred to avoid the subject of predestination. The former treats the issue only in his unfinished and somewhat (I think) inconsistent reply to *A Christian Letter,* a Puritan attack on *The Laws;*[21] the latter only in his commentary on the Lambeth Articles, written at the express demand of Archbishop Whitgift. Andrewes, in fact, begins by protesting his reluctance to deal with "these mysteries which I am not able to explain."[22] It is not necessary to wade too far into the technical difficulties these texts present. What seems clear is that both reject a strict Calvinist understanding of reprobation as an act of the divine will without foresight of sin. Andrewes quotes the first of Whitaker's original articles thus: "from eternity God

19. Andrewes, *Works,* 3:225, 229, 296; 5:457. On *Christus Victor* theology in Luther, see Pelikan, *Reformation,* pp. 162–63.

20. Andrewes, *Works,* 3:363.

21. On Hooker's reply, see Peter G. Lake, *Anglicans and Puritans? Presbyterianism and English Conformist Thought from Whitgift to Hooker* (London, 1988), pp. 183–97. Hooker argues that reprobation results from God's foresight of sin but salvation does not result from foresight of faith but is an act of gratuitous mercy—an Augustinian, if slightly inconsistent, position. See also Willem Nijenhuis, *Adrianus Saravia (c. 1532–1613),* Studies in the History of Christian Thought (Leiden, 1980), p. 187.

22. Andrewes, *Works,* 6:294.

predestinated some to life and reprobated some to death." To this Andrewes adds, "only so far as the reason does not seem the same on both sides, i.e., the reason of predestination the same as that of reprobation; if this is not fully evident, I would wish there be added that the former are predestined in one way, namely through Christ (Eph. 1:5), the latter reprobated in another, namely on account of sin."[23] When Hooker restates the Lambeth Articles at the conclusion of his reply to *A Christian Letter,* he simply drops any mention of reprobation, paraphrasing the first article to read, "That God hath predestinated certain men, not all men."[24] Both also reject the eighth article, which states that all men are not drawn by the Father to come to Christ. That is, both approach universalism, holding that God does offer all persons saving grace, which, however, because not irresistible, is not conferred upon all, or, as Hooker (after much struggle with this question) finally puts it, "that inward grace, whereby to be saved, is deservedly not given unto all men," where "deservedly" is Hooker's addition to the Lambeth formularies.[25]

Both men thus deny that God in any sense bears responsibility for damnation. Yet while this then becomes the consequence of individual sinfulness, neither Hooker nor Andrewes uses human freedom as a lever to intensify guilt, although the combination of "Arminianism" and moral rigorism later becomes characteristic of Anglican theology. They do not exculpate God in order to blame persons but to avoid the implication of Calvinist theology that God is either totally heteronomous or ruthlessly indifferent to human pain. The emphasis is exclusively on divine love. Hooker thus speaks of Christ:

> Nor do I think that any wound did ever strike his sacred heart more deeply, than the foresight of men's ingratitude, by infinite numbers of whom that which cost him so dear would so little be regarded; and that made to so few effectual through contempt, which he of tender compassion in largeness of love had provided to be a medicine sufficient for all.[26]

God can only helplessly struggle to save creatures whose freedom He will not violate, "freedom being a part of their very nature."[27] Such

23. Quoted in Andrewes, *Works,* 6:295.
24. Hooker, *Works,* 2:596.
25. Andrewes, *Works,* 6:300; Hooker, *Works,* 2:573, 583, 588, 590.
26. Hooker, *Works,* 2:574.
27. Hooker, *Works,* 2:567.

theology responds to the pastoral problem of desolation, the fear that God does not care. For Hooker and Andrewes, the end of God's working is not His own glory but the good of his creatures, "and according to our several wants we send to Him."[28]

Hooker and Andrewes also differ from the mainstream of English Protestantism in the importance they attribute to the sacraments, especially the Eucharist. For both, communion moves into the center of religious life because it offers the possibility of participation: "We then are at the highest pitch, at the very best we shall ever attain to on earth, what time we newly come from it; gathered to Christ, and by Christ to God."[29] The Eucharist overcomes the boundaries of time and space; in receiving, not Christ alone, "but He, as at the very act of His offering, is made present to us, and we incorporate into His death."[30] In the Eucharist the distance between God and humanity is bridged; Christ enters a troubled and isolated inwardness. Both thus stress not only the objective participation of natures but its psychological correlate: the deeply sensuous awareness of presence. There is only one *body* in these texts, the wounded body of Christ; the prose always becomes concrete, vivid, dramatic in depicting that body, making it present—not only as an object beheld, but touched, tasted, embraced, and with Himself returning the gaze, for so Andrewes tells his congregation to look upon the Crucified Christ "'till He look upon you again.' For so He will."[31] Body, sacrament, presence, and participation intertwine. Hooker thus concludes his discussion of the eucharistic controversies with a highly emotional prosopopoeia depicting the consciousness of the faithful communicant:

> the very letter of the word of Christ giveth plain security that these mysteries do as nails fasten us to his very Cross, that by them we draw out, as touching efficacy, force, and virtue, even the blood of his gored side, in the wounds of our Redeemer we there dip our tongues, we are dyed red both within and without, our hunger is satisfied and our thirst for ever quenched; they are things wonderful which he feeleth, great

28. Andrewes, *Works,* 3:176; compare Hooker, *Works,* 1:203.
29. Andrewes, *Works,* 1:283; compare Hooker, *Works,* 2:350–62.
30. Andrewes, *Works,* 2:302.
31. Andrewes, *Works,* 2:137. Caroline Bynum thus observes that medieval representations of the body of Christ are likewise vividly graphic and likewise not sexual. They are interested in the wounded, not the gendered, body—finding "in suffering (rather than in sexual temptation) the core of what it is to be human" ("The Body of Christ in the Later Middle Ages: A Reply to Leo Steinberg," *Renaissance Quarterly* 39 [1986]: 413).

> which he seeth and unheard of which he uttereth, whose soul is possessed of this Paschal Lamb and made joyful in the strength of this new wine.[32]

This sort of graphically physical participation seems driven by feelings of forsakenness and distance; the latter gives the former its almost histrionic urgency, the longing for contact being proportional to the terror of abandonment. The images of tasting and of literal "adherence" (the "nails" that "fasten us to his very Cross") connect this passage to Hooker's first sermon, sacramental participation to his participatory epistemology of belief. In both passages, presence and contact—a physical touching—articulate the substance of faith. One may also speculate that the retreat of sacred meaning from history and institutions, visible elsewhere in Hooker and his contemporaries, reinforces the need to stress interior presence. We will return to this point in the following chapters.

In rejecting reprobation and stressing the sacraments over preaching, Hooker and Andrewes depart from the Reformed tradition— that is, Calvinism plus subsequent modifications—what I am calling "Calvinist orthodoxy." A similar break appears in their treatment of religious subjectivity. In each case, the change responds to the pathos of doubt and loss. But with respect to subjectivity, Hooker and Andrewes seem part of a larger shift within English Reformation thought. For Spenser's Red Cross and for Bunyan's Christian the most terrible enemy is Despair. The failure of faith and assurance pervades the religious consciousness of the period, forcing it away from the *Institutes* and Lambeth Articles, although men who thought of themselves as good Calvinists often seem confused to the point of self-contradiction by the tension between authority and experience.

The search for "a final assurance that one was elect" lay at the center of the experimental predestinarianism characteristic of Puritan piety.[33] Already in the *Institutes* Calvin argues repeatedly for subjective assurance. The faithful "do not doubt at all about the good pleasure of God toward us," for faith (as opposed to hypocrisy) "requires full and fixed certainty, such as men are wont to have from things experienced and

32. Hooker, *Works,* 2:361.

33. Lake, *Anglicans and Puritans?,* pp. 121, 178; Kendall, *Calvin and English Calvinism,* passim.

proved" and a "feeling of full assurance." Hence "no place for doubting is left." Conversely, those who are "doubtful and perplexed as to whether they are to be heard" by God, call to Him "but effect nothing."[34] The same position appears in the sixth Lambeth Article: "A truely faithful man, that is, one endowed with justifying faith, is certain, according to the certitude of faith, concerning the remission of his sins and his eternal salvation through Christ."[35] Hooker and Andrewes, however, deny that being loved by God entails being certain of that love, because they are acutely sensitive to the lack of evidence, both historical and psychological. They therefore insist that disbelief and anguish do not necessarily signify reprobation.[36] In their separate restatements of the Lambeth Articles, Hooker totally omits article 6 and Andrewes heavily modifies it.[37]

The question of subjective assurance also lies at the heart of Hooker's first sermon, "Of the Certainty and Perpetuity of Faith in the Elect." The distinction between certainty of evidence and certainty of adherence is intended to confute Calvin's assertion that one can have the same certainty concerning the objects of faith that one has with respect to matters "experienced and proved." It was precisely this denial that caused the doctrinal explosion that erupted over this sermon and forced Hooker to defend himself to the archbishop. The sermon focuses on the prophet Habakkuk's bitterly skeptical com-

34. John Calvin, *John Calvin: Selections from His Writings,* ed. John Dillenberger (Missoula, Mont., 1971), pp. 274, 390–91, 416. On subjective assurance in Calvin and Puritan theology see Lake, *Anglicans and Puritans?,* pp. 121, 178; Richard Strier, *Love Known: Theology and Experience in George Herbert's Poetry* (Chicago, 1983), pp. 108–9; William J. Bouwsma, *John Calvin: A Sixteenth-Century Portrait* (Oxford, 1988), p. 101; Peter Munz, *The Place of Hooker in the History of Thought* (London, 1952), p. 22; Perry Miller, *The New England Mind: The Seventeenth Century* (New York, 1939; reprint, Boston, 1961), pp. 49–51, 370. Miller argues that Puritan theology tends to move away from the necessity of subjective assurance. Outside of the *Institutes,* Calvin also seems to allow for doubt and uncertainty in the Elect; see Strier, *Love Known,* pp. 177–78, 242–43. Donne, interestingly, frequently argues that the Elect may know their election and that to doubt that one is elect is evidence of one's damnation; see *The Sermons of John Donne,* ed. George Potter and Evelyn Simpson, 10 vols. (Berkeley, 1953–62), 2:9.488–97; 7:14.278–83; 8:2.259–63, 571–78.

35. Quoted in Andrewes, *Works,* 6:292.

36. Lake notes that Whitgift also rejects Cartwright's claim that election equals assurance (Peter G. Lake, "Calvinism and the English Church, 1570–1635," *Past and Present* 114 [1987]: 46; and Peter G. Lake, *Moderate Puritans and the Elizabethan Church* [Cambridge, 1982], pp. 216–17).

37. Hooker, *Works,* 2:596–97; Andrewes, *Works,* 6:299–300.

plaint, "Therefore the law is slacked, and judgment doth never go forth," and concerns two related problems: whether radical doubt concerning the goodness (existence?) of God is equivalent to unbelief and whether a person's doubt about God's goodness toward himself is as well.[38] That is, it concerns both philosophic and existential doubt. The opening of the sermon takes up the first question, arguing that doubt is inevitable (and therefore not sinful), since faith rests on a barely tasted sweetness rather than on empirical or logical evidence. The sermon then goes to the second issue and is here explicitly pastoral: "The question is of moment; the repose and tranquillity of infinite souls doth depend upon it. The Prophet's case is the case of many. . . . If in him this cogitation did extinguish grace, why the like thoughts in us should not take the like effect, there is no cause."[39] What Hooker argues is that saving faith may be experienced as loss of faith, a paradox that depends on severing cognition from truth. One need not *know* one's own faith, because, as in Herbert's "Holdfast," "ev'n to trust in him, was also his." Assurance is, to use theological language, objective, its substance residing in God's love for us rather than our faith in Him.[40]

Hooker thus focuses on the contradiction between introspection and actuality.

> Men in like agonies unto this of the Prophet Habakkuk's . . . lament as for a thing which is past finding: they mourn as Rachel, and refuse to be comforted, as if that were not, which indeed is, and as if that which is not, were; as if they did not believe when they do, and as if they did despair when they do not.[41]

Curiously, the discontinuity here between psyche and fact does not make subjectivity irrelevant. The prose instead weaves in and out of prosopopoeia, dramatizing the inner struggles of the mind that experiences itself as forsaken and faithless. The focus on subjectivity in fact

38. The same passage from Habakkuk was used as the lection for the sermon delivered before Charles I on November 29, 1648—the last sermon he ever heard. See Boyd M. Berry, *Process of Speech: Puritan Religious Writing and "Paradise Lost"* (Baltimore, 1976) p. 160.

39. Hooker, *Works,* 3:473.

40. Gene Edward Veith, Jr., *Reformation Spirituality: The Religion of George Herbert* (London, 1985), pp. 92–97.

41. Hooker, *Works,* 3:474.

intensifies precisely insofar as intellectual assent, the sort of consciousness that can be expressed propositionally, becomes drained of significance. The intellectual "contents" of faith become subordinate to affective inwardness—to the longings, griefs, anxieties, appetites that constitute life lived in the absent-presence of God. To the extent that faith is not propositional belief but a theocentric emotionality—an overriding need for God that may subsist with conscious disbelief in His existence or His love—it incorporates desolation as it incorporates joy.

> Better it is sometimes to go down into the pit with him, who, beholding darkness, and bewailing the loss of inward joy and consolation, crieth from the bottom of the lowest hell, "My God, my God, why hast thou forsaken me?" than continually to walk arm in arm with angels. . . . No, God will have them that shall walk in light to feel now and then what it is to sit in the shadow of death. A grieved spirit therefore is no argument of a faithless mind.[42]

The problem of subjective assurance reappears in Andrewes's sermons, especially the third and fourteenth Easter sermons on the visit of the Marys to Christ's tomb. They go to the tomb to weep over Christ whom they believe dead. What fascinates Andrewes is the possibility of love without faith. Mary Magdalene "believed no more than just as much as the High Priests would have had the world believe, that 'he was taken away by night.' " But here again, the need for God, for Christ, somehow consists with disbelief in His existence and becomes desolation. Mary weeps: "Whose presence she wished for, His miss she wept for; Whom she dearly loved while she had Him, she bitterly bewailed when she lost Him. *Amor amare flens,* 'love running down the cheeks.' "[43] Her love and that of the other Marys is sheerly irrational, purposeless. They go to embalm a body already embalmed; their way is blocked by an unbudgeable stone; the "party is dead" in any case.[44] What Andrewes insists on in both these sermons is that the women's foolish and faithless love is sufficient. Mary Magdalene believed Christ was dead; "there was error in her love, but

42. Hooker, *Works,* 3:474–75.
43. Andrewes, *Works,* 3:6–8.
44. Andrewes, *Works,* 2:228.

there was love in her error too." And "such love, and such labour would not be lost."[45] Christ, disguised as a gardener, sees Mary's agonized devotion, that "for the want of Jesus nothing but Jesus could yield her any comfort." Her love attracts His, for "*magnes amoris amor;* 'nothing so allures, so draws love to it, as doth love itself.'" Desire, as we have noted before, is self-warranting; it takes the place of evidence. Thus Christ "is no longer able to contain, but even discloses Himself" to her in the garden, calling her by name, and she falls at his feet.[46] The third Easter sermon ends with a celebration of Christ's merciful love for the faithless, weak, and sinful:

> Well, whatsoever become of other, Peter that so foully forsook, and forsware Him both, he shall never see Him more? Yes, Peter too, and Peter by name. . . . This is a good message for him, and Mary Magdalene as fit a messenger as can be to carry it, one great sinner to another. That not only Christ is risen, but content that His forsakers, deniers, forswearers, Peter and all, should repair to Him the day of His Resurrection; that all the deadly wounds of His Passion have not killed His compassion over sinners; that though they have made wrack of their duty, yet He hath not lost His mercy, not left it in the grave, but is as ready to receive them as ever. . . . Dying and rising, He is to sinners still one and the same, still like Himself, a kind, loving, and merciful Saviour. This is the last; Peter and all may see Him.[47]

It is instructive to compare these sermons with Calvin's treatment of the same scene in his commentary on the Gospel according to St. John. Calvin virtually never mentions Mary's love. Instead, he emphasizes the guilt of the women and the disciples for not believing. Jesus' own teaching and the testimony of the prophets should have proved sufficient evidence of the Resurrection. The women who stayed at the tomb therefore do not deserve praise; they are "filled with idle and useless weeping. In short, only a mixture of superstition and carnal feeling keeps them at the tomb." Mary has a "gross attitude" and is sent to the disciples as a "reproach, since they had been so slow and sluggish to believe," but both were "carnal and stupid."[48] Calvin holds that the word provides sufficient evidence, and therefore lack of cer-

45. Andrewes, *Works,* 3:12, 2:229.
46. Andrewes, *Works,* 3:20.
47. Andrewes, *Works,* 2:235.
48. John Calvin, *The Gospel according to St. John 11–21 and The First Epistle of John,* trans. T. H. L. Parker, Calvin's Commentaries (Edinburgh, 1961), pp. 193–200.

tainty concerning the objects of faith demonstrates a culpable blindness, the refusal of flesh—the carnal eye—to see. Calvin's epistemology is, as it were, forensic, while Andrewes's, like Hooker's, is erotic. The former operates in terms of evidence and assent, the latter in terms of desire.

The sensitivity of Hooker and Andrewes to the distance of God and the lack of external evidence for belief leads them to de-emphasize faith as the ground of salvation. While never explicitly rejecting salvation by faith alone, they end up making faith equivalent to the desire to believe, the longing for holiness and obedience. The requirement slips from the cognitive to the affective realm. Hooker argues that Roman Catholics can attain salvation because "they in all ages, whose hearts have delighted in the principal truth, and whose souls have thirsted after righteousness, if they received the mark of error, the mercy of God, even erring, and dangerously erring, might save them."[49] Andrewes makes the same point: "every error [is not] repugnant to God's election." Even for those who believe only "the Gentiles' creed," Christ "will not fail them that seek Him."[50] Not only dogma but obedience is also less important than desire. Hence, both Hooker and Andrewes exhibit no interest in covenant theology, a staple of English Reformed thought since Tyndale.[51] The critique of this contractual divinity is most explicit in Andrewes's third Pentecost sermon. It begins by asserting precisely such a covenant: Christ's promise of the Holy Spirit "is in manner of a deed; not absolute, but as it were with articles on both parts. . . . A covenant on His part, a condition on theirs," namely, keeping the commandments. If one does not keep these commandments, then one does not love Christ, for "if our love were not light, His commandments would not be heavy."[52]

But about halfway through, this line of thought suddenly begins to reverse itself. If salvation rests on obedience, on performing the conditions of the covenant, then it is unattainable:

> for who can do this, keep the Commandments? as good condition with us, to fly or walk on the sea. . . . So, upon the matter, all this promise

49. Hooker, *Works,* 3:526.
50. Andrewes, *Works,* 3:329, 339.
51. For the notion of covenant in Calvin and Calvinist orthodoxy, see Bouwsma, *Calvin,* p. 96; Armstrong, *Calvinism,* p. 49.
52. Andrewes, *Works,* 3:146, 150.

> falls out to prove nothing; the condition cannot be kept, and so the covenant void. No Holy Ghost or Comforter to be hoped for or had; we are but deluded.[53]

At this point Andrewes simply rejects the notion of covenant altogether; Christ requires neither an impossible obedience nor a perfect faith:

> If a bruise in the reed, Moses would break it quite. If the flax smoke and flame not out, he would quench it straight. So will not He. . . . To Mary Magdalene He ordained, that *fecit quod potuit* should serve, and He would require no more. *Credo, Domine, adjuva incredulitatem meam,* "I believe, Lord, help my unbelief:"—a belief mixed with unbelief, would never have endured Moses' assay; *in manu Mediatoris* it did well enough.

The disciples, Andrewes notes, denied Christ and fled and did not keep His commandments, "but this they kept, and so may we too: they were troubled, their hearts were troubled for not keeping them; and at the throne of grace that was accepted."[54] The grief itself supplies the place of certainty or righteousness. Hooker makes the same point. If those who despair are "grieved for their unbelief," that sorrow must come from "a secret love and liking which they have of those things that are believed," and no one can "love things which in his own opinion are not." Therefore, "by desiring to believe they prove themselves true believers."[55] The desperate love of God here, as in Andrewes's sermons on Mary Magdalene, bears witness to the persistence of a theocentric emotionality, which, well into the nineteenth century, made intellectual doubt such a devastating affair. In this context, the axiom shared by Hooker and Andrewes that "natural desire cannot utterly be frustrate" does not assert the unproblematic participation of the psyche in reality but conveys the fragility of the bond linking man to God.[56] The experience of desire is often the only certainty.

As mentioned previously, the contrast between Hooker and Andrewes, on the one hand, and Calvinism, on the other, quickly blurs at the edges, especially with respect to the problematics of subjectivity.

53. Andrewes, *Works,* 3:151.
54. Andrewes, *Works,* 3:152–53.
55. Hooker, *Works,* 3:475–76.
56. Hooker, *Works,* 1:257; compare Andrewes, *Works,* 2:262; 3:198.

The confusion over whether seventeenth-century religious lyric poets like Donne and Herbert were High Church or Low Church, Anglican or Calvinist, neomedieval or semiradical follows from the inherent difficulty of distinguishing these positions in their treatment of spiritual inwardness. This is not to deny that such labels pick out real differences. What I have called "Calvinist orthodoxy" differs from the thought of Hooker and Andrewes in several important respects, as the preceding paragraphs have tried to demonstrate. But by the late sixteenth century the situation has become more tangled. It is worth spending a moment on this confusion if only because the tendency to reify and rigidify party labels—and to assume that such distinctions are always conflictually structured—has encouraged considerable historical misstatement.

William Perkins's theological writings, works such as *The Golden Chain* and *The Foundation of Christian Religion,* give a harsh and systematic presentation of sixteenth-century Calvinist orthodoxy. His pastoral writings do not. This is particularly true of *A Grain of Mustard-Seed,* a little treatise subtitled *Or the Least Measure of Grace That Is or Can Be Effectual to Salvation,* published in 1597 and dedicated to the countess of Cumberland. The work treats the same question that exercised Hooker and Andrewes: whether subjective assurance is necessary for salvation. Perkins responds that "the desire to believe, in the want of faith, is faith"[57]—the argument of Hooker's first sermon. The same paradoxical syntax that identifies desire with fulfillment recurs repeatedly: "the desire of reconciliation with God in Christ is reconciliation itself: the desire to believe is faith indeed and the desire to repent, repentance itself."[58] Perkins offers two reasons for this curious argument that wanting is having. First, those who endeavor to apprehend "do indeed apprehend; God accepting the desire to do the thing, for the thing done."[59] Here, wanting is not the same as having but is simply accepted by God in defect of the latter. But he also argues that the "spiritual motions" whereby one desires God "are without doubt from the Spirit of God."[60] That is, those who "thirst after Christ," because they "feel themselves out of Christ," are not, in fact, separated from God at all, for their consciousness of absence is itself a sign of presence.

57. Perkins, *Work,* p. 399.
58. Perkins, *Work,* p. 398.
59. Perkins, *Work,* p. 401.
60. Perkins, *Work,* p. 398.

Perkins thus concludes, "to see and feel in ourselves the want of any grace pertaining to salvation, and to be grieved therefore, is the grace itself."[61] As in Hooker and Andrewes, the felt loss of presence generates desire for what has been lost, but that desire (unlike the Platonic eros) does not simply negotiate the poles of absence and presence but collapses them. Perkins grounds this collapse in the basic structures of religious existence. The treatise ends with the "rules" of the Lutheran theologian Victor Strigelius: "It is the principal art of a Christian to believe things invisible, to hope for things deferred, to love God when he shews himself to be an enemy and thus to persevere unto the end. . . . [For] all the works of God are done in contrary means."[62] Faith is structured by deferment and contradiction, but the logic of deferment does not eddy out into a vortex of endless expectations but circles back on itself to declare that what is deferred is also present.[63]

Perkins seems somewhat uncomfortable with this argument, and he attempts to resist its valorization of desire by insisting that this psychological formation belongs only to the early stages of faith, and therefore "the aforesaid beginnings of grace are counterfeit unless they increase."[64] This then leads him back to a detailed list of theological and moral virtues necessary for salvation. In Hooker and Andrewes, however, the conviction that spiritual suffering forms *the* problem of faith entails a marginalization of ethical concern. The virtues most commended in the sermons are those most relevant to the problem of inward pain and disbelief: patience, endurance, humility. In his catechism, for example, Andrewes lists "a grief for God's absence from us," "to be afraid to lose Him," "to be grieved when we think we have lost Him"; and again, "patience" and "perseverance," the "sorrow of bearing the cross" and the "tediousness of long delay."[65] Otherwise, the sermons contain very little moral content besides the utterly conventional (medieval) approbation of prayer, fasting, and alms, the

61. Perkins, *Work*, pp. 399, 402.

62. Perkins, *Work*, p. 410.

63. The same passages appear frequently in Protestant works of the period. See, for example, John Downame, *The Christian Warfare* (London, 1604; reprint, Amsterdam, 1974), pp. 120–22, 516–17; Kendall, *Calvin and English Calvinism*, pp. 96, 117, 123, 157.

64. Perkins, *Work*, p. 404. See David Little, *Religion, Order and Law: A Study in Pre-Revolutionary England* (Oxford, 1970), p. 117. This moralism also is characteristic of Calvinist orthodoxy, good works being the only reliable evidence of election. See Kendall, *Calvin and English Calvinism*, pp. 47, 81, 99, 123, 161.

65. Andrewes, *Works*, 6:111, 122.

conjunction suggesting that moral action (alms) does not belong to a separate category of virtues directed to one's neighbor but remains incorporate with theological duties. Neither Hooker nor Andrewes emphasizes vocation, the central organizing concept in Reformed social ethics. Conscience, likewise, plays only a minor role in their works. Moreover, especially in Andrewes, moral action is sharply distinguished from spiritual life. The former we spin out of ourselves, "as the spider doth her web," while holiness requires participation: "From without it cometh, from the Spirit of God, not our own spirit."[66] Although his sermons frequently are divided into doctrine and use, the "use" or "duty" of the text almost invariably turns out to be a passive reception rather than an active performing. One's duty is to be led, to receive communion, to allow oneself to be acted upon. The solution to the problem of faith lies in disclosing participation rather than in being good.

Thus far, our account of spiritual psychology in Hooker and Andrewes has disclosed a pervasive concern with affective inwardness, with the experiences of desire, confusion, fear, and so forth—as opposed to a concern with sin and morality, which seems to have been more typical in the period. This inwardness exists between the poles of desolation and participation and hence belongs to the larger polarity of rational and participatory habits of thought, insofar as the former tends to empty history, institutions, and signs of sacred presence. The foregoing then suggests a few more general observations.

First, the participation described in Hooker and Andrewes is not "primitive," that is, it does not express an unproblematic enchantment of the world where sacred meaning remains inextricably bound up with phenomenal experience.[67] Rather, as found in Hooker and Andrewes, participation presupposes a radical disenchantment; it functions precisely as a response to feelings of distance. The need to affirm some contact, some interpenetration of self and divine other, arises from the perception both of inner desolation and the forsakenness of history. This perception, of course, did not originate in the late six-

66. Andrewes, *Works,* 3:211; compare 3:159ff., 190, 204, 217.

67. Lucien Levy-Bruhl, *The "Soul" of the Primitive,* trans. Lilian A. Clare (New York, 1966), pp. 15–19; Lucien Levy-Bruhl, *How Natives Think,* trans. Lilian A. Clare (New York, 1979), pp. 44–45; Robin Horton, "African Traditional Thought and Western Science," in *Rationality,* ed. Bryan R. Wilson (Evanston, 1970), pp. 158–59.

teenth century—it fills the Psalms, prophets, and poetic books of the Old Testament—but it seems to have become particularly acute during this period.

Hooker especially manifests an acute consciousness of the contradiction between history and promise. He imagines Habakkuk as

> beholding the land which God had severed for his own people, and seeing it abandoned unto heathen nations; viewing how reproachfully they did tread it down, and wholly make havock of it at their pleasure; beholding the Lord's own royal seat made a heap of stones, his temple defiled, the carcasses of his servants cast out for the fowls of the air to devour, and the flesh of his meek ones for the beasts of the field to feed upon . . . the conceit of repugnancy between this which was object to his eyes, and that which faith upon promise of the law did look for, made so deep an impression and so strong, that he disputeth not the matter; but without any further inquiry or search inferreth, as we see, "The law doth fail."[68]

In Andrewes a similar sense of the opposition between temporal injustice and divine meaning appears in his repeated contrast between the brutality of human society and the inclusive plentitude characteristic of sacred order. On earth "begetting is, properly, but to life, and nothing else. . . . To inherit besides, not one of a thousand. Ask poor men's children, ask younger brethren." But, Andrewes continues, the harsh consequences of primogeniture do not obtain in the kingdom of heaven, where Christ begets us not only as children but as heirs.[69] Like its laws of inheritance, the hierarchical structure of English society also discloses its alienation from sacred order. Here, concerning "country, condition, birth, riches, honour, and the like," we see that "*in omni gente* men accept of this, and in a manner of nothing else but this; all goes by it. Well, with God it is otherwise, and with men it should be."[70] Despite Andrewes's vigorous royalism, he rarely speaks as though social existence reflected divine (although he does easily draw theological analogies from human institutions, especially legal ones). At least to some extent, the bonds of cosmological participation have been broken, exposing the "disorder" of history and soci-

68. Hooker, *Works,* 3:478.
69. Andrewes, *Works,* 2:377.
70. Andrewes, *Works,* 3:330; compare 5:322.

ety. To a greater or lesser degree, then, participation moves inward. Andrewes writes,

> When we behold the state of the world, and see that good men are trodden under feet, and the vessels of wrath and sin are exalted and prosper, then we may know that that is not the true Kingdom, and therefore we pray that God will set up His Kingdom in our hearts, and govern us by His Spirit.[71]

One is reminded of Milton's grave and poignant antinomy between history and inwardness at the end of *Paradise Lost,* where he contrasts a world "To good malignant, to bad men benign, / Under her own weight groaning" to "A paradise within thee, happier far."[72]

Second, this inwardness is itself constituted by the experience of absence and longing. Contra Foucault, one might say that in these works the self (soul) is not so much the creation of power but of desire.[73] As Bruno Snell observed many years ago regarding the early Greek lyric poets, the "personal soul" is the creation of frustrated eros; it is apprehended as "the source of the reactions which set in when the feelings are blocked. . . . Only the emotional discord released by unhappy love is truly personal," for happiness and successful love are felt as divine gifts poured into the self from without, while the emotions attendant upon failure are one's own—are one's self.[74] Unhappy sexual love and deferred religious desire have, as Plato observed, much in common. In Greek lyric and Renaissance sermons, longing and desolation differentiate an interior space that then becomes available to literary representation, but in the latter this interior space does not solidify into autonomous selfhood. The self that emerges in these sermons makes itself felt as absence and desire, and because the "self" emerges from desire for the absent other, it is also (potentially) the point of its indwelling presence. Hooker, Andrewes, and Perkins view inward existence as paradoxically structured by the desire for that which is absent and by participation in indwelling presence. That is,

71. Andrewes, *Works,* 5:393.

72. John Milton, *Paradise Lost,* in *John Milton: Complete Poetry and Major Prose,* ed. Merritt Y. Hughes (New York, 1957), 12.539–40, 587.

73. Michel Foucault, *Discipline and Punish: The Birth of the Prison,* trans. Alan Sheridan (New York, 1977), p. 29.

74. Bruno Snell, *The Discovery of the Mind in Greek Philosophy and Literature,* trans. T. G. Rosenmeyer (New York, 1982), p. 65.

the boundaries of the self are experienced as fluid and permeable, so that God or Christ or the Kingdom or Satan seems to dwell within the heart, but the self is also conscious of its solitude. The two experiences are related because the horror evident in these sermons at inner isolation indicates that participation is felt as normal. When autonomy came to feel normal, then the loss of indwelling was no longer critical. But this only happened gradually and never totally.

Finally, these texts do not mask or repress the problematics of faith. Instead, such contradictions govern the entire exploration of spiritual life in sermon after sermon. They insist upon the apparent lack of justice, the apparent lack of presence, the apparent lack of evidence that confront faith. That this doubt and grief always find some resolution does not mean that they are not exposed.

These points suggest a final observation. The spiritual psychology of Andrewes, Hooker, and (in some works) Perkins closely resembles features of seventeenth-century poetry, particularly that of Herbert. One notes in *The Temple* the same problems of absence and loss, the same need for touch and direct participation, the same affective inwardness. In addition, the separation of morality, spirituality, and history found in the prose seems reflected in the odd tripartite organization of Herbert's corpus. Finally, as in the prose, Herbert's poems do not mask the problematics of faith but center on them, in both the tensions between history and desire giving rise to a conflictual, problematized structure. The next chapter will investigate these resemblances, both as they illumine the perceived relations between self, society, and history in the Renaissance and as they inform the architecture of Herbert's *Temple*.

3

The Structure of *The Temple*

> Where the Spirit is, there is feeling; for the Spirit maketh us feel all things. . . . The life of a Christian man is inward between him and God.
>
> Tyndale, *The Wicked Mammon*

In 1615 Andrewes, then bishop of Ely, visited Cambridge where he met George Herbert, at that time a student at Trinity. According to Walton, "there fell to be a modest debate betwixt them two about predestination and sanctity of life." Afterward, Herbert sent the bishop a long letter written in Greek, which was "so remarkable for the language and reason of it, that, after reading it, the bishop put it into his bosom, and did often show it to many scholars . . . but did always return it back to the place where he first lodged it, and continued it so near his heart til the last day of his life." We do not know the substance of the debate or of the letter.[1] The story records a moment of personal contact between the aging bishop and the young aristocratic scholar and the rather touching aftermath where the twenty-two-year-old becomes master to England's most eminent theologian, and the old man treasures the youthful wisdom.

I have not begun with this anecdote in order to reclaim Herbert for the High Church party but to draw him into the discussion begun in the previous chapter, to see whether that analysis can illuminate the structure of *The Temple* and whether, in turn, this structure can throw further light on conceptions of self, society, God, and history available

1. Veith, who mentions the modest debate but not the letter or Andrewes's reaction to it, assumes that Herbert took a Calvinist stance over and against Andrewes's Arminianism (Gene Edward Veith, Jr., *Reformation Spirituality: The Religion of George Herbert* [London, 1985], pp. 35, 84). But the bishop's response rather strongly suggests that this was not the case. If anything, the fact that Andrewes singled out Herbert's letter seems to indicate that it said something significantly different from the stock arguments of either Calvinist or anti-Calvinist dogma. Herbert later dedicated his *Musae responsoriae* to Andrewes.

within the dominant culture. The problem of the structure of Herbert's *Temple* is reasonably obvious—the three main parts do not have much to do with each other. It is not only that "The Church Porch" treats ethics and social "behavior" in general; "The Church," inner devotional life; and "The Church Militant," ecclesiastical history, but additionally, the premises governing these three divisions seem incompatible. For example, the premium placed on self-control in "The Church Porch" seems oddly juxtaposed to the sense of human passivity and vulnerability in "The Church," while the intimacy and divine-human friendship of "The Church" does not square with the impersonal determinism of "The Church Militant." Attempts to posit some sort of unity based on an external scheme—whether the structure of a Hebrew temple, some sequence of biblical books (for example, Proverbs, Psalms/Canticles, Revelation), the Protestant Law-to-Gospel sequence, or catechistical elements—have not met with general acceptance.[2] Herbert's remarks on catechism in *The Country Parson* explicitly limit it to basic doctrinal instruction; the pragmatic social directives of "The Church Porch" scarcely resemble the Protestant conception of the Law that overwhelms the sinner with consciousness of guilt; and there could be few things less like Revelation than "The Church Militant."[3] Since modern critical practice no longer forces one to discover unity anyway, I would like to approach the problem from the other end and ask if the *disunity* of *The Temple* can be shown to be meaningful. By "meaningful" here I mean simply "historically meaningful"; that is, do the discontinuities perceptible in *The Temple* corre-

2. For a critique of various attempts to connect "The Church Militant" to the rest of *The Temple,* see Lee Ann Johnson, "The Relationship of 'The Church Militant' to *The Temple,*" *Studies in Philology* 68 (1971): 200–206. She also notes that in the Bodleian and Williams manuscripts, "The Church Militant" is separated from the rest of *The Temple* by five blank pages, concluding from this that "The Church Militant" was never meant to be part of *The Temple* at all. Annabel Endicott [Patterson] offers a similar argument in "The Structure of George Herbert's *Temple:* A Reconsideration," *University of Toronto Quarterly* 34 (1965): 236. This reading of the manuscript evidence, in turn, has been criticized by Stanley Fish in *The Living Temple: George Herbert and Catechizing* (Berkeley, 1978), p. 143. Citations from Herbert's *The Temple,* noted by line numbers parenthetically in the text, are taken from *George Herbert and Henry Vaughan,* ed. Louis L. Martz (Oxford, 1986).

3. Barbara Lewalski makes the parallel between Revelation and "The Church Militant" in her *Protestant Poetics and the Seventeenth-Century Religious Lyric* (Princeton, 1979), pp. 304–5; the catechism theory belongs, of course, to Fish's *Living Temple;* Veith argues for the Law-to-Gospel paradigm.

spond to felt dualities (or triplicities) discernible elsewhere within the culture, and might those then throw some light on the *implications* of the negative spaces in Herbert's text?

"THE CHURCH PORCH"

"Command thyself in chief" (215): "The Church Porch" assumes and teaches a self capable of and perfected by moral activity, and moral activity of a very specific kind. The precepts of "The Church Porch" are not strictly ethical imperatives but prudential rules for attaining both the dispositions and behaviors that will allow the "sweet youth" (1) Herbert addresses to function as a respected and worthy member of a competitive, courtly, albeit Christian, society. Self-command enables successful social praxis. As in classical ethics, the individual is conceived as both autonomous and social; being "good" means attaining control over one's appetites to fulfill one's role within a community. Morality, "self-fashioning," and social performance are closely linked.

In contrast, "The Church" generally conceives of the self as passive, incapable of self-control, and threatened by social norms. From "The Altar" to "Love (III)" it is dependent on God's fashioning. As a result, the prior emphasis on moral activity disappears, replaced by supplications for presence, healing, and redemption. Both autonomy and social performance must, with a certain amount of agony, be renounced, the self submit to its radical vulnerability to God, who wounds and torments it with failure. Moreover, the selfhood formed by divine power and love does not fulfill a social role. The poems on affliction and employment spell out with painful precision the calamitous effects on one's career and status resulting from getting involved with God's love. In "The Answer" Herbert allows society to evaluate him, and the report that comes back is harshly negative. In the perception of the community, Herbert is "pursy and slow," a vapor that "doth live and die / In that dark state of tears" (10–12).

The problem of the relation between "The Church Porch" and "The Church" thus centers on apparently contradictory conceptions of the self. In "The Church Porch" the self is autonomous, ethical, and social; in "The Church," dependent, passive, and private. This duality is, in fact, the subject of "Coloss. 3.3: Our Life is Hid with Christ in God," which contrasts the hidden life that obliquely winds toward God with the straight line of the life of the flesh. The Incarnation teaches the poet that "still one eye / Should aim and shoot at that which *Is* on high" (7–8), and the pun on "eye"/"I" seems intentional. There is one "I," one self, that aims toward God, but also another "diurnal" self, and it is these *two* that form the theme of Herbert's poetry: the poem begins, "*My* words and thoughts do both express this notion, / That *life* hath with the sun a double motion." There is both a hidden selfhood and a public one, and their double motion informs the discontinuity between the first two parts of *The Temple*.

To understand better this peculiar duality we can begin with William Perkins, the most celebrated of the reforming preachers and theologians in the Elizabethan church. In "A Dialogue of the State of a Christian Man," Perkins cites a passage that he borrows from Tyndale's *Exposition on Matthew*, which in turn derives from Luther's work of the same title. The quotation states the central thesis of Luther's *Zwei-Regimente-Lehre*, the two regiments under which a Christian lives.[4] Perkins observes that

> every person is a double person and under two regiments. In the first regiment I am a person of mine own self, under Christ and his doctrine, and may neither hate nor be angry . . . but must after the example of Christ humble myself, forsake and deny myself, and hate myself and cast myself away . . . and let every man go over me . . . and do me wrong. And yet I am to love them. . . . In the temporal regiment, thou art a person in respect of another. Thou art husband, father, mother, daughter, wife, lord, subject and there thou must do according to thine office. If thou be a father, thou must do the office of a father and rule, or else thou damnedest thyself.[5]

4. On the *Zwei-Regimente-Lehre* in Luther and Tyndale, see W. D. J. Cargill Thompson's "The Two Regiments: The Continental Setting of William Tyndale's Political Thought," in *Reform and Reformation: England and the Continent, c. 1500–c. 1750*, ed. Derek Baker (Oxford, 1979), pp. 17–33, and his *Studies in the Reformation: Luther to Hooker*, ed. C. W. Dugmore (London, 1980); Quentin Skinner, *The Foundations of Modern Political Thought*, 2 vols. (Cambridge, 1978), 2:14. See also William Tyndale, *Exposition of Chaps. v. vi. and vii. of St. Matthew's Gospel*, in *Expositions and Notes on Sundry Portions of The Holy Scriptures*, ed. Rev. Henry Walter, The Parker Society (Cambridge, 1849), pp. 60, 67. The notion is not prominent in Calvin's thought, but see John Calvin, *Institutes of the Christian Religion*, 2 vols., ed. John T. McNeill, trans. Ford Lewis Battles, The Library of Christian Classics (Philadelphia, 1960), 3.19.15.

5. William Perkins, *The Work of William Perkins*, ed. Ian Breward, The Courtenay Library of Reformation Classics (Appleford, Eng., 1970), p. 382.

Here we have a clear distinction between a private self ("a person of mine own self"), which is nevertheless "under" Christ, and a public, social self ("a person in respect of another"), which is constituted by its role or "office" within a hierarchical sociopolitical order. According to the first regiment, the self strives toward submission and love; according to the second, it exercises authority and endeavors "to bring all under obedience." For Perkins, both regiments are binding—one can go to hell for refusing to exercise power as well as by refusing to love—but they also (rather obviously) make largely antithetical demands. The self that struggles to cast itself away exists in tension with the social self that must perform its role in relation to others. The spiritual and social are seen as equally obligatory but also essentially separate realms.

Perkins's analysis of the dual persons within each person offers a starting point for an understanding both of Renaissance notions of selfhood and ultimately of the discontinuous structure of *The Temple,* which itself alludes to the Lutheran conception of "both Regiments; / The world's, and thine," in "Frailty" (9–10). Perkins's "person in respect of another" bears strong similarities to the conception of selfhood Greenblatt ascribes to the Renaissance in his "Psychoanalysis and Renaissance Culture." Citing Hobbes, Greenblatt argues that the period conceives of a person as a persona, a "theatrical mask secured by authority."[6] A persona is an actor, one who plays a role. One becomes a person, rather than "a chaos of unformed desire," by assuming or being given a social mask that then constitutes one's identity. But Hobbes represents a late stage in the formation of the concept of a social self. The same notion of a "person" appears in Andrewes, who defines it as "all by-respects that do personate, attire, or mask any, to make him personable; such as are the country, condition, birth, riches, honour, and the like." "Personal," he thus notes, is the opposite of "real."[7] But the isolation of this notion seems to occur much earlier, at the inception of the Renaissance, in a text that became a standard on Latin philology for over a century: the *Elegantiae linguae Latinae* of Lorenzo Valla.

6. Stephen Greenblatt, "Psychoanalysis and Renaissance Culture," in *Literary Theory/Renaissance Texts,* ed. Patricia Parker and David Quint (Baltimore, 1986), p. 223.

7. Lancelot Andrewes, *The Works of Lancelot Andrewes,* 11 vols., Library of Anglo-Catholic Theology (Oxford, 1854), 3:330.

Valla's article "In Boethium de Persona" argues that Boethius's definition of persona as an immutable, individuated substance refers to nothing except Boethius's faulty Latin. A persona is not, according to Valla, a substance but "a quality by which we differentiate one person from another." A person is then an individual, defined by his distinction from others. But the qualities that differentiate are not those of post-Romantic, post-Freudian individuality but social status, moral disposition, and physical characteristics; for example, one may possess the persona of a doctor, a miser, a woman, a pauper—or of all four, since, according to Valla, each individual possesses a *multiplex persona.* Such personae are explicitly, as in Hobbes, compared to theatrical roles: "So actors in a theater assume personae, when they play either a servant or handmaid or matron, or whore or senex" and so forth.[8] Striking in this account is the lack of discrimination between moral attributes and social function; liberality, timidity, fatherhood, wealth, nobility, strength are all personae, that is, individuating qualities or attributes that now constitute an "insubstantial" person, layers of a mask without a face beneath.

The conception of self as persona seems to inform Herbert's "The Church Porch," most evidently in its failure to demarcate ethical from pragmatic evaluation, moral from social precepts. The poem begins with the avowed intention to "Rhyme thee to good" (4), where "good" apparently means "morally good." But by the fifth stanza, and increasingly thereafter, the principle of evaluation shifts toward the social categories of "shame" (27), "honour" (152), and "glory" (335). In fact, most of the poem is not about being morally good at all, but about how to achieve the self-control, discretion, and manners necessary to perform one's role successfully. For example, stanza 53 observes,

> Calmness is great advantage: he that lets
> Another chafe, may warm him at his fire,
> Mark all his wand'rings, and enjoy his frets;
> As cunning fencers suffer heat to tire.
> (313–16)

As in Valla, the categories of moral good and social advantage fuse. The self that is to be rhymed to good is ineradicably politicized, a

8. Laurentius Valla, *Elegantiarum libri sex,* in *Opera omnia,* 2 vols., intro. Eugenio Garin (Turin, 1962), 1:215–16.

social performance. The lack of tension between ethical and pragmatic considerations appears nakedly in stanza 59, which begins with what appears to be an allusion to Christian charity: "Scorn no man's love, though of mean degree; / Love is a present for a mighty king." But two lines later the reason for such kindness is given in unmistakeably utilitarian terms: "The cunning workman never doth refuse / The meanest tool, that he may chance to use." Love, cunning, and use here belong to the same discourse.

The performative self of "The Church Porch" has two further characteristics. First, it seems relatively autonomous, that is, capable of self-control. One's mask is *secured* by authority, but a part may still be played better or worse. Many of the precepts advocate an inner command necessary for successful social functioning; for example, one should "rule" liquor "as thou list" rather than allow it to "tame" thee, since drunkenness may lead to "shame" (25–27). Such self-control involves not only internal government but manipulation of others; there are rules for pleasing (289), for making others desire one's company (325–26), for gaining affection (299–300). As Richard Strier notes, "the ideal is the cool, flexible, and socially uninhibited opportunist."[9] Second, such autonomy is totally enmeshed in a social context. Like morality, "self-fashioning" is not differentiated from social performance. The long middle section of "The Church Porch" focuses almost exclusively on questions of honor, shame, success, ambition—on questions, that is, of social action and evaluation, and these are not regarded as inadequate criteria: "Who says, I care not, those I give for lost; / And to instruct them, will not quit the cost" (347–48).[10] The concept of persona, available from Valla through Hobbes, sustains Herbert's notion of selfhood as a role or performance in which moral virtues like temperance or calmness appear as means for attaining honor and success. The self is "a person in respect of another," evaluated in relation to the requirements of his "office" or social function.

9. Richard Strier, "Sanctifying the Aristocracy: 'Devout Humanism' in François de Sales, John Donne, and George Herbert," *Journal of Religion* 69 (1989): 56.

10. The concern for one's reputation would not necessarily have felt "irreligious" or culpable to a seventeenth-century audience. Donne unhesitatingly gives the same advice in his sermons (*The Sermons of John Donne,* 10 vols., ed. George Potter and Evelyn Simpson [Berkeley, 1953–62], for example, 7:9.469–71; 4:8.419–20). Similarly, the pragmatic and cautious charity of "The Church Porch" (373) resembles Donne's counsel not to spend money on God until one has paid one's social and personal obligations (*Sermons,* 4:7.383–89). But see Strier's "Sanctifying the Aristocracy" for a harsh (and rather Kantian) critique of the "ethics" of "The Church Porch."

Before Hobbes, however, the "theatrical mask secured by authority" conceals not only chaotic desire but Perkins's second person, that of one's own self, under Christ. This self has no convenient name in modern English; "spiritual self" would be correct, since in Renaissance psychophysiology the spirits are the source of emotion, the immediate instruments of the soul, and receptacle of the Holy Spirit,[11] but "spiritual" has distressingly Neoplatonic connotations—perhaps it would be better to estrange the term slightly by Greekifying it to "pneumatic self," *pneuma* being the equivalent of the Latin *spiritus*. Herbert, like most Renaissance writers, refers to this self as either the "soul" or "heart," the two terms being almost identical, and this localization of the soul in the heart suggests that the pneumatic self is conceived in terms of spatial inwardness; it is "inside" and therefore both central and obscured. In "Coloss. 3.3" this self is the hidden life that winds obliquely toward God; in "The Sinner" it is "heav'n the centre" surrounded by "the circumference earth" (8).

As we have already seen, Perkins attributes two characteristics to the pneumatic self: a struggle to cast itself away and love. In order to amplify this analysis, we can turn back to the texts considered in the last chapter, for the pneumatic self forms the subject of almost all these works. Moreover, the selfhood depicted there seems strikingly close to the one imaged in "The Church." I am not, however, interested in sources but a shared conceptual model, one that is in many respects very old, although largely abandoned by the end of the century in favor of an alternative conception of selfhood based on introspection and self-reflexivity.[12] This conceptual model of pneumatic selfhood has several relevant features. First, in Andrewes's sermons, as in Herbert's lyrics, one notes a lack of interest in moral action. Andrewes generally divides his text into doctrine and duty, but almost invariably the "duty" turns out not to be a doing but a receiving. Thus, in the tenth Nativity sermon "our duty [is] to be led and to be fed by [Christ]." Similarly, in the first Andrewes argues that we must frame

11. Philip Melanchthon, *Liber de anima*, vol. 13 of *Opera quae supersunt omnia*, 28 vols., ed. Carolus Gottlieb Bretschneider, Corpus Reformatorum (Brunswick and Halle, 1834–60), p. 88.

12. For the failure to acknowledge different conceptions of selfhood, see Anne Ferry, *The "Inward" Language: Sonnets of Wyatt, Sidney, Shakespeare, Donne* (Chicago, 1983). The book is an important study of selfhood during the Renaissance but partially vitiated by the fact that she is exclusively interested in finding premonitions of the modern self rather than reconstructing Renaissance conceptions of selfhood.

"even some practice" from the text, but that practice is not an action but a "receiving" of the Eucharist. Likewise in the fifth, he asks "shall we not . . . perform some duty to *natus est.*" But, "to a gift the duty that belongeth properly, is to receive it. . . . How is that? how shall we receive Him? who shall give Him us? That shall One That will say unto us within a while, *Accipite,* 'Take, this is My Body.' "[13] This passive duty of reception replaces ethical activity, the latter becoming almost suspect, a form of self-assertion. "Good moral virtues," Andrewes thus remarks,

> will not serve to seal us against the day [of Judgment]. . . . That which is then to stand us in stead—let us not deceive ourselves—we spin it not out of ourselves, as the spider doth her web. . . . It is from without, as breathing and as sealing is.[14]

Morality is at best a preparative, enabling us "to dispose ourselves, and be ready wrought to receive the figure of His seal."[15]

The selfhood that interests Andrewes and Hooker is not the source of ethical judgment (that is, conscience) but of emotional response, for the hidden, private self is experienced as desire. That is why prosopopoeia, or the voicing of this pneumatic self, becomes the characteristic rhetorical figure in the sermons, corresponding to Herbert's lyric expressivity. Like Herbert, they focus on "what life feeleth,"[16] on the experience of lostness, grief, joy, love. The speaker of "Affliction (V)" claims "There is but joy and grief" (13), and this polarity governs the experience depicted in almost all the lyrics of "The Church." Thus the hymn that concludes "An Offering" begins: "Since my sadness / Into gladness / Lord thou dost convert" (25–27) or, in "The Glimpse," the inner presence of Christ is addressed as "delight":

> Whither away delight?
> Thou cam'st but now; wilt thou so soon depart,
> And give me up to night?
> For many weeks of ling'ring pain and smart
> But one half hour of comfort to my heart?

"Delight" is a sensation, but also a Person—or the psychological traces of a Person. The identification of the heart and soul here (and in Renaissance sacred texts generally) articulates a pneumatic selfhood

13. Andrewes, *Works,* 1:156, 16, 83.
14. Andrewes, *Works,* 3:211.
15. Andrewes, *Works,* 3:217
16. Herbert, "Repentence," 12.

structured by the affective polarities of joy and grief, sweetness and bitterness, delight and despair—but these emotional states in turn are contingent upon the presence or absence of the divine within the heart.[17] It is the Holy Spirit who "stirreth up our affections." The Spirit creates human love, and from that infused "love of God proceeds this love and affection in us that we desire Him."[18]

This identification of emotion with the inward activity of the Holy Spirit suggests the second characteristic of the pneumatic self—a lack of autonomy. The self is both permeable and passive. It is not solid but like a "house [that] will not stand empty long. One spirit or other, holy or unholy, will enter and take it up."[19] That is, the pneumatic self is not a "thing" or agent or individuality but the locus of presence. It is not a bounded *ego* but a space—a void, if you like—where God comes (or does not come). In Donne's words, "your *Soules* are holy, by the inhabitation of Gods holy spirit, who dwells in them. . . . Your *Bodies* are holy, by the inhabitation of those sanctified *Soules*."[20] This notion of a person as constituted by triple concentric spheres of body, soul, and Spirit recurs regularly, from the Middle Ages on.[21] But the inmost sphere, the "center," as it were, of selfhood, is *not* part of the self. Rather than being an enclosed monadic entity, the self is inhabited by an alien life, which is yet "natural," or as Levy-Bruhl writes, the premodern "individual is only himself by virtue of being at the same time something other than himself."[22] Hence Andrewes explains,

17. Richard Strier's claim that Herbert's "assertion of the special status of emotion in the relationship between man and God" brings him close to the radicals of the Civil War is therefore misleading (*Love Known: Theology and Experience in George Herbert's Poetry* [Chicago, 1983], p. 174ff.). The heavy stress on religious affectivity characterizes, as far as I can tell, *all* religious thought during the Reformation and its aftermath. It belongs to the revival of Augustinian psychology that dominates the whole spectrum of Christian spirituality during this period. See Debora Shuger, *Sacred Rhetoric: The Christian Grand Style in the English Renaissance* (Princeton, 1988), pp. 46–49, 132–39; William J. Bouwsma, "The Two Faces of Renaissance Humanism: Stoicism and Augustinianism in Renaissance Thought," in *Itinerarium Italicum: The Profile of the Italian Renaissance in the Mirror of Its European Transformations*, ed. Heiko A. Oberman with Thomas Brady, Jr. (Leiden, 1975), pp. 3–60.

18. Andrewes, *Works*, 5:336–37.

19. Andrewes, *Works*, 3:191.

20. Donne, *Sermons*, 4:15.13–16.

21. See, for example, Hugh of St. Victor, *On the Sacraments of the Christian Faith (De sacramentis)*, trans. Roy Defarrari (Cambridge, Mass., 1951), p. 167; William J. Bouwsma, *John Calvin: A Sixteenth-Century Portrait* (Oxford, 1988), p. 79; Andrewes, *Works*, 3:384.

22. Lucien Levy-Bruhl, *The "Soul" of the Primitive*, trans. Lilian A. Clare (New York, 1966), p. 202.

> Somewhat there is to be in us, more than a natural soul. *Φύσις* [nature] is one thing, *φύσησις* [inspiration] is another. Some inspiring needs, somewhat of *accipite*. . . . The spirit, not a habit gotten with practice, and lost again with disuse, as are the arts and moral virtues. . . . Christ's Spirit [is] not Hero's *pneumatica;* not with some spring or device, though within, yet from without; artificial, not natural; but the very *principium motûs* to be within.[23]

Christ's Spirit operates within, not like a windup toy (*pneumatica*) but as the "natural" source of all activity, and yet inspired from without rather than in some sense innate. Hooker makes the same point: Christ does not "only knock without, but also within assist to open"[24]—the "assist" perhaps giving Hooker away as an "Arminian" (that is, Thomist) but in no way negating the ancient sense of an inhabited self.[25] This belief that "somewhat there is to be in us," that the "natural soul" requires inhabitation by the divine similarly informs Herbert's depiction of selfhood. "Good Friday," "The Temper (II)," "Whitsunday," "Denial," "Home," and "Longing," to name only the most obvious, are all pleas for God to enter the inner space of the self, that "pile of dust, wherein each crumb / Says, Come."[26] The pneumatic self is not only permeable to presence but constituted by it; when presence is deferred, it collapses into suicidal chaos. Thus "Nature" begins, "Full of rebellion, I would die." As this passage suggests, the affective self possesses virtually no inner stability. Sometimes it "peer[s]" above "forty heav'ns," sometimes "fall[s]" to hell,[27] its wild oscillations responding to the approaches and retreats of divine presence. So Herbert writes in "The Search": "my grief must be as large, / As is thy space, / Thy distance from me." Alone and fallen, man is "A

23. Andrewes, *Works,* 3:274. The Stuart court was apparently fascinated by such ingenious machines and self-propelled gadgetry (for example, "moving statues of wood nymphs playing on organs powered by waterwheels"); see R. Malcolm Smuts, *Court Culture and the Origins of a Royalist Tradition in Early Stuart England* (Philadelphia, 1987), pp. 148–52.

24. Richard Hooker, *The Works of that Learned and Judicious Divine, Mr. Richard Hooker,* 3 vols., ed. Rev. John Keble, 7th ed. (Oxford, 1888; reprint, New York, 1970), 3:7.

25. Lucien Levy-Bruhl, *How Natives Think,* trans. Lilian A. Clare (New York, 1979), pp. 84, 91; Levy-Bruhl, *The "Soul" of the Primitive,* pp. 26, 68–71, 201; Emile Durkheim, *The Elementary Forms of the Religious Life,* trans. Joseph Swain (New York, 1915), pp. 305–6.

26. Herbert, "Longing," 41–42.

27. Herbert, "The Temper (1)," 5–8.

lump of flesh, without a foot or wing / To raise him to a glimpse of bliss: / A sick tossed vessel, dashing on each thing; / Nay, his own shelf."[28] As Andrewes notes, "if we desire to be delivered from whatsoever is evil, then from ourselves."[29]

Joy and goodness result from presence. The self, insofar as it is personal, is also passive. Again Andrewes:

> But, of all good, all our well-wrought works, of them, we say not only, *sine Me nihil potestis facere,* "We can do none of them without Him;" but further, we say with the Prophet, *Domine, omnia opera nostra operatus es in nobis.* In them He doth not only co-operate with us from without, but even from within; as I may say, in-operate them in us.[30]

Or, in Herbert's words, "Mothers are kind, because thou art, / And dost dispose / To them a part."[31] This radical passivity tends to intensify the problem of absence while simultaneously diminishing concern for ethical responsibility. It is utterly mistaken to view Herbert's lyrics as describing the "intrusion of grace into the tumultuous or complacent human soul."[32] The speaker in these poems pleads with something more like desperation than complacency for that grace, but because grace *is* the presence of the divine other, it can only be given, not found. So "The Search" begins:

> Whither, O, whither art thou fled,
>   My Lord, my Love?
> My searches are my daily bread;
>   Yet never prove.

The soul is scarcely complacent; it is just helpless, forced to wait until God "dost turn, and wilt be near" (53). Similarly in "The Flower" the speaker can only passively endure the alternations of absence and presence, "killing and quick'ning" (16), and try to accept his vulnerability and see the love behind that power, and, in Perkins's words, "hope for things deferred." The *promise* (not threat) of Reformation Christianity is that, although "to have nought is ours, not to confess / That we have nought," nevertheless "what Adam had, and forfeited

28. Herbert, "Misery," 74–77.
29. Andrewes, *Works,* 5:451.
30. Andrewes, *Works,* 3:392–93.
31. Herbert, "Longing," 14–16.
32. Veith, *Reformation Spirituality,* p. 52.

for all, / Christ keepeth now, who cannot fail or fall."[33] But this promise initially leaves the speaker "much troubled," not because it injures his self-esteem but because he cannot protect himself against desolation. That is why the friend reassures him by promising that "all things were more ours by being his" (12).[34]

As the pneumatic self is neither ethical nor autonomous, so it is not social. While radically contingent on presence, it cannot be touched by temporal power. "Somewhat there is still that comes from Christ, and none but Christ," Andrewes writes, "somewhat that as it comes higher, so it goes deeper, than any earthly power whatsoever. . . . The kings of the nations, send they can, and give power they can, but inspire they cannot."[35] Only grace can enter "the soul's most subtle rooms."[36] "The Church" appears to exist outside the state. This is, in fact, the radical substance of Luther's *Zwei-Regimente-Lehre.* Unlike Augustine's model of the two cities of man and God, which contrasts two opposing communities or invisible societies, Luther's two regiments divide a *private* and inward spiritual kingdom from the whole temporal order of society.[37] This formulation of the contrast between spiritual and temporal in terms of private versus public strongly influences the ecclesiology of the Church of England. Thus Whitgift distinguishes the "visible society and the external government" of the church from "the spiritual government of it by Christ in the heart and conscience of man." The magistrate is head of the church only in the former acceptation; in the latter, Christ alone can be the head, for, as David Little observes, to Whitgift "*all action as such* is external and indifferent and therefore subject to royal regulation. For him it is invisible inwardness that constitutes the realm of true religion."[38] The

33. Herbert, "The Holdfast," 9–10, 13–14.

34. See Donne, *Sermons,* 5:15.745–47: "God does all. Yet thus argues S. *Augustin* upon *Davids* words, *Tuus sum Domine,* Lord I am thine, and therefore safer then they, that thinke themselves their owne."

35. Andrewes, *Works,* 3:271.

36. Herbert, "The H. Communion," 22.

37. Cargill Thompson, "The Two Regiments," p. 22 and his *Studies in the Reformation,* pp. 46, 54. Compare Tyndale's comment: "The life of a Christian man is inward between him and God" (*The Wicked Mammon,* in William Tyndale, *Doctrinal Treatises and Introductions to Different Portions of The Holy Scriptures,* ed. Rev. Henry Walter, The Parker Society [Cambridge, 1848], p. 90).

38. John Whitgift, *Works,* 3 vols., ed. Rev. John Ayre, The Parker Society (Cambridge, 1852), 1:392; David Little, *Religion, Order, and Law; A Study in Pre-Revolutionary*

distinction between the two regiments thus defines and, by defining, half-creates the privatized "rooms" of the devotional lyric. Herbert, in fact, departs from contemporary Puritan theology (which did not make much use of the distinction between the two regiments) precisely because he has no sense of "the brethren," of an elect community supporting the soul in its earthly journey. Herbert's "Pilgrimage" is lonelier even than that of Bunyan's Christian.

When the state—Perkins's whole "temporal regiment"—does enter the poems, it is almost always threatening and dangerously enticing. Social values, the values largely accepted in "The Church Porch," become in "The Quip" the "merry world" assembled to "jeer" at the speaker; in "Frailty," the poet attempts to perceive "honour, riches, [and] fair eyes" as merely "dust," but the world's "regiment" fans its "glory and gay weeds," swelling like "a Babel . . . Commodious to conquer heav'n." "The Answer," the only poem that presents a social perspective on the self, depicts the eye of the other as confirming the poet's own fears that he is inadequate and a failure. Society is felt as a shame-culture—as it is in Hooker's discussion of confession in book 6 of *The Laws of Ecclesiastical Polity*. Hooker rejects the Puritan reestablishment of public confession to the community because other people are more than likely to "upbraid" the penitent for his sins, whereas God alone "will cure them."[39] The confessional intimacy of the divine-human encounter in Herbert fulfills the need for a relationship *not* available in society. Robin Horton's comment on African religious systems is applicable here:

> All social systems stimulate in their members a considerable diversity of such needs [for personal relationship]; but, having stimulated them, they often prove unwilling or unable to allow them full opportunities for satisfaction. In such situations the spirits function . . . as surrogate people providing opportunities for the formation of ties forbidden in the purely human social field.[40]

England (Oxford, 1970), p. 144; compare Richard Bancroft, *Tracts Ascribed to Richard Bancroft*, ed. Albert Peel (Cambridge, 1953), p. 93; John S. Coolidge, *The Pauline Renaissance in England: Puritanism and the Bible* (Oxford, 1970), p. 46; Peter G. Lake, *Anglicans and Puritans? Presbyterianism and English Conformist Thought from Whitgift to Hooker* (London, 1988), pp. 28, 40, 49. I will treat Hooker's development of this distinction in the next chapter.

39. Hooker, *Works*, 3:54.

40. Robin Horton, "African Traditional Thought and Western Science," in *Rationality*, ed. Bryan R. Wilson (Evanston, 1970), p. 161.

Social relations in the English Renaissance, as we have them both from Lawrence Stone and "The Church Porch," were competitive, pragmatic, and rather distant. "The Church," if we may anthropologize for a moment, then depicts a supplemental society of two: passionate, intimate, based on sacrifice, self-abnegation, and the paradox of gratuitous love.

Thus the discontinuity between "The Church Porch" and "The Church" corresponds to a parallel discontinuity in the cultural representation of selfhood. Each person is a dual person, on the one hand enmeshed in the social relations of power, hierarchy, and performance, yet relatively autonomous (that is, capable of both self-control and manipulation of others), on the other hand radically unstable and passive, yet outside of any social matrix, experienced neither as the reflexive "I" of the cogito nor as a mask but as the space of divine indwelling (or absence), and therefore of joy and grief. Such a correspondence between cultural representations and literary structures does not, perhaps, explain anything—at least if explanation equals disclosing causal relations. It does, however, suggest that the poetic discontinuity is significant, not the result of hasty patching together of juvenilia with more mature works,[41] but an articulation of the felt duality (even contradiction) of selfhood. The *explanation* of this duality seems to involve a gradual emptying of the temporal world, both physical and social, of divine presence.[42] Despite the rather last-ditch effort of divine-right theory, even conservative Anglican writers like Hooker and Whitgift show a distinct tendency to "secularize" social institutions and practices and a corresponding tendency to confine presence to inwardness, resulting in an intensification of private spirituality split off from a historicized and rationalized account of social and political behavior.

THE CHURCH MILITANT

The split also informs "The Church Militant." In this poem history is a predetermined failure. Sin chases Religion around the globe in "period[s] and prefixed time[s]" (59), and Sin always wins, even if only Pyrrhic victories. "The Church Militant" is, in fact, a rather ironic

41. Strier, "Sanctifying the Aristocracy."
42. Veith, *Reformation Spirituality*, p. 229.

title, since Herbert's church spends most of its time fleeing rather than fighting. The poem's fatalism, furthermore, seems to have little to do with the passionate immediacy of divine-human relations imaged in "The Church." Like "The Church Porch," "The Church Militant" suggests the withdrawal of presence from both *tempora* and *mores* into the pneumatic self. Indeed, several poems in "The Church" describe exactly such a withdrawal: "Whitsunday," "Decay," "Sion," "The Bunch of Grapes." "Decay" is the most explicit:

> Sweet were the days, when thou didst lodge with Lot,
> Struggle with Jacob, sit with Gideon,
> Advise with Abraham, when thy power could not
> Encounter Moses' strong complaints and moan:
>   Thy words were then, *Let me alone.*
>
> One might have sought and found thee presently
> At some fair oak, or bush, or cave, or well:
> Is my God this way? No, they would reply:
> He is to Sinai gone, as we heard tell:
>   List, ye may hear great Aaron's bell.
>
> But now thou dost thyself immure and close
> In some one corner of a feeble heart.
>
> (1–12)

Presence retreats from history to inwardness; God no longer inhabits "Solomon's temple," but "all thy frame and fabric is within."[43] This perception seems to have been rather generally felt in the period. For example, Hooker's treatment of historical causation and change in *The Laws* is almost exclusively concerned with immanent cultural process, but this secular analysis vanishes at two points: in his discussion of man's longing for happiness in book 1 and of the Eucharist in book 5—the two main sections where he treats individual religious experience. These sections represent spirituality, as "The Church" does, in terms of desire, participation, indwelling, joy, and mystical presence. As in *The Temple,* the discourses of history and inwardness split apart.

But nothing in Hooker corresponds to the determinism of "The Church Militant." There are loose parallels between Herbert's account

43. Herbert, "Sion," 2, 11. For a rather optimistic interpretation of these texts, see Chana Bloch, *Spelling the Word: George Herbert and the Bible* (Berkeley, 1985), pp. 139–40; Marion White Singleton, *God's Courtier: Configuring a Different Grace in George Herbert's "Temple"* (Cambridge, 1987), p. 201; Kenneth Alan Hovey, "Church History in 'The Church,' " *George Herbert Journal* 6 (1982): 9–12.

of the steady encroachment of Sin on Religion in Renaissance descriptions of universal decay or of the Church on earth as a persecuted pilgrim fleeing from city to city,[44] but neither of these topoi suggests the lawlike inevitability that Herbert's poem articulates, where all nations have "their period also and set times / Both for their virtuous actions and their crimes" (261–62), as Sin chases Religion westward until the whole sorry circle is negated by a literal deus ex machina. This inevitability is so alien to Protestant notions of divine providence, which stress the unpredictable, personal, and retributive interventions of God in the world, that it seems impossible to locate the conceptual model for "The Church Militant" in the framework of Reformation Christianity.[45] Herbert's determinism informs, to the best of my knowledge, only one other Renaissance text:

> Reflecting now upon the course of human affairs, I think that, as a whole, the world remains very much in the same condition, and the good in it always balances the evil; but the good and evil change from one country to another. . . . All the virtues that first found a place in Assyria were thence transferred to Media, and afterwards passed to Persia, and from there they came into Italy and to Rome. . . . After the fall of the Roman Empire . . . we . . . see them scattered amongst many nations, as, for instance, in the kingdom of France, the Turkish empire . . . and nowadays the people of Germany.[46]

So opens the second book of Machiavelli's *Discourses*. There are, of course, differences between this and Herbert's account: Machiavelli is talking about virtue and vice, not Religion and Sin; although the movement is generally east to west this is not specified. But both versions show the same deterministic procession from nation to nation, beginning in the East and shifting to Rome and from thence to the Western European nations. Yet it seems inherently implausible that Machiavelli would be Herbert's source; the absence of any interest in Christian providence in the former separates his work sharply from the poem's understanding of history. If Machiavelli were the source for "The Church Militant" (and intended to be recognized as such)

44. Lewalski, *Protestant Poetics*, p. 289.

45. See Herbert's own "The Parson's Consideration of Providence," in *A Priest to the Temple*, pp. 228–29.

46. Niccolò Machiavelli, *The Prince and the Discourses*, intro. Max Lerner (New York, 1950), p. 272.

then the poem would seem to subvert its own assertions, and Herbert is generally not, I think, a subversive poet, at least not subversive of religious meaning. In order to "locate" the conception of history that informs "The Church Militant," we must move back to the originally Christian paradigm implicit in both *The Discourses* and the poem.

We can begin by setting out the principal features of ecclesiastical history as presented in "The Church Militant." Very briefly, one may list the steady movement from east to west of empire, arts, and religion, concluding with the Apocalypse, with an almost mechanical, predetermined regularity. As Kenneth Hovey has observed, the movement of empire and the arts derives from the well-established notion of the *translatio imperii et studii*.[47] The idea that history exhibits a movement of empire and arts from east to west, from Assyria through Persia and Greece and finally to Rome and the barbarian West, goes back to antiquity and is a common property of Christian historiography from the fathers through the seventeenth century.[48] But, in general, this motif does not exhibit a deterministic apocalypticism nor is it associated with a *translatio religionis*.[49] In fact, there seems to be only a single work that contains all the main elements found in "The Church Militant": *The Chronicle or History of the Two Cities* by Otto von Freising, a twelfth-century German bishop, grandson of Emperor Henry IV and uncle of Frederick Barbarossa.[50] The work had three sixteenth-century editions (1515, 1569, and 1585) and was available in England; the 1605 Bodleian catalogue lists two copies, and Andrewes's will mentions the work. However, since *The Two Cities* also fell victim to the epidemic of unacknowledged borrowing that infects the entire Middle Ages and Renaissance, its observations could have

47. Kenneth Alan Hovey, " 'Wheel'd about . . . into Amen': 'The Church Militant' on Its Own Terms," *George Herbert Journal* 10 (1986): 75.

48. For all this information, I am indebted to Werner Goez, *Translatio Imperii: Ein Beitrag zur Geschichte des Geschichtsdenkens und der politischen Theorien im Mittelalter und in der frühen Neuzeit* (Tübingen, 1958).

49. Thus, for example, Melanchthon interprets the transfer of power as a punishment for sin, history thus exhibiting a strict poetic justice; in Calvin, the *translatio imperii* is contrasted with *religio,* which is nontransferable (Goez, *Translatio Imperii,* pp. 263–66, 272–74, 279, 374–77).

50. Otto von Freising, *The Two Cities: A Chronicle of Universal History to the Year 1146 A.D.,* ed. Austin P. Evans and Charles Knapp, trans. Charles C. Mierow (New York, 1928; reprint, New York, 1966). See Goez, *Translatio Imperii,* pp. 107–25.

reached Herbert through one or more layers of redaction. But whether Otto's history is the father of "The Church Militant" or first cousin several times removed, the similarity between the two texts offers a clue to the strange intellectual (intertextual?) provenance of Herbert's poem.[51]

The Two Cities is a theological world history from Adam to A.D. 1146. Despite its title, it is not merely a chronological list of events but a study of civilizational change. As a recent scholar has remarked, "the level of reflective historical writing reached by Otto of Freising was not reached again until the seventeenth and eighteenth centuries."[52] Otto structures his narrative according to the east-to-west movement of empire, of "earthly pomp and power departing with time, even as the heavens revolve from east to west."[53] *The Two Cities* describes how "human power . . . originating in the East, began to reach its limits in the West. . . . how it passed from the Babylonians to the Medes and the Persians and from them to the Macedonians, and after that to the Romans and then again to the Greeks under the Roman name . . . [and] was transferred from the Greeks to the Franks, who dwell in the West."[54] Like Herbert, Otto associates this *translatio imperii* with the *translatio studii* or *sapientiae:* "The careful student of history will find that learning was transferred from Egypt to the Greeks, then to the Romans, and finally to the Gauls and the Spaniards. And so it is to be observed that all human power or learning had its origin in the East, but is coming to an end in the West."[55] This conjoined progress of empire and arts is, as mentioned above, relatively common intellectual property. But Otto also includes a third *translatio* and here, except for Herbert, he stands alone. At the end of the seventh book he speaks about the rise of monasticism, concluding with the striking remark that monks "dwelt once in greatest numbers in Egypt . . . [but] are most numerous now in the regions of Gaul and Germany, so that one need not wonder at the transfer of power or of wisdom from the East

51. For the influence of *The Two Cities* on historians through the sixteenth century, see Mierow's introduction to *The Two Cities,* pp. 45–46.

52. Amos Funkenstein, *Theology and the Scientific Imagination from the Middle Ages to the Seventeenth Century* (Princeton, 1986), p. 267.

53. Otto, *The Two Cities,* p. 358.

54. Otto, *The Two Cities,* p. 322.

55. Otto, *The Two Cities,* p. 95.

to the West, since it is evident that the same transfer has been effected in matters of religion."[56]

Like "The Church Militant," *The Two Cities* ends with the Last Judgment, the first seven books taking world history up to the twelfth century, the final book depicting the end of all history at the Apocalypse. This eschatological structure grows out of the bishop's deep historical pessimism. History is, in Otto's words, tragedy—a tedious record of war, suffering, and "sorrow-burdened insecurity" designed by divine providence to drive men from "the wretchedness of this fleeting life" to hope for the life to come.[57] Empire succeeds empire with a predetermined, almost mechanical regularity according to the inscrutable will of God:

> If the Lord, who is the judge and arbiter of the world, holding a cup in His hand, first making Babylon drunken humiliated it at last at the hands of the Medes and, when the Medes had been brought low by the Persians, the Persians in turn by the Greeks, and the Greeks finally by the Romans, wished for a time to exalt Rome, which was also in its turn to be put down, if, weighing in balanced scales all human events, He weaves such changes as those, will it be possible for the Creator to be blamed by His creature?[58]

Otto's conception of history has therefore very little ethical import. The transferal of empire is not a punishment for sin but simply follows the fixed law of spatiohistorical change. The Romans are not better than the Greeks, just further west. Otto therefore never suggests that increased moral or spiritual effort might reverse the steady diurnal movement of history. Instead, every moment of hope for respite and peace swiftly turns into loss. He thus describes the collapse of Charlemagne's brief empire: "earthly power which, fleeing so to speak from east to the west, had at last, so men fancied, found stability and peace, must in accordance with the saying of the Evangelist be brought to desolation."[59] Otto's characterization of church history seems particularly close to the dual progress of Religion and Sin in "The Church

56. Otto, *The Two Cities*, p. 448. According to Goez, in every other instance from antiquity through the seventeenth century, *translatio religionis* signifies only the transfer of true religion from the Jews to the Gentiles (*Translatio Imperii*, pp. 378–79).

57. Otto, *The Two Cities*, pp. 89, 94–97.

58. Otto, *The Two Cities*, p. 222.

59. Otto, *The Two Cities*, p. 358.

Militant": every time the church finally triumphs over persecution and begins to expand and prosper, the devil, following on its heels, enters and assails it from within.[60] As in Herbert, the forces of both good and evil are more or less personified and therefore impersonal; Religion and Sin, church and devil seem to operate autonomously according to the laws of the *translatio*.

That Otto's *Two Cities* would have appealed to Herbert is not surprising. There is much in it that would have seemed relevant to any Englishman in the 1620s, for the earlier work traces the beginning of the Investiture Controversy, the first phase of the great struggle between church and state that eventuates in the English Civil War. Moreover, as *The Two Cities* is informed by the failure of the medieval church to renovate history, so "The Church Militant" reflects the failure of the Reformation:

> The second Temple could not reach the first:
> And the late reformation never durst
> Compare with ancient times and purer years;
> But in the Jews and us deserveth tears.
> (224–27)

But if *The Two Cities* with its austere and disillusioned apocalyptic determinism (and perhaps the secular determinism of Machiavelli's *Discourses*) provides the overall scheme for "The Church Militant," then the second and third parts of *The Temple* fissure. The emotional intimacy of divine/human relations in "The Church" gives way to a picture of history divested of that direct and personal providential control which was, for Calvin, the ground of all assurance, comfort, and felicity.[61] And this fissuring cannot be smoothed over by Hovey's platitudinous formula that "amid this outward decline the Church has made inner progress."[62] Herbert did not draw on what might be the most depressing account of world history ever written in order to say something so pat. Instead, the brief "L'Envoy," which follows "The Church Militant" and concludes *The Temple,* expresses a barely contained anguish at the apparent silence of history. The poet pleads with God:

60. Otto, *The Two Cities,* pp. 351, 283, 323.
61. Calvin, *Institutes,* 1.17.7–11.
62. Hovey, "Church History," pp. 11–12.

Let not Sin devour thy fold,
Bragging that thy blood is cold,
That thy death is also dead,
While his conquests daily spread;
That thy flesh hath lost his food,
And thy Cross is common wood.
(5–10)

As in Otto's grim chronicle—and Hooker's sermons—the perception that history provides little empirical evidence of divine grace becomes profoundly disturbing. "The Church Militant" is, as Fish notes, "pessimistic, inconclusive, and anticlimactic."[63]

The Temple then falls into three discontinuous parts, indicative of some general cultural fragmentation, splitting social, spiritual, and historical discourses into "divided and distinguished worlds." That fragmentation is sharply etched in the flagrantly nonempirical epistemology of "Faith," which flaunts the identification of faith, fiction, and wish fulfillment. Faith makes what one imagines or desires to be true, true—submitting the appearances of things to the desires of the mind. (Herbert was, one cannot help remembering, the friend and translator of Bacon.)

Hungry I was, and had no meat:
I did conceit a most delicious feast;
I had it straight, and did as truly eat,
As ever did a welcome guest.
(5–8)

This practice, quite clearly, only works for spiritual meat—which is precisely the point: the laws of supernature do not resemble the laws of nature. So too "The Church" is related to "The Church Porch" and "The Church Militant" by an absence of relation, for spiritual experience has nothing to do with either social behavior or history.

THE CHURCH

Of course, that is not the whole story. Without denying the discontinuity among the three parts of *The Temple,* I would like to suggest that the divisions are not absolute; furthermore, some of the crucial proble-

63. Fish, *The Living Temple,* p. 144.

matics of "The Church" stem from the *imperfect* separation of social, spiritual, and historical paradigms. I will begin with one instance of such entanglement between history and spirituality and then briefly examine a few intertwinings of spirituality and social praxis.

As mentioned previously, in "The Church Militant" Herbert portrays ecclesiastical history as a failure, "Sin and darkness follow[ing] still / The Church and sun with all their power and skill" (272–73). This downward temporal process has no immanent telos; there is no fulfillment in history—the end of the story is not part of the story but takes place after the termination of history at the Last Judgment. The providential conclusion, that is, is largely extrinsic to the temporal process, although not wholly so, since "the Church by going west / [did] Still eastward go; because it drew more near / To time and place, where judgement shall appear" (275–77). This sequence of temporal failure redeemed only after and outside of time seems to be not only the pattern of history but also of biography. The lyrics of "The Church" repeatedly struggle with temporal disaster, and repeatedly the resolution to these problems of "unemployment," sickness, and grief is deferred to a point after and outside of time. "The Pilgrimage" is exemplary here. The speaker travels "a long . . . and weary way" through some threatening allegorical scenery to get to "the hill, where lay / My expectation" (1–3). Having arrived, "A lake of brackish waters on the ground / Was all I found" (23–24). The pilgrimage ends in failure, and the speaker cries out, "Alas my King! / Can both the way and end be tears?" (27–28). The reply comes: the true hill is further off, but "*None goes that way / And lives*" (33–34), at which point the poet confesses that "After so foul a journey death is fair, / And but a chair" (35–36). All his hiking is from one vale of tears to another; the end is not accessible on foot. The switch in modes of transportation emphasizes the lack of narrative continuity between the temporal pilgrimage and its telos. Herbert's view of both history and individual experience is surprisingly similar and surprisingly bleak. In heaven God shall "look us out of pain" but not until then.[64] Even "The Dawning," which celebrates the joy of Christ's resurrection, ends with the empty tomb and a sense that all we have left of Christ to comfort us and dry our eyes are the strips of burial cloth that signify both His triumph and His absence.

64. Herbert, "The Glance," 21.

Arise, arise;
And with his burial-linen dry thine eyes:
  Christ left his grave-clothes, that we might, when grief
  Draws tears, or blood, not want a handkerchief.

There is no progress, meaning, or fulfillment within the temporal order in either "The Church Militant" or (often) "The Church"; the poet can only gesture outside of time, to the place where he will be "past changing" and rid of "hope and fear"—although even these desires for the Church Triumphant remain subject to correction.[65]

The analysis of spiritual experience in "The Church" is also related to the analysis of social performance in "The Church Porch." To some extent, this relation is one of opposition. "The Church Porch" perceives social interaction in terms of personal success achieved, at least partly, by the manipulation of others. That is, one practices courtesy, "respective boldness," or civility toward other people in order to ingratiate oneself and use them for one's own purposes. This need for success and reward also frequently appears in "The Church," but usually only to be denied. In lyrics such as "Affliction (I)," "The Collar," and "Artillery" the speaker struggles with his inability to manipulate God to his satisfaction, with the absence of reward or any "harvest but a thorn,"[66] but rebellion finally collapses into paradox: a love that demands nothing except to love, in response to the Love that gives nothing except love. Yet the speakers who demand "cordiall fruit" in Herbert's poems are not, as Bloch would have it, "men of little faith, stiff-necked, self-righteous."[67] Critics of Herbert generally seem rather too eager to fault the speakers of the poems for their demands and complaints, as if human pain were somehow evitable and to feel it sinful.[68] While there is certainly precedent in Calvinism for equating murmuring with infidelity, Herbert generally displays only sympathy—and identification—with his personae. Like their biblical predecessors—Job, Jeremiah, Habakkuk, Esdras, and the psalmist—they are struggling with *the* question of the Bible: the suffering of

65. For example, "The Temper (1)," 20, and "The Flower," 22.

66. Herbert, "The Collar," 7.

67. Bloch, *Spelling the Word,* p. 149.

68. For example, Veith, *Reformation Spirituality,* pp. 34, 40, 61; Strier, *Love Known,* p. 238; Bloch, *Spelling the Word,* pp. 42, 94, 127, 145ff. But see William Sessions's fine essay, "Abandonment and the English Religious Lyric in the Seventeenth Century," in *"Bright Shootes of Everlastingnesse": The Seventeenth-Century Religious Lyric,* ed. Claude J. Summers and Ted-Larry Pebworth (Columbia, Mo., 1987), pp. 1–19.

God's children. So in the Old Testament Jeremiah speaks to God:

> Ah, Lord God! surely thou hast greatly deceived this people and Jerusalem, saying Ye shall have peace; whereas the sword reacheth unto the soul. . . . I sat not in the assembly of the mockers, nor rejoiced; I sat alone because of thy hand. . . . Why is my pain perpetual, and my wound incurable, which refuseth to be healed? wilt thou be altogether unto me as a liar, and as waters that fail?
>
> (4:10, 15:17–18)

The bitter questioning and the need for reward is not sinful; it is just that God requires an almost inhuman submission, an abjuration of interest and prudential motive: "Ah my dear God! though I am clean forgot, / Let me not love thee, if I love thee not."[69]

Yet in several poems one also finds the rueful acknowledgment that this submission itself conceals a deeper manipulation, that "The distance of the meek / Doth flatter power" for "the poor do by submission / What pride by opposition."[70] Michael Schoenfeldt observes of these lines: "devotional postures of submission [are] continually contaminated by the subtle forms of opposition or ambition they both enable and disguise. Surprisingly, the submission of the poor and the opposition of the proud have the same outcome, however different they may be in appearance and intention: the flattery of might and power, whether secular or sacred."[71] So Herbert's description of Holy Scripture as "Subject to ev'ry mounter's bended knee" implies that such humble posture may be posturing, may serve an ambitious intent.[72] In these poems there is no escape from the prudential, social self; even submission is only the poor man's attempt to ingratiate himself with power. So too, prayer is in part "Engine against th'Almighty . . . Reversed thunder," a direct assault disguised as supplication.[73]

69. Herbert, "Affliction (1)," 65–66.

70. Herbert, "The Priesthood," 39–42.

71. Michael Schoenfeldt, " 'Subject to Ev'ry Mounters Bended Knee': Herbert and Authority," in *The Historical Renaissance: New Essays on Tudor and Stuart Literature and Culture*, ed. Heather Dubrow and Richard Strier (Chicago, 1988), p. 244. See also both his "Submission and Assertion: The 'Double Motion' of Herbert's 'Dedication,' " *John Donne Journal* 2 (1983): 39–47, and "Standing on Ceremony: The Comedy of Manners in Herbert's 'Love (III),' " in "*Bright Shootes of Everlastingnesse*," pp. 116–33.

72. Herbert, "The H. Scriptures. I," 14.

73. Herbert, "Prayer (1)," 5–6. The notion of prayer as agon appears frequently in Donne; see his *Sermons* 2:1.175, 735; 2:8.245.

Such wobbling between a demand for purity of motive and a sense that interest is inevitable pervades Christian thought. Andrewes, for example, repeatedly returns to the question of whether one must love God sheerly for His own sake or whether such love can only be motivated by hope of a reward, even if a deferred one. Thus in his ninth sermon on the Lord's Prayer, he begins by saying that Christ requires us "when we come to pray to Him for our necessities we be carried away with such a desire of the glory of our heavenly Father, that we forget our own selves and desire only that His name may be sanctified." Here love of God entails self-forgetfulness, but within two pages one finds the observation, "And reason it is that we should esteem of God's name, for . . . in time of trouble *turris altissima nomen Domini,* 'the name of the Lord is a strong tower.'"[74] Self-interest, thrust out of doors, comes in at the window. Hooker simply accepts as a fact that in this life "we now love the thing that is good, but good especially in respect of benefit unto us," selfless love being possible only in heaven.[75] The same reluctant acceptance appears in Herbert's *The Country Parson,* interestingly, in the chapter entitled "The Parson's Courtesy":

> [the parson] oftenest invite[s] those whom he sees take best courses, that so both they may be encouraged to persevere, and others spurred to do well, that they may enjoy the like courtesy. For though he desire that all should live well and virtuously, not for any reward of his, but for virtue's sake, yet that will not be so: and therefore as God, although we should love him only for his own sake, yet out of his infinite pity hath set forth heaven for a reward to draw men to piety, and is content, if at least so, they will become good, so the country parson, who is a diligent observer and tracker of God's ways, sets up as many encouragements to goodness as he can, both in honour, and profit, and fame.
>
> (206)

It is not that impurity of motive subverts or even contaminates love, reducing it to a kind of vulgar "magical" manipulation—the kind Protestants often attributed to Roman Catholics. In "Gratefulness" the

74. Andrewes, *Works,* 5:381–83; compare 6:107–10.

75. Hooker, *Works,* 1:256. There is, however, another strain of Reformation Christianity that tends (not always consistently) to lump together and reject all forms of self-interest, including supernatural self-interest. See Little, *Religion, Order, and Law,* p. 115; Tyndale, *Exposition on Matthew,* in *Doctrinal Treatises,* pp. 30–31 and *The Wicked Mammon,* in *Expositions and Notes,* pp. 62, 71–73.

"beggar" who "works on [God] . . . / By art" (3–4), is not wheedling God for temporal gain but pleading for a "thankful heart" (27), "whose pulse may be / Thy praise" (31–32). But the recognition that even the "bended knee" implies the desire to "mount" reconnects the social and pneumatic selves. In deeply differing ways, both are upwardly mobile.

This reconnection also occurs in the consideration of love and service. In "The Church Porch," serving and pleasing others, what Herbert there terms "humbleness" (337), is implicated in the desire for power and superiority: "in service, care or coldness / Doth rateably thy fortunes mar or make" (255–56). That love and service are in some sense a form of self-assertion frequently appears in Renaissance texts (usually drawing on the *Nicomachean Ethics*). In his *De anima,* Juan Luis Vives thus writes:

> Just as a benefactor is loved, so the benefactor also loves the one he benefits as his own handiwork; so a father [loves] his son and a teacher his student. Indeed it often turns out that the love of the one who helps and gives is more ardent than that of the one who receives the benefit. For the love of the former derives from his goodness, of the latter from his need. In the former is honor and glory, as the greater and more powerful [of the two]; in the latter, however, a certain (as it were) shame, as the inferior. . . . It is rightly said that although love has the nature of fire, yet it descends rather than ascends. A parent loves his child more . . . than the reverse; and the greatest and most ardent of all loves is that of God toward us.[76]

Such love is unselfish insofar as it seeks to give to the other, but that desire to give is bound up with the desire for power and preeminence, since love descends from the higher to the lower. The corresponding disgrace of being loved motivates the agon of "The Thanksgiving." The poet will "revenge me on thy love" (17), try to love Christ back and so regain some measure of equality, if not "victory" (48). The ambitions of the social self insinuate themselves into the desire to love. Similarly, such ambitions infiltrate service.[77] As "Love (III)" makes abundantly clear, the one who serves is the superior; only the owner of

76. Juan Luis Vives, *De anima et vita* (Basel, 1538; reprint, Turin, 1959), p. 159.

77. On the connection between service and ambition in the secular courtesy literature of the period, see Frank Whigham, *Ambition and Privilege: The Social Tropes of Elizabethan Courtesy Theory* (Berkeley, 1984), pp. 103–4.

the inn can invite someone else for dinner. In the lyrics that treat the poet's own disastrous career the problematics of service are a central motif. In "Employment (II)," for instance, the desire to be able to serve God, to be an "orange-tree" and so "never want / Some fruit for him that dressed me" (21, 24–25) is complicated and rendered less innocent by the political analysis of the third stanza:

> When th'elements did for place contest
> With him, whose will
> Ordained the highest to be best,
> The earth sat still,
> And by the others is oppressed.

The ability to serve belongs to the highest, not the oppressed. So in "The Cross" this ability is explicitly referred to as "my power to serve thee" (10), where both "my" and "power" require emphasis. In the next lines, service derives from "my abilities, my designs." In fact, in the thirty-six lines of the poem, "my" is repeated eighteen times—although in the submission of the final line, "my words" merge with Christ's words: *Thy will be done.* "The Cross," like many of the other poems, moves from a desire to serve to self-abnegation precisely because, as Perkins notes, the pneumatic self can only escape the social self by the ruthless casting of oneself away. The very radicalism of this self-negation suggests that the discourse of "The Church Porch" cannot easily be shut out of "The Church."

The structure of Herbert's *Temple* exhibits the same discontinuities visible in contemporary religious prose: the contrast between the apparent emptiness of history and inward presence, the segregation of social and ethical behavior from pneumatic inwardness. In both the poetry and prose, the locus of the sacred shrinks to the private spaces of the psyche, which remains permeable to presence but also tormented by a sense of desolation, and yet this anguish paradoxically discloses the indwelling of grace as it carves out the center of the self, creating the neediness only it can fill. The lack of continuity between this selfhood, the subject of "The Church," and the social self of "The Church Porch" involves more than simply the juxtaposition of inconsistent viewpoints (or the juxtaposition of unrelated poems); it is a theorized inconsistency, as Perkins's discussion of the *duplex persona* and dual regiments indicates. The pneumatic and social selves imply each other, emerging simultaneously from the failure of post-Reformation Europe to create forms of social existence shaped by spiritual needs, from the failure, that is, of monasticism and Erasmianism.[78] Instead, the competition, ambition, and superficiality of the Stuart court would seem to have both stimulated and frustrated the desire for community—for communion. In modern, secular culture these social conditions produce the psychiatric self; in the theocentric environment of the seventeenth century they fostered its pneumatic equivalent—both being marked by deprivation, solitude, and the need to be loved. The failure of the Reformation to renew history likewise intensified the privatization of the sacred, a process narrated in Herbert's "Decay" and "Church Militant." Yet the discontinuities between social, spiritual, and historical experience are not absolute. History and biography show strange homologies, and the strategies of social climbing insinuate themselves into devotional practice. Inside and outside *The Temple* there appears a "double motion": on the one hand, a withdrawal of divine presence from the realms of social behavior and historical process into "some one corner of a feeble heart," and, on the other, the discovery of both that social behavior and that historical process well entrenched in some of its other corners.

78. More's *Utopia* is one such attempt to imagine a society whose institutions would give public shape to ethical and spiritual imperatives. There are thus, as has often been noted, no private spaces in More's commonwealth.

4

Holy Church and Sacred King

As *Constantine's* Court, *Ecclesiae instar,* a little *Universitie,* compassed with *Learned* men in all professions; and his Majesty in the middest of them.

Barlowe, *An Answere*

Et ipse magistratus sanctus est, non profanus, sanctaque illius potestas, sanctae leges, et sanctus gladius.

Wolfgang Musculus, *Loc. comm.*

This chapter will consider the relation between politics and religion, the city of man and the city of God, under Elizabeth and James. Once again we will focus on Hooker and Andrewes as representative of the two central approaches to this subject, the constitutional and the absolutist. The connections between politics and religion during this period have, of course, been subject to extensive analysis, but usually only with respect to the political implications of theological factions and especially how such divisions paved the road for the Civil War.[1] But if theology had political implications, then politics also had theological ones, and in two senses. First, the Henrican restructuring of the ecclesiastical polity raised in acute form the problem of the relation between temporal institutions and divine presence. Second, the rise of *iure divino* absolutism could not but affect the conceptualization of heaven's lord and king. This chapter will focus on the institutional implications of the English union of state and church under the headship of the sovereign; the subsequent chapters will then consider the implications of this arrangement for the understanding of God.

The structural discontinuities of *The Temple* reflect the historic

1. For example, Nicholas Tyacke, "Puritanism, Arminianism, and Counter-Revolution," in *The Origins of the English Civil War,* ed. Conrad Russell (New York, 1973); J. P. Sommerville, *Politics and Ideology in England, 1603–1640* (London, 1986); Christopher Hill, *Intellectual Origins of the English Revolution* (Oxford, 1965); Lawrence Stone, *The Causes of the English Revolution, 1629–1642* (New York, 1972).

problem of the Church of England and, more generally, of Protestantism. In Protestant countries, the Reformation meant the loss of a visible, universal church, of a sacramental and sacred institution at least theoretically independent of the state. And that loss destabilized the traditional relations between the holy and its manifestations, between, that is, God, church, state, and soul. The state was, in general, the winner. Throughout the Middle Ages, princes and heretics had contested papal claims, and the union of these two oppositional forces at the Reformation divested the medieval church of much of its power and potency. The Reformers needed support against the papacy and thus tended to shelter under the one available alternative pair of wings, those of the prince or magistrate. But such proto-Erastianism harmonized poorly with other impulses at work in the Reformation, especially the longing to reshape and purify society along biblical lines and the conviction that one knew how this should be done. In any case, a good many magistrates, particularly those in Italy, France, and the Holy Roman Empire, declined to protect the Protestants from the pope.

In Protestant countries, the loss of the imperial church raised certain obvious questions of authority, both spiritual and temporal. It was not immediately clear who had the right to interpret the Bible or ascertain doctrine, polity, and worship. But it would be a mistake to construe the collapse of the universal catholic church exclusively in terms of authority, whether we take it in the bureaucratic or epistemic sense. "The Middle Ages," Tillich writes, "were dominated by one problem, namely, to have a society which is guided by a present reality of a transcendent divine character. . . . This was the problem of the Middle Ages—to have the holy present."[2] The medieval church could plausibly claim to be such a present reality: a visible institution mediating objective grace through sacraments. Thus when medieval heretics wanted to attack the church they unerringly focused on the Mass, the place where the holy was felt to be most present. The English Reformers, from Cartwright through Milton, likewise reviled and ridiculed ceremony, sacrament, rite—all the visible manifestations of present holiness—in their attempt to dislodge sanctity from its current institu-

2. Paul Tillich, *A History of Christian Thought from Its Judaic and Hellenistic Origins to Existentialism,* ed. Carl Braaten (New York, 1967), pp. 154–55.

tional embodiments in order to reinvest it elsewhere. The ferocity of these attacks suggests that the problem of the Reformation was not altogether different from that of the Middle Ages: the need for a visible locus of the sacred. As such it concerns the nature of institutions and, more specifically, whether the institutions of church and the state possess a sacramental or transcendent divine character. The difference, of course, between the Middle Ages and the Reformation lay in the answer to this problem.[3]

Viewed one way, Protestantism represents a denial of the need for visible, institutional holiness. In opposition to Catholics like Sir Thomas More who stressed the visibility and continuity of the Roman church, Protestants tended to redefine the "holy, catholic, and apostolic church" of the Creed as the invisible church of the predestined. Thus the church could not be identified with any specific historical church; it was not an institution but "the whole multitude of the faithful."[4] The split between Spirit and structure appears most clearly in the Radicals, who, according to Luther, supposed they had "swallowed the Holy Spirit feathers and all," and therefore denied the need of any official (that is, clerical) church.[5] But even mainline Reformers like Oecolampadius and Zwingli attempted to separate both word and sacrament from the presence of God, to separate, that is, the visible from the holy. Greenblatt quotes a lovely passage from Tyndale that vividly sets forth the early Protestant longing for an unmediated, noninstitutional relation to the divine: "Who taught the eagles to spy out their prey? Even so the children of God spy out their Father; and Christ's elect spy out their Lord, and trace out the paths of his feet, and follow; yea, though he go upon the plain and liquid water, which will receive no step, and yet there they find out his foot."[6] Or as Jewel says

3. On the problem of "residual needs" for sacred meaning and the difficulty of shaking off the "inherited questions" of the Middle Ages, see Hans Blumenberg, *The Legitimacy of the Modern Age,* trans. Robert M. Wallace, Studies in Contemporary German Social Thought (Cambridge, Mass., 1983), p. 65.

4. Peter G. Lake, *Moderate Puritans and the Elizabethan Church* (Cambridge, 1982), p. 105.

5. Quoted in Jaroslav Pelikan, *The Christian Tradition: A History of the Development of Doctrine,* 5 vols., vol. 4, *Reformation of Church and Dogma, 1300–1700* (Chicago, 1984), p. 175.

6. Stephen Greenblatt, *Renaissance Self-Fashioning from More to Shakespeare* (Chicago, 1980), p. 99.

less poetically, "God's grace is promised to a good mind and to one that feareth God, not unto sees and successions."[7]

But somewhat paradoxically, the Protestant impulse to deny the sacred a visible locus led to (or at least coexisted with) a massive endeavor to instantiate the holy in some sort of institutional form. That is the essence of English Presbyterianism. For men like Cartwright and Travers, church and state must be organized and run according to the precise letter of God's word. Were the discipline installed, the sacred and the social would recompact, and Christ would sit "not only in his chair to teach but also in his throne to rule, not alone in the hearts of everyone by his spirit, but also generally and in the visible government of his church, by those laws of discipline he hath prescribed."[8] The Anabaptists at Münster, Zwingli at Zurich, Calvin at Geneva, the English Separatists at Amsterdam all likewise undertook to create institutional forms that would manifest a "transcendent divine character," not, of course, the hierarchic, sacramental character of the medieval church but (with the exception of Münster) a more aural, ethical, pedagogic holiness. But the difference in "character" should not obscure the fact that for the Reformers, as well as for their predecessors, it seemed crucially important that the visible order express the divine down to the smallest details of marriage ring and surplice.[9] Therefore, both Puritans and Roman Catholics had difficulties with the notion of a comprehensive, national church based

7. John Jewel, *An Apology of the Church of England,* ed. John E. Booty, Folger Documents of Tudor and Stuart Civilization (Charlottesville, Va., 1963), p. 128.

8. Cartwright in John Whitgift, *Works,* 3 vols., ed. Rev. John Ayre, The Parker Society (Cambridge, 1852), 3:315; quoted in Peter G. Lake, *Anglicans and Puritans? Presbyterianism and English Conformist Thought from Whitgift to Hooker* (London, 1988), p. 31.

9. Recent scholarship on the politics of the body offers some suggestions that help clarify why the seemingly indifferent matters (*adiaphora*) of ritual and gesture so easily became the focus of dissent. In *Outline of a Theory of Practice,* Pierre Bourdieu thus observes that "the social formation of the body is the more effective because it extorts the essential while seeming to demand the insignificant: in obtaining the respect for form and forms of respect which constitute the most visible and at the same time the best hidden (because most 'natural') manifestation of submission to the established order, the incorporation of the arbitrary abolishes what Raymond Ruyer calls 'lateral possibilities,' that is, all the eccentricities and deviations which are the small change of madness." Quoted in Peter Stallybrass, "Patriarchal Territories: The Body Enclosed," in *Rewriting the Renaissance: The Discourses of Sexual Difference in Early Modern Europe,* ed. Margaret W. Ferguson, Maureen Quilligan, and Nancy J. Vickers (Chicago, 1986), p. 123.

on the Erastian principle of *cuius regio, eius religio,* whose forms were compulsory—"for order's sake"—but not obviously sacred. As the English Separatist John Robinson put it in 1610, in matters of religion there are no *adiaphora,* no things indifferent; either rite and ceremony conform to God's will or they do not.[10] From Whitgift on, English Conformity was faced with the task of showing that its institutions were not a political compromise but possessed a truly sacramental, numinous character or, if they did not, trying to understand and justify that loss or—in Weber's famous phrase—*Entzauberung.*

The controversies of the English Reformation are too often treated exclusively with respect to their political consequences. In fact, however, they were religious in the fullest sense of the word. They concerned, above all else, the relation between God and the world, the transcendent character of social institutions. Such controversies inevitably centered on the question of participation—the mystical relation between the apparently separate. If the final outcome of such debates was to deny the sacral character of society, the intermediate stages present no such clear picture. Rather, under the Stuarts a concerted effort was made to "remystify" church, state, and the social order.

Yet the religious dimension of Reformation controversy cannot be separated from the political. The ecclesiastical controversialists did not, in Whitgift's phrase, "dream of such a church, as Plato did of a commonwealth,"[11] but dealt with a church embedded in a specific sociopolitical environment, and they were perforce brought to reflect on the fundamental political issues of the age: patriarchy, absolutism, law, hierarchy. The linkages between religion (qua religion) and politics, however, pertain to more than just shared subject matter. Greenblatt speaks of More's *concensus fidelium* and Tyndale's New Testament as "forms of power."[12] The phrase seems apt because the holy is a form of power, what anthropologists of the last century used to call *mana.*[13] Such power is not exclusively political power, power as a mechanism of social stability and institutional control. The holy

10. J. W. Allen, *English Political Thought, 1603–1660,* 2 vols. (London, 1938), 1:151.
11. Whitgift, *Works,* 1:23.
12. Greenblatt, *Self-Fashioning,* p. 97.
13. G. van der Leeuw, *Religion in Essence and Manifestation,* 2 vols., trans. J. E. Turner (London, 1938; reprint, New York, 1963), 1:24–26.

possesses power because it orders the individual and community in relation to the divine and only secondarily in relation to institutions. In general, to claim that something is sacred entails that its power is not political, that is, not a matter of human needs and interests but inherent—a part of its essence. Yet once a thing or institution loses holiness it loses political power; *In Praise of Folly* opened the door to the Reformation, as the compilers of the *Index librorum prohibitorum* well knew. Therefore, in the aftermath of the Reformation the problem of social locus of the sacred was not only a religious problem, a question of how God manifests Himself in the world, but a political one, a question of whether a particular institution is holy and therefore powerful. The Crown resisted Presbyterianism in part because, like Roman Catholicism, it seemed to weaken the state by denying its sacrality.[14]

In England, the space vacated by the collapse of the universal church of the Middle Ages was filled by a state-church under royal headship. In 1534 Henry VIII was declared supreme head of the Church of England. The royal supremacy resulted from one problem and led to another. The English church accepted the king's control because it needed the king's protection if it were not to go the way of the monasteries.[15] It also needed the Crown to enforce ecclesiastical law and privilege: to punish heretics, to authorize tithes, to compel attendance.[16] The dependence of the church on the Crown, however, had problematic consequences. Machiavelli was not alone in seeing religion as a branch of civil policy, essential for preserving order, which, in the Renaissance, usually meant keeping the have-nots from having. In fact, writers during this period were remarkably open about affirming the connection between religion and social control. Sir John Eliot thus notes that "religion it is that keeps the subject in obedience,

14. Lake, *Moderate Puritans,* p. 21; Sommerville, *Politics and Ideology*, pp. 214–17; Douglas Macleane, *Lancelot Andrewes and the Reaction* (London, 1910), pp. 3, 39, 105, 219.

15. In *Religion, Order, and Law,* however, David Little notes that even before the Reformation, the English king maintained considerable control over the English church (*Religion, Order, and Law: A Study in Pre-Revolutionary England* [Oxford, 1970], p. 133).

16. Sommerville, *Politics and Ideology*, p. 10; Christopher Hill, *The Collected Essays of Christopher Hill: Religion and Politics in Seventeenth-Century England* (Amherst, Mass., 1986), pp. 38, 64; Patrick Collinson, *The Religion of Protestants: The Church in English Society, 1559–1625* (Oxford, 1982), p. 13.

as being taught by God to honour his vicegerents." Thomas Taylor (d. 1633) says about the same thing: "If Christian religion confirm civil authority, then the way to bring men to become subject to superiors is to plant the gospel."[17] The ease and frequency with which such comments were made suggests that the conviction of the social utility of religion, pace Machiavelli, did not imply the subversive perception that religion is *merely* useful. Besides, social order was generally held to be a positive good. Yet Machiavellian glimmerings and a sense of the basically irreligious and pragmatic nature of the Tudor state-church do surface from time to time. Donne clearly believed that a cynical notion of the function of the church commanded widespread assent: a sinner "hears the Ordinance of *Preaching* for salvation in the next world, and he cals it an invention of the State, for subjection in this world."[18] Both continental Protestants and Roman Catholics found the notion of royal headship questionable. Calvin called it blasphemy.[19] In his *True, Sincere and Modest Defence of English Catholics* (1584), William Allen remarks upon the religious consequences of the church's loss of independent authority: "But now and ever when the superiority temporal hath the preeminence, and the spiritual is but accessory, dependent, and wholly upholden of the other, error in faith is little accounted of, whatsoever their pulpit men (to make themselves and their patrons sport) bawl of such matters."[20]

With the royal headship, the Church of England forfeited the Augustinian vision of the pilgrim church, living "like a captive and a stranger in the earthly city" and enduring "reproaches for that city of God which is hateful to the lovers of this world."[21] This notion of a pilgrim church, fundamentally alien to all the cities of men, all human institutions and temporal powers, persists in the Church of England into the mid-sixteenth century. It is the theme of Foxe's *Book of Martyrs*. Even Whitgift admits that the church is likely to be "purest"

17. Quoted in Hill, *Collected Essays*, pp. 14–15.

18. John Donne, *The Sermons of John Donne*, 10 vols., ed. George Potter and Evelyn Simpson (Berkeley, 1953–62), 2:3.701–3; compare 2:8.344–45; 2:18.6–12.

19. John Calvin, *Comm in Amos*, quoted in Richard Hooker, *The Works of that Learned and Judicious Divine, Mr. Richard Hooker*, 3 vols., ed. Rev. John Keble, 7th ed. (Oxford, 1888; reprint, New York, 1970), 3:385n.

20. Quoted in Charles McIlwain, "Introduction," in *The Political Works of James I* (Cambridge, Mass., 1918; reprint, New York, 1965), p. xxix.

21. Aurelius Augustine, *On the Two Cities: Selections from the City of God*, ed. F. W. Strothman (New York, 1957), pp. 18, 65, 103.

during times of persecution.[22] The very unradical Bishop Jewel begins his *Apology of the Church of England* (1562) with a history of the truth that "wandereth here and there as a stranger in the world." Thus he quotes Hilary to the effect that the true church is not a matter of walls and roofs, of visible institutions; rather "hills, woods, pools, marshes, prisons, quavemires [*sic*] . . . [are] places of more safety; for in these the prophets, either abiding of their accord or forced thither by violence, did prophesy by the Spirit of God."[23] The violence that forced the prophets into the wilderness was wielded by the authorities of church and state. The history of the church, for Jewel, is largely a record of official persecution:

> Hereupon kings and princes . . . killed all the prophets of God, letting none escape—Isaiah with a saw, Jeremiah with stones, Daniel with lions, Amos with an iron bar, Paul with the sword and Christ upon the cross—and condemned all Christians to imprisonments, to torments, to the pikes, to be thrown down headlong from rocks and steep places, to be cast to wild beasts, and to be burnt; and made great fires of their quick bodies, for the only purpose to give light by night, and for a very scorn and mocking-stock; and did count them no better than the vilest filth, the offscourings and laughing-games of the whole world. Thus (as ye see) have the authors and professors of the truth ever been entreated.[24]

Jewel sees the powers-that-be as the historic persecutors of truth, although he does not explicitly relate this paradigm to the English situation where such powers were now officially in charge of protecting her. Later in the century, Puritans like Cartwright would claim the paradigm for themselves; they were the persecuted, pilgrim church struggling against the indifference or hostility of official institutions. For by the end of the sixteenth century, the Church of England was no longer a pilgrim but very much established. And this change in status brought a change in images—no longer the wandering and persecuted *viator* of the Augustinian tradition but the imperial *ecclesia* of Constantine. Foxe's *Book of Martyrs* occupies the threshold of this transformation, for while the text details the persecutions of *ecclesia viatrix,* the

22. Whitgift, *Works,* 1:385; compare John Calvin, "Prefatory Address to King Frances," in *Institutes of the Christian Religion,* 2 vols., ed. John T. McNeill, trans. Ford Lewis Battles, The Library of Christian Classics (Philadelphia, 1960).

23. Jewel, *An Apology,* p. 72; compare Lake, *Anglicans and Puritans?,* p. 155.

24. Jewel, *An Apology,* pp. 7, 10.

dedication and the closing pages summon up the figure of Elizabeth as the new Constantine, who has again brought the church out of the wilderness into the safety of the court.[25]

The parallel between the church under Constantine and the Church of England was, however, more of an ideal than a reality. Any understanding of Hooker's defense of the Elizabethan Settlement depends on the realization that under the Tudors the church was suffering from an acute loss of power, status, and revenue. Priests and bishops were generally despised. In 1589 Bishop Cooper speaks of "the loathesome contempt, hatred and disdain that *the most part* of men in these days bear . . . toward the ministers of the church of God."[26] Sommerville refers to the rampant anticlericalism of post-Reformation England.[27] Hooker, of course, could not find a publisher for *The Laws* apparently because booksellers felt that no one would be interested in reading a defense of episcopacy. According to Hill, the royal supremacy was popular only because it gave the Crown and landed classes access to the church's wealth.[28] Elizabeth was no Constantine.

RICHARD HOOKER: SUPERNATURAL AND POLITIC SOCIETIES

Hooker did not think the Church of England would survive a century.[29] The final two books of *The Laws* repeatedly refer to the calamitous situation of the church under Elizabeth. The clergy daily suffer "manifold intolerable contempts and indignities" from their parishioners.[30] The episcopate no longer commands authority or respect among either the common people or the aristocracy: "It is a long time sithence any great one hath felt, or almost any one much feared the edge of that ecclesiastical severity, which sometime held lords and dukes in a more

25. On Foxe, compare Collinson, *The Religion of Protestants,* p. 2; Frances A. Yates, *Astrea: The Imperial Theme in the Sixteenth Century* (London, 1975), pp. 42–43. The same Constantinianism also appears in Saravia; see Willem Nijenhuis, *Adrianus Saravia (c. 1532–1613),* Studies in the History of Christian Thought (Leiden, 1980), pp. 215, 256.

26. Hill, *Collected Essays,* p. 52 and passim.

27. Sommerville, *Politics and Ideology,* p. 212; compare Collinson, *The Religion of Protestants,* p. 41; Lake, *Anglicans and Puritans?,* p. 92.

28. Hill, *Collected Essays,* p. 64.

29. Macleane, *Andrewes,* p. 169.

30. Hooker, *Works,* 3:273.

religious awe than now the meanest are able to be kept,"[31] but "it may be men have now found out, that God hath proposed the Christian clergy as a prey for all men freely to seize upon; that God hath left them as the fishes of the sea, which every man that listeth to gather into his net may."[32] Bishops have been stripped of their revenues, so that "a mean gentleman that hath but an hundred pound land to live on, would not be hasty to change his worldly estate and condition with many of these so over abounding prelates."[33] Indeed, like Christopher Hill, Hooker locates the appeal of Puritanism to the landed classes in its promise to transfer to them the remaining power and wealth of the church.[34]

The loss of clerical status was partly a financial problem, partly a social one. Hooker notes with nostalgia that in the past men were "willing to live in dutiful awe and subjection unto the pastor of their souls," but now they imagine themselves so able "to teach and direct all others, that none of us can brook it to have superiors."[35] Again, the problem concerns the locus of the sacred. In an interesting footnote, Hooker relates the church's loss of "holiness" to its relation to the Crown. In the past, he notes, kings assumed sacerdotal status because its prestige would help "for the countenance of secular power." But now such prestige has been lost, and the priesthood no longer enhances the king, but the king must protect and countenance the clergy.[36] Despite its own nascent clericalism, English Puritanism expressed the laity's desire for power and spiritual independence from their sacerdotal governors, with the consequent rejection of any special sacrality or mystique inherent in the priesthood. This popular anticlericalism made the church unable convincingly to provide a mystical legitimation for the state,[37] yet made the state doubly necessary for the church as its sole protector. Under Elizabeth, however, such protection was

31. Hooker, *Works,* 3:310; compare 3:143.
32. Hooker, *Works,* 3:316.
33. Hooker, *Works,* 3:324.
34. Hooker, *Works,* 3:319–20; compare 1:157–58. See also Hill, *Collected Essays,* p. 64, and his *Economic Problems of the Church from Archbishop Whitgift to the Long Parliament* (Oxford, 1956).
35. Hooker, *Works,* 3:261.
36. Hooker, *Works,* 3:250n. For the sixteenth-century tendency to view the English bishops as merely crown-appointed civil servants, see Collinson, *Religion of Protestants,* p. 3.
37. Sommerville, *Politics and Ideology,* p. 212.

indifferent at best. With studious indirection, Hooker observes that the Crown has encouraged the depredation of the church by appointing mediocre and unworthy bishops, allowing sees to remain vacant for long periods, and appropriating ecclesiastical revenues.[38]

For Hooker, the problem faced by the Elizabethan church concerns the loss of spiritual authority. But it can only regain such authority by accepting secular standards and values. With considerable reluctance and regret, Hooker argues that the church must possess the tangible, social signs of power—land, money, titles, retainers—in order to hold secure any vestige of moral authority, because people acknowledge power only if coded in the symbols of secular status.

> Let the people be asked who are the chiefest in any kind of calling? who most to be listened unto? who of greatest account and reputation? and see if the very discourse of their minds lead them not unto those sensible marks, according to the difference whereof they give their suitable judgment, esteeming them the worthiest persons who carry the principal note and public mark of worthiness. If therefore they see in other estates a number of tokens sensible, whereby testimony is given what account there is publickly made of them, but no such thing in the clergy; what will they hereby, or what can they else conclude, but that where they behold this, surely in that commonwealth, religion and they that are conversant about it are not esteemed greatly beneficial? Wherupon in time the open contempt of God and godliness must needs ensue.[39]

Thus, he argues, the episcopacy requires both wealth and secular power "that their credit and countenance may by such means be augmented," for the church's loss of sacrality entails that "the glory of God is constrained even to stand upon borrowed credit" and "to make bishops poorer than they are, were to make them of less account and estimation than they should be."[40] The argument is somewhat paradoxical: the church is popularly despised as being too worldly, but the only way to quell such contempt is to increase its worldly involvement.

Hooker is clearly nervous about the paradox. In the long section on tithing in book 7 he contends that the issue is not economic but

38. Hooker, *Works,* 2:521–22; 3:430. Collinson notes that of the first cohort of Elizabethan bishops 45 percent died poor (*Religion of Protestants,* p. 39).

39. Hooker, *Works,* 3:275.

40. Hooker, *Works,* 3:241–42, 317.

spiritual. Tithes are not wages but gifts of thanksgiving to the glory of God.[41] While admitting that authority is contingent on wealth, he struggles against a strictly secular, economic analysis of the relation between clergy and laity. The money granted the clergy is "homage and tribute due unto the Lord Christ."[42] This mystification, however, cannot and is not meant to disguise the admission that once the church has become a branch of the state it can no longer base itself on values opposed to those of civil society. In a society based on rank, wealth, and honor there can be no Franciscans—nor any Diggers and Anabaptists. It is not that Hooker considers secular values particularly admirable; they are simply the only values anybody really takes seriously.

If the church needs status and money to regain spiritual authority, then it must look to the Crown. As Henry VIII decisively showed, if the king wants ecclesiastical goods, there is little to prevent him from taking them. Expropriating church land and income often proved useful for Tudor monarchs, habitually strapped for money. The only way to stop this depredation was to convince the monarch that the church was more useful to the state living than dead. James I's famous formula "no bishop, no king" suggests the depth of his conviction on this matter, but Elizabeth at times seemed harder to persuade. At least in part, *The Laws of Ecclesiastical Polity* directs its argument less toward the Puritans than toward the queen and her government, attempting to demonstrate the value of the church, and religion in general, to the state. The reason Hooker gives is the one universally given: religion promotes obedience, justice, and virtue.[43] Religious persons better perform their civic duties, serve the common good more conscientiously, are "willinger to obey" their superiors.[44]

Hooker's defense of the civic utility of religion is, however, neither wholly convincing nor theologically unproblematic. It is not convincing for two reasons. First, as he spells out with great clarity in the preface to *The Laws,* religion possesses considerable potential for social destabilization or, in his words, "the mind once imagining itself to seek the execution of God's will, laboureth forthwith to remove both

41. Hooker, *Works,* 3:295.
42. Hooker, *Works,* 3:295.
43. Hooker, *Works,* 2:13–19. Puritans tended to be equally socially conservative; compare Lake, *Moderate Puritans,* pp. 27–28, 35, 169; Hill, *Collected Essays,* 11–18.
44. Hooker, *Works,* 2:14.

things and persons which any way hinder it from taking place."[45] Second, the argument is open to a Machiavellian interpretation. Hooker explicitly addresses this issue: people see that there is "a politic use of religion" and conclude "that religion itself is a mere politic device, forged purposely to serve for that use."[46] To this he replies that false religion cannot have the desired utility since "treachery, guile, and deceit are things, which may for a while but do not use long to go unespied."[47] Once people perceive the trick, "religion" loses its efficacy. The problem with this reply is, of course, that false religions have survived quite a long time and been perhaps as effective a means of social discipline as Christianity. Hooker himself acknowledges this in the discussion immediately preceding his criticism of Machiavelli; he thus remarks that all religions possess some truth, and while their errors condemn their votaries to damnation, "yet the other [that is, their truth] had many notable effects as touching the affairs of this present life."[48] In other words, since the basic principles of religion concerning virtue and obedience are known to all peoples (the *concensus gentium* argument of book 1), non-Christian religions teach and enforce sociologically useful truths quite similar to those upheld by Christianity.

The theological (or ecclesiological) problem is more serious, however, and more significant for Hooker's overall conception of the church; for the claim that the state should support religion because religion supports the state entails the loss of the prophetic role of the church. Unlike Jewel and Foxe, Hooker never writes of the visible church as exile, pilgrim, voice crying in the wilderness. Indeed, he notes with a certain amount of scorn and dismay how these images have become the rhetorical property of the radicals, who now apply to themselves whatever "scripture hath in the favour of innocency persecuted for the truth," whereupon "the people's common acclamation unto such deceivers [is] . . . 'These are verily the men of God, these

45. Hooker, *Works,* 1:182.

46. Hooker, *Works,* 2:21.

47. Hooker, *Works,* 2:23. Andrewes takes a different tack and argues that religion could not have been invented to secure support for law because civil law is subsequent to religion and was invented to control those whom the authority of God could not constrain (Lancelot Andrewes, *The Works of Lancelot Andrewes,* 11 vols., Library of Anglo-Catholic Theology [Oxford, 1854], 6:23).

48. Hooker, *Works,* 2:17.

are his true and sincere prophets.'"[49] Hooker's own images for the English church derive from the Old Testament priesthood or the caesaropapalism of the Empire under Constantine and thereafter.[50]

Hooker thus tends not to oppose the true church to the official institution. Instead, he views the church (or, more properly, the episcopal organization of the church) largely as a judicial body necessary for dealing with heretics and schismatics. Whereas Jewel and Foxe (following the Lutheran *Centuries*) represented church history as the embattled survival of the faithful few—Hussites, Lollards, Waldensians, and so on—constantly menaced by the corrupt hierarchy centered in Rome, Hooker views the history of the church as the long struggle of an institution against doctrinal error and schismatic pride. The church as a coercive, hierarchical institution originates in the "emulations, strifes, and contentions" that arose within decades after Pentecost, "whereof there could be no sufficient remedy provided, except . . . some one were endued with episcopal authority over the rest, which one being resident might keep them in order."[51] Hooker returns to this theme repeatedly. Thus, quoting St. Augustine, "It was for a remedy of schism that one was afterwards chosen to be placed above the rest; lest every man's pulling unto himself should rend asunder the Church of Christ."[52] The enemy is not the institution but the individual, and the problem is not persecution but heresies caused by ambition and the lust for power.

Hooker's psychology, like that of most of his contemporaries, is basically Hobbesian. Everyone wants to be top dog (or, alternatively, alpha male), and this social aggressiveness leads to doctrinal chaos because one obvious way of attaining prestige is by claiming to have a superior handle on the truth.[53] Only an institution that rigidly designates and enforces rank can restrain this centrifugalism, because people

49. Hooker, *Works,* 1:154, 188; compare Richard Bancroft, *Tracts Ascribed to Richard Bancroft,* ed. Albert Peel (Cambridge, 1953), pp. 54–55.

50. Hooker, *Works,* 3:292–93, 411, 423–25.

51. Hooker, *Works,* 3:156.

52. Hooker, *Works,* 3:158; compare 3:163, 179, 188, 195, 219.

53. Hooker, *Works,* 3:200. On the *libido dominandi* or desire for preeminence as the basic sin, see William Tyndale, *Exposition on Matthew,* in *Expositions and Notes on Sundry Portions of The Holy Scriptures,* ed. Henry Walter, The Parker Society (Cambridge, 1849), p. 117; William J. Bouwsma, *John Calvin: A Sixteenth-Century Portrait* (Oxford, 1988), p. 51; Andrewes, *Works,* 2:408–9; 6:213, 267–68; Lake, *Anglicans and Puritans?,* p. 27; Bancroft, *Tracts,* p. 136; Nijenhuis, *Saravia,* p. 246.

are less likely to challenge strong and clearly marked authority than to struggle for preeminence in an amorphous and mobile situation.[54] However, although people may not attack entrenched prerogative, they usually resent it. Hooker has no illusions about the fact that most people prefer to be on the top of the heap and dislike those who are: "the manner of inferiors is to think that they which are over them always have too much."[55] This resentment does not derive, at least not necessarily, from the wickedness of those in power but is intrinsic to any hierarchical structure. The observation of the Spanish humanist Juan Luis Vives, cited in the previous chapter, is illuminating in this regard: "It often turns out that the love (*charitas*) of the one who helps and gives is more ardent than that of the one who receives the benefit. For the love of the former derives from his goodness, of the latter from his need. In the former is honor and glory, as the greater and more powerful [of the two]; in the latter, however, a certain (as it were) shame, as the inferior."[56] Although hierarchical institutions arise from the need to curb the *libido dominandi,* they in turn occasion it by producing "inferiors" who then resent even their superiors' goodness. But the view that all people desire power takes the ethical sting out of protests against subordination, for such protests are interpreted as the expression of personal ambition rather than the results of structural inequity.[57]

We will return to this Hobbesian psychology and its relation to Renaissance patriarchalism in the last chapter. It is relevant here, because it underlies Hooker's conception of the church as a coercive institution designed to control dissent and faction.[58] As such, it is a judicial and administrative body rather than a mystical or sacramental one. It therefore does not pertain directly to the faith or salvation of the individual but to the individual as he "liveth joined with others in

54. Hooker, *Works,* 3:359.

55. Hooker, *Works,* 3:297.

56. Juan Luis Vives, *De anima et vita* (Basel, 1538; reprint, Turin, 1959), p. 159.

57. This is nicely put in a 1658 broadside, entitled *A Worthy Panegyrick upon Monarchy;* according to the relevant verse, kingship is "Disown'd of None, but them whose Minds aspire, / And Envy One should have what *All* desire; / For be't a Few or Many we live under, / Such shall repine, still, whilst not of the Number." Quoted in W. H. Greenleaf, *Order, Empiricism, and Politics: Two Traditions of English Political Thought, 1500–1700* (London, 1964), pp. 46–47.

58. For similar views of the church among sixteenth-century Conformists, see Lake, *Anglicans and Puritans?,* pp. 90–91.

common society, and belongeth unto the outward politic body of the Church," the "law of nature and the law of God" being sufficient with respect to "what belongeth unto each man separately, as his soul is the spouse of Christ"—Luther's two regiments again.[59] For Hooker, as for Luther and the antipapal theorists of the late Middle Ages, the visible church performed a functional and administrative role. The conciliarist claim that the pope was not the "lord (*dominus*)" but only the "administrator (*dispensator*)" of the church is paralleled in Hooker's discussion of the royal headship.[60] As head of the English church, the king can call assemblies, authorize laws pertaining to religion, appoint bishops, and exercise judicial authority, but Hooker carefully and sharply divides Christ's headship over the mystical body of the Church from the regiment "outwardly administered by them whom Christ doth allow to be the rulers and guiders of his Church."[61] There is no trace of a sacerdotal kingship in Hooker. Even his treatment of the episcopate emphasizes its functional and pragmatic aspect rather than its role as mediating sacramental grace or representing cosmological order.[62] While he approaches the High Church position of Saravia and the Jacobeans concerning the apostolic origins of the episcopate, he nevertheless insists that it is not inviolably sacred; if bishops disregard the common good for which they were instituted, the church can abolish them.[63] He therefore also has very little sympathy with the Puritan need to ground the visible church on some sort of absolute and unalterable platform.

This draining of sacrality is the price paid for the demystification of power, particularly royal power over both church and state. Although Hooker emphatically denies that the state is a wholly secular body, concerned with the temporal welfare of its citizens to the exclusion of their spiritual well-being, he equally repudiates the notion that the king can "participate that sanctified power which God hath endued his

59. Hooker, *Works,* 3:400. Harold J. Berman thus writes, "Where Lutheranism succeeded, the church came to be conceived as invisible, apolitical, alegal; and the only sovereignty, the only law (in the political sense), was that of the secular kingdom or principality" (*Law and Revolution: The Formation of the Western Legal Tradition* [Cambridge, Mass., 1983], p. 29). Hooker's separation of church and state (including state-church) is not this drastic, although configured along the same lines.

60. Pelikan, *Reformation,* pp. 80, 174.

61. Hooker, *Works,* 3:389; compare 3:341.

62. Hooker, *Works,* 3:198.

63. Hooker, *Works,* 3:165.

clergy with."[64] Although the state is not secular, the king is not sacred. For Hooker, power and authority are only indirectly given by God. While kings can be said to rule by "divine right" insofar as all government derives from God, yet (except in the case of military conquest) their authority derives from the consent of the governed and can only be justified in terms of the common good.[65]

Hooker virtually never thinks of royal power as participation in the divine but as an authority able to constrain people to perform their duties, something they might otherwise not wish to do. But since every "independent multitude" originally has "full dominion over itself," it cannot be subject to this coercive power except by its own consent.[66] If that consent was granted upon conditions—and Hooker supposes that this is always the case, except where power has been won by force or specially appointed by God—then those conditions remain binding on the sovereign, as do all subsequent positive laws and customs.[67] The king is therefore under the law and dependent upon the body politic for his power.[68] In fact, Hooker's whole discussion of royal power focuses on its limitations, especially the need to limit power by law. "Happier that people," he writes, "whose law is their king in the greatest things, than that whose king is himself their law."[69] In particular, the kings of England are under the law: "The axioms of our regal government are these: 'Lex facit regem:' the king's grant of any favour made contrary to the law is void; 'Rex nihil potest nisi quod jure potest.'"[70]

Despite his enthusiasm for the law, Hooker is no more inclined to

64. Hooker, *Works,* 3:329, 332, 419. Hooker's view is similar to Selden's and the early Andrewes. Compare William Lamont and Sybil Oldfield, eds., *Politics, Religion, and Literature in the Seventeenth Century* (London, 1975), p. 13; Macleane, *Andrewes,* p. 37.

65. Hooker, *Works,* 3:345.

66. Hooker, *Works,* 3:267, 343, 404. For the medieval origins of this idea, see Sommerville, *Politics and Ideology,* p. 59; Peter Munz, *The Place of Hooker in the History of Thought* (London, 1952), p. 99; Ernst H. Kantorowicz, "Kingship under the Impact of Scientific Jurisprudence," in Ernst H. Kantorowicz, *Selected Studies* (Locust Valley, N.Y., 1965), pp. 157–59.

67. Hooker, *Works,* 3:350–51.

68. Hooker, *Works,* 3:342, 346.

69. Hooker, *Works,* 3:352.

70. Hooker, *Works,* 3:353; W. D. J. Cargill Thompson, "The Philosopher of the 'Politic Society': Richard Hooker as a Political Thinker," in *Studies in Richard Hooker: Essays Preliminary to an Edition of His Works,* ed. W. Speed Hill (Cleveland, 1972), pp. 59–63.

mystify this, whether along the lines of the medieval jurists with their *sacerdotium temporale* or those of Coke and the common lawyers,[71] than to sanctify the Crown. The reason royal power should be limited by the law is that the law embodies popular consent. "Against all equity it were," Hooker remarks, "that a man should suffer detriment at the hands of men, for not observing that which he never did either by himself or by others, mediately or immediately, agree unto. . . . In this case therefore especially that vulgar axiom is of force, 'Quod omnes tangit ab omnibus tractari et approbari debet.'"[72] Hooker's constant awareness that all forms of power, whether secular or ecclesiastical, oblige people either to do what they might not choose or else "suffer detriment" leads him to insist that the subjects of such power must also be its authors. Laws governing the church, therefore, receive their force neither from prince nor Parliament "but from power which the whole body of this realm being naturally possessed with, hath by free and deliberate assent derived unto him that ruleth over them."[73] That is, neither prince nor Parliament nor even the clergy has the independent authority to prescribe matters of religion; insofar as such matters affect everyone, they must be approved by the "consent of the whole Church, which is the only thing that bindeth each member of the Church, to be guided by them."[74] It is perhaps not necessary to add that if by "consent" we mean an active consent—the right to participate directly or through elected representatives in political and ecclesiastical life—then no such "general consent" existed in Tudor England, where only a very small percentage of the populace had any voice in church or state. But for whatever reason, Hooker seems not to have observed this fact; at least, he never mentions it.

Hooker's attempt to assert the supremacy of law over the king founders at the very end of *The Laws*. This is a difficult passage to untangle, partly for textual reasons. The last three books of *The Laws*, not published until 1648 (books 6 and 8) and 1662 (all three books), were apparently either never completed or the final draft was lost or mutilated. The whole discussion of church elders, apparently intended

71. Kantorowicz, "Kingship," in Kantorowicz, *Selected Studies*, p. 162; Sommerville, *Politics and Ideology*, p. 87.
72. Hooker, *Works*, 3:404.
73. Hooker, *Works*, 3:412.
74. Hooker, *Works*, 3:410.

for book 6, has disappeared; we only know of its prior existence from critical notes Sandys and Cramner made on it.[75] Book 8, the last book, breaks off abruptly in the middle of a discussion as to whether kings are subject to ecclesiastical censure, but this whole passage appeared neither in the 1648 nor the 1662 edition of Hooker; it derives from a single manuscript, first published by Keble in 1836.[76] The passage opens with a promise to treat the subject *in utramque partem* without making any final determination, leaving "the wise" to judge which of the two sides is "likeliest to be true." Hooker first takes up the negative pole, that "the highest magistrate should not be judged of any, saving God alone."[77] The manuscript, however, ends before presenting the other side. Yet it seems as though Hooker had changed his plan midway through discussing the first position, for by the end of this fragment he appears to be endorsing the view that no one can judge the highest magistrate rather than merely presenting it for consideration. The final sentence of *The Laws* is reasonably explicit: "For which cause, till better reason be brought, to prove that kings cannot lawfully be exempted from subjection unto ecclesiastical courts, we must and do affirm their said exemption lawful."[78] It sounds from this that Hooker himself is not intending to suggest any "better reason," that is, he is not going to set forth the positive side of the argument. Thus it is difficult to ascertain Hooker's final view with any certainty; nevertheless this concluding fragment deserves consideration because it exposes the characteristic tension in Hooker's thought.

The debate over excommunication of the sovereign has two aspects. One concerns the question of civil allegiance, the other the spiritual authority of the church. When the pope excommunicated Elizabeth in 1570, he thereby released her Catholic subjects from their obedience to the English Crown, indirectly, at least, sanctioning the numerous attempts against the lives of both Elizabeth and James. After the Gunpowder Plot, discussions of royal excommunication largely centered on whether such ecclesiastical censure could ever legitimate

75. These notes are printed following book 6 of *The Laws* in the Keble edition.

76. For the textual history of books 6 through 8, see P. G. Stanwood's introductory essay to the third volume of *The Folger Edition of the Works of Richard Hooker*, 4 vols., general ed. W. Speed Hill (Cambridge, Mass., 1981).

77. Hooker, *Works,* 3:444–45.

78. Hooker, *Works,* 3:455.

rebellion against the excommunicated ruler. Hooker, however, does not deal with this aspect of the problem. Rather, he is concerned with the issue of what we now call Erastianism, the view that the church has no spiritual authority over the sovereign and therefore cannot excommunicate him or her. Puritans, following Calvin, rejected this position, holding that qua Christian, the sovereign was a member of a congregation and subject to the same discipline as any other member. This is not merely a technical question of church discipline. As Hooker puts it, "in the mighty upon earth . . . what may we look for, considering the frailty of man's nature, if the world do once hold it for a maxim that kings ought to live in no subjection: that, how grievous disorders soever they fall into, none may have coercive power over them?"[79] Erastianism opens the door to absolutism by removing any effective check on royal power; moreover, it reduces the church to an arm of the Crown with no prophetic authority to pass spiritual judgment on it. It thus greatly weakens the church's claim to represent a truth higher than the will of the prince. Holiness, as previously noted, cannot be separated from power, and if the church does not have power to excommunicate the sovereign, then its sanctity is only that of Varro's civil religion, which is not sanctity (at least in the Judeo-Christian sense) at all.

In the fragment of the conclusion to book 8 that we have, Hooker appears to defend the Erastian position, basically on the grounds that "punishments proceed always from superiors," but if the king had a superior, that superior would also need a superior to judge him, and so on "infinitely in a circle."[80] Order, however, requires that there be "a supreme head of justice, whereunto all are subject, but itself in subjection to none." Therefore "on earth" princes are rightly "not accountable to any," including the church.[81] But then Hooker proceeds to make a crucial exception. Those who rejected Erastianism based part of their argument on Ambrose's famous excommunication of the Emperor Theodosius for ordering the massacre at Thessalonika.

79. Hooker, *Works,* 3:445.

80. Hooker, *Works,* 3:445. Cargill Thompson, however, points out that Hooker was not an Erastian in the modern sense; the king could be head of the church *only* if he were a Christian; in any other case, the church had the authority to govern itself ("The Philosopher of the 'Politic Society,'" in Hill, ed., *Studies in Hooker,* pp. 65–66).

81. Hooker, *Works,* 3:445–46.

Hooker denies that Ambrose's act should be interpreted as excommunication, because it was not an official act of the church as a judicial institution. There was no hearing, no deliberation; Ambrose simply shut the church door on Theodosius and told him he could not come in. It was a spontaneous, personal action, not a church censure, and to this "dutiful, religious, and holy refusal to admit notorious transgressors . . . unto the blessed communion of saints," Hooker affirms, "every king [is] bound to abide at the hands of any minister of God wheresoever through the world."[82] The spiritual authority of a priest as minister of the sacraments thus transcends the authority of the church as an institution. The "power of the ministry of God" in Hooker remains wholly numinous; it "translateth out of darkness into glory, it raiseth men from the earth and bringeth God himself down from heaven, by blessing visible elements it maketh them invisible grace, it giveth daily the Holy Ghost . . . when it poureth malediction upon the heads of the wicked they perish, when it revoketh the same they revive."[83] But this sacramental and spiritual power cannot be translated into institutional forms designed to maintain order and stability, and thus prophetic authority remains awkwardly half within, half without ecclesiastical jurisdiction.[84] So in Herbert, "The Church," including both "Aaron" and "The Priesthood," is separated from "The Church Militant" by several blank manuscript pages.

The division between priestly and ecclesiastical authority conforms to the distinction we have previously noted in Hooker between the pneumatic and historical. This distinction, reminiscent of Luther's *Zwei-Regimente-Lehre*—is central to Hooker's ecclesiology, in which the church is both a "society supernatural" and a "politic society," a "body mystical" and a "Church visible."[85] The sacraments, the mystical body, the life of faith—all that is inward, invisible, and private—are experienced as sacred and spoken of in the language of participation and presence, whereas the visible arenas of history and institutions are analyzed in terms of coercion, politics, contingency, and secondary

82. Hooker, *Works*, 3:454. Similar distinctions between St. Ambrose's action against Theodosius and official excommunication occur frequently in Anglican apologetics; see Collinson, *Religion of Protestants*, pp. 24–26; Lake, *Anglicans and Puritans?*, pp. 224–25.

83. Hooker, *Works*, 2:456.

84. Little, *Religion, Order, and Law*, pp. 145, 152–54.

85. Hooker, *Works*, 1:275–76, 338–39; Cargill Thompson, "The Philosopher of the 'Politic Society,'" in Hill, ed., *Studies in Hooker*, pp. 53–57.

causality.[86] The old medieval sacramental holiness that had seeped through politics, historiography, biography, natural history, interpretations of pagan classics, and jurisprudence is drained out and confined to a realm at once more inward and more overtly "religious" (as opposed to secular)—the sacraments and liturgy. Institutions, whether political or ecclesiastical, no longer serve as carriers of ultimate value or signification.

A ROYAL PRIESTHOOD

By the time the first installment of *The Laws* was published in 1594, Hooker's views on ecclesiastical polity were rapidly becoming outdated.[87] As has often been noted, in the last decade of Elizabeth's reign, political theology, especially—but not exclusively—among the higher clergy, began moving in the direction of divine-right absolutism.[88] Although J. P. Sommerville has shown that Jacobean absolutism can be seen as a coherent and rational theory about the origins of political power, it was never, I think, primarily a political *theory*. Instead, to a great extent it was a polemical instrument forged in the age of regicide.[89] Jesuit and radical Protestant political theory legitimated resistance against a wicked king on the grounds that kings were instituted to serve the common good; if they became wicked and no longer served that good, they could be deposed: as the medieval proverb goes, "Qui non recte regit, non regit." In a period of sectarian religious tension, such legitimation could be construed to mean that any ruler who embraced a religion some of his subjects considered false could be killed by the self-appointed representative of said subjects. Henry III and Henry IV of France fell victim to this construction; Elizabeth and James almost did. The doctrine of the divine right of kings was designed to discourage regicidal tendencies by refuting their theoretical justification. The primary target for this refutation became the principle, which the Jesuits and Protestant radicals inherited from the Mid-

86. Lake, in particular, stresses the extent to which Hooker invested ritual with religious significance, departing from earlier Conformists who tended to enforce ritual practices on largely political grounds (*Anglicans and Puritans?*, p. 214).

87. Sommerville, *Politics and Ideology*, p. 11.

88. On the popularity of absolutist ideas, see Sommerville, *Politics and Ideology*, p. 46.

89. Sommerville, *Politics and Ideology*, pp. 10, 35, 46.

dle Ages, that rulers derive their authority from the people,[90] a principle that had been widely held by sixteenth-century English political writers, including Hooker.[91] While neo-Thomist writers like Suárez (and Hooker) maintained that the fact that rulers *originally* derived their power from the populace does not necessarily imply that the populace retains any right to reclaim it, that caveat proved insufficient to repress the radical implications of theories of popular sovereignty. And insofar as the affirmation of the popular origins of sovereignty was perceived to legitimate resistance, it became desirable to abandon it. Instead, divine-right theorists argued that the authority of a king came from God alone and therefore did not depend on the consent of the governed. No one could depose a king, no matter how wicked.

Divine-right absolutism, thus stated, was a polemical instrument, a response to Jesuit-inspired sedition and regicide. But it was something more. What this something was can best be seen in the political sermons of Andrewes, the sermons preached before King James on the anniversaries of the two major attempts against his life: the Conspiracy of the Gowries and the Gunpowder Plot. Altogether, these two series comprise eighteen sermons, preached between 1606 and 1623. While these sermons reiterate the basic arguments of absolutist theory, they entwine this with an extraordinary and persistent concern over the location of "sacredness" in history and social structure. Like Hooker's *Laws,* although in a radically different way, they thus respond to the secularization of the church implicit in the English subordination of church to state and to the secularization of the state characteristic both of papal and Calvinist ecclesiastical politics. While Hooker largely accepts this desacralization—and uses it to enable a realistic analysis of mundane institutions—Andrewes turns in the opposite direction and attempts a large-scale restoration of the archaic symbolism of the Davidic sacerdotal kingship and the cosmological empire. This solves

90. On the Conciliarist, legal, and Thomist developments of a notion of popular sovereignty and its relation both to the legitimation of popular resistance and to the indirect power of the pope to depose unjust or heretical rulers, see Quentin Skinner, *The Foundations of Modern Political Thought,* 2 vols. (Cambridge, 1978), 2:114–84, and his "The Origins of the Calvinist Theory of Revolution," in *After the Reformation: Essays in Honour of J. H. Hexter,* ed. Barbara Malament (Manchester, Eng. 1980), pp. 309–30; Sommerville, *Politics and Ideology,* pp. 25–26; J. W. Allen, *A History of Political Thought in the Sixteenth Century* (London, 1928), pp. 320–28, 359–66.

91. Sommerville, *Politics and Ideology,* p. 11.

the problem of secularization by erasing it; the king is sacred, there is no secular space.

Andrewes, of course, did not invent the idea of transferring the biblical sacred kingship to Western societies. The notion of a priestly or liturgical monarchy pervaded the Middle Ages, with the introduction of Roman law becoming fused with the jurists' concept of a *sacrum imperium*. In the twelfth, as in the seventeenth century, the assertion of sacred kingship occurs in the context of struggle between the "state" and the papacy, a contest that runs from the Investiture Controversy to the conflict between Guelf and Ghibelline and thence to the late medieval Conciliarist movement and finally the Reformation, only to culminate, in a distinctly minor key, with Hobbes's *Leviathan* and its mortal god.[92] But this tradition of political *theology* unfolds in contrast to the better-known evolution of political *theory* from antiquity through Augustine, Aquinas, Marsilius, and the early English political writers—Fortescue, Smith, and Hooker, all of whom were less concerned with the divinity that hedges a king than the empirical functions of power in maintaining order and prosperity.[93]

The problem, as we have said, with the secular understanding of the state characteristic of political theory was that, when applied to post-Reformation England, it placed the church under the control of a layperson and thus seemingly transgressed the boundaries between the spiritual and the profane. Instead of the two sources of sacred power—king and pope—of the Middle Ages, England seemed to be governed by a ruler whose authority rested on popular consent and by some crown-appointed civil servants, for tradition's sake still referred to as bishops. This loss of social sacrality was, I think, felt to be intolerable.

92. Kantorowicz, "Deus per naturam, Deus per gratiam: A Note on Medieval Political Theology," in Kantorowicz, *Selected Studies,* p. 124; Kantorowicz, "Kingship," in Kantorowicz, *Selected Studies,* p. 161–63; Kantorowicz, "Mysteries of State: An Absolutist Concept and Its Late Medieval Origins," in Kantorowicz, *Selected Studies,* p. 382; see also his *The King's Two Bodies: A Study in Medieval Political Theology* (Princeton, 1957), pp. 15–19, 197, 207–8. Also, Yates, *Astrea,* pp. 1–87; Macleane, *Andrewes,* p. 218; Marc Bloch, *The Royal Touch: Sacred Monarchy and Scrofula in England and France,* trans. J. E. Anderson (London, 1973), pp. 196–200; John N. Figgis, *The Divine Right of Kings,* 2d ed. (Cambridge, 1922); Geoffrey R. Elton, *Studies in Tudor and Stuart Politics and Government,* 2 vols. (Cambridge, 1974), 2:193–214.

93. In Hobbes, of course, these two strands coincide. The coexistence of political theory and theology from the Middle Ages on means that one cannot read Shakespeare's mature history plays as describing the transition from "traditional" political theology to "modern" political theory—at least not if these terms are taken chronologically.

Recusancy and Presbyterianism both expressed the need for *iure divino* institutions, whether the papal church or apostolic elders. But this need seems most acutely and strangely articulated in the Church of England and its reversion after 1590 to political theology.

Andrewes's political sermons center on the divinization of the king. The king has both a sacred and priestly character. Thus royalty participates in divinity; as Christ "saith, 'My Father in Me, and I in Him;' so [kings] . . . in Him, and He in them. . . . For as it is true they reign in and by Him, so is it likewise true He reigns in and by them. They in God, and God in them, *reciproce*."[94] Like early medieval theorists, Andrewes associates the king's sacredness with his ritual anointing at his coronation.[95] The king is the anointed one (*christus*) and thus mystically connected to Christ, the Anointed Son of God. Thus Andrewes writes, "His very chiefest Name, Christ, He imparteth to [kings] . . . And that is not without mystery, to shew their near alliance to Him."[96] Because they are anointed, kings have a sacerdotal sanctity: "their calling is sacred, sacred as any, even the best of them all. From whence the Priests have theirs, thence and from no other place the King hath his,—from the Sanctuary both. The anointing is one and the same. All to shew that sacred is the office whereunto they designed, sacred the power wherewith they endued, sacred the persons whereto it applied."[97] Therefore, since their calling is "holy," kings are properly entrusted with holy things, properly called to be heads of the church: "How fond it is to imagine them to be 'anointed with holy oil,' to deal only in unholy matters, and not to meddle with any thing that holy is?"[98]

Like the Puritans, Andrewes models his ideal of church and state on the Bible—not, however, on the primitive church depicted in Acts and the Pauline Epistles, but the levitical priesthood and the Davidic kingship.[99] King David is, for Andrewes, more than simply a normative

94. Andrewes, *Works,* 4:285.

95. James was the last English king to be anointed with the ancient oil preserved in the Tower and only used for coronations (Macleane, *Andrewes,* p. 96).

96. Andrewes, *Works,* 4:284.

97. Andrewes, *Works,* 4:55.

98. Andrewes, *Works,* 4:84.

99. On the sacerdotal kingship in the Old Testament, see A. R. Johnson, "Hebrew Conceptions of Kingship," in *Myth, Ritual, and Kingship: Essays on the Theory and Practice of Kingship in the Ancient Near East and in Israel,* ed. S. H. Hooke (Oxford, 1958), pp. 207, 212–13, 222.

exemplar of the proper relation between ruler, nation, and church; he is, quite literally, the antitype in a royal typological system. Andrewes repeatedly takes biblical passages traditionally interpreted as pertaining to David as a type of Christ and, emptying them of their Christic signification, makes James instead a type of David. For David was "not *persona Regis* only, 'the person of a King,' but *persona Regum,* 'a person representing all Kings' to come after him. . . . We do safely therefore, what is said to him, apply to them all, since he is the type of them all."[100] Many of the sermons work out these typological parallels in detail, frequently insisting that James's deliverance from his enemies is not only like David's but more miraculous, more impressive: "in far greater peril was His Majesty, far greater than ever was David. . . . I dare confidently affirm it, I may well I am sure, God's hand was much more eminent in this, than in that:—praised be His name for it."[101] God's rescues of James have "not the like in the 'chronicles' of Persia; nay, not of the Kings of Judah or Israel; but are *sine exemplo,* ours, none coming home, all falling short of them."[102] At one point James's deliverance even becomes a type of the Crucifixion, for "ours did come near to the great delivery of the world by Christ, what time the world little thought either of their own peril or of His pains and passion That delivered it."[103]

The events of the Jacobean court belong to sacred history—not to the history of European power politics. The energy behind these sermons is the longing for mystification, a perhaps overly insistent desire to transform mundane institutions and events into manifestations of the divine. For Andrewes, this entails denying that kings either originated from common consent or are essentially oriented toward the common good.[104] These sermons therefore present nothing that could be called a political theory, at least not in the sense of defining power with respect to human needs or social function. "The 'crown' is in God's 'hand,' saith Esay, and His hand sets it on David's, sets in [*sic*] on all their heads that lawfully wear it."[105] It is not only that royal

100. Andrewes, *Works,* 4:77.
101. Andrewes, *Works,* 4:22.
102. Andrewes, *Works,* 4:147.
103. Andrewes, *Works,* 4:369.
104. Andrewes, *Works,* 4:38, 52, 79, 280, 302.
105. Andrewes, *Works,* 4:114.

power derives directly from God, but the events of James's reign continue sacred history. Andrewes thus treats the Gowrie Conspiracy and Gunpowder Plot not as part of the ideological and political struggle between the papacy and the Crown but as part of a cosmic battle between good and evil, with God taking an active role on the English side. James's deliverances are "miraculous," "miraculous divine preservations."[106]

The denial of politics is not accidental. The whole "point" of these sermons is that the chronicles of kings express the *magnalia Dei,* that the age of miracles is not over, sacred history is not confined to the canon of Holy Scripture. Hence the repeated insistence on seeing James's deliverances as acts of God and responding in thankfulness: "'Great' were the things, and very great; they chanced not, they were 'done;' done by 'God,' He was the doer. . . . and we the people for whom these great things were done . . . and so a people deeply bound to magnify Him for all His mercies, but for this above all, that all the world speaks of."[107]

These sermons were preached before James and hence might be considered a species of interested flattery, James, of course, controlling all important ecclesiastical appointments. That Andrewes himself considered them something more than flattery appears in an anecdote related in Plume's *Life of Hacket,* which tells how "the most religious Bishop Andrewes once fell down upon his knees before King James and besought his Majesty to spare his customary pains upon that day [the anniversary of the Gowrie Conspiracy], that he might not mock God unless the thing were true."[108] Andrewes seems to have taken the matter very seriously, and that is of course the point. We tend to think of power and the mystifications of power as fictions imposed upon their subjects and not for their benefit. Clearly both Elizabeth and James used pageantry and ceremony to sustain their power by investing it with an aura of divinity. Yet other evidence also indicates a widely held desire to preserve that social sacrality, a desire perhaps partly created by royal ideology, but people tend to believe only those official fictions they want to believe; mystification is usually a group

106. Andrewes, *Works,* 4:212, 269, 350, 395.
107. Andrewes, *Works,* 4:238.
108. Quoted in Macleane, *Andrewes,* p. 101.

effort, and thus the paradigm that opposes official belief to popular subversion/skepticism tends to oversimplify.[109] This seems true with regard to the sacred kingship, where "official" opinion split dramatically, Parliament taking quite a different view of the king's divinity than he himself did. On the other hand, when James tried to back away from some of the traditional "sacred" powers attached to the Crown, particularly administering the royal touch (thought to cure scrofula), he apparently met with enough popular opposition to force him, albeit reluctantly, to continue the practice. Even when held prisoner by the parliamentary army, Charles I was besieged by crowds of the sick waiting for his touch, and in the early 1680s over eight thousand people came to Charles II for healing within the space of one month. This testimony to popular belief in royal magic endured, in fact, into the eighteenth century.[110] And it was not some credulous sixteenth-century peasant but Samuel Pepys who, in 1662, found himself disappointed and disillusioned that King Charles could not control the rain.[111] So too in 1686, Richard Baxter noted in a manuscript not designed for publication that "Christian Princes are as Sacred persons as priests."[112] These are just isolated bits of evidence, but they suggest a widespread desire to preserve the sacral character of English kingship, to preserve the link between social forms and divine order. James, no doubt, found Andrewes's sermons personally gratifying, but they would also have appealed to a communal need, one the preacher apparently shared, to affirm the archaic association of divinity with politics.

In light of this, Andrewes's political treatises, the *Tortura torti* (1609) and the *Responsio ad apologiam Cardinalis Bellarmini* (1610), come as a surprise. Written at the king's command to defend the Oath of Allegiance, which required Recusants to deny that the pope could deprive rulers of their subjects' obedience, the treatises cover much the same ground as the political sermons. But while the sermons proclaim the

109. For a criticism of the recent tendency to depict popular religion as fundamentally opposed to official, "high culture," orthodoxy, see Collinson, *Religion of Protestants,* pp. 190–95.

110. Bloch, *The Royal Touch,* pp. 190–92, 207–20; Keith Thomas, *Religion and the Decline of Magic: Studies in Popular Beliefs in Sixteenth- and Seventeenth-Century England* (London, 1971), pp. 192–96.

111. Kantorowicz, "Kingship," in Kantorowicz, *Selected Essays,* p. 166.

112. Lamont and Oldfield, *Politics, Religion,* p. 6.

sacerdotal character of the king and thus erase the distinction between secular and sacred realms, the treatises insist upon this distinction. Roman Catholic subjects may sign the oath because it pertains only to civil obedience, not to matters of faith.[113] Andrewes accuses Bellarmine of doing precisely what Andrewes does in the sermons, namely conflating secular and spiritual jurisdictions. Bellarmine, who was no fool, noticed the discrepancy between James's claim to be "preserver and defender of the true, Christian, Catholic, Apostolic Faith and of the true and primitive Church" and Andrewes's assertion that the king required only civil obedience. If there is any humor in these treatises, it appears in the cardinal's insistence on challenging James's ecclesiastical pretensions, while Andrewes struggles to avoid this issue and bring the discussion back to matters "of civil loyalty (*fides*), of the loyalty of citizens to the King, concerning which alone it is incumbent upon the Cardinal to speak here."[114] Particularly in *Tortura torti,* temporal dominion is viewed as wholly distinct from ecclesiastical concerns; thus a pagan ruler has "true temporal power" because "dominion is not grounded in faith (*fides*)."[115] Obedience to the king is therefore "only civil" and "merely political," a purely secular affair. It follows that the king is not priestly: "neither he nor we think it lawful for him to lay hands on that which pertains to the sacerdotal office."[116] Nor should he claim competence in spiritual matters, although he may interfere in questions of "exterior discipline."[117] And while Andrewes occasionally introduces the example of the Israelite sacerdotal kings and the notion of the king as a vicar of Christ, the main argument of these endlessly long polemics rests on the firm distinction between the sacred and the profane, with kingship falling in the latter category.[118]

Many years ago, Charles McIlwain, the editor of King James's political writings, noted the same anomaly. Despite James's own proclamation of his sacred and quasi-sacerdotal status, the conflict with Bellarmine over the oath forced him and his ideological supporters to accept Bellarmine's premise, namely the separation of the secular from

113. Andrewes, *Works,* 7:11, 14.
114. Andrewes, *Works,* 8:6, 74.
115. Andrewes, *Works,* 7:49.
116. Andrewes, *Works,* 7:467.
117. Andrewes, *Works,* 7:199–200.
118. Andrewes, *Works,* 7:211, 446; 8:97.

the sacred—a premise that Bellarmine shared with the ultra-Calvinists, and one that Andrewes's sermons had fiercely rejected.[119] The English controversialists had to make the separation, because to deny it would have meant that obedience to the king had religious implications, that it was not merely a political act, and therefore that Roman Catholics could not profess loyalty to the state without compromising their faith. But by arguing that such loyalty was compatible with recusancy, Andrewes and his associates implicitly accepted the separation of church and state and therefore the possibility that all members of the English commonwealth were not (and need not be) members of the Church of England, despite Hooker's claim to the contrary.

But in Andrewes, the emergent differentiation of secular and sacred seems to have a further motive. Alongside his deep attraction to the figure of the anointed king who unites the temporal and spiritual swords, one notes a revulsion from the implications of this union, namely that the temporal sword can be used against spiritual offenses.[120] Both the treatises and sermons attack Bellarmine's claim that the early church submitted to persecuting emperors only because it lacked military power to overthrow them.[121] Andrewes himself is extremely reluctant to admit that Christianity should ever be sustained by violence or that spiritual wrongs should be corrected by corporeal punishment.[122] And this seems to entail an absolute separation of civil from ecclesiastical government. In his 1609 sermon on the Gunpowder Plot he thus asks, "What then? shall not Christ be received?" To which he gives his own answer:

> Yes; He is most worthy so to be. I add, they that refuse it are worthy any punishment; but that every man is to be dealt with as he is worthy, would prove but a hard piece of divinity. . . . The Samaritans, they received not Christ; they were gone, burnt all. . . . When He came to Jerusalem, how was He received there? Why, there He was murdered, worse used than in Samaria. Then we must call for more fire, Jerusalem must be burnt too. Now for the disciples, James and John, how carried they the matter? It is true, they had received Him, but when most need

119. McIlwain, "Introduction," in James I, *Political Works*, pp. xx, xlix–lii.

120. Compare Yates, *Astrea*, p. 83. Andrewes's position seems similar to that of Henri III, who endeavored to create a mystical sacred empire, one that, unlike the military imperialism of Spain, would not be based on the power of the sword.

121. Andrewes, *Works*, 4:354–55; 7:40; 8:80.

122. Andrewes, *Works*, 7:249–50; 3:254–56.

> was, thrust Him from them, renounced Him, utterly denied that ever they knew Him. Then we must trouble Heaven once more, call for fire for James and John too. Nay then, "the world was made by Him, and the world knew Him not," nor "received Him not;" why then the world is at an end . . . all a heap of ashes if this doctrine go forward. Best take Phaeton out of the chariot, that he set not all on fire.[123]

Andrewes is moving toward a rejection of the basic principle underlying the royal headship: that the king has the responsibility for enforcing religious uniformity. That principle entailed that the king could and should use coercion—fines, imprisonment, execution—to punish those who did not receive Christ in the prescribed manner.[124]

Andrewes's aversion to the political inclines him toward both religious toleration and mystification. His anxiety about the use of force in religious matters is of a piece with his tendency to strip the discourse of sacred institutions, whether royal or ecclesiastical, from sociopolitical or economic contexts—contexts that, as Hooker acknowledged, limit and compromise any attempt to institutionalize the sacred. Instead, Andrewes endeavors to irradiate the center of power with divinity, to affirm participation, presence, and miracle. It is an interpretation of power that, in his own words, "made the Emperors to stamp their coin with a hand coming out of the clouds, holding a crown and putting it on their heads."[125] Yet this endeavor runs counter to his need, as James's spokesman against Bellarmine, to find a basis for loyalty to the king not contingent on religious affiliation. So Andrewes's antipapal writings allow a secular, political arena to settle out from the cosmological compactness of the sermons. In these works, the king is generally treated as a layperson authorized to govern only the external affairs of the church. Likewise loyalty is viewed as exclusively political and hence compatible with religious diversity—for, as Sir Thomas More and Henry VIII and everyone else knew, sacred institutions must be, at least in principle, hegemonous.

123. Andrewes, *Works,* 4:255.

124. Even the more radical Protestants, who denied that the king could be head of the church, accepted the magistrate's coercive power over the moral and religious behavior of his subjects; see Cartwright in Whitgift, *Works,* 1:386. At times, Andrewes also portrays the king as the vicar of the church, able to inflict *poena civilis;* see, for example, *Works,* 8:99.

125. Andrewes, *Works,* 4:114.

THE DENIAL OF POLITICS

Paul Tillich once remarked that "the problem of the church was the most unsolved problem which the Reformation left to future generations. The reason is that the Catholic system was not replaced and could not be replaced definitively by a Protestant system of equal power."[126] In England, the problem of the church was equally a political problem because the doctrine of the royal headship effectively incorporated the church into the state, and sixteenth-century political thinkers had very few illusions about the holiness of the state.[127] This incorporation could not but affect the holiness of the church. The widespread anticlerical and antiepiscopal sentiments of the Elizabethan era thus indicate a pervasive feeling that the established church had forfeited its special sanctity.

Hooker attempts to "solve" this problem by dividing the church into a "body mystical" and "politic society," a ghostly community of the faithful in the machine of the comprehensive state-church.[128] This move frees him to analyze the church as a political institution based on coercion and enmeshed in the social order and also to see it as a "supernatural society" of "God, Angels, and holy men,"[129] linking heaven to earth via the sacramental priesthood.

Hooker's effort to distinguish the sacred from institutional forms without repudiating either aligns him with late medieval conciliarist thinking, as well as with the Lutheran *Zwei-Regimente-Lehre*.[130] Such delicate balancing was perhaps uncongenial to an era chasing after *iure divino* institutions, whether presbyterian, episcopal, papal, separatist, or monarchal. Hooker's "Baconian" solution, confining the sacred to the nonempirical, granted too little *mana* to state and church for them to compete against the high claims of papacy and presbytery. Before

126. Tillich, *Christian Thought*, p. 252.

127. Machiavelli was scarcely the only political realist in the sixteenth century. English political thought during the period is markedly nontheological and pragmatic; see Sir John Fortescue, *The Governance of England (c. 1471–1476)*, ed. Charles Plummer (Oxford, 1885); Sir Thomas Smith, *De republica Anglorum*, ed. Mary Dewar, Cambridge Studies in the History and Theory of Politics (Cambridge, 1982); and Skinner, "Calvinist Theory."

128. Cargill Thompson, "The Philosopher of the 'Politic Society,'" in Hill, ed. *Studies in Hooker*, pp. 53–57.

129. Hooker, *Works*, 1:273.

130. Pelikan, *Reformation*, p. 80.

the turn of the century, earlier strains of medieval and premedieval thought had begun to dominate English political theology—particularly the absolutist notions of Roman law and images of sacred kingship developed during the Investiture Crisis. As Frances Yates has shown, even under Elizabeth the "tradition of sacred empire" formed the polemical basis for the royal supremacy.[131] This shift seems to have been driven by a longing for the sacred, especially in a visible, institutional form, and by the need to isolate the sacred from politics. Englishmen detested the Jesuits precisely because they refused to transcend politics but accepted the fact that the church might have to use intrigue, faction, equivocation, and assassination.

The tendency to sacralize and thereby depoliticize institutions appears in a variety of forms and certainly belongs to no one ideological party. It is evident in the tendency to ground political and ecclesiastical arrangements in the will of God, Holy Scripture, and immemorial custom. In Neoplatonic guise, it enters into the court masques. Royal pageantry under the Tudors and Stuarts, with its evocations of Marian, imperial, chivalric, and Christian symbols, likewise laid a sacred patina over what Stephen Orgel calls the "inelegant realities of military power . . . and the mundane details of administrative efficiency."[132] Even writers not particularly interested in "the king's matter" display a similar inclination toward grounding institutions in the absolute. Thus for the Elizabethan Puritan conformist William Perkins, "God himself is the author and beginning of callings," for "God hath ordained and disposed all callings, and in his providence designed the persons to bear them."[133] This claim effectively sanctifies the whole socioeconomic order (and thus denies its socioeconomic character). A person knows that God has ordained him for a particular calling because that is the calling society assigns, or at least allows, him to perform.[134]

131. Yates, *Astrea,* pp. 39–41.

132. Stephen Orgel, "The Spectacles of State," in *Persons in Groups: Social Behavior as Identity Formation in Medieval and Renaissance Europe,* ed. Richard Trexler, Medieval and Renaissance Texts and Studies (Binghamton, N.Y., 1985), p. 109.

133. William Perkins, "A Treatise of the Vocations or Callings of Men," in *The Work of William Perkins,* ed. Ian Breward, The Courtenay Library of Reformation Classics (Appleford, Eng., 1970), pp. 447–49.

134. Perkins, *Work,* p. 461.

These attempts at holy depoliticization are admittedly ideological in the strong sense; they mask interest and power. But, it may be claimed, all cultural symbolisms are ideological, and therefore the term is of little value in accounting for the *specific* and curious nature of political theology in this period. It cannot account for the turn toward archaic cosmological symbolization, "the mythical expression of the participation . . . of the order of society in the divine being that also orders the cosmos."[135] Fictions designed to sustain social order need not involve the massive divinization of that order. The myth of equal opportunity that legitimates the contemporary status quo and the truth of the *libido dominandi* that justified existing social arrangements in Augustine's account of the city of man show no traces of such divinization. The next chapter will be a very partial and tentative attempt to understand why the recompacting of heaven and earth acquired such psychocultural plausibility in the early seventeenth century.

Before entering this murky terrain, I want to look very briefly at the premier instance of political divinization: the divine-right absolutism of King James. As mentioned previously, if, in one sense, divinization denies the political, in another sense, it intensifies it; that is, it intensifies power in that figure or institution perceived as sacred. The holiness of power creates the power of holiness. In terms of James's political thought, this means that the assertion of the king's divinity underlies his claim to absolute power. James's politics will figure importantly in the following chapters, so here I will simply summarize some relevant aspects.

Throughout his life, James associates himself with God. The introductory poem to his first political work, the *Basilikon Doron,* begins, "God gives not Kings the stile of *Gods* in vaine, / For on his Throne his Scepter doe they swey."[136] Two decades later, the same note sounds in his 1616 speech in the Star-Chamber: "Kings sit in the Throne of GOD, and they themselves are called Gods."[137] What James meant by this conjunction may be seen in his address to Parliament in 1609, where he affirms

135. Eric Voegelin, *Israel and Revelation,* vol. 1 of *Order and History,* 5 vols. (Baton Rouge, 1956), p. 27.

136. James I, *Political Works,* p. 3.

137. James I, *Political Works,* p. 326.

> Kings are justly called Gods, for that they exercise a manner or resemblance of Divine power upon earth: For if you wil consider the Attributes to God, you shall see how they agree in the person of a King. God hath power to create, or destroy, make, or unmake at his pleasure, to give life, or send death, to judge all, and to be judged nor accomptable to none: To raise low things, and to make high things low at his pleasure, and to God are both soule and body due. And the like power have Kings.[138]

As this quotation indicates, James's divine exemplar is not Hooker's law-abiding deity but the God of late medieval voluntarism (and of Calvinism), whose absolute power (*potentia absoluta*) is not necessarily limited to his will revealed in nature and Scripture (*potentia ordinata*). So too, James claims an absolute and mysterious prerogative unconstrained by "the Kings revealed will in his Law."[139] In this respect, James's understanding of sacred kingship also differs, at least in emphasis, from Andrewes's. The latter dwells on the sacred origin and aura of the Crown, but the only practical implication he draws from this is that no one may depose or kill the king on any pretext. James, however, is primarily concerned with the power implied by his "sparkles of the Divinitie,"[140] power he generally portrays in highly theological language of mixing "Justice with Mercie," of "fatherly love," and of shepherding his flock.[141]

Jacobean absolutism rests on the notion of sacred kingship, but not primarily the Davidic *christus* of the Old Testament. Instead, as Kantorowicz has argued, Stuart absolutism derives from Roman law complexly mediated through medieval canonists and jurists. In particular, the Roman conception of the "prince above the laws" (*princeps legibus solutus*) stands behind James's assertion that "the King is above the law, as both the author and giver of strength thereto."[142] Therefore, while a just king will obey his country's laws—and James professes every

138. James I, *Political Works,* pp. 307–8.

139. James I, *Political Works,* p. 333. Ockham had identified *potentia absoluta* with the power of the pope to contravene laws he had established; subsequently this interpretation seems to have been quite common. See Francis Oakley, *Omnipotence, Covenant, and Order: An Excursion in the History of Ideas from Abelard to Leibniz* (Ithaca, 1984), pp. 56–57, 108–9; Elton, *Studies in Tudor,* 2:210–11.

140. James I, *Political Works,* p. 281.

141. James I, *Political Works,* pp. 20, 27, 272.

142. James I, *Political Works,* p. 63.

intention of doing so—"yet is hee not bound thereto but of his good will."[143] The king's observance of the law displays his goodness and selflessness, but he is not obliged to do so unless he binds himself.[144] As McIlwain observes, this Roman view of the king as *legibus solutus* entails that the king has no legally enforceable duties toward his subjects, but their relation to him "must consist entirely of duties, and duties to which no limits can be put; of the 'rights of subjects' it is idle, even impious to speak."[145] In James's words, the king has "right & power," his subjects owe "allegeance & obedience."[146] So too a king is "a Judge set by GOD over [his subjects] . . . having power to judge them, but to be judged onely by GOD"—a maxim that James apparently borrows from papal Rome, and in particular from the assertion of the Decretists that "Sancta Sedes omnes iudicat, sed a nemine iudicatur."[147]

Roman (in both senses) also is James's assertion of "the mysterie of the Kings power" and his "absolute Prerogative"—the secrets of state (*arcana imperii*) which no subject may discuss or dispute. The Jacobean *arcana* derive from the late Imperial law equating the questioning of the prince's judgment with sacrilege, which law then winds its way into the thought of the papal canonists, where it becomes the *arcana ecclesiae,* and from thence to James's "mystery of State."[148] Thus Jacobean kingship rests on a pontifical legacy, or, in Kantorowicz's words, "literally, the absolute Prince had stepped into the shoes of the Roman Pontiff."[149] In James, this "mystery" is equated with "what a King may do in the height of his power,"[150] that is, with his *potentia absoluta* and perhaps also with the Tacitean *arcana imperii,* where it is implied that the prince's prerogative is not only sacred (*arcana* is a religious

143. James I, *Political Works,* p. 63.

144. James I, *Political Works,* p. 309. For medieval antecedents, see Kantorowicz, *The King's Two Bodies,* pp. 105, 136.

145. McIlwain, "Introduction," in James I, *Political Works,* pp. xlii–xliii.

146. James I, *Political Works,* p. 64.

147. James I, *Political Works,* p. 61; Kantorowicz, "Mysteries of State," in Kantorowicz, *Selected Studies,* p. 387; Brian Tierney, *Religion, Law, and the Growth of Constitutional Thought, 1150–1650* (Cambridge, 1982), p. 14.

148. James I, *Political Works,* p. 332; Kantorowicz, "Mysteries of State," in Kantorowicz, *Selected Studies,* pp. 382–85.

149. Kantorowicz, "Mysteries of State," in Kantorowicz, *Selected Studies,* p. 388.

150. James I, *Political Works,* p. 310.

term) but involves a disparity between "declared policy and actual strategy," what Tacitus terms *species* and *vis*.[151]

Next to the analogies between the king and God, the most frequent comparison in James is that between king and father. This comparison, as is well known, pervades royalist politics, but in James it has quite a different significance than it does in, let us say, Filmer's *Patriarcha,* where it is used to show that kingly authority derives from the father's absolute power over his children. Only once in James does fatherhood connote patriarchal (and hence royal) domination; everywhere else it explicitly refers to a relation based on love and nurturing. The king is like a father for James, because like a father he cares for the well-being of his subjects and regards their happiness as his chief goal. Thus a good king will be a "naturall father" to his people and thus think that "his greatest contentment standeth in their prosperitie." He will act "as a loving Father . . . caring for them more then for himselfe."[152] James uses the analogies of husband to wife and head to body in the same way; they are, as it were, variants on the central patriarchal image of loving power. Whereas the traditional distinction between a king and a tyrant lay in the fact that a king ruled according to law, while a tyrant followed his own whims and appetites, James subjectifies the contrast: a good king, although above the law, rules with "fatherly love," while a tyrant, equally above the law, rules in his own interest. The distinction is moral and affective rather than legal and institutional.

James is thus God, pontiff, father. And, of course, these three images were historically interconnected: God is our father; the pope represents God and is a father to his flock; and so forth. James invests his power with all the traditional sacred associations accruing to these figures in the (rather unsuccessful) attempt to fill the place of Holy Church with a cosmological empire. James's absolutism is, I think, less important than his need to depict political relations as sacred and fatherly. The world is full of absolute rulers—military dictators, party chairmen, colonial governors—and James, in any case, rarely exercised any extralegal powers or ever claimed an intention to do so.[153]

151. Donald R. Kelley, *The Beginning of Ideology: Consciousness and Society in the French Reformation* (Cambridge, 1981), p. 4; Tacitus *Annales* 2.36.

152. James I, *Political Works,* pp. 18, 55.

153. Allen, *English Political Thought,* 1:4–6.

What he, like Andrewes, wanted was to ground society in the divine, to reconnect visible institutions with sacred order, and to transform political relations—understood as relations based on coercion and rights, force and law—into quasi-religious ones, where power would be both utterly absolute and wholly benevolent, where subjection would become "the mysticall reverence, that belongs unto them that sit in the Throne of God,"[154] where "the magistrate is holy and not profane, his authority holy, his laws holy."[155]

If Jacobean politics was largely theological, then Jacobean theology absorbed a considerable dose of politics. The analogy between God and king has traditionally operated in both directions; the Bible calls kings "gods" and God a king. If the first half of the equation pertains primarily to the nature of actual institutions (that is, the sacrality of church or Crown), the second has to do with the cultural symbolization of religious experience: how does temporal authority mediate the understanding of the divine? It should be noted that there is no *necessary* relation between them. On the one hand, an oppressive political order may give rise to a contrastive spirituality. This inversion has, in fact, characterized certain strains of Christianity from Augustine's two cities to liberation theology. Franciscan and Joachimite ideals are based on the unlikeness between the social order and the spiritual. In *Pearl* the egalitarian social arrangements of heaven come as a distinct shock to the dreamer. Conversely, Milton combined republicanism with a rather absolute heavenly monarchy. On the other hand, ingrained habits of analogy encouraged cosmological parallels between temporal and divine order, between God and king. The celestial hierarchies of the Pseudo-Dionysius mirror ecclesiastical ones, and Anselm's God has a feudal sense of honor. Inasmuch as analogical thinking flourished in the Renaissance, the dominant ideology tended to perceive relations between social and spiritual orders as duplicative. Thus English religious texts during the sixteenth and seventeenth centuries consistently and relentlessly employ economic, legal, royal, familial, and hierarchical metaphors.

But such analogizing poses rather than solves the problem. Recent

154. James I, *Political Works*, p. 333.
155. Whitgift, *Works*, 1:389.

critics have argued that the staple orthodox analogies carried "potentially subversive implications" capable of serving very diverse ideological interests.[156] And while the alternatives of "orthodox" and "subversive" are unhelpfully limited, it seems clear that the cultural significance of analogies is rarely transparent. What does it mean in the age of absolutism to say that God is like a king? In *Renaissance Self-Fashioning* Greenblatt observed that Henry VIII is eerily like the Protestant God. Calvin and Luther noted the same resemblance with something approaching horror, Calvin calling the royal headship "blasphemy" and Luther remarking that "squire Henry meant to be God and do as he pleased."[157] But while the Reformers may not have liked this Tudor version of the divine image, the question remains as to why they depicted a God who bore such an evident resemblance to Henry VIII.

This seems to be the central issue. Reformation theology showed little interest in celestial hierarchies and thus in the relation between the social order as a whole and the spiritual order. What they did overwhelmingly emphasize was the absolute sovereignty of God, and therefore it is the cultural significance of this emphasis, with its implicit analogy between God and kings, that must be the center of investigation. I have chosen to look at John Donne in this regard not because his theology is markedly different from the mainstream of English Protestantism but because he frames his understanding of God insistently and explicitly in terms of a distinctly Stuart variety of royal absolutism.

156. Thomas Sorge, "The Failure of Orthodoxy in *Coriolanus*," in *Shakespeare Reproduced: The Text in History and Ideology*, ed. Jean Howard and Marion O'Connor (New York, 1987), p. 227.

157. Greenblatt, *Self-Fashioning*, p. 116; for Calvin, see Hooker, *Works*, 3:385n; for Luther, see Macleane, *Andrewes*, p. 224.

5

Absolutist Theology
The Sermons of John Donne

Dominus Deus
Rex Coelestis
Pater Omnipotens

The corollary to the Jacobean mystification of kingship is the theology of absolutism; as the first sacralizes the political, so the second politicizes the sacred. Hence one notes the extraordinary tendency to analyze and legitimate religious ritual as an analogue of courtly ceremony. The arch-presbyterian Walter Travers, for example, explains that in Holy Communion "the Lord's Table [is] furnished as the royal table of a king at the marriage of his son"; similarly, Bishop Hall justifies kneeling at communion on the grounds that men kneel to kiss the king's hand.[1] Sacred symbolism appears as a variant of political gesture. This absence of sharp symbolic differentiation points to the survival of the ancient sense of consubstantiality between God and king. "In the primitive world," remarks G. van der Leeuw, "the king is the power bearer, the saviour; and for quite a long time he remained so. . . . indeed he is one of the first and oldest gods."[2] The analogy between God and king continued to have more than metaphoric significance down through the Renaissance, as witnessed by the persistent belief in the curative powers of the royal touch. Indeed, it would seem that instead of being a mere verbal residue of earlier cosmological cultures, the perceived relation between divinity and kingship in-

1. Christopher Hill, *The Collected Essays of Christopher Hill: Religion and Politics in Seventeenth-Century England* (Amherst, 1986), p. 23; Peter G. Lake, *Moderate Puritans and the Elizabethan Church* (Cambridge, 1982), p. 66.

2. G. van der Leeuw, *Religion in Essence and Manifestation,* 2 vols., trans. J. E. Turner (London, 1938; reprint, New York, 1963), 1:115, 120.

tensified after the Reformation; the emphasis on the sovereignty of God grew hand in hand with the claim for the divinity of the sovereign.[3] One thus senses a return, in both directions, toward archaic divine Power.

Perhaps "return" is too ahistoric a term. In the Renaissance the duplication of political order in the conceptualization of the divine did not lead to the reemergence of Dionysian hierarchies modeled on the late imperial court but to Protestant voluntarism, where the absolute power of the king found its equivalent in the divine *potentia absoluta,* or rather the reverse, since the emphasis on divine sovereignty preceded the consolidation of royal absolutism. The duplication of the political in the sacred, whatever the causal mechanisms involved, produced a theology based on reciprocally implied principles of power and submission, domination and obedience. This theology finds its most characteristic expression in Calvin's *Institutes* with their insistent stress on the "majesty of God" that "compel[s] us to obey."[4] Calvin's emphasis on the sovereignty of the divine will pervades English Protestantism.[5] While it seems connected to the replacement of the papacy with the temporal magistrate as governor of the church, the French historian Jean Delumeau has suggested that this theology of domination and submission may have been characteristic of all European Christianity in the aftermath of the Reformation and Council of Trent. The early-eighteenth-century French priest who wrote that Marseilles could be saved from the plague only by "an entire submission of mind and heart to the . . . Church, which are the sure and only means of staving off the hand of a wrathful God"[6] sounds not very unlike William Perkins, who told his congregation at Stourbridge Fair in 1593,

> Repent, or else certainly God will take vengeance. . . . I am in my conscience persuaded to fear . . . that a plague and a judgment, and that

3. Hill, *Collected Essays,* p. 27.

4. John Calvin, *Institutes of the Christian Religion,* 2 vols., ed. John T. McNeill, trans. Ford Lewis Battles, The Library of Christian Classics (Philadelphia, 1960), 1.7.4; compare 1.6.2–3, 1.8.11, 1.12.1, 3.7.1–2. On the polarities of rebellion and submission in Calvin's thought, see also William J. Bouwsma, *John Calvin: A Sixteenth-Century Portrait* (Oxford, 1988), p. 183.

5. Lake, *Moderate Puritans,* p. 119.

6. Quoted in Jean Delumeau, *Catholicism between Luther and Voltaire: A New View of the Counter-Reformation,* trans. Jeremy Moiser (London, 1977), p. 229.

> most fearful, hangs over England . . . and shall be as certainly executed, without a visible reformation. . . . O then entertain the word of God into thy heart, submit thy soul unto it. . . . Our long peace, plenty and ease have bred great sins, so great that they reach to heaven and provoke God's majesty to his face and so strong they will violently draw down judgments from God upon us.[7]

Perkins, of course, speaks about submitting to the word rather than to the church, but that is in some ways a difference of detail.

It should be declared from the outset that such theological absolutism is not simply an ideological lever for naturalizing royal power, although it certainly had this potential. Men like Calvin and Travers, however, were scarcely royalists. This chapter is intended as an investigation into the meaning of this theology of power, but such an investigation is futile unless we assume that we are dealing with a *theology,* an attempt to understand the nature of God and not a cloak for legitimating a certain regime. This does not imply that the proximity of God and monarch in this politicized theology is unproblematic. On the contrary, its drastic fusion of the historical and sacred disallowing any secular space, its emphasis on guilt, its stark reduction of spirituality to power relations generated the crisis of Western Christianity. Socinianism and Deism react against the oppressive politics of Reformation theology. Delumeau has convincingly argued that the fascination with divine power and penal coercion in the end effected the "de-christianization" of Europe as people became increasingly repelled by the moral implications of the "God of power and might," whether in Calvinist or Tridentine guise.[8] Moreover, if absolutist theology presented ethical problems to the seventeenth century, its psychocultural significance has become even more opaque in an age that equates power with oppression and oppression with all that is evil—slavery, sexism, feudalism, colonialism. Thus Kenneth Min-

7. William Perkins, *The Work of William Perkins,* ed. Ian Breward, The Courtenay Library of Reformation Classics (Appleford, Eng., 1970), pp. 295–99. See also Keith Thomas, *Religion and the Decline of Magic: Studies in Popular Beliefs in Sixteenth- and Seventeenth-Century England* (London, 1971), pp. 83, 110–11.

8. Delumeau, *Catholicism,* pp. 229–31; C. F. Allison, *The Rise of Moralism: The Proclamation of the Gospel from Hooker to Baxter* (New York, 1965), p. 205. In *The Legitimacy of the Modern Age,* Hans Blumenberg similarly views the origins of modernity in the transition from nominalism to "self-assertion" (trans. Robert M. Wallace, Studies in Contemporary German Social Thought [Cambridge, Mass., 1983]).

ogue argues that contemporary theory (which he calls "ideology") "is a form of social analysis which discovers that human beings are the victims of an oppressive system, and that the business of life is liberation."[9] To the extent that we cannot but perceive "oppressive systems" as bad and liberation as good, we are confused by a spirituality based on the duplication of political relations of domination and submission, one valorizing obedience, guilt, and fear. As Peter Laslett observes, "it is the symbolic life of our ancestors which will be the most difficult to handle, and especially their symbols of status."[10]

Absolutist theology belongs to larger cultural and discursive patterns, which deserve brief mention since they suggest some of the interpretive dilemmas involved in tracing the connections between politics and religion. It is a (rather discredited) commonplace to observe that Renaissance thought is analogic, yet the concept of analogy leads to the center of our problem, understanding by "analogy" here the exchange of symbols and concepts from the secular realm to the sacred and vice versa. The conceptual exchange between God and kings both informs and follows from the historical practice whereby, from the early Christian era on, "the *imitatio imperii* on the part of the spiritual power was balanced by an *imitatio sacerdotii* on the part of the secular power."[11] In Renaissance culture this *communicatio idiomatum* pervades symbolic expression.[12] And such extensive cross-pollenization between secular and sacred makes it very hard to fix boundaries between social and transcendent meanings. When King James, for instance, tells his son to remember that "yee differ not in stuffe, but in use, and that onely by . . . [God's] ordinance, from the basest of your people,"[13] the language turns the prince into a sacrament, for in Reformed theology, the eucharistic bread differs from base "stuffe" "only in regard of the use"; or, in Donne's words, the bread is "appro-

9. Kenneth Minogue, *Alien Powers: The Pure Theory of Ideology* (New York, 1985), pp. 37–38.

10. Peter Laslett, *The World We Have Lost: Further Explored,* 3d ed. (London, 1983), p. 52.

11. Ernst H. Kantorowicz, "Mysteries of State: An Absolutist Concept and Its Late Medieval Origins," in Ernst H. Kantorowicz, *Selected Studies* (Locust Valley, N.Y., 1965), p. 381.

12. Blumenberg, *The Modern Age,* pp. 70–72, 92–94.

13. James I, *The Political Works of James I,* intro. Charles McIlwain (Cambridge, Mass., 1918; reprint, New York, 1965), p. 41.

priated by God, in that Ordinance to another use."[14] Kings are like sacraments, and sacraments, as Travers indicates, like royal banquets. Yet if such comparisons were pervasive they also stirred at times the uneasiness registered in Andrewes's claim that "the world and the Holy Ghost speak not one language."[15] One of Donne's sermons hints at the problems to which this habitual bidirectional analogizing might give rise. Its final paragraph begins with a wholly typical eucharistic metaphor: "Let us . . . receive the testimony of Gods Privy Seale . . . and that leads us to the Great Seale, the full fruition of all." But as Donne starts to describe this fruition he stops himself short with the telling phrase, "[I] can finde no words, but such, as I my selfe have mis-used in lower things."[16]

Again in Donne's words, "God and Kings are at a near distance."[17] The oxymoron suggests the unsettled combination of likeness and unlikeness present in analogy that gives rise to interpretive problems. For while analogy, by articulating relation, provides a language of analysis, it does not supply the analysis itself. The formal parallelism of analogic structure need not entail similarity at the level of meaning—which is just to say that not all analogies are of the Neoplatonic, great-chain-of-being variety. For instance, Peter Brown observes that although the ancient Christian saints were modeled on the *patronus* and *dominus* of late Roman society, yet this isomorphism underscores the contrast between the "good, 'clean' power" of the martyr and the "'dirty'" power of the society that put him to death.[18] But Renaissance analogy generally does not show this antithetic structure, where formal parallelism emphasizes contrasting substance. Instead it affirms duplication, but duplication of a problematic rather than an idealized Platonic variety. Thus, as Michael Schoenfeldt has argued, the dialogue between Love and soul in Herbert's "Love (III)" presents "the discourse between God and man in the strategically submissive yet subtly coercive vocabulary of courtesy," where "both the host's gra-

14. John Donne, *The Sermons of John Donne,* 10 vols., ed. George Potter and Evelyn Simpson (Berkeley, 1953–62), 7:11.557–63; Perkins, *Work,* p. 215.

15. Lancelot Andrewes, *The Works of Lancelot Andrewes,* 11 vols., Library of Anglo-Catholic Theology (Oxford, 1854), 3:364.

16. Donne, *Sermons,* 7:13.844–47, 862–63.

17. Donne, *Sermons,* 7:17.358.

18. Peter Brown, *Society and the Holy in Late Antiquity* (Berkeley, 1982), pp. 16–18.

cious invitation and the speaker's equally gracious protestations of unworthiness register an intense concern with propriety, precedence, and prestige."[19] But if social transactions are like spiritual ones, then it becomes difficult to see how the pride and manipulative strategies that characterize the former do not also contaminate the latter.[20] In typical medieval analogies of the "four cardinal virtues equal the four rivers of paradise equal the four elements" variety this problem does not arise. It occurs frequently in the characteristic Renaissance analogy between the sociopolitical and the sacred. But if we grant that the dialogue in "Love (III)" "is actually a battle for political superiority," disclosing the "analogous political pressures" operative in devotional and social submission,[21] then we are left with the perplexing function of such an analogy. Why would Herbert implicate piety in politics?

The problem does not concern only a single poem but the whole tendency to draw analogies between the sacred and sociopolitical. And this brings us again to our primary question: what is the function of the analogy between the *rex coelestis* and Stuart kings? that is, how are social forms of power used to understand the nature of God? What meaning is being constructed?

There can be no single answer to this question. But Donne's sermons are unusually instructive in this regard, since they present the analogy in its most extreme and explicit form. Donne consistently and insistently deploys language associated with absolute monarchy in his treatment of the divine, and he stresses precisely that aspect of absolutism most alien to the modern mentality: the configuration of ideal relations in terms of domination and submission. Yet Donne is not an eccentric convert but in many ways representative of the mainstream of English Reformation theology. Whatever the biographical origins of his religious temperament—a subject that John Carey has investigated with perspicacity and intelligence—his theology is characteristic of the "High Church Calvinism" of men like Downame, Bridges,

19. Michael Schoenfeldt, "Standing on Ceremony: The Comedy of Manners in Herbert's 'Love (III),'" in *"Bright Shootes of Everlastingnesse": The Seventeenth-Century Religious Lyric,* ed. Claude J. Summers and Ted-Larry Pebworth (Columbia, Mo., 1987), p. 117.

20. Schoenfeldt, "Standing on Ceremony," in Summers and Pebworth, eds., *"Bright Shootes,"* p. 127.

21. Schoenfeldt, "Standing on Ceremony," in Summers and Pebworth, eds., *"Bright Shootes,"* pp. 121, 126.

Carleton, Hall, and Montague (James, not Richard), although—like many English Calvinists—he is "soft" on predestination.[22] He could not have preached successfully from the major pulpits of his day—Lincoln's Inn, St. Paul's, Whitehall, St. Dunstan's—if his religion had not seemed to his contemporaries acceptably orthodox and pious.[23]

COMMUNICATIO IDIOMATUM

Measure God by earthly Princes
Donne, *Sermons*

Donne's religious writings differ from those of his contemporaries primarily in the *degree* to which he stresses the analogy between God and kings.[24] Even in the erotic poetry, he is fascinated by kingship. Often in the sermons, the analogy is quite casual, just indicative of a general habit of mind that perceives the divine in terms of royal and courtly associations. Thus he likes to point out that as one would never dare to offer the king a defective gift, so one should not presume to pawn damaged goods off on God.[25] Elsewhere he notes in passing that "the Kings pardon flowes from his meere grace, and from his brest . . . [as] does faith from God," or, somewhat humorously, that God's coming to the individual resembles a visit by the king: "an honour . . . yet [not] without removes, and troubles, and charges."[26] Occasionally one finds not unexpected traces of the ancient correspondences between sociopolitical and supernatural order. "God is a Mon-

22. On predestination in the English church, see Peter White, "A Rejoinder," *Past and Present* 115 (1987): 221–25; Lake, *Moderate Puritans*, p. 209; for the strong Calvinist view of predestination, see Jaroslav Pelikan, *The Christian Tradition: A History of the Development of Doctrine*, 5 vols., vol. 4, *Reformation of Church and Dogma, 1300–1700* (Chicago, 1984), pp. 221–22; Perkins, "A Golden Chain," in *Work*, pp. 183–86, 250–51. On "High-Church Calvinism," see Patrick Collinson, *The Religion of Protestants: The Church in English Society, 1559–1625* (Oxford, 1982), pp. 10–21. The similarities between Donne's theology and Puritanism can be seen by comparing Lake's description of Puritan practical divinity with Donne's own sermons (Lake, *Moderate Puritans*, pp. 116–68).

23. My one criticism of John Carey's excellent *John Donne: Life, Mind, and Art* (New York, 1981) is that he tends to see Donne's theology as so closely intertwined with his personality and neuroses as to be "not in any distinctive sense religious" (p. 220). The reception of his sermons suggests that this perception could not have been shared by Donne's original audiences.

24. On the analogy between God and kings in Calvin, see Bouwsma, *Calvin*, p. 163.

25. Donne, *Sermons*, 2:11.340–50; 5:7.289–302; 9:10.155–61.

26. Donne, *Sermons*, 7:10.203–5; 5:18.248–51.

arch alone"; "Heaven is a kingdome, and Christ a King"; the "Heaven of Heavens" is "the Presence Chamber of God himselfe"; as Christ is the mediator between God and man, so King's counselors are mediators "between Princes and People."[27]

Donne's references to kings are frequently, however, more significant and more specific. Whether speaking about literal or metaphoric kings he almost invariably echoes the main themes of Jacobean royalism.[28] Like Andrewes and James himself, he refers to the king as the image of God and as a god on earth.[29] His authority therefore does not derive from the people but directly from God; like Christ, a true king is a hereditary not an elective monarch.[30] Hence royal power does not simply inhere in a divinely sanctioned social *role,* but the king is in a real sense a sacred person, one who participates in the divine in such a way that "the Kings acts are Gods acts." Thus "Sedition and Rebellion [are] Sacriledge; for, though the trespasse seeme to be directed but upon a man, yet in that man, whose office (and consequently his person) is sacred, God is opposed, and violated."[31] As in Andrewes and James, one sees the same connection between the Davidic priest-king and the royal headship of the Church of England. Like David, the king (Charles, in this case) "institutes those Orders, which the Church is to observe in the publique service of God" for "the King is King of men; not of bodies onely, but of soules too."[32]

A principal difference between Donne and Andrewes appears in the theological scope of their politics. Although both were unquestionably royalists of a high Stuart variety, the latter only rarely and very conventionally depicts God in monarchal terms. The reverse is true of Donne, for whom the ideal structure of the king/subject relation set forth in James's own writings is replayed in spiritual politics. Donne, that is, depicts divine/human interaction as analogous to seventeenth-century absolute monarchy. Thus he regularly thinks of sin as a political offense, as "Treason," as "disloially" breaking "our Allegeance,"

27. Donne, *Sermons,* 4:4.450; 7:4.391; 4:1.76; 8:15.159–67.

28. On the parallels between James's own politics and Donne's opinions, see Carey, *John Donne,* pp. 113–15; Jonathan Goldberg, *James I and the Politics of Literature: Jonson, Shakespeare, Donne, and Their Contemporaries* (Baltimore, 1983), p. 213.

29. Donne, *Sermons,* 7:14.301; 8:4.183; 8:15.34, 159.

30. Donne, *Sermons,* 7:17.459; 8:13.401–4.

31. Donne, *Sermons,* 8:4.190–91, 234–37.

32. Donne, *Sermons,* 8:4.177–80.

and as "a rebellion against that soveraignty which God hath instituted . . . and an ambition of setting up another Prince."[33] Donne's God, like James's, possesses *arcana imperii,* which no one may presume to investigate. As "it is enough for a happy subject to enjoy the sweetnesse of a peaceable government, though he know not *Arcana Imperii,* The wayes by which the Prince governes; So is it for a Christian to enjoy the working of Gods grace . . . though he inquire not into Gods bed-chamber, nor seek into his unrevealed Decrees."[34] It is not merely unnecessary to probe God's secrets, but "Libell" to publish them, "an injury to God, and against his Crowne."[35] God's unrevealed decrees here are insistently political. Donne does not think of the *arcana* as *religious* mysteries, although this would be good classical usage. Rather they are "secrets of his State" and "Cabinet Decrees," metaphors drawn from Jacobean absolutist rhetoric.[36] "These are acts of [God's] . . . Regality, and of his Prerogative; and as Princes say of their Prerogative, *nolumus disputari.*"[37] Like James, Donne thus associates the *arcana* with royal prerogative and "absolute power."[38] The *arcana imperii* belong to the discourse of absolutism precisely because they imply that there exists a reserve of power behind the ordinary lawful operations of the monarch (or divinity) that can neither be questioned nor limited. Thus, for Donne, miracles constitute acts of God's "absolute prerogative" because they break the law of nature.[39]

Unlike Hooker, Donne has little interest in divine law, in law as a mediating structure between transcendent will and temporal phenomena. He focuses on the direct, immediate power of God, who will not be content "with a Consulship, with a Collegueship, that he and the world may joyn in the government," but demands "absolute power."[40] The Gospel inscribes the "Law of Liberty" in the same sense that James refers to England as a "free monarchy": it "leaves God at his liberty."[41] Freedom derives from absolute power. There is, moreover,

33. Donne, *Sermons,* 5:3.81; 5:16.550–51; 2:3.782–84.
34. Donne, *Sermons,* 9:10.517–22.
35. Donne, *Sermons,* 4:12.78–81.
36. Donne, *Sermons,* 8:5.860–61.
37. Donne, *Sermons,* 8:5.868–69.
38. Donne, *Sermons,* 1:6.131.
39. Donne, *Sermons,* 8:13.421.
40. Donne, *Sermons,* 2:8.353–60.
41. Donne, *Sermons,* 8:15.540.

no appeal from God's judgment, for "to whom should we appeal from the Soveraign."[42] When Donne does acknowledge the "lawfulness" of God, it is invariably in the specifically Jacobean sense that the sovereign may choose to obey the law but has no obligation to do so: "God, as absolute Lord, may damn without respect of sin, if he will. . . . But God is pleased to proceed with us, according to that Contract which he hath made with us, and that Law which he hath given to us, in those two Tables."[43] The nominalist distinction between *potentia absoluta* and *potentia ordinata,* which absolutist theory had taken over, thus reemerges in a theological context but without shedding its political connotations.[44] God, Donne admits, allows himself to be tried by laws, but only by the law of which he himself is author and interpreter, that is, Holy Scripture[45]—again, a position remarkably close to James's. To attempt to try God by "the Light and Evidence of [human] . . . Reason," however, is "a presumpteous thing, and a contempt against God."[46]

THE POWER OF GOD

> Ita fit, ut religio et maiestas et honor *metu* constet.
> Lactantius, *De ira Dei*
>
> [God] is more terrible and frightful than the Devil.
> Luther

Donne's politicization of the divine image leads to a spirituality based on awe and subjection. One must have "a reverentiall feare" and "a fearfull reverence."[47] Hence "no man may thinke himselfe to bee come to that familiar acquaintance with God, as that it should take away that reverentiall feare which belongs to so high and supreme a Majesty."[48]

42. Donne, *Sermons,* 2:15.222.
43. Donne, *Sermons,* 1:4.434–38.
44. The sixteenth-century Puritan Laurence Chaderton thus argues that God "is above all law absolutely free" (quoted in Lake, *Moderate Puritans,* p. 154). The notion that God voluntarily limits His absolute power in covenanting with humanity is the basis of federalist theology. Even in New England, this self-limitation evokes royalist metaphors: within the Covenant, as "in all other royall patents, and grants of princely grace and bounty," God's promises hold firm (Perry Miller, *The New England Mind: The Seventeenth Century* [New York, 1939; reprint, Boston, 1961], pp. 376–80).
45. Donne, *Sermons,* 8:12.416–21.
46. Donne, *Sermons,* 1:2.75–77.
47. Donne, *Sermons,* 2:10.440, 730.
48. Donne, *Sermons,* 2:10.646–47.

A person comes before God with the "reverence" with which people come "to the Kings presence."[49] Hence, Donne stresses the distance between God and man rather than their intimacy. He thus associates High Church ritual—kneeling at communion, genuflecting, baring the head—not with adoration or humble love but with the marks of submission to one's social superiors: "we must not be too familiar, too fellowly, too homely with God, here at home, in his house."[50] Rather there must be "a due consideration of greatness, a distance, a distinction, a respect of Rank, and Order, and Majestie," not, apparently, unlike the reverential gestures required in the presence of the king.[51] Along with "respect of Rank" God requires unquestioning obedience, the "silence of reverence, silence of subjection" that restrains one "from questioning any thing ordained by God."[52]

It should be clear from the foregoing that Donne's theology is "absolutist" not by implication or inference but quite literally and explicitly. The sermons insist on the analogy between God and king and furthermore locate the point of contact in *power*. Kings are called gods "by participation of Gods power"[53]—a power characterized by secret decrees, *potentia absoluta,* freedom from law, and the distant fearfulness of majesty. Moreover, as the following discussion will attempt to demonstrate, this analogy involves more than a simple comparison between temporal and spiritual centers of authority. It is a psychagogic rather than cosmological analogy; that is, Donne presses the absolutist qualities of divinity in order to generate terror, insecurity, and guilt. God is the utterly absolute monarch a Stuart could only dream of being.

The theological corollary of royal absolutism is radical monotheism, the total concentration of power into a single figure. Such a conception of God, as Donne is aware, verges on moral incomprehensibility and paradox. To the "naturall man" there is "no burden . . . so insupportable, no consideration so inextricable, no secret so inscrutable, no conception so incredible, as to conceive One infinite God, that should do all things alone, without any more Gods."[54] If God does "all things alone," then He is responsible for all things; but "That that God that settles peace, should yet make warres . . . That the conquered

49. Donne, *Sermons,* 9:5.810.
50. Donne, *Sermons,* 8:5.313–14.
51. Donne, *Sermons,* 1:4.415–17.
52. Donne, *Sermons,* 9:12.322–24.
53. Donne, *Sermons,* 2:9.143.
54. Donne, *Sermons,* 8:14.604–10.

God, and the victorious God, should be both one God, That that God who is all goodnesse in himselfe, should yet have his hand in every ill action, this the naturall man cannot digest, not comprehend."[55] This final implication is the most significant. Donne's monotheism abolishes the mythic dualism of Andrewes's *Christus Victor* theology, in which responsibility for "ill action" devolves onto Satan and the powers of darkness, thus eliminating the paradox of a good God who directly causes evil. Donne, however, insists upon the paradox: "all the evill (that is, all the *penall* ill, all plagues, all warre, all famine,) that is *done* in the World, God doth."[56] There is no cosmic battle between God and Lucifer but instead a "strange warre, where there are not two sides . . . for, God uses the Devill against us, and the Devill uses us against one another . . . so that God, and the Devill, and we, are all in one Army, and all for our destruction."[57] God does not cause evil in the loose or deistic sense of establishing natural laws that may produce unpleasant side effects for some persons nor in the Catholic (and Arminian) sense of mere permission; rather, human suffering is "*penall* ill," it is intended to hurt and punish. If God requires man to keep his distance, yet God himself is painfully present in His "judgements . . . speedily enough executed upon thy soul and body together, every day."[58] Donne's "Calvinism" is at work in the reiterated claim that "War, and Dearth, and Sickness, are the Weapons of Gods displeasure; and these he pours out of his Treasury, in this world," but Calvin himself tends to emphasize the comfort and safety to be derived from the notion of supernatural control rather than God's punitive capacity.[59] In his stress on the latter, Donne seems closer to the English Calvinists and, perhaps, to Luther.[60]

Donne's monotheism includes two related elements: the unlimited power of God and the representation of such power as terrifying and

55. Donne, *Sermons,* 8:14.614–20.

56. Donne, *Sermons,* 7:14.610–12.

57. Donne, *Sermons,* 4:11.322–26.

58. Donne, *Sermons,* 1:2.337–38.

59. Donne, *Sermons,* 9:7.409–11; Calvin, *Institutes,* 1.17.11. See also Bouwsma, *Calvin,* p. 171.

60. Van der Leeuw notes that this conception derives from the near-demonic Javeh of the Old Testament (*Religion in Essence,* 2:636–37). On God's absolute control over all temporal events in English Puritanism, see Lake, *Moderate Puritans,* pp. 103, 124. For the nonrational, nonlegal aspects of Luther's notion of providence, see Paul Tillich, *A History of Christian Thought from Its Judaic and Hellenistic Origins to Existentialism,* ed. Carl Braaten (New York, 1967), p. 259.

destructive. James expresses Donne's meaning precisely when he concludes that kings exercise "Divine power upon earth" insofar as "they have power to . . . make of their subjects like men at the Chesse; A pawne to take a Bishop or a Knight, and to cry up, or downe any of their subjects, as they do their money."[61] So for Donne, God is "such a Lord, as is Lord and Proprietary of all his creatures, and all creatures are his creatures; And then, *Dominium est potestas tum utendi, tum abutendi,* sayes the law; To be absolute Lord of any thing, gives that Lord a power to doe what he will with that thing. God . . . may give and take, quicken and kill, build and throw downe, where and whom he will." Or, as Donne elsewhere puts it more simply: "his Power hath no limitation but his owne Will."[62] Even when Donne makes a point not in itself disturbing, he couches it in the language of *potentia absoluta.* Thus, in his hands the statement that Christ founded the Church becomes "*Ego vici mundum,* sayes Christ, I have conquered the world, and comming in by conquest, I may establish what forme of Government I will."[63]

Divine power fascinates Donne largely in its destructive and catastrophic aspect.[64] "With one *Pereat,* he can destroy all."[65] God is the "*Terribilis Rex,*" the terrible king, who falls upon the sinner like "hailestones . . . as shall grinde them to powder."[66] The images used highlight the direct and deliberate nature of God's infliction of pain. He thus paraphrases Psalm 38:2, "Thy hand hath wounded mee, and that hand keeps the wound open." Elsewhere he speaks of God's hand as "pushing away, and keeping downe." God is like an archer who "bends his bow, and whets his arrows, and at last he shoots." Again, "all the wounds that I have, come from thy hand, all the arrowes that stick in me, from thy quiver."[67] Such passages on divine punishment, anger, striking, shooting occur with oppressive regularity and very

61. James I, *Political Works,* p. 308.

62. Donne, *Sermons,* 7:1.555–61; 8:1.744–45. One should contrast this with Hooker's claim: "They err therefore who think that of the will of God to do this or that there is no reason besides his will. Many times no reason known to us; but that there is no reason thereof I judge it most unreasonable to imagine" (Richard Hooker, *The Works of that Learned and Judicious Divine, Mr. Richard Hooker,* 3 vols., ed. Rev. John Keble, 7th ed. [Oxford, 1888; reprint, New York, 1970], 1:203).

63. Donne, *Sermons,* 5:13.262–65.

64. Carey, *John Donne,* pp. 122–23.

65. Donne, *Sermons,* 8:2.180.

66. Donne, *Sermons,* 7:12.661; 2:8.571–72.

67. Donne, *Sermons,* 2:1.649–50; 9:12.671–72; 8:14.164–65; 7:1.206–7.

little rationalist softening—a methodical onslaught on security.[68] To cite just one more example:

> But if the Lord be angry, he needs no Trumpets to call in Armies, if he doe but *sibilare muscam,* hisse and whisper for the flye, and the Bee, there is nothing so little in his hand, as cannot discomfort thee, discomfit thee, dissolve and powr out, attentuate and annihilate the very marrow of thy soul. Every thing is His, and therefore every thing is Hee; thy sicknesse is his sword, and therefore it is Hee that strikes thee with it.[69]

Donne lays particular weight on man's utter vulnerability, both physical and psychological, to divine aggression. God can make people perish while they are in the middle of trying to repent. He can totally abandon them, forgetting all his prior "paternities," all his "filiations" to them.[70] All human attempts at independence and rational control are illusory, since external events and psychic life are at the mercy of God, who can, with a word, "reduce them to *nothing* againe": "*Navyes* will not keepe off *Navies,* if *God* be not the *Pilot,* Nor *Walles* keepe out *Men,* if *God* be not the *Sentinell.* . . . as long as the Testimonies of GODS anger lye at the dore of the *Conscience,* no man can returne to peace there."[71] The famous *pondus gloriae* passage from Donne's second Prebend sermon forms a nightmarish rhapsody on man's exposure to divine power.[72] God imposes intolerable burdens, "infinite waights of afflictions that oppresse us here." The prose stresses divine responsibility: "God calls in but the fly, to vexe Egypt, and even the fly is a heavy burden unto them. . . . It is not onely *Jeremy* that complains . . . That God made their fetters and their chains heavy to them, but the workmen in harvest complaine, That God had made a faire day heavy unto them. . . . all is waight, and burden, and heavinesse, and oppression." The pain is not just external. The psyche is likewise vulnerable to divine wrath, with the result that what appeared to be a proprietary selfhood can be ripped away and vanish in an instant:

68. This emphasis on the wrath of God has affinities with Luther. See Pelikan, *Reformation,* p. 132; Tillich, *Christian Thought,* p. 240.

69. Donne, *Sermons,* 2:2.520–26.

70. Donne, *Sermons,* 8:8.487–92; 8:13.333.

71. Donne, *Sermons,* 7:2.258–63, 282–83.

72. Donne, *Sermons,* 7:1.73–219.

> But when I shall trust to that, which wee call a good spirit, and God shall deject, and empoverish, and evacuate that spirit, when I shall rely upon a morall constancy, and God shall shake, and enfeeble, and enervate, destroy and demolish that constancy; when I shall think to refresh my selfe in the serenity and sweet ayre of a good conscience, and God shall call up the damps and vapours of hell it selfe, and spread a cloud of diffidence, and an impenetrable crust of desperation upon my conscience . . . except hee put in that *pondus gloriae,* that exceeding waight of an eternall glory, with his owne hand, into the other scale, we are waighed downe, we are swallowed up, irreparably, irrevocably, irrecoverably, irremediably.

And this is not deserved punishment for sin, but "still the best men have had most laid upon them." And, as Donne acutely notes, such agony is often not medicinal but produces aversion and drives us away from God, making us unable to hear His voice or He ours.[73]

Although Donne generally depicts divine punishment as retribution for sin and therefore explicable, if terrifying, he also will play with the notion of undeserved suffering, or suffering that seems far in excess of the offense. He thus observes that first God hurts us and then punishes us for complaining; we "are whipt if we cry."[74] Similarly, the fear that God is angry with us—a fear Donne makes every effort to inculcate—will make Him angry. In fact, this terror at inscrutable punishment guarantees its execution, since "nothing can alienate God more from thee, then to think that any thing but sin can alienate him."[75] Divine logic operates with dilemmas and conundrums, rendering every human action potentially subject to penalty. Donne is, in fact, intrigued by all the things one can be punished for. If prayer is not made "in faith," if it is "discontinued, intermitted, done by fits," if "it be not vehement," such prayer "shall not only be ineffectuall, but even . . . *an abomination;* And not only an abomination to God, but destruction upon themselves." If one receives the Sacrament unworthily—and Donne inserts parenthetically that almost everyone does so—"at the last day, we shall be ranked with *Judas*."[76] Similarly, if one loves God's creation in an ordinate manner and loves God "as a great and incomprehensible power," but does not love (because he does not

73. Donne, *Sermons,* 5:16.678–80.
74. Donne, *Sermons,* 7:1.115.
75. Donne, *Sermons,* 8:15.397–99.
76. Donne, *Sermons,* 7:12.685–94, 770–84.

know) Christ, then, Donne concludes, "let him be accursed, for all his love."[77] The proximity of divine curse and human love seems particularly unsettling here. God's gifts of prayer and sacraments, His gift of His Son, turn out, in Donne's hands, to be snares and traps. With like rigorism, Donne dwells on the catastrophic results of dogmatic error. At the Last Judgment, the penalty for sins of "not cloathing, not visiting, not harbouring the poore" will be mild compared to that due for the "high treason . . . of denying or doubting of the distinct Persons of the holy, blessed, and glorious Trinity," without which "all morall vertues are but diseases."[78] Indeed, "for matter of beleefe, he that beleeves not all, *solvit Iesum* . . . he takes Jesus in peeces."[79] More explicitly, "He that beleeves not every Article of the Christian faith, and with so stedfast a belief, as that he would dye for it, *Damnabitur,* (no modification, no mollification, no going lesse) He shal be damned."[80]

Donne also plays with the notion of damnation without personal guilt. His discussions of Original Sin and the condemnation of the invincibly ignorant underscore the mysterious and illogical implications of traditional doctrine on these matters. Thus in the second sermon he preached before Charles I, Donne begins by considering the economics of sin; sin is a sort of selling, a bad bargain whereby one gives up immortality and the love of God for temporal benefits. But as he attempts to apply this model to Original Sin, the analogy conspicuously breaks down: "But what had *I* for *Heaven? Adam* sinnd, and *I* suffer; I *forfeited* before I had any *Possession,* or could claime any *Interest;* I had a *Punishment,* before I had a *being,* And *God* was displeased with *me* before *I* was *I.*"[81] Original Sin fascinates Donne, but fascinates him because it is heteronomous and morally unintelligible. In other passages the illogic works itself into the rhythms of the prose. His funeral sermon for Lady Danvers, for example, contains the following

77. Donne, *Sermons,* 1:5.225–28.

78. Donne, *Sermons,* 8:1.812–18, 834–35.

79. Donne, *Sermons,* 8.5.584–85.

80. Donne, *Sermons,* 7:12.618–21. A similar rigorism operates in Calvin; see Bouwsma, *Calvin,* pp. 49, 141. It is again instructive to compare this with Hooker's assertion that "they be not all faithless that are either weak in assenting to the truth, or stiff in maintaining things any way opposite to the truth of Christian doctrine" (*Works,* 3:500).

81. Donne, *Sermons,* 7:2.174–77.

passage: "For *his mercies are new every morning;* and his later mercies are his largest mercies. How many, how great *Nations* perish, without ever hearing the name of *Christ.*"[82] The space, the *aporeia,* between the first and second sentence seems intolerably large; the typographic relation between God's "mercies" and the fact that whole nations "perish" both demands and resists explanation. These are uneasy passages, exhibiting both an edge of moral revulsion and the determination to rub the hearer's nose in the terrifying reality of divine wrath and inexplicable rigor. They simultaneously force and forbid the perception of injustice. They assault the congregation with the destructive and alien power of God.

Yet however heteronomous, Donne's God never escapes the representational web of sociopolitical analogy. In His "psychological makeup," if the phrase may be used in this context, He strongly resembles a Renaissance nobleman. He is, above all, concerned to maintain His superiority. He thus jealously guards His honor, "which Honour consists much in our honouring of him," hence punishing people primarily to make them aware that they are being punished, to compel the acknowledgment of His power.[83] Christ too "deliver[s] his own Honour, by delivering [a] . . . sinner to malediction."[84] Like Calvin and almost all Reformed theologians, Donne holds that "Gods first purpose was his owne glory," a self-directed intentionality he associates with princes.[85] In a thoroughly aristocratic manner, God resents whatever threatens to derogate from this glory. Donne makes the sociological parallel totally explicit:

> In benefits that pass from men of higher ranck, to persons of lower condition, it is not the way to get them, to ground the request upon our own merit; Merit implies an obligation, that we have laid upon them; and that implies a debt. And a Petition for a due debt is an affront.[86]

82. Donne, *Sermons,* 8:2.506–8.
83. Donne, *Sermons,* 5:3.79–80; 5:16.440–41.
84. Donne, *Sermons,* 7:14.541–42.
85. Donne, *Sermons,* 4:12.88–89; 2:14.130–31. That God does everything for His own glory is a central principle of Reformed theology; see Tillich, *Christian Thought,* p. 266; Pelikan, *Reformation,* p. 207; Bouwsma, *Calvin,* p. 163; Calvin, *Institutes,* 1.15.8. Again, Hooker voices the opposition, arguing that the "general end" of God's working is "the exercise of his most glorious and most abundant virtue. . . . Not that any thing is made to be beneficial unto him, but all things for him to shew beneficence and grace in them" (*Works,* 1:203).
86. Donne, *Sermons,* 1:7.86–90.

God refuses to allow human merit because he finds it offensive to His noblesse oblige. God's sense of His own honor requires people to pay honor to Him. As Donne several times remarks, "God takes it as ill to be slighted, as to be injur'd," and again there is no attempt to conceal the social analogy.[87] Rather, he notes that "as man doth, so [God] . . . takes it worse to be neglected, then to be really injured."[88] Hence one must acknowledge God's power in order to avoid being crushed by it, for "when God cannot breake us by breaking our backs . . . nor by breaking our hearts . . . then he comes to breake us by breaking our necks."[89]

The relation between God and man in Donne thus operates along the axis of power and submission. God possesses ineluctable and overwhelming might designed to inspire fear and impel obedience. This relation recapitulates the structure of absolutist rule, as Donne makes perfectly clear, although intensifying precisely those aspects of royal absolutism that appalled members of Parliament and the common lawyers: sovereign will unconstrained by law, the taboo on probing the *arcana imperii,* the yawning distance between ruler and subjects. It is not enough to say that such power dynamics do not constitute the totality of Donne's theology. They are at the center of his conception of God, and an accurate understanding of that totality requires some comprehension of *why* Donne would choose to fashion divine/human relations along such harsh and politicized lines.

CALVIN AND PELAGIUS?

> Every man fears the mighty: for what he will do, we know not; what he can do we know.
>
> Andrewes

Donne attempts to stabilize the terrifying freedom of God vis-à-vis mankind by denying reprobation. He departs noticeably from Calvinist orthodoxy by claiming that Christ died for all persons and therefore damnation is not necessitated by any eternal decrees but is a conse-

87. Donne, *Sermons,* 9:7.126.
88. Donne, *Sermons,* 9:10.150–51.
89. Donne, *Sermons,* 2:8.514–18.

quence of sin.[90] At times Donne moves close to the Catholic position that grace is offered equally to all, and people are then free to accept or resist it.[91] More often, he seems to adhere to the position of moderate English Protestantism, which holds that divine condemnation is always with respect to sin, without affirming the universality of grace. While Donne clearly opposes supralapsarian Calvinism, it seems precipitous to label him an Arminian, especially since Peter Lake has shown that even "strong" Calvinists like Laurence Chaderton tended to take a less austere position in the pulpit.[92]

Donne reinforces his rejection of the arbitrary deity implied in supralapsarian Calvinism by stressing the covenant or contract that places divine/human relations within a lawful, predictable context. By this contract "hath God expressed his love to us," since it has "manifested to us a way, to come to him."[93] Since God is "*fidelis,* a faithful God," He will perform the covenant He has made; in other words, although God is an "absolute Lord," He will "proceed with us, according to that Contract which he hath made with us, and that Law which he hath given to us."[94] God has *potentia absoluta* but governs the world according to His *potentia ordinata*—a distinction common to both the nominalists and the Stuarts.[95] Insofar as the relation between God and human beings is contractual, it is also conditional. The condition on God's side is fidelity to His promise, on the human side, obedience: in Donne's words, "*If you obey you shall live, if you rebell you shall die.*"[96]

90. Donne, *Sermons,* 2:6.275–310, 5:1.700–715, 7:2.67–79, 9:17.687–700. See also Carey, *John Donne,* pp. 240–42. Carey notes that Donne's theology teeters between the Thomist conception of God as just and reasonable and the Calvinist monster—perhaps an oversimplified contrast. It is so easy to find Calvinism morally obnoxious and so hard to understand why an earlier era embraced it.

91. Donne, *Sermons,* 5:1.712–14.

92. Lake, *Moderate Puritans,* pp. 151–53.

93. Donne, *Sermons,* 10:4.150–52.

94. Donne, *Sermons,* 1:8.409–11; 1:4.434–39.

95. On the nominalist distinction between *potentia absoluta* and *ordinata,* see Francis Oakley, *Omnipotence, Covenant, and Order: An Excursion in the History of Ideas from Abelard to Leibniz* (Ithaca, 1984), pp. 52–59; Heiko A. Oberman, "The Shape of Late Medieval Thought: The Birthpangs of the Modern Era," pp. 12–13; and William Courtney, "Nominalism and Late Medieval Religion," pp. 37–43, both in *The Pursuit of Holiness in Late Medieval and Renaissance Religion,* ed. Charles Trinkaus with Heiko A. Oberman (Leiden, 1974). For the Reformation sequel see Oberman, "*Via antiqua* and *Via moderna:* Late Medieval Prolegomena to Early Reformation Thought," *Journal of the History of Ideas* 48 (1987): 23–40; Miller, *New England Mind,* pp. 376–80.

96. Donne, *Sermons,* 7:14.210.

This conditionality, however, undermines the attempt to establish the relation between God and humans on a predictable and workable footing. The divine promises remain contingent on obedience, for "all Gods promises have a *Si audieritis, si volueritis,* if *I hearken,* if *I obey,* I shall eat the good things of the land; otherwise I shall sterve, body, and soule."[97] But Donne sets the standard of obedience so high that no one can perform his part of the bargain. As in Perkins, any fault is, in God's eye, a capital offense.[98] Thus, for example, in an early sermon preached before Queen Anne, Donne argues,

> If thou hast lov'd thy self, or any body else principally; or so, that when thou dost any act of love, thou canst not say to thine own conscience, I do this for Gods sake, and for his glory; if thou hast loved so, thou hast hated thy self, and him whom thou hast loved, and God whom thou shouldest love.[99]

That is, if one does not love God to the exclusion of all else, then one hates God; there is no middle ground. This passage is typical of Donne's association of obedience with purity of motive. Although a firm moralist, he rarely makes the link between moral perfection and fulfilling the divine conditions on salvation. Instead, the connection between obedience and promise involves the more intangible and perhaps more impossible requirement of sincerity.[100] That is, "if when we eat and drink, or sleep or wake, we do not all to the glory of God . . . he will divorce."[101] Any trace of "selfness" totally contaminates an act or intention, no matter how good. Donne thus remarks, "If I would not serve God, except I might be saved for serving him, I shall not be saved though I serve him; My first end in serving God, must not be my selfe, but he and his glory."[102] What is striking here is not the claim that one should intend God's glory—something no religious person would deny—but that the desire for one's own bless-

97. Donne, *Sermons,* 7:16.686–88.

98. Perkins, "A Faithful and Plain Exposition," in *Work,* p. 288. The same covenantal rigorism can already be found in Tyndale; see, for example, William Tyndale, *Exposition on Matthew,* in *Expositions and Notes on Sundry Portions of The Holy Scriptures,* ed. Henry Walter, The Parker Society (Cambridge, 1849), p. 6.

99. Donne, *Sermons,* 1:5.267–71.

100. Sincerity of intention also forms the principal requirement on man's side in federalist theology. See Miller, *New England Mind,* p. 387.

101. Donne, *Sermons,* 9:10.601–3.

102. Donne, *Sermons,* 2:14.796–98.

edness should be seen as a fatal perversion of saving love. Human action is viewed in black-and-white terms, and the "white" portion squeezed by a spiritual rigorism into nonexistence.

Hence, Donne's emphasis on covenants and contracts generally does not stabilize the relation between God and man. Since the human partner fails to fulfill his end of the bargain, the whole *instrumentum* falls to the ground. Instead such bilateral promises serve primarily to exculpate God while simultaneously incriminating man; "the justification of God . . . is accomplished at the expense of man."[103] Donne describes God as setting up the Gospel so that "we might be absolutely inexcusable" if we continue to sin. God always does "all that is necessary"; our suffering is our fault.[104]

Donne's substitution of a contractual divinity for hard-line reprobation seems further problematized by his habitual association of God's eternal decrees (that is, the decrees of election and reprobation) with the *arcana imperii*. For Donne never denies that God has "*Arcana ejus,* The secrets of his State . . . unrevealed Decrees."[105] The fact that people are forbidden from discussing God's secrets implies that they exist. The nature of these secrets is not wholly clear. They may be the old religious *arcana*, mysteries too high or holy to be disclosed; but Donne generally uses the phrase *arcana imperii,* thus locating these secrets in a political context rather than a sacred one. And, from Tacitus on, reference to these political *arcana* suggests that the public, official account of things does not correspond to the real story. Hence, Donne's association of the divine decrees with the *arcana* allows room for the vertiginous possibility that the promises God makes in Holy Scripture have only a flexible relation to what He really intends to do. This possibility seems to be the prima facie meaning of Donne's statement: "we are not to consider God in those Decrees, wherein we

103. See Calvin, *Institutes:* "Since, then, we see the flesh panting for every subterfuge by which it thinks that the blame for its own evils may in any way be diverted from itself to another, we must diligently oppose this evil intent. Therefore we must so deal with the calamity of mankind that we may cut off every shift, and may vindicate God's justice from every accusation" (1.15.1). This shift of responsibility derives from Augustine. As Blumenberg notes, in Augustine and thereafter, the justification of God "is accomplished at the expense of man, to whom a new concept of freedom is ascribed expressly in order to let the whole of an enormous responsibility and guilt be imputed to it" (*The Modern Age,* p. 133).

104. Donne, *Sermons,* 7:12.229–301; 8:13.351.

105. Donne, *Sermons,* 8:4.120–21.

cannot consider him as *fidelem Deum;* In those Decrees, which are not revealed to us, we know not whether he be faithfull, or no."[106] Donne goes on to say that God will perform the promises revealed in Holy Scripture, but that God's secret decrees might equivocate on His express statements remains a latent possibility and impenetrable fear.[107]

THE POLITICS OF GUILT

Despite Donne's emphasis on obedience and duty, which derives both from his notion of the covenant and from his stress on vocation, the role of ethical activity in these sermons is far less important than it is not only in the works of a truly Pelagian moralist like Sebastian Castellio but even in the writings of more typical Protestants like Tyndale and Perkins, where the insistence on human sinfulness quickly passes to quite practical recipes for improved behavior. In Donne, the drive toward moralism is undermined by the valorization of guilt.[108] The sermons characteristically lay less stress on moral reformation than on remorse and shame, on the necessity of apprehending one's culpability. Such guilt is not simply the prelude to a *conversio* but almost an intrinsically desirable condition, for "he that stinks most in his owne . . . is the best perfume to Gods nostrils."[109] Furthermore, divine grace is experienced as acute guilt. Thus Donne remarks that while he passes his time "sociably and merrily in cheerful conversation, in musique, in feasting, in Comedies, in wantonnesse" he remains unconscious of impinging spiritual presences, but "alone,

106. Donne, *Sermons,* 1:8.431–34.

107. On God's secret will in Reformation theology, see Pelikan, *Reformation,* p. 219; Bouwsma, *Calvin,* p. 42; Miller, *New England Mind,* p. 379; Calvin, *Institutes,* 1.17.2. The Remonstrants (or Arminians) denied the existence of this hidden will, as does Hooker (Pelikan, *Reformation,* p. 234; Hooker, *Works,* 2:563).

108. In *The Transformation of Sin: Studies in Donne, Herbert, Vaughan, and Traherne* (Montreal, 1974), Patrick Grant discusses the history of "guilt-culture" from antiquity through the Reformation (pp. 1–39).

109. Donne, *Sermons,* 7:11.229–31. The same association of guilt with salvation (and conversely of security with damnation) appears in Perkins, "A Faithful and Plain Exposition": "Ask the devil, he will tell thee all is well and that thou art in an excellent estate; and God loves thee and thou art sure of heaven. . . . Ask our own flesh and our own hearts and natures and they will answer and say that all is well and safe and that we have believed and loved and feared God all our days. . . . [But] the first rule is that every man . . . sinned in the sin of Adam . . . [and] thou art guilty of it before God. . . . The second rule to be known is that in every man are all sins. . . . The third rule . . . is that every man . . . is by nature the child of wrath and God's enemy" (in *Work,* pp. 289–90).

between God and me at midnight, some beam of his grace shines out upon me, and by that light I see this Prince of darknesse, and then I finde that I have been the subject, the slave of these powers and principalities, when I thought not of them."[110] Grace illuminates the demonic, exposing one's own guilt and sin. This fusion of guilt and grace also informs Donne's understanding of the conscience, which is felt both as accusatory and as the locus of divine presence. This psychology, which differs radically from the association of interior presence with joy and love examined in chapter 3, derives from Calvin, who defines the "inward mind" as "the forum of conscience," or the "sense of divine judgment, as a witness . . . which does not allow them to hide their sins from being accused before the Judge's tribunal."[111] For Donne, the Holy Ghost is the soul within the soul, but this participation manifests itself as a "sense of sin."[112] This indwelling Spirit resembles the Freudian superego, the introjected punitive Other that generates conscience, rationality, and guilt. Donne thus explains, "every man hath a kinde of God in himselfe, such a conscience, as sometimes reproves him," a conscience Donne also identifies with *recta ratio*.[113]

This psychological formation where grace and presence manifest themselves as guilt is good because it is good to feel at fault. One should, Donne writes, be "Afraid that I have not said enough against my self, nor repented enough; Afraid that my sorrows have not been sincere."[114] "Every humble christian" must therefore constantly conclude that he is "in an evident danger of being the greatest sinner."[115]

110. Donne, *Sermons,* 10:1.541–47; compare 4:6.216–20.

111. Calvin, *Institutes,* 3.19.15; Little, *Religion, Order, and Law,* p. 123. For the equation of an essentially prohibitory conscience with the inner voice of God, see van der Leeuw, *Religion in Essence,* 2:466–67.

112. Donne, *Sermons,* 7:8.258–60.

113. Donne, *Sermons,* 7:8.73–75; 1:7.531. Donne's notion that God "is able as a Judge to minister an oath unto us, and to draw evidence from our own consciences against ourselves" (*Sermons,* 2:15.283–85) seems to align the deity with the operations of the High Commission (the chief ecclesiastical court in England), which could impose an ex officio oath upon defendants, obliging them to confess their own guilt. This oath violated one of the basic principles of common law, namely, that no one could be forced to accuse himself. See J. P. Sommerville, *Politics and Ideology in England, 1603–1640* (London, 1986), p. 192.

114. Donne, *Sermons,* 8:15.323–25. Likewise Perkins writes, "Labour to be displeased with thyself" ("A Grain of Mustard-Seed," in *Work,* p. 406).

115. Donne, *Sermons,* 1:9.638–39.

This consciousness of being at fault has particular spiritual value for Donne because it entails the perception that suffering is punishment. That is, guilt functions as a psychological lever not for reform but propitiation. One must see that all suffering results from "offending . . . God," that it is "laid upon me by the hand of God," and then "thou wilt come to him in teares."[116]

Donne freezes the posture of the individual before God into a tableau of remorse and self-reproach because spiritual relations, like economic ones, are governed by the law of scarcity; goodness and honor are limited commodities, always attained at another's expense. Hence the "literall sense" of Scripture always is "what may most deject and vilifie man, what may most exalt, and glorifie God."[117] The mutual entailment of these upward and downward pressures becomes explicit in a similar passage from another sermon where Donne observes, "the more I vilifie my selfe, the more I glorifie my God." God's honor requires human guilt, for "*Adversum me,* is *Cum Deo.*"[118] Donne valorizes guilt because whatever "layes flat the nature of man" likewise "most exalts the Grace and Glory of God."[119] But to the extent that guilt constitutes the proper attitude of a person with respect to God then Donne's contractualism is largely a fiction; if one could perform the conditions it would somehow detract from God's glory.

The spiritual importance Donne attributes to guilt also rests on his understanding of selfhood. The sermons come close to equating the self with sin. "All the imaginations of the thoughts of our hearts," he writes, "are only evill continually." All goodness comes from without the self, but "Our sins are our *own.*"[120] Donne thus represents the moment of spiritual *anagnorisis* as the discovery of the monster behind the facade of moral decency. God's punishments bring a person "into company with himselfe," where he realizes, "Lord! how have I mistaken my selfe, Am I, that thought my selfe, and passed with others,

116. Donne, *Sermons,* 8:8.340–43.

117. Donne, *Sermons,* 9:16.410–11.

118. Donne, *Sermons,* 9:13.527–28. See Calvin, *Institutes,* 1.1.2, 1.11.9, 1.12.3.

119. Donne, *Sermons,* 9:13.568–69. Charles Trinkaus thus comments on the theological requirement for moral failure in Protestantism: "With only a limited amount of exaggeration it could be said that Luther and Calvin in their separate ways sought to show how one could not lead a Christian life and still remain a Christian" (*The Scope of Renaissance Humanism* [Ann Arbor, 1983], p. 318).

120. Donne, *Sermons,* 2:6.345–47; 2:3.242; compare 9:13.419.

for a sociable, a pleasurable man, and good company; am I a leprous Adulterer, is that my name? Am I, that thought my selfe a frugall man, and a good husband . . . am I an oppressing Extortioner, is that my name?"[121] The devil occupies a surprisingly small place in Donne's theology seemingly because the self replaces Satan as the origin of evil. The two figures at times almost coalesce, the self becoming a *Spontaneus Satan,* a *Spontaneus Daemon,* for "every man hath a devill in himselfe,"[122] where "in" may mean not only "within," as if the devil were an alien presence inside the self, but also "intrinsically" (as in the phrase "lying is bad in itself"), with the implication that the devil *is* the self.

The depravity of fallen man is a Reformation commonplace,[123] but Donne's sense of personal sinfulness gains intensity because his royalism prevents moral aggression from turning outward to attack a corrupt social order. Such projection of guilt onto the demonic other characterizes the more radical or disaffected Protestants of the period,[124] but Donne almost always internalizes the enemy.[125] He thus rejects the prophetic model of preaching as a critique of power in favor of moral denunciation, where "enemies" become "sins."[126] In his fifth Prebend sermon, Donne defends this denial of politics: "I direct not your thoughts upon publique Considerations; It is not my end; It is not my way: My way and end is to bring you home to your selves, and to consider there, That we are full of weakenesses in our selves, full of enemies, sinfull tentations about us."[127] Aggression toward the self substitutes for prophetic politics. Such internalization seems habitual

121. Donne, *Sermons,* 9:13.139–49.

122. Donne, *Sermons,* 9:13.529; 2:3.418; 7:8.71–72.

123. The notion of the fallen self as demonic is particularly associated with the hard-line Lutheranism of Flacius Illyricus but can be found in Calvin as well. See Pelikan, *Reformation,* pp. 142–43; Bouwsma, *Calvin,* p. 142.

124. Donne's endless attacks on Roman Catholicism, however, can be construed as this sort of projection.

125. On the criticism of the social and ecclesiastical order in Puritan divinity, see Lake, *Moderate Puritans,* pp. 18–19; Thomas, *The Decline of Magic,* pp. 148–50; as well as Cartwright's diatribes, reproduced in John Whitgift, *Works,* 3 vols., ed. Rev. John Ayre, The Parker Society (Cambridge, 1852). Bouwsma thus notes that Calvin denounced ambition, wealth, sex, drunkenness, women, rulers, France, Spain, Henry VIII, courtiers, great merchants, cities, the lower orders, war, luxury, etc. (Bouwsma, *Calvin,* pp. 51–58). The term "demonic other" comes, of course, from Stephen Greenblatt, *Renaissance Self-Fashioning from More to Shakespeare* (Chicago, 1980).

126. Donne, *Sermons,* 2:14.589–600; 8:8.567.

127. Donne, *Sermons,* 8:4.681–85.

in Donne's thought; thus his repeated claim that suffering is punishment for sin manifests the same tendency to introject external badness rather than the more familiar strategy of projecting internal hostility.

Yet this depoliticized treatment of sin at the literal level enables Donne's characteristic politicized theology. Political discourse shifts from temporal to spiritual existence, shaping the analysis of sin and guilt along absolutist lines. Hence Donne speaks of sin as the violation of an "infinite Majesty."[128] It is like throwing down the statue of a king, which the king himself had set up in the middle of his own city, and, Donne asks, "How will this King take it, . . . to have his statue thrown down? . . . How would this King take it . . . if any other Statue, especially the Statue of his enemy, should be set up in this place?"[129] Sin is not merely wrongdoing or even the violation of a law but a personal affront to a powerful royal Other. As such it must be negated by an equally personal and political submission: "The Worme [must] . . . licke his foote that treads upon him."[130]

Donne's valorization of guilt, his depiction of a demonic selfhood, and vilification of man belong to the discourse of absolutist theology. They define the human end of a relationship based on the principles of power and submission. Although I do not want to discuss Donne's treatment of social relations at any length, it seems worth pointing out that he represents the same principles as operating in the temporal sphere. That is, like most Renaissance social theorists, he configures society into a vertical system based on superiority and inferiority, the governors and the governed.[131] But Donne differs from someone like Hooker by depicting these hierarchical relationships less in terms of order than of domination. Hence, while most Renaissance thinkers saw the family as the primary social unit, Donne considers the master/slave relation to be the primal human bond. An undated christening sermon argues that "because the principall foundation, and preservation of all States . . . is *power* . . . the first relation was between *Prince*

128. Donne, *Sermons*, 8:8.839–40.

129. Donne, *Sermons*, 9:2.534–43.

130. Donne, *Sermons*, 5:18.227–28.

131. For example, the *Shorter Catechism* of 1644 expounds the fifth commandment as requiring "the preserving the honour and performing the duties, belonging to every one in their several places and relations, as Superiors, Inferiors or Equals" (quoted in Laslett, *The World We Have Lost*, p. 218).

and *Subject*." Donne goes on to note that the second relation was between husband and wife, the third between parents and children. He then paraphrases the foregoing: "from that beginning to the end of the world, these three relations, of *Master* and *Servant, Man* and *Wife, Father* and *Children,* have been . . . the elements of all society."[132] Apparently, the relation between prince and subject is interchangeable with that between master and servant, and this is the original human relationship because the most evidently structured by power.[133] Donne's assertion of the priority of relations based on domination and subordination informs his depiction of man's prefallen condition, for, he notes, man was given power over the beasts before the creation of Eve. He thus imagines Paradise as the perfect subjection of emotions, animals, and women.[134] In particular, understanding is power, and thus man's primal dominion over animals derives from his superior intelligence; by "understanding them, and comprehending them, we master them." Knowledge allows enslavement of the other by concealing from that other its true condition; hence creatures "are content to thanke us, if we afford them any rest, or any food; who, if they understood us, as well, as we doe them, might teare our meate out of our throates; nay teare out our throates for their meat."[135]

Donne likewise treats marital relations in terms of power. He thus glosses woman's inferiority to man as signifying that "she must *not Governe*" but "*be content to learn in silence with all subjection,*" and he immediately equates female subjection with social subordination. Women and the poor must learn to "content" themselves "with that manner and that measure that [God] . . . gives."[136] Even marital love operates in the categories of hierarchical power: "the love of husband to the wife, is a burthen, a submitting, a descent"[137]—and it is also a form of political control. As the prince must lower himself to consider

132. Donne, *Sermons,* 5:5.13–24.

133. The notion that even Edenic relations were structured by "superioritie and subjection" seems to have been widespread in English Reformation thought. See Sommerville, *Politics and Ideology,* pp. 17–19; Peter G. Lake, *Anglicans and Puritans? Presbyterianism and English Conformist Thought from Whitgift to Hooker* (London, 1988), p. 135; and, of course, *Paradise Lost.*

134. Donne, *Sermons,* 7:14.346–53.

135. Donne, *Sermons,* 9:2.570–95.

136. Donne, *Sermons,* 2:17.74, 347–48, 364–65.

137. Donne, *Sermons,* 5:5.68–69.

the safety of his subjects, so "such a subjection is that of a Husband, who is bound to study his wife, and rectify all her infirmities."[138] "Study" here is reminiscent of Donne's equation of understanding and power mentioned above; the husband endeavors to comprehend his wife so he can "rectify" her—and keep her from tearing his throat. Donne does insist that both political and marital domination be moderated by compassion, but the reason he offers is telling: "if the servant, the wife, the sonne be oppressed, worne out, annihilated, there is no such thing left as a Master, or a husband, or a father."[139] That is, the superior needs an inferior in order to exercise his superiority.

A complete picture of Donne's "sociology" would produce a less harsh effect. Like many Protestant thinkers, Donne's notions on this matter can generally be summed up under the heading of vocation. He repeatedly argues that everyone (including young aristocrats) must have a vocation and must perform it faithfully and honestly, not cheating, not oppressing, not exploiting others. His sermons thus exhibit far more interest in social morality than those of either Andrewes or Hooker. But the passages discussed above suggest that alongside this ethics of vocation, Donne holds a view of social relations parallel to his view of spiritual (and political) ones, a view based on the dynamics of power and submission.

THE RELIGION OF GUILT

> Das Schaudern ist der Menschheit bestes Teil.
> Goethe

> Those are my best dayes, when I shake with feare.
> Donne, *Holy Sonnets*

These dynamics push Donne's conception of God close to the demonic or tyrannical, a conclusion he recognizes and resists—apparently successfully since he was not tried for heresy but became one of the most acclaimed preachers of his day. Donne always maintains with unequivocal clarity that God is not immoral or cruel.[140] In fact, he precludes such an inference with a theological catch-22: it is the wicked

138. Donne, *Sermons,* 5:5.136–39.
139. Donne, *Sermons,* 5:5.39–41.
140. For example, *Sermons,* 5:4.306–8; 7:2.45, 67; 8:15.400–402; 9:13.344–45.

who see God as a tyrant, and hence those who claim that God oppresses them unjustly prove, by their complaint, the justice of their punishment.[141] But Donne's denial that God is a monster does not answer the problem of why he allowed such suspicions to arise.

At times, the threateningly absolute power of God in these sermons seems contained by the conventional Protestant Law-to-Gospel dialectic, where the God of the Old Testament is cast as punitive justice in contrast to Christ's love revealed in the New.[142] Donne will therefore sometimes portray the relation between Christ and man in a wholly nonpolitical, nonanalogical fashion. For instance, he depicts the agon between Job and God in forensic terms, but as he starts to consider God as Christ the judicial analogy undergoes a sea change; Christ is the judge, but he is also the witness for the defendant, and he is not only judge and witness but the defendant himself:

> He that is my Witnesse, is my Judge, and the same person is my Jesus, my Saviour, my Redeemer; He that hath taken my nature, He that hath given me his blood. So that he is my Witnesse, in his owne cause, and my Judge, but of his owne Title, and will, in me, preserve himselfe.[143]

When Donne speaks of Christ, he will begin to draw on the language of participation characteristic of Andrewes: "we are not onely His, but He"; "Christ is *Idem homo cum te,* the same man that thou art, so thou art *Idem spiritus cum Domino,* the same spirit that he is."[144] In such passages, identity replaces power as the mode of relation.

But Donne's theology is not uniformly Christocentric in this sense. Rather, he portrays Christ in the context of absolutist power relations as often as those of paradox and participation. An early Lincoln's Inn sermon thus observes that "by Christs taking my sins, I am made a *servant of my God . . .* a *vassall,* a *Tributary* debtor to God."[145] Redemption thus entails enslavement. In general, Donne perceives Christianity as having increased man's moral burden, placing him under heavier obligations. In a late sermon preached at St. Dunstan's, he makes what appears to be an original claim (at least, I have never

141. Donne, *Sermons,* 9:18.418–23.
142. Donne, *Sermons,* 2:8.194–96; 8:8.532–45.
143. Donne, *Sermons,* 9:9.594–617.
144. Donne, *Sermons,* 9:16.690–91; 2:12.262–64.
145. Donne, *Sermons,* 2:5.261–63.

seen it elsewhere) that human suffering is a "re-crucifixion" imposed as a penalty for our crucifixion of Christ. Therefore, although "we think to enjoy" the death of Christ, "God would have us doe it over again. . . . All being guilty of Christs death, there lies an obligation upon us all, to fulfill his sufferings. And this is the *generality* of afflictions, as we consider them in their own nature."[146] Guilt, pain, fear, domination, servitude are as much part of Donne's understanding of specifically Christian relations as they are of his theology as a whole.

The meaning of absolutist theology does not lie in its Christian negation but can best be approached by returning to the function of guilt. Guilt, in Donne, arises from the combination of a demand for obedience with a denial of its possibility or, even, insofar as it implies merit and self-sufficiency, desirability. One must be and cannot be perfect. The tension between the demand and the denial creates an impasse catapulting the individual out of the categories of morality back into the psychodynamics of personal power, where even the anger of God "hath a *face*."[147] Moral failure then creates guilt, but guilt here is not paralyzing but creative insofar as it forces the sinner to seek God's face.[148] Guilt, that is, propels the individual into the *personal* relations of propitiation, dependency, and submission—the struggle to pacify God by repentance, the desire to approach God in tears and have Him wipe them away, the humble pleading not for pardon but only a reprieve, the endeavor to please.[149] Moreover, such submission of the guilty self expresses not only fear of divine power but the longing for it; so Donne pleads "but yet Lord, looke more particularly upon me, and appropriate thy selfe to me, to me . . . as I am I, as I am this sinner that confesses now . . . that begs thy mercy now."[150] G. K. Chesterton has elegantly expressed this crucial connection between the apprehension of power as *personal* and prostrate submission:

> As long as a tree is a tree, it is a top-heavy monster with a hundred arms, a thousand tongues, and only one leg. But so long as a tree is a tree, it does not frighten us at all. It begins to be something alien, to be some-

146. Donne, *Sermons*, 10:9.161–79.
147. Donne, *Sermons*, 2:2.146.
148. In the opening chapter of the *Institutes*, Calvin similarly argues that the recognition of our own miserable sinfulness drives us to seek God. See also van der Leeuw, *Religion in Essence*, 2:523.
149. Donne, *Sermons*, 8:8.341–49, 831; 5:15.355–62; 9:17.481–82.
150. Donne, *Sermons*, 5:15.400–403.

> thing strange, only when it looks like ourselves. When a tree really looks like a man our knees knock under us. And when the whole universe looks like a man we fall on our faces."[151]

The configuration of spirituality in such highly personal and relational terms does not, of course, remove it from the context of absolutist politics, where all the ancient symbolism and pageantry surrounding the monarch visibly maintained the association of power with an individual figure. This is, after all, the age of personal rule. On every level, from the household to the nation, power adhered in and was exercised by individuals rather than through large impersonal, bureaucratic systems.[152] When such power threatened, one responded in personal terms by attempting to appease and propitiate the hostile figure—not in systemic terms by forming a union. Perkins's *A Dialogue of the State of a Christian Man* preserves a remarkable vignette of such social dynamics. One Timotheus complains to his religious preceptor, Eusebius, that his landlord is raising rents and driving him to beggary; to which Eusebius replies,

> And my counsel is that you give your landlord now and then a capon, now a goose and, if you are able, a lamb or a calf; and let your wife visit your landlady now and then with spiced cakes, with apples, pears, cherries and suchlike; and be you ready with your oxen or horses, five or six times in the year, to fetch home their wood, to plough their land. Then, no doubt, God may soften their hearts and move them to have some pity and compassion on your poor estate.[153]

One wonders why God requires these preliminary services. (One also wonders exactly what the tenants of the earl of Pembroke were thinking when they brought their rural cakes and nuts to Penshurst.) But what is relevant for our purposes is Perkins's apparently unquestioning acceptance of the model of propitiation as a strategy for dealing with power.

151. G. K. Chesterton, *Heretics,* p. 152; quoted in van der Leeuw, *Religion in Essence,* 1:90.

152. Laslett, *The World We Have Lost,* p. 17.

153. Perkins, "A Dialogue," in *Work,* p. 384. The passage is taken from Tyndale, *Exposition on Matthew* in *Expositions and Notes,* pp. 21, 59. See also Greville's 1603 letter to Cecil, quoted in Ronald Rebholz, *The Life of Fulke Greville, First Lord Brooke* (Oxford, 1971), pp. 156–57. Such propitiation seems to have been a regular part of social relations between inferiors and superiors.

In Renaissance society, power was almost always personal power. Jobs were secured by patronage instead of standardized tests, as Donne knew only too well.[154] Most businesses were family affairs, servants and apprentices being counted as members of the household rather than employees. If this society was stratified and authoritarian, it was also very small-scale and intimate by modern standards, and such personalization of power within small, relatively stable units cannot but have affected power relations by embedding them within a complex psychosocial web of needs and desires. The English monarchy and English society located authority within personal relationships and thus bound power to the basic human desire to be "in relation."

This bond is fundamental to Donne's theology. Insofar as guilt drives the sinner into a relationship with power, it is felt as a positive emotion, where the need for personal contact outweighs the fear of punishment. Donne thus imagines King David responding to God's threats of "afflictions and tribulations": "Nay but Lord, doe Thou doe it, do it how Thou wilt, but doe Thou doe it: Thy corrosives are better then others fomentations; Thy bitternesses sweeter then others honey."[155] The experience of guilt is terrifying because it threatens the loss of love, of relation, while simultaneously intensifying the need for it. The offense committed (or even contemplated) against a loved one—and this is visible even in children and dogs—produces both fear of rejection and a longing for pardon and restoration of bonds. In contrast to modern attempts to extricate theological guilt from this psychological matrix,[156] Donnean spirituality remains suffused with primary, almost primal, affectivities. The fear of being left alone and the corresponding desire for any contact with God, even painful, forms a steady refrain in Donne's writings. In a sermon preached before King Charles he exclaims, "let *God* handle me how he will, so hee *cast* mee not out of his hands: I had rather *God* frownd upon mee,

154. On Donne's sense of overwhelming dependence on his patrons, especially King James, see Goldberg, *James I*, pp. 211ff. John Stachniewski draws a suggestive parallel between Donne's experience of the Jacobean patronage system and his dark and uneasy Calvinism ("The Despair of Donne's Holy Sonnets," *English Literary History* 48 [1981]: 702–3).

155. Donne, *Sermons*, 5:15.369–71.

156. For example, John McKenzie defines a "healthy sense of guilt" as motivated not by the fear of losing the love of one's parents but by the sense that what one has done is morally wrong (*Guilt: Its Meaning and Significance* [New York, 1962], p. 47). Donne would not have made such a distinction.

then not looke upon me; and I had rather God pursued mee, then left mee to my selfe."[157] A similar passage occurs in one of the undated sermons on the penitential psalms: "As long as I have God by the hand, and feele his loving care of me, I can admit any waight of his hand; any fornace of his heating."[158]

Guilt forces one into dependence on a power felt as both overpowering and personal and therefore as "aweful" in both its ancient and modern senses. The cultural basis for this apprehension of power manifests itself in James's quite conventional analogues for his own authority: father, husband, head. As noted previously, these metaphors all connote both absolute dominion over the other (child, wife, body) and loving care for that other. In particular, the father has both *patriae potestas,* the power of life and death, over his children and a deep natural affection for them; he cares for them more than for himself. The royal metaphors thus depict a power that is inherently ambivalent, a fusion of unlimited, fearful authority and protective love. But this cultural representation throws us back on the problem of bivalent co-option, for the particular ambivalence of Stuart absolutism was in no sense a Stuart invention but has a long history. Absolutist theology opens out on to what Rudolph Otto called the "idea of the holy."

Ambivalence permeates the human response to holiness. It itself has deep psychological roots. The infant who screams for his mother's breast simultaneously experiences love, aggression, and dependence. Desire for the all-powerful yet terrifyingly absent parent, anger at her absence, and a sense of one's helpless dependency present themselves to consciousness at the same moment.[159] This original ambivalence seems to structure the human encounter with the divine parent. According to the two seminal studies of religious phenomenology, Otto's *Idea of the Holy* and G. van der Leeuw's *Religion in Essence and Manifestation,* religion originates in the apprehension of absolute and mysterious Power. It "starts from a consciousness of the absolute superiority or supremacy of a power other than myself. . . . 'par le

157. Donne, *Sermons,* 7:2.345–48; compare 10:9.717–22.

158. Donne, *Sermons,* 5:16.624–26. The same longing for domination appears in Andrewes's *Private Devotions:* "Hold me in with bit and bridle, when I keep not close to Thee. *P. Hos.* ii.6. O Lord, compel me to come in unto Thee. *S. Luke* xiv.23" (*Works,* 11:256).

159. Joan Riviere, "Hate, Greed, and Agression," in Joan Riviere and Melanie Klein, *Love, Hate, and Reparation* (New York, 1964), pp. 8–9; McKenzie, *Guilt,* pp. 29–34.

sentiment d'une *domination* universelle, invincible.'"[160] This confrontation with Power produces fear, horror, dread, and aversion—and the attempt either to propitiate or escape its *tremenda majestas*. The sacred is dangerous, taboo, demonic.[161] The appropriate response to such Power is, of course, the only response to absolute power—submission. Van der Leeuw's description of this response reverts almost inevitably to the political analogies inseparable from (but not causally prior to) the confrontation with sacred Power: "before Power man humbles himself. God is *Lord*. . . . He is the king who owns the land and whom all men must serve . . . [who requires] not only complete submission but also readiness for service, obedience."[162] But (and this is the crucial part) sacred Power simultaneously evokes what would seem to be incompatible emotions. Van der Leeuw writes,

> In the human soul, then, Power awakens a profound feeling of awe which manifests itself both as fear and as being attracted. There is no religion whatever without terror, but equally none without love, or that *nuance* of being attracted. . . . Physical shuddering, ghostly horror, fear, sudden terror, reverence, humility, adoration, profound apprehension, enthusiasm—all these lie *in nuce* within the awe experienced in the presence of Power.[163]

As in infancy terrifying dependence and desire arise together, so religious fear contains an element of love, and love an element of fear, or as Donne himself puts it: "those who have Authority over others [cannot] . . . be lov'd so as they should, except they be fear'd. . . . If you take away due Fear, you take away true Love."[164] The relation of man to Power thus betrays an essential ambivalence, although one that post-Enlightenment theology, with its harmlessly benevolent deity, attempted to mask. But in the presence of God, primitives and Protestants were "seized with dread," and yet loved their dread and worshiped it and desired to be united to it.[165] The paradoxical ambivalence that constitutes the experience of the holy lies at the center of the theology of power and submission—Donne's absolutist theology.

160. Rudolph Otto, *The Idea of the Holy*, trans. John W. Harvey (New York, 1958), pp. 21–22; van der Leeuw, *Religion in Essence*, 1:27.

161. Van der Leeuw, *Religion in Essence*, 1:44, 47.

162. Van der Leeuw, *Religion in Essence*, 2:472.

163. Van der Leeuw, *Religion in Essence*, 1:48; compare Otto, *Idea of the Holy*, p. 31.

164. See Donne, *Sermons*, 1:4.388–90; Van der Leeuw, *Religion in Essence*, 2:465.

165. Van der Leeuw, *Religion in Essence*, 1:49; 2:456; compare Otto, *Idea of the Holy*, p. 22.

For Donne, sacred Power demands a submission that must be understood in the context of this ambivalence. Submission here is not a half-resentful, half-defiant obedience to an oppressive system, the master/slave model implicit in most modern discussions of power relations, but almost a mode of desire. The terror at divine power is bound up with a longing to be overpowered. The language of spiritual politics in Donne is thus suffused by an erotic and infantile affectivity. The self longs for a childlike passivity. Donne imagines God urging the self toward autonomy and independence, to which the self replies in horror, "*Domine Tu,* Lord put me not over to the catechizing of Nature . . . but take me into thine owne hands, do Thou, Thou, that is to be done upon me."[166] This self (or soul), which Donne at times considers "female," desires dependence and submission because they entail "being mastered," being cared for by God: "God is the Potter: if God will be that, I am well content to be this: let me be any thing, so that I am be from my God. I am as well content to be a sheep, as a Lion, so God will be my Shepheard."[167]

This desire for passivity at times modulates into a dramatic, and occasionally macabre, eroticism. Donne speaks of desiring to "awake at midnight, and embrace God in mine armes," although he immediately attempts to deny the sexual implications of this image by glossing "embrace" as "that is, receive God into my thoughts."[168] Similarly he speaks of wanting to "Dye in [God's] . . . armes,"[169] where the secondary, sexual meaning of "die" is heightened by the physicality of "armes." The longing to be almost sexually overcome is particularly associated with Christ's body. His body "covers me by touching me," "cover," like "die," frequently having erotic undertones in the seventeenth century.[170] Christ covers sin, "by comming to me, by spreading himself upon me . . . Mouth to mouth, Hand to hand."[171] Some-

166. Donne, *Sermons,* 5:337–48.
167. Donne, *Sermons,* 9:12.190–200; 9:1.577–80.
168. Donne, *Sermons,* 9:8.249–50.
169. Donne, *Sermons,* 9:11.833.
170. Donne, *Sermons,* 9:11.421. There is also perhaps an allusion here to the husband's "coverture" of his wife, "coverture" being a legal term referring to a husband's protection of and authority over his wife. See Caroline Walker Bynum, "The Body of Christ in the Later Middle Ages: A Reply to Leo Steinberg," however, for the crucially important distinction between premodern sensuous spirituality and our own tendency to read such sensuousness as repressed sexuality (*Renaissance Quarterly* 39 (1986): 406–7 and passim).
171. Donne, *Sermons,* 9:11.416–18.

times it is the soul that spreads itself on Christ: "so when my crosses have carried mee up to my Saviours Crosse, I put my hands into his hands, and hang upon his nailes, I put mine eyes upon his. . . . I put my mouth upon his mouth."[172] Almost the same passage occurs at the end of Donne's final sermon, *Death's Duel:* "There wee leave you in that *blessed dependancy,* to *hang* upon *him* that *hangs* upon the *Crosse,* there *bath* in his *teares,* there *suck* at his *woundes.*"[173] With "suck," the erotic image of covering coalesces with that of infantile dependency. The desire to hang upon the beloved's mouth or to suck at his wounded side, the desires of the gendered anima and the infant, are parallel: cravings for submission to power, for intimacy and union with the dread beloved.[174]

Donne neither rejects nor rationalizes his depiction of God as destructive power; rather, these passages simply stand alongside those of "blessed dependancy." As in Otto and van der Leeuw, fear and love are inextricable rather than antithetical responses to the holy. Such ambivalence intensifies when the images of violence and love fuse, when God's love borders on rape. The Holy Ghost falls upon men "as a Hawk upon a prey, it desires and it will possesse that it falls upon; as an Army into a Countrey, it Conquers, and it Governes where it fals."[175] As in *Holy Sonnet* 14, "Batter my Heart," the self desires God to force and ravish it; God's love is a mode of power. "He loves us, but with a Powerfull, a Majesticall, an Imperiall, a Commanding love; He offers those, whom he makes his, his grace; but so, as he sometimes will not be denyed."[176] The irresistibility of grace reflects God's masculine potency—a sort of absolutist erotics. But the fear aroused by the sense of imminent violation is deflected by the longing for violence, a sexual violence significantly associated with the political discourse of majesty, empire, and command. For Donne as for James, king, husband, and father (and, correspondingly, subject, wife, and child) interchangeably express the same substance of power.

172. Donne, *Sermons,* 2:14.480–85.

173. Donne, *Sermons,* 10:11.668–70.

174. For the medieval antecedents of such images, see Caroline Walker Bynum, *Jesus as Mother: Studies in the Spirituality of the High Middle Ages* (Berkeley, 1982), pp. 123, 152. Stachniewski interprets these longings for passivity as "masochistic strivings"—a term that seems to stigmatize rather than elucidate them ("Despair," pp. 688–89).

175. Donne, *Sermons,* 5:1.511–13.

176. Donne, *Sermons,* 9:3.430–33.

Donne's understanding of the divine/human relation is most clearly articulated in one of the late sermons on the penitential psalms. Toward the end he begins a long passage on the terrifying, crushing pressure of God's hand, "pushing away, and keeping downe." For those who forget or only half-detest their sins, "The hand of God will grow heavy upon them. . . . The hand of God shall grow heavy upon a silent sinner." If he tries to comfort himself with riches or friends or philosophy, "the hand of divine Justice shall grow heavy upon him," and so forth, until there is no refuge: "The hand of God will grow heavy upon them every way, and stop every issue, every posterne, every sally, every means of escape." Then follows a remarkable passage:

> But that which is peculiar to the Children of God, is, That when the hand of God is upon them, they shall know it to be the hand of God, and take hold even of that oppressing hand, and not let it goe, till they have received a Blessing from it, that is, raysed themselves even by that heavy and oppressing hand of his, even in that affliction.[177]

The ideal moment, the moment of spiritual "success," is figured in terms of drastic confrontation with personal power, with that anthropomorphic "hand" characteristic of Donne's theological imagination.[178] The children of God cling in utter submission yet with all the urgency of their need. The act of submission is at the same time aggressive; the children refuse to let go until they have gotten what they desire—and yet the aggression itself expresses a kind of wild trust that the demonic oppressor can be appeased.[179] They thus grasp the hand of the torturer as it pushes them down and away, and this gesture of vulnerability to its heavy pressure simultaneously "rases" or obliterates the self and "raises" it.[180]

The intersection of dependence, terror, and adoration here pertains both to the ontogeny as well as the phylogeny of faith—to its sources in the original deprivation of the maternal breast as well as to the

177. Donne, *Sermons,* 9:12.670–712.

178. Interestingly, Donne also uses the hand metaphor to describe King James's role in his life. See Goldberg, *James I,* pp. 212–14.

179. The passage is an allusion to the story of Jacob wrestling with the angel in Gen. 32:24–30. The notion of prayer as an agon appears frequently in Donne's sermons, for example, 2:8.243–48; 2:10.254–60; 5.18.1–15; 5:11.269–74.

180. See Greenblatt, *Self-Fashioning,* p. 123.

phenomenologists' "idea of the holy" with its interpenetration of dread and love. Donne preserves the full ambivalence and complexity of a seemingly primal experience of the Other, which while based on the dynamics of power and submission, can scarcely be called political in the modern sense. Rather, he seems to be drawing on more archaic and elemental strata of psychic life, privileging, as it were, a drastic affectivity permeated with infantile and erotic longings and, above all, the desire for personal relation.[181] This is scarcely Anglican moralism or Anglican reticence, although it is easy to see the rise of rational religion, both in its latitudinarian and deistic strains, as an "oppositional discourse" to this theology of suffocatingly immediate contact and fierce emotionality. Rational religion, like rational politics, is based on law, on morality. For Donne, the need to feel the power of God's hand and the protection of His covering body—and also to feel His distant and kingly majesty—remains paramount. As Hans Blumenberg has remarked, "rationalism . . . can base its mode of operation on impersonal 'mechanisms.' . . . Voluntarism is necessarily dependent on a subject, be it only a fictional one. Hence it requires 'persons.'"[182] This is messy religion, religion still implicated in social forms and subconscious needs.

This messy religion has its counterpart in messy politics; James is no more inclined to sever kings from nursing fathers, loving husbands, and a voluntarist God than Donne is inclined to dissociate God from kings, fathers, and husbands. But Donne's God is both duplicate and supplement, the latter in two senses. That is, while theological relations, like political ones, rest on the dynamics of power and submission, in theology these dynamics are idealized and unrestrained. They are idealized in that, unlike Perkins's landlord, God never betrays those who seek Him; if one turns to Him "his mercy shall returne to thee."[183] And while "The Kings of the earth are faire and glorious resemblances of the King of heaven," the former always refuse to forgive some offenses, but the latter "sweares by himselfe, That there

181. The excitement and joy of being forced to obey also appears in Calvin, for example, "By this power [of divine majesty] we are drawn and inflamed, knowingly and willingly, to obey him, yet also more vitally and more effectively than by mere human willing or knowing" (*Institutes*, 1.8.5).

182. Blumenberg, *The Modern Age*, pp. 99–100.

183. Donne, *Sermons*, 5:18.222.

is no sinner but he can, and would pardon."[184] Donne's frustrations as a courtier and seeker of patronage among the great may lie behind his insistence that submission to God—licking the foot that treads on you—invariably releases love, acceptance, and forgiveness. Donne can risk the full play of power relations in his depiction of God, because here—and "if true, here only"—James's ideal figure of the good father-king exists.[185] But the relations between man and God in Donne are also supplemental in the same way that they are in Herbert. They permit an emotional space unconstrained by cultural suspicions and repressions because *coram Deo* human self-exposure and vulnerability are not penalized; if a person confesses to a judge, he will be punished, but "The mystery of the Kingdome of heaven, is, That onely the Declaring . . . of my sins, possesses me of the Kingdome of heaven."[186] This mystery gives "political theology" its psychological "point" because it allows submission unrestrained by fear of opprobrium, allows the longings for passivity and dependence, the expressions of need, fear, self-loathing, misery, childlike trust, guilt, and so forth—all affects generally prohibited in ordinary social or political interaction, where defensiveness seems to have been the norm.

THE EYE OF THE BEHOLDER

In Donne, the idealization of power relations is never innocent. Andrewes's prose creates the impression that participation is an experiential given, an intuited relation rather than an explanation imposed on the contents of perception. This is not the case with Donne, who makes it quite clear that correct understanding of divine power depends on a prior interpretive act. The goodness of God is not a given but follows from a conscious mystification of power relations. Like Calvin—and like King James—he holds that absolute authority must be *perceived* as loving and caring.[187] This perception is the premise of all patriarchal models of power—that the one who rules and therefore

184. Donne, *Sermons*, 5:3.284–94.

185. John Milton, *Paradise Lost*, in *John Milton: Complete Poetry and Major Prose*, ed. Merritt Y. Hughes (New York, 1957), 4.251.

186. Donne, *Sermons*, 9:13.6–12.

187. See, for example, Calvin, *Institutes* 1.3.2. Compare Trinkaus, *The Scope*, pp. 318–19.

punishes also loves. If God slays his people, "yet, that God, their Father weepes over the slaughter."[188] The *rex tremendae maiestatis* is also the *fons pietatis,* and Donne always insists on the identity of the God who strikes and the God of love and mercy. His punishments are always medicinal; "God strikes so, as that when he strikes, he strikes a fire, and lights him a candle, to see his presence by."[189]

But, in addition, Donne identifies the crucial responsibility of the believer as apprehending this identity of father and oppressor. If one can see pain as love, if one can, that is, mystify power, then one belongs to the elect.[190] The godly "finde" that their suffering comes from "Gods hand"; they "finde the hand of God in adversity, and love it," for it is "not every mans case, to mend by Gods corrections; onely *the poore of the sheep,* the broken-hearted, the contrite spirit . . . could make that good use of affliction, as to finde *Gods hand.*"[191] The repeated "finde" suggests that God's presence is not a datum of consciousness but a reconstruction of an experience that could be constructed differently. In similar fashion, Donne elsewhere affirms that the faithful must "feele the hand of a father" and "know" its meaning or be able to "say" that tribulations are sacraments and "see" that they enable salvation.[192] The verbs "say," "feel," "find," and "see" all suggest the active role of the believer in carrying out this mystification of the power that inflicts suffering. Such suffering must become one's "owne *red glasse*" through which one can then "see Christ, in that colour too."[193] Meaning is never simply given in experience but depends on interpretation.

Yet at times a certain amount of ambiguity emerges here, for interpretation is not always in one's own control; one cannot, that is,

188. Donne, *Sermons,* 7:9.222–24.

189. Donne, *Sermons,* 4:6.365–66; compare 8:8.681–98.

190. This seems to have been a regular feature of Puritan preaching. In *Moderate Puritans,* Peter Lake thus writes, "This difference in God's intentions in chastising the righteous and the wicked was paralleled by the very different subjective response of those two groups to the experience of affliction. . . . God's people, confronted by the seemingly impenetrable palimpsest of events had to preserve an interpretation of these events, and in particular of their own fate within them, that centred on the providence of God. . . . But they had to do this in the face of rival interpretations put forward by the ungodly. External reality was not theirs by right, rather they had to appropriate it" (pp. 124–26).

191. Donne, *Sermons,* 9:18.625; 9:12.739; 10:9.437–40.

192. Donne, *Sermons,* 8:14.307–12; 8:2.297–305.

193. Donne, *Sermons,* 4:6.426–27.

determine how or what he will see or how God will appear to him. This uncertainty follows from Donne's general insistence on the vulnerability of psychic life, making both emotional and cognitive states contingent on divine activity.

> I am not able of my selfe to dye that glasse, that spectacle, thorow which I looke upon this God, in what colour I will; whether this glasse shall be black, through my despaire, and so I shall see God in the cloud of my sinnes, or red in the blood of Christ Jesus, and I shall see God in a Bath of the blood of his Sonne, whether I shall see God as a Dove with an Olive branch . . . or as an Eagle, a vulture to prey, and to prey everlastingly upon mee . . . whether his purpose bee to restore mee, or to consume me, I, I of my selfe cannot tell. I cannot look upon God, in what line I will, nor take hold of God, by what handle I will.[194]

For Donne, as for Luther, as we see God so He is for us; the dove and the vulture constitute equally "real" divine self-presentations.[195] Mystification is essential because it forms the precondition for divine love, but, in this passage at least, it is not something one can choose.

Donne, however, rarely toys with these ambiguities of perception. Instead, his interests lie in stressing the paradoxical results of interpretation. That is, a person must see and feel not only that the power that inflicts pain is also loving, but that the very act of striking is a gesture of love. Human suffering results from divine *caritas,* for the "Sharp arrowes" which wound us come "out of the sweet hand of God."[196] God's arrows contain "a *Canticle,* a *love-song,* an *Epithalamion,* a *marriage song* of God, to our souls, wrapped up, if wee would open it, and read it."[197] Domination and punishment in theology are like objects approaching the speed of light; they lose their ordinary nature, and suddenly the relations of time and space, of power and pain, become paradoxical and unfamiliar. While Donne's radical Protestant monotheism leads him to see God as the cause of suffering, God's terrifying power, in turn, transmutes into tenderness. The torturer is also the healer, or, perhaps more accurately, one must see the torturer as the healer. Hence faith is largely a matter of being able to appreciate paradoxes: that God cuts us "into peeces" in order to sew us together

194. Donne, *Sermons,* 8:4.486–98.
195. Tillich, *Christian Thought,* p. 246.
196. Donne, *Sermons,* 8:8.879–80.
197. Donne, *Sermons,* 2:1.698–700.

again, that He breaks our bones "to set them strayter."[198] While we "are fishes reserved for that great Mariage-feast," and therefore presumably designed to be consumed, each fish is "a ghest too," for "whosoever is served in at the table, sits at the table."[199] Such paradoxes are rooted not only in the conviction that God controls all events, both good and bad, but also that all events are signs of His love and justice and mercy. God causes everything and everything He causes is significant. Thus Donne writes, "All comes from Gods hand; and from his hand, by way of hand-writing, by way of letter, and instruction to us."[200] But if all events are divine messages—and in the passage immediately preceding this quotation Donne names the defeat of the Armada, the Gunpowder Plot, and the cessation of the plague—then there is no space left for the operations of natural law.[201] Indeed, the attempt to propose natural explanations, as, for example, to "say the winds delivered us" from the Armada, implies a disbelief in God's power and "present judgements."[202]

Insofar as events are signs—and mostly encoded, paradoxical signs—they require interpretation. One must break open the arrow and read the love message hidden inside. But if paradox and interpretation are related to each other, they are also both related to power. Insofar as divine self-presentation is darkly encoded, a message "delivered mysteriously, and with much reservation, and in-intelligiblenesse," it is a form of power, creating "halfe-horror and amazement." Thus "Parables, and comparisons of a remote signification, were called by the Jews, *Potestates,* Powers, Powerfull insinuations." Interpretation likewise is a form of power. The priests who know the meaning of the "dark sayings" possess authority over others, placing "a necessity upon [their followers] . . . of returning againe to them, for the interpretation and signification of those darke Parables."[203] But interpretation also involves submission. "Many a man," Donne remarks, "lets the *Bible* dust, and rust, because the Bible hath a kinde of majesty, and prerogative, and command over a man, it will not be jested

198. Donne, *Sermons,* 9:9.139–40; 7:2.341–42.

199. Donne, *Sermons,* 2:14.833–35.

200. Donne, *Sermons,* 8:13.497–99.

201. Calvin, *Institutes,* 1.16.2; 1:17.7–10; Tillich, *Christian Thought,* p. 259; Bouwsma, *Calvin,* pp. 33, 164; Thomas, *The Decline of Magic,* pp. 79, 83.

202. Donne, *Sermons,* 8:13.471–88.

203. Donne, *Sermons,* 7:12.526–77.

withall."[204] To undertake to interpret implies the prior acknowledgment that one dwells within a master narrative in which all events are pedagogic signs, for if there were no narrative, there would be nothing to interpret. Conversely, God's power is manifest in His ability to make signification; He not only does everything but ascribes meanings and plots the didactic narrative of crime and punishment that constitutes national history and individual biographies. "God writes to the King," but only the king can give the "interpretation of that judgement"; nevertheless "God writes to me too; and that letter I will open, and read that letter; I will take knowledge that it is Gods hand to me, and I will study the will of God to me in that letter."[205] By reading events, one discovers the authorial intention behind them, but since "intention" here means "will," reading necessarily involves submission to *author*ity.

ESCAPE TO FREEDOM

Donne's treatment of sin in fact makes clear this connection between authority and authorship. While he frequently depicts sin politically as rebellion against divine law and governance, he will also speak of it as the attempt to escape from a claustrophobic governing narrative. Sin is the refusal to interpret, to admit that the event is a sign. And it becomes "desperate and irrecoverable" precisely when the offender refuses to see God's punishments as punishments rather than bad luck. Then "God cannot breake us with his corrections, but that we will attribute them to some naturall, to some accidentall causes, and never thinke of Gods judgements, which are the true cause of these afflictions."[206] The sinner is the secular individual, who when "Thunder from heaven burns his Barns," says, "What luck was this? if it had fallen but ten foot short or over, my barns had been safe: whereas his former blasphemings of the Name of God drew down that Thunder upon that house, as it was his."[207] Although Donne never dissociates

204. Donne, *Sermons,* 4:6.111–14.
205. Donne, *Sermons,* 8:13.504–14.
206. Donne, *Sermons,* 2:8.510–13.
207. Donne, *Sermons,* 1:2.523–26. See Herbert's similar critique of rural secularism in "The Parson's Consideration of Providence" in *The Country Parson,* in *George Herbert and Henry Vaughan,* ed. Louis L. Martz (Oxford, 1986), p. 228.

sinfulness from wrong actions, he views its essence as the preference for meaninglessness, the desire for an "empty" cosmos and correspondingly for human freedom to write one's own story. It is thus the desire to be alone in the universe, a belief in "an imaginary possibility" of standing by oneself "without any farther relation, or beholdingnesse to God." "We had rather [Christ] . . . had left us to our libertie and discretion." For to acknowledge that an event "is a judgment, and not an accident" makes "God too imperious over us," since it admits His power to create meaning.[208]

The association Donne makes between faith and submission to meaning inclines him to mistrust reason in its native capacity to interpret the world according to its own best lights and interests. The worst sins are "peccata cum ratione," sins justified on a rational basis.[209] Following Augustine, he describes heresy as attempting to overthrow the foundations of the church "upon the appearance, and pretence, and colour of *Reason,*" by arguments, that is, based on probability and verisimilitude rather than on the text of Scripture.[210] There can, however, be no independent moral or empirical criteria for truth and goodness. Donne is thus almost always hostile to philosophy, viewing it as a culpable attempt at self-sufficiency: "to think that we can believe out of *Plato,* where we may find a God, but without a Christ, or come to be good men out of *Plutarch* or *Seneca,* without a Church and Sacraments . . . this is pride, and the pride of the Angels."[211] Philosophy is demonic because it allows humans rather than God to determine the means of salvation; it is also futile since "the first breath of his indignation blowes out thy candle . . . disorders thy *Seneca,* thy *Plutarch,* thy *Tacitus,* and all thy premeditations."[212] The authors Donne mentions were the favorites of Renaissance neo-Stoicism, but he is not critiquing Stoicism here except as symptomatic of what Hans Blumenberg calls "self-assertion" (and sees as constitutive of modernity): the notion that human "premeditation" and planning can protect man from the world.

Whether he speaks of it as rebellion, self-sufficiency, or rational

208. Donne, *Sermons,* 2:14.253–54; 2:8.402; 8:13.474–76.
209. Donne, *Sermons,* 1:4.58.
210. Donne, *Sermons,* 8:2.377–86.
211. Donne, *Sermons,* 9:17.292–96.
212. Donne, *Sermons,* 2:18.209–12.

autonomy, sin for Donne is an escape from power into a secular, "sovereignless" world.[213] Moreover, he assumes that this is the world in which most people live. A sermon preached at Whitehall in 1627 acknowledges the pervasive secular temper of the court. Already instinctive naturalists, the aristocracy discuss religion in the categories of psychopathology. A devout courtier will find that family and friends "think thy present fear of God, but a childishness and pusilanimity, and thy present zeal to his service but an infatuation and a melancholy, and thy present application of thy self to God in prayer, but an argument of thy Court-despaire, and of thy falling from former hopes there."[214] (One senses some residual autobiography here.) Donne is in fact fascinated and horrified by the possibility of experiencing existence without reference to the absolute, of an existence free from dependency and constraint, where "The jingling and ratling of our Chains and Fetters, makes us deaf."[215] Sin is secularization, the attempt to avoid the drastic personal confrontation between absolute power and one's own guilty, wormlike selfhood by refusing to hear the constraints such power imposes. It is moreover *the* Protestant sin, first sharply articulated in Luther's angry attack on Erasmian free will and codified in the Law-to-Gospel spirituality of virtually all the Reformers, according to which the recognition of one's total sinfulness, misery, and liability to punishment must precede redemption. And the resemblance of sin (so conceived) to modernity seems more than fortuitous. Both in politics and theology, modernity entails the rejection of the absolutist paradigm based on the polarities of power and subjection and therefore of the psychocultural formation which made this paradigm acceptable. At a certain point in Western history, guilt, dependence, and longing for passivity and for being "in relation" to personal power—the whole complex of archaic/infantile emotions valorized in Donne—became offensive. As Christopher Hill remarked, "we are all Pelagians now."[216] But that is another story, for although Donne lived in the last generation of full-blooded Augustinians and sacred monarchs, he did not know it.

213. The same association of liberty with rebellion, the same preference for Christian servitude over Christian freedom, appear in Calvin; see Bouwsma, *Calvin,* p. 86.

214. Donne, *Sermons,* 8:7.307–12.

215. Donne, *Sermons,* 1:2.504–5.

216. Hill, *Collected Essays,* p. 133.

PASTORAL POLITICS

What function is so noble, as to bee
Embassadour to God and destinie?
Donne, "To Mr. Tilman"

A final implication of Donne's absolutist theology deserves mention. As noted previously, Donne tends to view God's self-communication as paradoxical, dark, as signs that require interpretation and decoding. This has consequences for both his exegetical and homiletic practice. Unlike most of his contemporaries, Donne seems curiously eager to point out the uncertainties of biblical interpretation, to bring up textual and interpretive problems without resolving them. For example, a sermon preached before King Charles in 1626 begins,

> There are occasions of Controversies of all kinds in this one Verse; And one is, whether this be one Verse or no; For as there are Doctrinall Controversies, out of the sense and interpretation of the words, so are there Grammatticall differences about the Distinction, and Interpunction of them: Some Translations differing therein from the Originall, (as the Originall Copies are distinguished, and interpuncted now) and some differing from one another.[217]

Donne then gives the different readings of Tremellius, the Syriac version, Beza, Piscator, and "Divers others," only to conclude, without explanation, that "we find no reason to depart from that Distinction and Interpunction of these words, which our own Church exhibits to us."[218] The passage raises numerous questions, including the parenthetical suspicion that extant "originals" do not faithfully represent their archetypes, and then cuts them off with a "no reason."

This consciousness of textual difficulties can look like a humanist concern for philological accuracy, but, as D. C. Allen has shown, Donne has little interest in scholarly rigor or exactitude;[219] he dwells on the problems and disagreements, not their resolution. The same destabilizing sense of multiple, incompatible options appears in his handling of biblical commentaries. In place of the normative consensus of antiquity, he tends to emphasize the disagreements among the

217. Donne, *Sermons,* 7:4.1–7.
218. Donne, *Sermons,* 7:4.28–30.
219. Don Cameron Allen, "Dean Donne Sets His Text," *English Literary History* 10 (1943): 225–29.

church fathers. Discussing the words of the "good thief" to Christ in Luke 23:40, he thus notes that

> *Hilary* raises and builds a great point of Divinity upon it. . . . He raises positive and literall Doctrine. And *Theophylact* raises mystical and figurative Doctrine out of it. . . . S. *Hierome* inclines to admit a figure in S. *Matthews* words. . . . Onely S. *Augustine* is confident in it, that this Thief never reviled Christ.[220]

At times he throws the whole notion of consensus and tradition into doubt, remarking that the early church held the necessity of infant communion, believed that there would be an earthly millennium, and claimed that the souls of the departed would not ascend into heaven until after Judgment: "This we have heard, and from so many of them of old, as that the voyce of that part is louder, then of the other. And amongst those reverend and blessed Fathers, which straied into these errors, some were hearers and Disciples of the Apostles themselves."[221] Again, Donne does not even attempt to remove the appearance of doctrinal uncertainty such disagreement generates, instead launching into an attack on the papacy for ignoring the patristic consensus he has just apparently discredited.

The repeated references to textual difficulties, disagreements among the fathers, differences between ancient and modern expositors seem designed to erode belief in a single, accessible meaning of the holy text. Donne's own hermeneutic furthers this destabilization by replacing the spiritual senses of medieval exegesis with the principle of accommodation.[222] The text has one genuine sense—the literal;[223] but this sense can then be "accommodated" to various situations. Donne, however, never suggests that these applied meanings exist in any sense *in* the text as opposed to being useful inferences made *from* it. Discussing the first chapter of Acts, he observes, "*Christ* spoke the words of this *Text,* principally to the *Apostles* . . . but they are in their just extention, and due accomodation, appliable to our present occation of

220. Donne, *Sermons,* 1:6.212–30.

221. Donne, *Sermons,* 7:4.160–66.

222. "Accommodation" is also a technical term in Calvinist theology, where it describes God's condescension to us in using language accessible to our limited and sense-based intellects, for example, the anthropomorphisms of Holy Scripture (Calvin, *Institutes,* 2.6.4; 2.10.6). Donne does not use the term in this sense.

223. Donne, *Sermons,* 1:7.572–73; 10:9.63–64.

meeting heere."[224] The accommodated meaning corresponds to the old tropological sense but relocated from the spiritual recesses of the text to the mind of the interpreter who applies the letter to the "present occasion." Donne similarly subsumes typology under the rubric of accommodation; he thus explains that

> Upon that pious ground that all Scriptures were written for us, as we are Christians, that all Scriptures conduce to the proofe of Christ, and of the Christian state, it is the ordinary manner of the Fathers to make all that *David* speaks historically of himselfe, and all that the Prophet speaks futurely of the Jews, if those places may be referred to Christ, to referre them to Christ primarily, and but by reflection, and in a second consideration upon *David,* or upon the Jews.[225]

Typology rests on pious rather than historical grounds. Hence elsewhere he affirms that "We may justly accommodate . . . those words of *Jeremie,* to God the Sonne, *Behold, and see, if there be any sorrow, like unto my sorrow.*"[226] Donne keeps the traditional reading of the verse, but the pivotal "accommodate" renders the relation between this reading and the "real" meaning of the text ambiguous. The notion of accommodation allowed Donne to exploit a good deal of medieval or quasi-medieval exegesis—for instance, the "fair, and just accommodation of the words ['Let us make man in our image']" to "the foure quarters of the world"—while simultaneously exposing its subjective character.[227] How loose and arbitrary the relation between text and meaning could become is suggested by his claim that a passage he recognizes to be a post-biblical interpolation may nevertheless "for our use and accommodation . . . well be accepted by us."[228] It finally seems not to matter much whether the meaning is *in* the text or even whether the text is *in* the Bible, as long as a useful lesson can be derived from it, yet it would be wrong to cast Donne's hermeneutic as a sort of pragmatic moralism. Earlier forms of biblical exegesis also could turn even the most unpromising passages into treasures of instruc-

224. Donne, *Sermons,* 4:10.36–39.

225. Donne, *Sermons,* 4:1.566–72. He does, very occasionally, retain the terminology of the multiple senses of Scripture and of Augustinian hermeneutics, for example, in *Sermons,* 9:3.105–35, 299.

226. Donne, *Sermons,* 8:12.13–16.

227. Donne, *Sermons,* 9:1.64–65.

228. Donne, *Sermons,* 8:4.34–35.

tion. The language of accommodation additionally functions to half-conceal, half-reveal the ungroundedness of this turn.

By destabilizing the text and interpretation of Holy Scripture, Donne stimulates epistemic anxieties—as he stimulates moral anxieties in his depiction of the *ira Dei*. He opens forbidden vistas onto the uncertainty of text and tradition, as onto the demonic power of God, and then slams the door, demands that the doubts thus aroused be repressed. The sermons do not resolve the problems of interpretation they engender but instead deny them. Rather, they produce anxieties in order to disclose the power of the priest and to create a dependency on that power. The denaturalization of text and dogma reinforces authority by breeding doubts and fears that then yearn for closure and intelligibility. One escapes from uncertainty by submission to personal power, especially priestly power. The fourth Prebend sermon lays out this connection between textual uncertainty and authority. The "Order of Doctors amongst the Jews" that taught "people by Parables and darke sayings . . . were the powerfullest Teachers amongst them, for they had their very name (*Mosselim*) from power and dominion." Their obscurity bred power because it "created an admiration, and a reverence in their hearers, and laid a necessity upon them, of returning againe to them, for the interpretation and signification of those darke Parables."[229] So Christ taught in parables to gain power, and so in both Testaments God leaves "evermore something reserved to be inquired after, and laid up in the mouth of the Priest, that the People might acknowledge an obligation from him, in the exposition, and application thereof."[230] The ability to determine meaning is here again a form of power.

Thus, despite Donne's deep desire to submit to God, he also has no small interest in associating himself with divine authority. The two tendencies may not be unrelated, for even "slavish humiliation may facilitate an excessive intensification of self-respect in being the servant of such a master, just as to serve, with the arrière pensée of being able to rule all the more effectively, repeatedly appears in human experience."[231] Whatever his subconscious motives, Donne places church and priest rather than some objective and relatively impersonal text at

229. Donne, *Sermons,* 7:12.549–57.
230. Donne, *Sermons,* 7:12.564–84.
231. Van der Leeuw, *Religion in Essence,* 2:472.

the center of the redemptive process as it unfolds in history.[232] The power of the Church of England and its preachers finds a place in virtually every one of Donne's sermons. The minister and "indeed, the whole frame, and Hierarchy of the Christian Church" is "the Mediator betweene Christ and Man."[233] The "established Church" is "a Church endowed with a power, to open the wounds of Christ Jesus to receive every wounded soule." Christ cannot speak to a person until he hears His voice "in a setled Church, and in the Ordinance of preaching." The mysterious beasts in Revelation "concurre to the Qualification of a Minister." The preacher "speaks in the person of God himselfe."[234] A preacher is like a king, Donne's highest form of compliment: "What a Coronation is our taking of Orders, by which God makes us a Royall Priesthood? And what an inthronization is the comming up into a Pulpit, where God invests his servants with his Ordinance."[235] As John Carey and William Mueller have shown with abundant evidence, Donne never tires of reminding his congregations of the majesty, dignity, and authority of the preaching ministry; he places far less emphasis on its sacramental role.[236]

Donne reports Christ as telling His Apostles, "*Hee that beleeves not your Preaching shall bee damned.*"[237] As the preacher shares in the divine power, so the sermon recapitulates the strategies of sacred absolutism. It does not teach a doctrine but operates rhetorically, affectively—a sort of psychagogic warfare: "Preaching is *Gods* ordinance, with that *Ordinance* hee fights from heaven, and batters downe all errors."[238] Like Donne's God, his sermons strike and stroke, assaulting the congregation with its guilt and sins, then reaching out in tenderness. Or in

232. On Calvinist clericalism see Pelikan, *Reformation,* p. 313; Lake, *Moderate Puritans,* pp. 88–89. In this respect Donne differs sharply from liberal theologians like Hales, Chillingworth, and Falkland, all of whom emphasized the right of private judgment and the duty of the individual to interpret Holy Scripture for himself, without clerical supervision. See John Tulloch, *Rational Theology and Christian Philosophy in England in the Seventeenth Century,* 2 vols. (Edinburgh, 1872), pp. 30, 161–64, 248, 328.

233. Donne, *Sermons,* 10:1.266–71; compare 8:1.230–32.

234. Donne, *Sermons,* 8:13.599–601; 7:5.601–2; 8:1.158; 8:6.513.

235. Donne, *Sermons,* 7:4.591–94.

236. Carey, *John Donne,* pp. 124, 134; William Mueller, *John Donne: Preacher* (Princeton, 1962), pp. 41–49.

237. Donne, *Sermons,* 4:7.550–51.

238. Donne, *Sermons,* 4:7.480–81. On Christian versions of the agonistic grand style, see Debora Shuger, *Sacred Rhetoric: The Christian Grand Style in the English Renaissance* (Princeton, 1988).

Donne's own piscatory metaphor, the Gospel preached is a net that "hath leads, that is, the denouncing of Gods judgements, and a power to sink down, and lay flat any stubborne and rebellious heart, And it hath corks, that is, the power of absolution, and application of the mercies of God."[239] While the preacher speaks, "there shall be a noyse, and a commotion, a horrour of their former sins, a wonder how they could provoke so patient, and so powerfull a God, a sinking down under the waight of Gods Judgements, a flying up to the apprehension of his mercies."[240] "The parson," George Herbert affirmed, "is a diligent observer and tracker of God's ways.[241] Donne, apparently taking some such precept to heart, structures his sermons following the jagged tracks of a God who "that He may raise . . . throws down," snatching from a person any security based on his ability to predict or control either himself or the world, yet promising the security of *being* controlled and covered by a "majesticall" love. Which is in effect to say that the perceived structures of human existence govern homiletic form, much as they do narrative.

Both as strategy and substance, then, theology duplicates politics. Donne's God, his preaching, and his king are all analogously related, all participants in absolutist structures of domination and submission. It is therefore not surprising that Donne never refers to the *duplex regimen* that separates the realm of power from that of inwardness; for him, the inner and outer man are both constructed politically. This interpenetration of politics and theology rests on Donne's attitude toward power, an attitude which belongs to the mystifying traditions of political theology, not to the realistic ones of political theory. The power that structures divine/human relations is not the rather simple self-interested *libido dominandi* of post-Hobbesian theory. Power is for him a "rich" concept, including connotations of oppressive cruelty and protective gentleness, dread and awe, fearful majesty and parental embrace, violence and love. Above all power is experienced as relatedness, as "being in God's hands" and bending under their pressure. The terrifying force of His *potentia absoluta* engenders paralyzing guilt, driving the human subject from autonomy to submission, but submis-

239. Donne, *Sermons,* 2:14.758–62.
240. Donne, *Sermons,* 7:3.818–21.
241. Herbert, *The Country Parson,* in *George Herbert and Henry Vaughan,* p. 206.

sion too is a "rich" concept—abjection releases an emotionality shot through with what appear to be archaic and infantile ambivalencies. Submission involves fear, the desperate attempt to propitiate the Other, aggression, longings for dependence and passivity, the desire to be touched and overpowered.

There is very little rationalistic softening here, little effort to substitute legal/contractual or ethical categories for personal and affective ones, despite Donne's awareness that religious perception involves an *interpretation* of the secularized contents of an already almost instinctive rationalism.[242] Original Sin, the damnation of the heathen, and other manifestations of the apparent amorality of the divine will worry him, but he almost always chooses to accept these consequences rather than relax God's grasp on the world. It is only when the notion of power has been flattened into its present meaning, that such a grasp becomes intolerable—again both in politics and theology. This is obvious in Deism's revulsion from both forms of absolutism, its preference for legal structures over those based on personal power, and its neo-Stoic moralism. But the critique of absolutist theology and absolutist politics also emerges within Donne's own Calvinist and courtly culture, most visibly in the difficult and problematic writings of Fulke Greville, Lord Brooke (1554–1628). We can end this chapter with a brief consideration of Greville's most important play, *Mustapha,* as a radical criticism of the mystification of power in both its sacred and profane manifestations, this dual focus itself witnessing to the deep analogical bonds that connected the politics of domination and submission to its theology.

POLITICS UNMIRACLED

Mustapha is a Senecan closet drama with its predictably melodramatic plot. In order to place her own child on the throne, the second wife of Solyman, the Turkish sultan, tries to convince him that Mustapha, his son by his first wife, is plotting rebellion. Solyman is torn between the suspicions aroused by his wife, Rossa, and his love for his child, who

242. For the view that Donne was basically a liberal and latitudinarian Christian Platonist, see Roy W. Battenhouse, "The Grounds of Religious Toleration in the Thought of John Donne," *Church History* 11 (1942): 217–48; Grant, *Transformation of Sin,* pp. 65–72.

is pious, virtuous, and obedient. His daughter and a good counselor argue for Mustapha's innocence. Finally, Solyman's wife kills the daughter in order to prove to Solyman that she would sacrifice anything to preserve his safety, and, convinced by this, he resolves to kill Mustapha. In the meantime, Mustapha learns of his father's intentions but, as a dutiful child, goes unarmed and unaccompanied to the sultan and is killed. His dying words beg his father's forgiveness. Upon learning of Mustapha's death, Rossa's own son commits suicide. Popular rebellion breaks out but is stilled by the good counselor, who, after long debate, decides that anarchy is worse than tyranny. The play ends with Solyman still in power, although the rebellion has not been decisively quelled. The plot, however, is not the point. Like all Greville's work, *Mustapha* is reflective and analytic rather than dramatic. Little action is shown onstage; instead the play consists largely of debate and analysis, each act punctuated by a different chorus—Priests, Converts, Bashas, Tartars, Time, Eternity—commenting on the political and religious implications of the events.

In *The Life of Fulke Greville,* Rebholz, I think rightly, suggests that Solyman represents King James.[243] Although the play is not an allegory, it is throughout concerned with the implications of Jacobean absolutism, especially the divinization of the king. As in English political theology, sacred predicates cluster around the ruler. Solyman possesses "universall providence," (2.2.39), "Omnipotence" (2.2.74), "grace" (4.4.9).[244] Characters not only talk about the sultan in religious terms, but at times one cannot easily tell whether the speaker is referring to God or Solyman, an apparently deliberate ambiguity. Thus Solyman's remark, "I see inferior wheeles of practice move, / Yet they prevaile not on the Powers above" (1.2.209–10), seems initially to refer to divine "Powers"; not until midway through the speech does it become clear that Solyman here refers to his own position. Similarly, Rosten, one of the bashas, tells Rossa: "But turne your eyes up to the will of one" (3.1.49); again, the language *sounds* as if it should be religious, although it is in fact political. But the likeness is reciprocal.

243. Rebholz, *Greville,* pp. 200–202.

244. All references are to Geoffrey Bullough's edition of the 1633 text of *Mustapha,* which almost certainly represents Greville's final intentions for the play; Fulke Greville, *Poems and Dramas of Fulke Greville, First Lord Brooke,* ed. Geoffrey Bullough, 2 vols. (Edinburgh, 1939).

If Solyman is formed in the image of God (as well as King James), then God, or at least the God of absolutist theology, Himself bearing the imprint of Jacobean politics, is formed in the image of the sultan. God is like Solyman because, as the chorus of priests confesses, "we fashion / God, as if from Powers Throne he tooke his being" (Chorus Secundus, 97–98). The priest who counsels Mustapha to rebel against his father directs his invective not only against the sultan but against God, for they are mirror images of each other: "False *Mahomet!* Thy Lawes Monarchall are, / Unjust, ambitious; full of spoyle, and blood, / Having not of the best, but greatest Care" (4.4.32–34).[245]

The disillusioned priest, Heli, goes on to pray that the people will "stirre, and teare away this veyle / Of pride from Power; that our great Lord may see / Unmiracled, his owne Humanity" (4.4.205–7). The characters in the play know that divinization merely covers the ruthlessness of political power. The bashas admit that they are "Exhausters of fraile Mankind . . . / To make them poore, and consequently base," who use "idle visions" for "trafficking mens mindes / To humble moderation, in all kindes / Till under false stiles of Obedience, / We take from Mankinde all, but suffering sense" (Chorus Primus, 33–40). Greville, like Donne, structures his analysis by the antinomies of power and submission, but because he regards absolute power as tyranny, he (or his characters) view submission as servility. Mankind, "by crafty power opprest," thinks "Thrones in all their practise true." Trusting in this royal truth, like "milde Earth," men allow themselves to be "plough'd, manur'd, and overthrowne" (Chorus Secundus, 193–98). To believe kings is to permit oneself to be oppressed. To instill such belief is "the Art of powerfull Tyrannie," which undermines "mans native libertie" (Chorus Primus, 169–70).[246]

Mustapha places particular emphasis on the role of religion in sustaining this mystification. Kings seek from the church the "rites of deitie," and the church, to enhance its own "supremacie," justifies the tyrant.[247] Heli confesses that "We Priests, even with the mysterie of words, / First binde our selves, and with our selves the rest / To

245. In Islamic thought, Mohomet is of course not God, but I suspect Greville was not sensitive to the distinction.

246. For the background of Greville's political thought and especially his debt to Etienne de La Boétie, see David Norbrook, *Poetry and Politics in the English Renaissance* (London, 1984), pp. 159–62.

247. Chorus Quartus, 41–42; Chorus Primus, 105–6; Chorus Quartus, 16–18.

servitude, the sheath of Tyrants sword" (4.4.41–43). The chorus of bashas makes this mystery of words more explicit: the priests are masters at "guilt-inflictions," oppressing and perplexing the conscience by making alternately "doctrines large, strict, milde, severe" in order to increase emotional dependency on "Power"—precisely the same point Donne makes. These psychological manipulations "prove to Thrones . . . a supporting cause" (Chorus Primus, 65–77). In the end, when she has nothing to lose, Rossa makes the darkest objection; the virtues instilled by religion (and the list seems to be Christian rather than Moslem) create, and are intended to create, subjection to power. Religion is the opiate of "weake Soules" and "humble Hearts," tricking them into "bearing yokes of Tyrants skill" by making political docility a theological virtue (5.4.117–22).

In the beginning of the fourth act, divinity enters the play *in propria persona*. Solyman receives a vision, or what may be a vision, since he is not sure whether what he sees is "Rays'd from within, or from above descending" (4.1.5–6). In any case, the vision apparently tells him, "*Safetie, Right, and a Crowne, / Thrones must neglect that will adore Gods light. / His will, our good*" (4.1.9–11). The vision demands that the sultan ignore his own safety and instead trust in God, but Solyman claims he is unable to "comprehend" these instructions, for they condemn his "Power [as] a Turret, built against my Maker" and make his "Empire" appear as "shaddowes." The vision castigates the struggle for power and security that controls the sultan. Sacred values thus appear to contradict secular ones, leading Solyman to exclaim in frustration, "The Earth drawes one way, and the skie another" (4.1.38). But in fact the opposition only conceals an underlying congruence. Confronted by the vision, Solyman must either submit to an incomprehensible superior who requires total vulnerability or commit the dark sin of self-reliance: "*Kings must looke upwards still, /And from these Powers they know not, choose a will.* / Or else beleeve themselves, their strength, occasion" (4.1.39–41). Solyman chooses rebellion—the escape to the fiction of secular autonomy—rather than submission, to believe himself rather than yield to an unknown Power. But the options disclose that the relation of God to man recapitulates the relation of king to subject; the same absolutist structures of power and submission, the same choice of rebellion or subjection, govern divinity as well as politics.

Religious submission, rather than political, constitutes the central issue of the play. Although he appears only in one scene, the play (as its title suggests) is about Mustapha, not Solyman. The two concluding choruses explore the meaning of Mustapha's death, not Solyman's decision to kill him—nor the permissibility of overthrowing a tyrant. This emphasis is crucial because it changes the significance of the work. Its politics could be seen as conservative—critical of tyranny but in the end rejecting popular rebellion. But Greville's treatment of Mustapha keeps the play from being "an *exemplum* of political immorality,"[248] drawing it into a disturbingly open-ended questioning of the values of sacrificial suffering and obedience—the virtues constitutive of "Donnean" Christianity.

From beginning to end, the play insists upon Mustapha's piety and dutifulness. We first hear of him in the messenger's description, which begins, "With zeale he doth adore the Powers above; / With zeale inferior duties paid him are" (1.2.142–43). At the end, we are told, "he obeying died" (5.2.65). In his one scene on stage, he ardently defends "Christian" otherworldliness and selfless submission to the paradoxes of redemptive pain. He responds to the priest, who has seen through the mystifications of power with outrage and is now trying to convince Mustapha either to escape or combat his father's murderous intentions:

> Shall I a Sonne, and subject seeme to dare,
> For any Selfenesse, to set Realmes on fire,
> Which golden titles to rebellions are?
> *Heli*! even you have told me, Wealth was given
> The wicked, to corrupt themselves, and others:
> Greatnesse, and health, to make flesh proud, and cruell.
> Where, in the good, Sicknesse mowes downe desire;
> Death glorifies; Misfortune humbles.
> Since therefore Life is but the throne of Woe,
> Which sicknesse, paine, desire, and feare inherit,
> Ever most worth to men of weakest spirit:
> Shall we, to languish in this brittle Jayle,
> Seeke, by ill deeds, to shunne ill destinie?
> And so, for toyes, lose immortalitie?
>
> (4.4.125–39)

248. Rebholz, *Greville,* p. 201.

But the priest, Heli, replies that this is the faith of "servile Men" who believe "false visions" and refuse to "see, / The art of Power" such faith is created to sustain (4.4.141–47). As far as Heli is concerned, the true God, unlike the fables of power, commands people to recover their freedom and pursue what is good for them, even if by force (4.4.45–51, 148–57).

What Heli sees is that "orthodox" religion has been so welded to the necessities of state that otherworldliness is no longer a possible attitude; to reject the world is tacitly to embrace its political structures, for submission to God's will cannot be distinguished from legitimation of temporal power. This ambiguity permeates Mustapha's strange death speech. The good counselor reports that:

> His last words were; *O Father! Now forgive me;*
> *Forgive them too, that wrought my overthrow:*
> *Let my Grave never minister offences.*
> *For, since my Father coveteth my death,*
> *Behold, with joy, I offer him my breath.*
> (5.2.84–88)

The lines are a pastiche of Christ's last words in the Gospel according to Luke. But the "Father" whom Christ addresses from the Cross cannot be confused with powers and principalities—Herod, Caiaphas, Pilate—authorizing the Crucifixion. In Greville, one cannot tell which father Mustapha intends. The first "Father" could refer either to God or Solyman, although the echo of Christ's "Father, forgive them," encourages an initial assumption that he is speaking to God. But the second "Father" seems to be Solyman, since we have no reason to think God coveted Mustapha's death. But then the final line, alluding to Christ's "Father, into thy hands I commit my spirit," would also refer to Solyman, which does not make much sense. And the ambiguity of reference is the subject of the play. The muddied allusions to the New Testament force the reader to traverse the distance between its supernatural ethos and Greville's dark worries about the uses which this passive heroism serves. Mustapha's imitation of Christ is, as it were, political suicide. And Christ's death may be political suicide, too, for the ambiguities of reference in Mustapha's *imitatio Christi* slide over to the biblical text. It is not finally clear that God the Father, "who gave His only-begotten Son," did not in some sense ordain, even "covet," Christ's death or authorize the Crucifixion. Who is Mustapha talking to?

Only once, and then very guardedly, does the play suggest that God rewards such obedience. At the end of the Chorus Tertius, Eternitie promises "Mine shall subsist by Me." She (he? it?) does not elaborate on this subsistence, and the final choruses unequivocally deny it. The Chorus Tartarorum is throughout an indictment of "Vast *Superstition*" (in earlier versions "Religion") as "Weaknesse" that disguises falsehoods under the title of paradox. Thus, as Mustapha had already claimed, the "blessings" of superstition (religion?) are "sicknesse . . . Miserie, thy triall; / Nothing, thy way unto eternall being; / Death, to salvation." Only Mustapha believed the paradoxes, while this chorus rejects redemptive suffering in the name of courage, reason, and nature, whose "mysteries are read without Faiths eye-sight" and who never "*promis'd any man, by dying, joy.*" The Chorus Sacerdotum, which immediately follows and ends the play, denies the goodness of nature affirmed in the previous chorus but does nothing to restore faith in eternal recompenses. The priests say they teach "*of Heavens wonders, and delights*" in order to get "*Promotion,*" but "*when each of us, in his owne heart lookes, / He findes the God there, farre unlike his Bookes.*" The priests do not say what that internal God is—a monster? the self?

Mustapha reads like a gloss on the conclusion to Stephen Greenblatt's *Renaissance Self-Fashioning,* a dramatization of the "peculiarly intense *submission* whose downright violence undermines everything it was meant to shore up"[249]—a narrative strategy both Shakespeare and Greville could have learned from Euripides. But it also reads like a commentary on Donne's sermons, with their analogies of king and God, their structures of power and obedience, and their paradoxes of redemptive submission. The play, of course, has nothing to do with Donne, the first version having been written long before he even took orders. Rather, it seems to interrogate the groundwork of royalist Calvinism, whose theological structure Donne by and large reproduced.[250] Interrogate rather than repudiate, for Greville was un-

249. Greenblatt, *Self-Fashioning,* p. 254.

250. I thus disagree with Rebholz, who argues that *Mustapha* is clearly saved and therefore that the play upholds a dark but orthodox Christianity (*Greville,* pp. 203–5); likewise I have difficulties with Jonathan Dollimore's notion that Greville meant to

doubtedly a devout and stern Calvinist—no one has ever questioned that—although finally, like Milton, a church unto himself. In his later years, and the revised *Mustapha* probably dates from 1607–10, Greville came to embrace a Christianity devoid of all visible, institutional embodiments, cut off from all analogy.

Or all but one. *Mustapha* consistently contrasts the figures of father and king. From the opening scene on, the decision whether or not to kill Mustapha presents itself to Solyman as a choice between acting as a parent or monarch; as he himself says, "Two States I beare: his Father, and his King; / These two, being Relatives, have mutuall bonds" (2.2.15–16). But the bonds are different, the latter consisting of power, the former of love. And therefore the question Rossa asks her husband concerns "how it fitts a King to be a lover" (1.2.118). The love between father and son is the one relation in the play that does *not* duplicate absolutist structures and therefore threatens them. Love makes one weak, makes one risk one's own safety for the sake of the other and thus destroys the security promised by absolute power: "kindnesse lessen[s] Kings authority" (1.1.12). Solyman has to choose between acting as a king or father, for "*Father*-language fits not Kings" (2.2.38). The contrast between king and father here splits the analogic unity observed in the political works of King James, where the king is the father. Both the contrast and the unity belong to a larger discourse on the interrelations among kings, father, and God—the discourse of patriarchalism—whose analogies and disanalogies probe the borders of love and power, private and public, self and other. The next chapter will explore this subject further.

---

reproduce orthodox teachings, but the play, apparently accidentally, "disconfirms its own attempts at formal and ideological coherence" (*Radical Tragedy: Religion, Ideology, and Power in the Drama of Shakespeare and His Contemporaries* [Chicago, 1984], p. 123).

6

Nursing Fathers
Patriarchy as a Cultural Ideal

Kings and fathers are very different things.
Milton

Over the past twenty years, berating Renaissance patriarchy has become almost a scholarly topos, a series of variations on Lawrence Stone's claim that the Renaissance family was "patriarchal in that the husband and father lorded it over his wife and children with the quasi-absolute authority of a despot."[1] Greville's contrast between kings and fathers seems puzzling because such scholarship, following Stone's magisterial footsteps, has generally assumed that the Renaissance considered the two roles analogous. Or rather three roles, for to father and king we may add God. These are held to have constituted a triple-tiered patriarchy, an authoritarian and repressive system of male dominance, where the subordination of subject to ruler mirrors the subjection of wife and child to the father, both being justified and "naturalized" by the monarchal patriarchy of heaven.[2] Moreover, it is argued, since patriarchy equals *male* despotism, it privileges masculine attributes like reason, control, and authoritarian order, devaluing emotion and gentleness, since these are female traits.[3] Yet *Mustapha*

1. Lawrence Stone, *The Crisis of the Aristocracy, 1558–1641*, abridged ed. (London, 1967), p. 271.

2. Lawrence Stone, *The Family, Sex, and Marriage in England, 1500–1800*, abridged ed. (New York, 1977), pp. 109–10; Leah S. Marcus, *Childhood and Cultural Despair: A Theme and Variations in Seventeenth-Century Literature* (Pittsburgh, 1978), p. 29.

3. Marianne Novy, *Love's Argument: Gender Relations in Shakespeare* (Chapel Hill, 1984), pp. 3–9; Marilyn French, *Shakespeare's Division of Experience* (New York, 1981), pp. 16, 21–24; Coppélia Kahn, *Man's Estate: Masculine Identity in Shakespeare* (Berkeley, 1981), pp. 11–16, and her "The Absent Mother in *King Lear,*" in *Rewriting the Renaissance: The Discourses of Sexual Difference in Early Modern Europe*, ed. Margaret W. Ferguson, Maureen Quilligan, and Nancy J. Vickers (Chicago, 1986), p. 39; Bryan S.

obviously does not fit this scheme. Instead of conflating patriarchy with royal authoritarianism, it seems to assume that a father's relation to his child is essentially different from political relations of submission, domination, and the struggle to acquire power. It assumes that "father" means something very different from "despot." It is possible that Greville's work is simply anomalous, but it is also possible that Stone overstated his case.

"Patriarchy" does not primarily refer to the actual behaviors of fathers toward their wives and children but rather to a cultural ideal. The English Renaissance was a patriarchal society because fatherhood came to symbolize an ideal of domestic, political, and religious order. That ideal was not unrelated to actual behavior, but it is the normative and symbolic value of fatherhood during this period, its significance as a conceptual category, that designates the culture as patriarchal. It follows that patriarchy principally refers to the relation between father and child, not husband and wife. Renaissance writers describe the latter relation as a variant of the former, not the reverse. For instance, in the mid-sixteenth century, Thomas Becon argues that a husband should be to his wife "even such one as a gentle and tender father is toward his most dear and sweet child."[4] The relation of father to child is paradigmatic, not only for marital order but for all other forms of social subordination. In Tyndale, the master should "nurture" his servants "as thy own sons," landlords should "be as fathers unto your tenants," and a king should not seek any other thing from his people "than a father seeketh in his children."[5] The relation between husband and wife rarely provides a model for other social relations, almost never for spiritual ones—a radical departure from the medieval analogies of *sponsus* and *sponsa*. This shift seems related to the fact that English Protestantism ignored both the matrilinear Holy Family

---

Turner, *The Body and Society: Explorations in Social Theory* (Oxford, 1984), pp. 139–40; David Leverenz, "The Woman in *Hamlet:* An Interpersonal View," in *Representing Shakespeare: New Psychoanalytic Essays,* ed. Murray M. Schwartz and Coppélia Kahn (Baltimore, 1980), pp. 115–21.

4. Quoted in Alan Macfarlane, *Marriage and Love in England: Modes of Reproduction, 1300–1840* (Oxford, 1986), p. 182.

5. William Tyndale, *The Obedience of a Christian Man* (1528), in *Doctrinal Treatises and Introductions to Different Portions of The Holy Scriptures,* ed. Rev. Henry Walter, The Parker Society (Cambridge, 1848), pp. 201–2.

(Anne, Mary, Jesus) and the nuclear one (Joseph, Mary, Jesus) in favor of the relation between the Father and the Son.[6]

Patriarchy, therefore, cannot be equated with male dominance over women (although these are scarcely unrelated). As a cultural ideal and center of analogic correspondences it pertains to a relation between parents, primarily the father, and children. In order to explore the meaning of patriarchy thus understood, I will once again focus on Andrewes and Hooker, but because the meaning of fatherhood seems to have remained relatively unchanged throughout the sixteenth and seventeenth centuries, I will also draw on texts from Tyndale through Milton, including some continental works of neo-Latin scholarship—the kind of theoretical material that tended not to be written in English until the latter part of the seventeenth century.

THE NURTURING PARENT

It is not difficult to find evidence for the accepted view of patriarchy as authoritarian male domination: Tyndale's *Obedience of a Christian Man,* Perkins's *Christian Oeconomy,* and Filmer's *Patriarcha,* for example, understand fathers in terms of hierarchical authority and control over their household and, by analogy, the king's authority over his subjects. But this is by no means the only or even the most common interpretation of the paternal figure. Instead, as the quotations from Becon and Tyndale have already hinted, "father" usually does not connote authority, discipline, rationality, law, and so on, but rather forgiveness, nurturing, and tenderness. This is almost always the case in discussions of God the Father. In fact, in reference to God the import of paternal images seems virtually identical to that of maternal ones, often both occurring in the same passage. Tyndale in particular specializes in delicate and realistic portrayals of parental love as the single analogue for the unmerited *caritas* of God. Thus he describes how a child owes his life and maintenance to his parents and yet

> is not able to recompense that it oweth to father and mother by a thousand parts. And though it be not able to do his duty, nor for

6. On the transition from the matrilinear to the nuclear Holy Family in Roman Catholic countries, see John Bossy, *Christianity in the West, 1400–1700* (Oxford, 1985), pp. 10–11.

> blindness to know his duty, yet the father and mother promise more gifts still without ceasing, and that such as they think should most make it to see love, and to provoke it to be willing to do part of his duty.

When the child acts badly and is sorry, his parents "not only forgive that is past, and fulfil their promise nevertheless, but promise greater gifts than ever before, and to be better father and mother to it than ever they were."[7] In his sermons Hooker similarly stresses the analogy between divine fatherhood and the gentle and forgiving love of parents for their children:

> God will not be termed that which he is not. . . . Were not his affection most fatherly, the appellation of a Father would offend him. . . . "If a mother forget her child, (O love inexplicable!) art thou my son? of thee I will never be unmindful." Fathers, if they be provoked unto anger, conceive not unappeasable wrath: do not the tears of their children . . . wring out oftentimes tears from their eyes?[8]

Likewise, Andrewes combines maternal and paternal images in exploring the phrase, *viscera miseracordiae:*

> [These] are the bowels or vessels near the womb, near the loins; in a word, not *viscera* only, but *parentum viscera,* the bowels of a father or mother. . . . See them in the parable of the father towards his riotous lewd son. . . . See them in the better harlot of the twain; out of her motherly bowels, rather give away her child quite, renounced it rather than see it hurt. . . . *O paterna viscera miserationum!* when we have named them, a multitude of such mercies as come from a father's bowels, we have said as much as we can say or can be said.[9]

God is a "tender-bowelled father" and "as a father pitieth his own children"; there is in Him "that faithfulness that is in a mother towards her children, for as a woman cannot but pity her own child and 'the son of her womb,' so the Lord 'will not forget' His own people."[10]

7. William Tyndale, *Exposition on Matthew,* in *Expositions and Notes on Sundry Portions of The Holy Scriptures,* ed. Rev. Henry Walter, The Parker Society (Cambridge, 1849), pp. 74–75.

8. Richard Hooker, *The Works of that Learned and Judicious Divine, Mr. Richard Hooker,* 3 vols., ed. Rev. John Keble, 7th ed. (Oxford, 1888; reprint, New York, 1970), 3:628.

9. Lancelot Andrewes, *The Works of Lancelot Andrewes,* 11 vols., Library of Anglo-Catholic Theology (Oxford, 1854), 4:272.

10. Andrewes, *Works,* 11:304, 309; 5:472.

Even the male body seems to partake of the nurturing warmth commonly associated exclusively with the female. Both images again are used with reference to God. Thus speaking of divine love, Andrewes writes, "The breasts that are full have as great pleasure in being drawn, as the child that draweth them."[11] But elsewhere Andrewes depicts this intimacy in terms of the patriarchal body: the Father receives man "with arms spread, as was the lost child in the Gospel."[12] So Hooker asks "Where should the frighted child hide his head, but in the bosom of his loving father?"[13] He "taketh up in his arms, he lovingly embraceth, he kisseth . . . with more than fatherly tenderness."[14]

Often the tender and compassionate parent is identified with the father alone. According to Andrewes, "Fathers stand thus affected towards their children, that they are hardly brought to chasten them; and if there be no remedy, yet they are ready to forgive, or soon cease punishing,"[15] and again, "mercy accords well with a Father; no compassion, no bowels like his."[16] So he notes that the Hebrew word for father, *abba,* means "he that hath a care or desire to do good."[17] Even Calvin's *Institutes,* a work not known for its sentimental warmth, consistently associates fathers with pity and nurturing care: a quick scan through the first three books thus yields "fatherly kindness," "fatherly love," "fatherly favor toward us," "fatherly favor and beneficence," "fatherly care," "fatherly gentleness," and "merciful Father."[18] None of this, of course, tells us how Renaissance fathers actually behaved; but what we are interested in is the meaning of patriarchy, the ideal image of the father's role—and therefore also in what the Renaissance meant in describing God and king as father. These descriptions of tender and forgiving fathers (and mothers) suggest not only that patriarchy means a good deal more than male despotism but that current notions of gender differentiation may post-

11. Andrewes, *Works,* 1:100.
12. Andrewes, *Works,* 3:298.
13. Hooker, *Works,* 3:652.
14. Hooker, *Works,* 3:521. Hooker is actually speaking of St. Paul here.
15. Andrewes, *Works,* 5:367–68.
16. Andrewes, *Works,* 2:370.
17. Andrewes, *Works,* 6:175.
18. John Calvin, *Institutes of the Christian Religion,* 2 vols., ed. John T. McNeill, trans. Ford Lewis Battles, The Library of Christian Classics (Philadelphia, 1960), 1.5.8; 1.14.2; 1.16.2, 5; 1.17.1, 6; 3.19.5.

date the Renaissance.[19] The passages cited above seem to assume that fathers are and should be tender, nurturing, affectionate, and emotional—qualities that recent scholarship, including some feminist scholarship, classifies as female.[20] Conversely, the common nineteenth-century assumption that women are more compassionate, pious, and loving than men does not seem to have been an important part of Renaissance ideology. And this leads to the suspicion that modern gender differentiation is not a historical constant. The Renaissance obviously also specifies gender distinctions, but different ones: women are weaker, more sensual than men, and therefore less suited to govern. The "emasculation" of traits like gentleness and emotion seems to occur later and for reasons that are not directly related to gender roles but rather to the subsequent attempt to throw off the burden of inherited Christian values.[21] By "feminizing" mercy, gen-

19. In "The Body of Christ in the Later Middle Ages: A Reply to Leo Steinberg," Caroline Walker Bynum likewise observes that "for all their application of male/female contrasts to organize life symbolically—medieval thinkers and artists used gender imagery more fluidly and less literally than we do. . . . Medieval thinkers, however, saw not just the body of Christ but all bodies . . . as both male and female. . . . theologians and natural philosophers assumed considerable mixing of the genders" (*Renaissance Quarterly* 39 (1986): 434–35). See also her *Jesus as Mother: Studies in the Spirituality of the High Middle Ages* (Berkeley, 1982), pp. 148–49.

20. A recent study in cross-cultural psychology seems to corroborate the existence of maternal qualities in Christian symbolizations of the father and God. The study was largely based on responses to a questionnaire given to college-age Roman Catholics from a variety of countries. Very simply, the questionnaire gave them a list of attributes, containing mostly either "typically" maternal or "typically" paternal characteristics (for example, law, tenderness, intimacy), and asked the subjects to ascribe these characteristics to the figure of the mother, of the father, and/or of God. In almost every instance, the subjects ascribed maternal characteristics to the figure of the mother, but the figure of the father was characterized by maternal as well as paternal characteristics—the former to a lesser extent—while maternal and paternal characteristics mingled almost equally in the subjects' representation of God, although the maternal component was of slightly greater importance. While such modern evidence need not apply to the Renaissance, my intuition is that it does, that is, that fathers, and especially divine fathers, are deeply endowed with what we call maternal attributes. See Antoine Vergote and Alvaro Tamayo, *The Parental Figures and the Representation of God: A Psychological and Cross-Cultural Study*, Religion and Society (The Hague, 1981).

21. For example, Elaine V. Beilin notes that during the Renaissance one can find male authors describing women as deficient not only in intelligence but also piety (*Redeeming Eve: Women Writers of the English Renaissance* [Princeton, 1987], p. 15). Similarly, Margaret Olofson Thickstun observes that seventeenth-century religious writers held that "in the spirit the sexes achieve equality . . . because in the spirit there is only male: 'She is a woman only in her body'" (*Fictions of the Feminine: Puritan Doctrine and the Representation of Women* [Ithaca, 1988], p. 20). But the trend toward feminizing Christianity may have already been underway during this period. Ruth Kelso thus argues that

tleness, forgiveness, and so forth—all essentially Christian virtues—one could devalue them: Real Men don't get crucified. That loving fathers in the Renaissance so often appear in a religious context (that is, in relation to God the Father) indicates a more than adventitious connection between gender and belief. Furthermore, this connection does not entail that social constructions of gender are automatically reflected in belief systems but rather that changes in the latter can reconfigure the former.[22]

LOVE IN THE WESTERN WORLD

The Renaissance idealization of the father and the tendency to stress domestic order as the paradigm of both divine and social relations belong to a crucial (and largely unnoticed) redefinition of the nature of love. There are two well-known paradigms for love in Western Christianity: one that models love on sexual desire, and one that views it in terms of friendship. Love, that is, can be viewed either as *eros* or *philia*. From Plato on, thinkers who regard love as eros define it as the desire for possession of the good and beautiful. Such love is a movement toward union with the beloved object, originating in lack and propelled by desire.[23] Eros is thus the love of the weaker for the stronger,

---

"the ideal set up for the [Renaissance] lady is essentially Christian in its character, and the ideal for the gentlemen essentially pagan," although she (somewhat misleadingly) tends to equate chastity and silence with the sum of Christian ideals (*Doctrine for the Lady of the Renaissance* [Urbana, 1956], p. 25).

22. The contrast designated by the modern differentiation of male and female, when it appears in the Renaissance, usually belongs to the opposition between basically Stoic (reason, law, control) and basically Augustinian (emotion, passivity, love) ideals. It therefore need not have gendered connotations. See William J. Bouwsma, "The Two Faces of Humanism, Stoicism and Augustinianism in Renaissance Thought," in *Itinerarium Italicum: The Profile of the Italian Renaissance in the Mirror of Its European Transformations,* ed. Heiko A. Oberman with Thomas Brady, Jr. (Leiden, 1975), pp. 3–60. Alternatively, Milton associates machismo not with males but with romances, contrasting the "long and tedious havoc [of] fabl'd Knights / In Battels feign'd" with the "higher Argument" of Christian "Patience and Heroic Martyrdom" (*Paradise Lost,* in *John Milton: Complete Poetry and Major Prose,* ed. Merritt Y. Hughes [New York, 1957], 9.30–42). These instances exemplify the converse of Blumenberg's paradigm of historical change: the continuity of substance with change of function rather than continuity of function with change of substance.

23. Plato, *Symposium,* trans. Michael Joyce, in *The Collected Dialogues of Plato,* ed. Edith Hamilton and Huntington Cairns (Princeton, 1961), 203b–5d.

of the less for the more perfect, of the creature for the creator.[24] Insofar as the lover seeks his own happiness and fulfillment in the possession of the beloved, such love is egocentric (a term that ought not be understood negatively, since it is absolutely proper for a creature to seek the perfection and joy for which it was created). The Platonic eros is by far the most pervasive model for love throughout the Middle Ages, but a second tradition emerges in St. Thomas, whose discussion of love in the *Summa* draws on Aristotle's account of friendship or *philia*. The model for love in this sense, what Thomas calls *amor amicitiae,* is the nonsexual, mature relationship between equals, a freely chosen willing of the good for another person for his/her sake—not for one's own utility or pleasure. While in Thomas *amor amicitiae* may describe the love between man and God, in Aristotle this possibility is explicitly ruled out—*philia* can only exist between equals.[25]

However, while both Aristotle and Thomas generally think of *philia* in terms of adult friendship, the former twice offers the curious observation that the love of a mother (explicitly not father) for her child may be the purest form of *philia,* insofar as maternal love is for the sake of the child, with no reward or even reciprocity demanded.[26] In the Renaissance, this observation seems to have become the germ of an important and widespread redefinition of love modeled on parental affection. Renaissance writers often refer to this love by its Greek name—*storge* or *storge phusike*[27]—or its English equivalent, "natural

24. *Symposium* 210b–11c; Aristotle, *Metaphysics,* trans. W. D. Ross, *The Complete Works of Aristotle,* 2 vols., ed. Jonathan Barnes (Princeton, 1984), 12.7.1072ab. The classic discussion of eros in Christian thought from Augustine to the Renaissance can be found in the second volume of Anders Nygren's *Agape and Eros: The History of the Christian Idea of Love,* 2 vols., trans. Philip Watson (London, 1939).

25. Aristotle, *Nicomachean Ethics,* trans. W. D. Ross, revised by J. O. Urmson, in *The Complete Works,* 8.7.1159a; St. Thomas Aquinas, *Summa theologiae,* 60 vols., vol. 19 trans. Eric D'Arcy, vol. 34 trans. R. J. Batten, O.P. (New York, 1963) 1a.2ae.26, 4; 2a.2ae.23,1.

26. Aristotle *Nicomachean Ethics* 8.8.1159a, 9.4.1166a, 9.7.1168a. On the theological uses of maternal (still not paternal) love in the Middle Ages, see Bynum, *Jesus as Mother,* pp. 116, 133, 144.

27. This term was not important in Greek thought. The only ancient work on the subject, Plutarch's "On Affection (*philostorgia*) for Offspring," does not appear to have been the source for Renaissance discussions. Compare Bruno Snell, *The Discovery of the Mind in Greek Philosophy and Literature,* trans. T. G. Rosenmeyer (New York, 1953), p. 168. It also is used once in the Greek New Testament, at Romans 12:10: "devoted to one another (*philostorgoi*) in brotherly love."

affection." In a significant number of Renaissance texts, *storge* largely replaces eros and *philia,* the love of parents for children becoming the primary metaphor for divine love.[28] In these the basic notion of love, both human and divine, derives from the mutual love of a parent—now usually the father—for his child, and, by extension, the ideal community becomes not the heterosexual union of lovers but the family. Thus Melanchthon describes *storge* as Mary's love for the infant Jesus and, by analogy, as the psychological ground of our awareness of God's love for His Son and for mankind. "In Elisabeth and Mary are στοργαὶ toward [their] sons"; for God has implanted "στοργαὶ in [our] heart . . . to remind us of the love of God toward his Son and toward us."[29] Similarly Lancelot Andrewes defines it as "love, but in a higher degree than that which is due to every one; the name of it is στοργὴ, which is a natural affection, either ascending or descending . . . as a son to the father."[30]

Despite Andrewes's claim that *storge* both ascends and descends, the latter direction tends to be emphasized. Andrewes himself admits as much in another passage, where he observes that "it is natural for every thing to have στοργὴν, 'a natural love,' toward that which it bringeth forth."[31] Among religious writers, *storge* thus becomes equivalent to *caritas,* the unmerited and gratuitous love of the higher for the lower, the stronger for the weaker. For Tyndale, the analogy between God and parents holds precisely because both love their children even when they are evil and without expecting any recompense.[32] But the assumption that love descends seems to have been a cultural commonplace outside of any Protestant context. Vives, as we have seen, notes that love generally descends from father to son and from God to man rather than the reverse. In *The Trew Law of Free Monarchies,* King James similarly observes in passing that "wee see by the

28. Bynum notes a similar phenomenon in the Middle Ages, where texts that use the *Brautmystik* motifs do not use maternal imagery and vice versa (*Jesus as Mother,* p. 141).

29. Philip Melanchthon, *Liber de anima,* vol. 13 of *Opera quae supersunt omnia,* 28 vols., ed. Carolus Gottlieb Bretschneider, Corpus Reformatorum (Brunswick and Halle, 1834–60), pp. 134–35.

30. Andrewes, *Works,* 6:176.

31. Andrewes, *Works,* 6:34.

32. Tyndale, *The Parable of the Wicked Mammon,* in *Doctrinal Treatises,* p. 107; *Exposition on Matthew,* in *Expositions and Notes,* pp. 74–75, 127.

course of nature, that love useth to descend more then to ascend."[33] In his *Matrimoniall Honour* (1642), Daniel Rogers acknowledges the same truism, "love must descend, not ascend." Rogers, however, goes on to make an important connection between this psychological pattern and its socioeconomic consequences: "its not natural (saith Paul) for children to provide to parents, but for parents to provide for them, therefore invert not providence . . . be sure to hold stroke sufficient in your hand, for the securing of love and duty from your children."[34] Although parents gladly provide for their offspring, the reverse is not the case, and therefore parents should be careful not to give so much to their child that they become dependent on him. Nor is Rogers being overly cynical (or Shakespearean). In Renaissance England, aged parents rarely were (or expected to be) supported by their offspring. Parents gave to children, not children to parents. It was thus an established principle in English law that property "always descended and never ascended."[35] Hence, as Alan Macfarlane concludes, "it came to be taken as axiomatic that obligations, like emotions, flowed down."[36] Protestant theology and cultural practice thus both reinforced an anti-Platonic notion of love flowing downward from the tender and nurturing parent to the child but less frequently or securely springing upward in return.

PATRIARCHY VERSUS POLITICS

The representation of divine/human relations in terms of descending paternal affection tended to amalgamate spiritual and domestic structures. The location of *political* relations with respect to this patriarchal complex is more ambiguous. The analogy between kings and fathers goes back to antiquity.[37] In the Renaissance the analogy could be used

33. James I, *The Political Works of James I,* intro. Charles McIlwain (Cambridge, Mass., 1918; reprint, New York, 1965), p. 64; compare Macfarlane, *Marriage,* p. 82.

34. Quoted in Macfarlane, *Marriage,* pp. 110–11.

35. Macfarlane, *Marriage,* p. 99.

36. Macfarlane, *Marriage,* p. 82.

37. For example, *Nicomachean Ethics* 8.10.1160a–61a. A fine survey of the political contexts of patriarchal thought can be found in Gordon J. Schochet's *Patriarchalism in Political Thought: The Authoritarian Family and Political Speculation and Attitudes Especially in Seventeenth-Century England* (Oxford, 1975).

to naturalize absolute monarchal authority by equating the power of the king with the unlimited authority fathers were held to possess over their children.[38] This, however, is not its principal use. It is not how King James uses it. As previously noted, he often recurs to the analogy of kings and fathers but "the authority and status of a king for James were unrelated to the monarch's being a father of his people or having derived his position from the power of a patriarch." Instead, like Hooker and Andrewes, James represents the father—and therefore the king—as a "maternal," nurturing figure, a "loving nourish-father."[39] This representation, however, has been viewed by Jonathan Goldberg and others as an ideological concealment of oppressive power relations; that is, James's depiction of the king as a loving father naturalizes (or attempts to naturalize) the absolutist demand for obedience and subordination.[40] We will subsequently look at James's father-king and the question of ideological masking, but it should first be observed that this identification of kings and fathers is by no means inevitable. Greville obviously refuses to identify them. The conforming Elizabethan Puritan, William Perkins, similarly contrasts the political and paternal; thus he notes that while God seems a "cruel tyrant" to the unregenerate, the Christian perceives Him as "a merciful father, that would consider my infirmity and weakness"; thus having sinned, only the memory of the Father's "old kindness would not let me despair, howbeit all the world could not see [set?] mine heart at rest . . . until I heard the voice of my father, that all is forgotten."[41] Somewhat surprisingly, Andrewes (James's court preacher throughout his reign and a fierce royalist) also consistently and explicitly opposes the two

38. J. P. Sommerville, *Politics and Ideology in England, 1603–1640* (London, 1986), pp. 29–30.

39. Schochet, *Patriarchalism*, pp. 87–88; James I, *Political Works*, p. 24; compare pp. 18, 27.

40. Jonathan Goldberg, "Fatherly Authority: The Politics of Stuart Family Images," in Ferguson, Quilligan, and Vickers, eds., *Rewriting*, pp. 3–5, 18; also Stephen Orgel, "Prospero's Wife," in Ferguson, Quilligan, and Vickers, eds., *Rewriting*, p. 59; E. Pearlman, "George Herbert's God," *English Literary Renaissance* 13 (1983): 100; Stone, *The Family, Sex, and Marriage*, p. 105. For a trenchant analysis of the modern tendency to reduce all social relations to practices of domination and oppression, see Kenneth Minogue, *Alien Powers: The Pure Theory of Ideology* (New York, 1985).

41. William Perkins, "A Dialogue of the State of a Christian Man," *The Work of William Perkins*, ed. Ian Breward, The Courtenay Library of Reformation Classics (Appleford, Eng., 1970), pp. 364, 373. Perkins's *Christian Oeconomy*, included in the same volume, is a good example of the more familiar authoritarian patriarchalism.

figures, associating the king with power and subordination, the father with unconditional love and inclusion. For Andrewes, God is both king and father, both commanding and loving—but the two metaphors are not identified or confused. For, he writes, "the excellency of God's love appeareth herein, that He is not described to be God under the name of a King or great Lord. . . . But this is it that contents us, that He describes His goodness under the term of Father, in which regard how wickedly soever we deal, yet still we may say with the evil child, 'I will go to my Father.'"[42] Elsewhere he notes, "as love to a father, so fear to a lord, doth belong most properly."[43] In other passages, Andrewes contrasts the hypocritical civility of the king with God's paternal love: "whereas earthly princes may perhaps afford a good countenance but will not grant the thing that is sought for at their hands, Christ saith that 'the Father of lights' is not only affable but liberal; so that albeit we be . . . wretched sinners unworthy to be heard . . . 'yet He will not cast out our prayers nor turn His mercy from us.'"[44]

Other Renaissance texts similarly affirm this distinction between kings and fathers. The opposition between royal power and the "natural affection" binding father and child thus informs William Roper's biography of his father-in-law, the *Lyfe of Sir Thomas Moore,* written in about 1556. The contrast between political relations and the reciprocal love of father and child structures the three pivotal scenes of physical contact, of a bodily intimacy that seems to rupture the isolations of rank, decorum, and competition. The first describes Henry VIII's surprise visit to More at his home in Chelsea. Roper recalls that "after dinner, in a faire garden of his, [the king] walked with him by the space of an houre, holdinge his arme aboute his necke."[45] Roper, excited by this honor paid his father-in-law, later congratulates More. More's response, the first premonition of the ensuing catastrophe, is "howbeit, sonne Roper, I may tell thee I have no cawse to be prowd thereof, for if my head could winne him a castle in Fraunce . . . it

42. Andrewes, *Works,* 5:367.

43. Andrewes, *Works,* 4:381. In *Jesus as Mother,* Bynum notes several instances where lord/ruler (*dominus*) is contrasted to *mother,* but not to father (pp. 117–18).

44. Andrewes, *Works,* 5:322.

45. William Roper, *The Lyfe of Sir Thomas Moore, Knighte,* ed. Elsie V. Hitchcock, Early English Texts Society (London, 1935), pp. 20–21.

should not faile to goe."[46] This insight into the power politics of kingly embraces is set in contrast to two further episodes. The earlier of these occurs after More has been made Lord Chancellor. Roper reports that whenever More passed

> by the courte of the kinges Benche, if his father, one of the Judges thereof, had bine sate ere he came, he wold goe into the same courte, and there reverently kneeling downe in the sight of them all, duly aske his fathers blessinge. . . . And for the better declaration of his naturall affection towards his father, he not only, while he lay on his death bedd . . . ofte times . . . most kindly came to visite him. But also at his departure out of the world with teares taking him about the necke, most lovingly kissed and imbraced him.[47]

As before, "natural affection" refers to the bond between child and parent that transgresses status distinctions and creates the depoliticized space of bodily and emotional intimacy.

The final incident is the climactic moment of the *Lyfe.* As More returns to the Tower for the final time, his daughter (and Roper's wife) meets him in a mimetic reenactment of More's meetings with his father.

> Assone as she sawe him, after his blessing on her knees reverently receaved, Shee hastinge towards him, and, without consideracion or care of her self, pressinge in amonge the middest of the thronge and company of the garde that with halberdes and bills wente round aboute him, hastely ranne to him, and there openly, in the sight of them all, imbraced him, toke him about the neck, and kissed him. Who, well liking her moste naturall and deere daughterlye affection towardes him, gave her his fatherly blessinge.

She steps back and then, in Roper's words, "being all ravished with the entyre love of her deere father," runs to him again and "tooke him about the neck, and divers times together most lovingly kissed him, and at last, with a full heavy harte, was fayne to departe from him."[48] A week later, More writes to her, "I never liked your manner towardes me better then when you kissed me last. For I like when daughterly love and deere charitye hath no leysure to looke to worldly courtesye."[49] These are his last written words; the next day he is

46. Roper, *The Lyfe,* p. 21.
47. Roper, *The Lyfe,* p. 44.
48. Roper, *The Lyfe,* pp. 98–99.
49. Roper, *The Lyfe,* pp. 99–100.

executed. This piece of "naturall and deere daughterlye affection" is worth insisting on if only because scholars have concluded from this passage that Roper here reveals the secret of incest between More and his daughter. The *Lyfe,* according to this reading, records Roper's voyeuristic and ambivalent presentation of his wife's incestuous involvement with his father-in-law, which finally comes to the surface in the abandon of these final moments.[50] But the text is explicit: Margaret's love expresses "naturall" (not unnatural) affection and "deere charitye," the kind of love that binds Christ and mankind. This asexual *storge,* so unfamiliar to us, is not the product of Roper's repression but a dominant model for love throughout the Renaissance and the antithesis of the treacherous "worldly courtesye" of Henry's politic embrace.

The contrast between political and filial spheres in Roper's *Lyfe* also informs *Paradise Lost.* The central thematic axis in the epic runs through Satan, Christ, and Eve. All three are slightly subordinate, excellent in themselves but one rung below true headship.[51] As Eve is to Adam, so Satan is to Christ, and Christ to the Father. Milton's subordinationism is thus crucial to the theme of *Paradise Lost.* For our purposes, what is significant is that Satan and Christ display two alternative responses to their subordination, and these alternatives form the interpretive framework for Eve's actions. Satan views subordination *politically;* he is the first new historicist, regarding his relation to God in terms of power. His first speeches make this abundantly clear: God is a tyrant, supreme only by force (1.124, 248);[52] the only available options are to be slave or master (1.263), to "submit" or "not to be overcome" (1.108–9); power relations are inherently oppressive, for "to be weak is miserable / Doing or Suffering" (1.157–58). It is only one of the manifold ironies of *Paradise Lost* that Satan himself

50. Jonathan V. Crewe, "The '*Encomium Moriae*' of William Roper," *English Literary History* 55 (1988): 300–301.

51. On the parallel between Eve and Christ, see Joseph H. Summers, *The Muse's Method: An Introduction to "Paradise Lost"* (Cambridge, Mass., 1962), pp. 176–85; Barbara Lewalski, "Milton on Women—Yet Once More," *Milton Studies* 6 (1974): 19; Joan Webber, "The Politics of Poetry: Feminism and *Paradise Lost,*" *Milton Studies* 14 (1980): 18; Diane McColley, *Milton's Eve* (Urbana, 1983), pp. 35, 51; Thickstun, *Fictions,* pp. 84–85. On the parallel between Eve and Satan, see Sandra Gilbert, "Patriarchal Poetry and Women Readers: Reflections on Milton's Bogey," *Publications of the Modern Language Association* 93 (1978): 372–74.

52. Milton, *Paradise Lost;* subsequent citations will appear in the text.

becomes the archpolitician, a master of colonialist practice and reasons of state.

Christ's response to his subordination supplies the alternative to demonic politicization, an alternative defined as "Filial obedience" (3.269). While Milton's Father has obvious affinities with the authoritarian patriarch, these do not govern the relation between Father and Son. Instead this relation is suffused with mutual love, with tenderness, affection, and a willing of the other's good. The Father gives "all Power" to the Son (3.317); the Son responds that he "gladlier shall resign" such power "when in the end / Thou shalt be All in All, and I in thee / For ever" (6.731–33). The Son's speeches in particular express the joyful obedience and love that distinguishes familial from political bonds.

> O Father, O Supream of heav'nly thrones,
> First, Highest, Holiest, Best, thou alwayes seekst
> To glorifie thy Son, I alwayes thee,
> As is most just; this I my glorie account,
> My exaltation, and my whole delight,
> That thou in me well pleas'd declarst thy will
> Fulfill'd, which to fulfil is all my bliss.
> (6.723–29)

The Father's responses to this devotion display an unreserved warmth. He answers Christ's plea for mercy on fallen humanity with "O Son, in whom my Soul hath chief delight, / Son of my bosom" (3.168–69). Similarly, Christ's offer of himself for man's sin is met with "O thou in Heav'n and Earth the only peace / Found out for mankind under wrauth, O thou / My sole complacence!" (3.274–76). Filial obedience and paternal love, as in More, do not recapitulate but are explicitly contrasted to the political model of subordination and its discourse of power, equality, ambition, and domination.[53] The assumption governing *Paradise Lost* is precisely opposite to that prevalent in recent criticism: as the latter presupposes that the rhetoric of the loving father and obedient child occludes power relations,[54] so in Milton Satan's

53. Stevie Davies, *Images of Kingship in "Paradise Lost": Milton's Politics and Christian Liberty* (Columbia, Mo., 1983), pp. 166–75.

54. See, for example, Kathleen McLuskie, "The Patriarchal Bard: Feminist Criticism and Shakespeare: *King Lear* and *Measure for Measure*," in *Political Shakespeare: New Essays in Cultural Materialism*, ed. Jonathan Dollimore and Alan Sinfield (Ithaca, 1985), pp. 88–108. Although McLuskie acknowledges that "when Lear enters, bearing his dead

political reading of the divine economy is a highly interested and deliberate masking of "Heav'ns free Love dealt equally to all" (4.68).

Since women and children occupied a similar cultural place in Renaissance England, the question of filial subordination can easily be transferred to the marital arena. That Eve's reasoning at the Fall is couched in political terms, her reconciliation with Adam in those of obedient love—that she passes under the influence of grace from Satanic ambition to Christlike submissiveness—is too obvious to be insisted on. Here, as before, the political reading is both wrong and catastrophic, the paternalist both right and productive of forgiveness, mutuality, and joy. The two discourses are strictly separated, and, while no one would accuse Milton of naiveté or political innocence, the proponents of realpolitik and demystification turn out to have pulled the wool over their own eyes.

These contrasts between the images of king (or tyrant) and father raise the possibility that paternal and political discourse are not, at least not inevitably, isomorphic. The image of the father need not belong to the realm of power and oppression but to an explicitly opposed arena of love and forgiveness. In other words, not all patriarchal discourse concerns whitewashing coercive power relations—unless we want to

---

daughter in his arms, we are presented with a[n] . . . emblem of the natural, animal assertion of family love," she goes on to argue that feminist criticism must resist and subvert the "patriarchal relations" which such a scene endorses, by revealing that the text is produced "within the contradictions of contemporary ideology and practice" and that issues of filial bonds cannot be separated from those of "economic justice" and "material circumstances" (pp. 102–6). For the pervasive tendency of recent criticism to analyze Renaissance texts in terms of the idealizing/mystification (bad) of power relations versus their exposure/subversion (good), see Jonathan Dollimore, *Radical Tragedy: Religion, Ideology, and Power in the Drama of Shakespeare and His Contemporaries* (Chicago, 1984) passim, and also his introduction to Dollimore and Sinfield, eds., *Political Shakespeare,* where "Tillyard's world picture" becomes "an ideological legitimation of an existing social order" (p. 5) and beliefs function to legitimate "the existing relations of domination and subordination" (p. 7); see also Paul Brown, "'This Thing of Darkness I Acknowledge Mine': *The Tempest* and the Discourse of Colonialism," in Dollimore and Sinfield, eds., *Political Shakespeare,* pp. 48, 59–61, 68–69; Leonard Tennenhouse, "Strategies of State and Political Plays: *A Midsummer Night's Dream, Henry IV, Henry V, Henry VIII,*" in Dollimore and Sinfield, eds., *Political Shakespeare,* p. 110; Stephen Orgel, "Making Greatness Familiar," in *The Forms of Power and the Power of Forms,* ed. Stephen Greenblatt, Genre Special Topics 7 (Norman, Okla., 1982), pp. 42–43. In general Marxist criticism, even in its revisionist forms, is led to equate the ideal (including all expressions of faith, love, and harmony) with the imaginary, the exposure of its material and ideological bases with the real. Compare Edward Pechter, "The New Historicism and Its Discontents: Politicizing Renaissance Drama," *Publications of the Modern Language Association* 102 (1987): 294–95, 301–2.

make an a priori claim that denies the contrast the text takes pains to enforce.

If the image of the loving father does not, in these texts, seem to be about legitimating male power, what is its function? Why does it partially or wholly replace eros and *philia*? Andrewes again suggests a possible answer: "The master may cease to be a master, so may a servant; the husband may cease to be a husband, so may the wife by means of divorce; but God can never cease to be 'our Father' though He be never so much offended, and we cannot cease to be His sons how wicked soever we be; and therefore God doth by an immutable term signify unto us the immutability of His affection."[55] Fatherhood is an immutable term. That is, unlike economic, marital, or erotic relations, parental affection is not based on choice or merit; it is unconditional and instinctive. Parents do not stop loving their children. Melanchthon and Vives make the same point: *storge* is natural rather than voluntary;[56] unlike eros, it does not depend on the excellence of the beloved but reaches out to what is deformed, weak, pitiable.[57]

This stress on the instinctive, unconditional aspect of parental love provides a clue to its psychosocial significance. Unlike eros and *philia*, it seems to express a longing for security, for the infant's guaranteed protection and nurturing, for a return to the family. Despite Stone's influential assertion that affective domesticity and the notion of family as refuge from the fray of the public and political postdate the Renaissance, whose family structure he depicts as authoritarian and autocratic,[58] these texts suggest that such *concepts* have acquired considerable currency by the sixteenth century. Nor does it seem plausible that

55. Andrewes, *Works,* 5:367.

56. Melanchthon, *De anima,* 13:132. "Quidam adfectus seu inclinationes natura insunt animantibus sine deliberatione, ut *στοργαὶ φυσικαὶ* in parentibus erga sobolem."

57. Juan Luis Vives, *De anima et vita* (Basel, 1538; reprint, Turin, 1959), pp. 169–70, 179.

58. See Stone, *Family, Sex, and Marriage,* pp. 81–82, 109–10, 116–26; Jonathan Goldberg, *James I and the Politics of Literature: Jonson, Shakespeare, Donne, and Their Contemporaries* (Baltimore, 1983), p. 86. Goldberg supports his case by citing numerous recent studies which argue that the notion of the family as a retreat from the public world is a postindustrial phenomenon (pp. 258–60). Stone, on the other hand, connects the rise of affective domesticity with the Reformation, although he feels that affective familial relations really began to replace authoritarian ones only after the middle of the seventeenth century (pp. 93–94, 100–101, 149–50). The contrast implicit here between the family as a social organism and the family as an affective unit may in fact be illusory. In *When Fathers Ruled: Family Life in Reformation Europe* (Cambridge, Mass., 1983),

humanists and preachers would appeal so confidently to parental tenderness if such emotions were culturally unavailable. More recent scholarship has, in fact, strongly contested Stone's thesis. In particular, Alan Macfarlane's *Marriage and Love in England, 1300–1840* claims not only that Renaissance parents showed a deep and abiding affection for their children but that the parent/child relation was significantly and qualitatively different from all other relations. According to Macfarlane, in the English Renaissance children were useless. Children provided their parents with no economic, social, or political benefits. They were simply loved, loved for the pleasure they brought their parents rather than for any ulterior advantage. And the majority of children left home between eight and fifteen,[59] a fact that may explain the intense nostalgia for familial bonds visible in Renaissance texts.

Moreover, the uniquely nonutilitarian basis of parental love allowed that relation to be perceived as essentially different from all other social ties. Therefore it seems possible to argue that in both ideology and praxis, the loving parent and family emerge by the sixteenth century in response both to the increasingly mobile and competitive conditions of Renaissance society and to the rather arbitrary power of the state.[60] In the texts we are examining, the parent is perceived as having a natural, noncontractual relation to the child, whereas all other relations—lordship, marriage—are social and therefore contingent. The Renaissance family, in these accounts, is not the domestic reflection of its monarchy, but the counterpart: a response to power politics and cultural complexity. The significance of *storge* lies precisely in establishing a space outside the political; a hierarchy where the stronger loves and cares for the weaker, where forgiveness and tenderness are unconditionally given. This space is not a mystification of the political but, if anything, the mystification (or, less judgmentally, articulation) of a need to escape political relations felt as coercive

---

Steven Ozment comments that sixteenth-century parents appear to have been affectionate, often (to the dismay of the moralists) indulgent, and deeply emotionally involved with their children, although equally concerned with discipline and socialization (pp. 132–35, 166–72). A similar conclusion is reached by Linda A. Pollock in *Forgotten Children: Parent-Child Relations from 1500 to 1900* (Cambridge, 1983).

59. Macfarlane, *Marriage,* pp. 52–90.

60. So Schochet suggests that the emergence of patriarchal political theories in the seventeenth century may have resulted from the tentative beginnings of a differentiation between "the political and social realms of human experience" (*Patriarchalism,* p. 54).

and contingent. Leah Marcus has similarly argued that the emphasis on the child in Renaissance devotional works seems a response to "profound feelings of doubt and social dislocation" created by the social changes of the early modern period.[61] The textual representations of the dutiful child and loving father symbolize the desire to establish a relationship exempt from coercion, mutability, and struggle. If, as social ideology, this model of filiation leads to the privatized domesticity of the bourgeois family, as theology, it articulates a relation of inequality radically different from all political relations because grounded in an instinctive and unmerited love.

THE MIRROR OF PARTICIPATION

Furthermore, the relation between parent and child retains traces of participation, the boundaries between self and other fading into (infantile) compactness. The longing for participation suffusing Renaissance texts thus seems linked to the valorization of parental bonds as the expression of noncontractual, nonnegotiable relatedness. In English law, the child is *pars patris*. He remains "part" of the father rather than being perceived as a clearly individuated and separate entity.[62] Andrewes thus observes that "to beget is an act of nature, and is ever determined in the identity of the same nature with him that did beget."[63] Often this participation is expressed in terms of imaging; the beloved child reflects the father and is loved as his reflection. So Donne writes that, "God loves nothing more then the Image of himselfe, in his Sonne, and then the Image of his Sonne Christ Jesus, in us."[64]

But the notion of parental love as love of one's own image is not unproblematic. At first glance, it would seem that since *storge* is the love of the stronger for the weaker, it is not self-interested. The parent loves the child for the child's sake, not because he or she derives any particular benefit from the child. According to Vives, "when something is loved for its own sake, because it is good in itself, taking away all consideration of our own interest, this is true and sincere

61. Marcus, *Childhood and Cultural Despair,* pp. 93 and passim.
62. Davies, *Images of Kingship,* p. 164.
63. Andrewes, *Works,* 1:291.
64. John Donne, *The Sermons of John Donne,* 10 vols., ed. George Potter and Evelyn Simpson (Berkeley, 1953–62), 9:2.854–55.

love . . . the clearest example of which we perceive in [the love] of a parent towards a child."[65] In this, *storge* closely resembles Aristotle's account of friendship.[66] But this selflessness is immediately complicated by the fact that parental love is a form of self-love.[67] The problem is set out most explicitly by Vives and Hooker. Almost immediately following the quotation just cited, Vives notes, "From the love of ourselves arises love towards our children, as if towards a part of ourselves . . . For likeness is the cause of love, as if toward another self. Thus children embrace and kiss mirrors in which they view their image because they think another child like themselves to be inside."[68] Parental love is the love of one's own image or likeness. The same point appears in Hooker: people love their children because they see themselves contained in them; in fact, we naturally love those on whom we bestow good things because we see in them the effects of our own virtue. Therefore, Hooker continues, God loves His own creation and the Father loves the Son—in each case, the beloved is loved as an image of the lover, as an extension or reflection of himself.[69] So here we have a love that is both selfless and self-love—one that apparently resembles both Christian agape and Lacanian narcissism.

To resolve this apparent paradox we need to look more closely at Vives. Following St. Thomas, Vives divides all love into *cupiditas* and true love (of which Thomas's friendship is a part). True love seeks the good for the sake of the beloved, cupidity for the benefit of the lover. As examples of true love, he selects God and parents, but then, curi-

65. Vives, *De anima,* p. 154.

66. *Nicomachean Ethics* 8.3.1156b.

67. This problem is also Aristotelian, although the Renaissance solution is significantly different since Aristotle sees true self-love as the person's desire to attain virtue, excellence, and nobility, as opposed to selfish love, that is, the desire to acquire good "things," like wealth or power, for one's self (*Nicomachean Ethics* 9.4.1166a, 9.8.1168a–69a). Aquinas follows Aristotle closely here: "amor quo quis diligit seipsum, est forma et radix amicitiae. . . . amantes seipsos vituperantur inquantum amant se secundum naturam sensibilem, cui obtemperant. Quod not est vere amare seipsum secundum naturam rationalem, ut sibi velit ea bona quae pertinent ad perfectionem rationis. Et hoc modo praecipue ad caritatem pertinet diligere seipsum" (*ST* 2a.2ae.25,5).

68. Vives, *De anima,* p. 155.

69. Hooker, *Works,* 2:246–47, 305. Likewise in Milton, the relation of the Father to the Son is consistently described in terms of mirroring and reflection; compare *Paradise Lost,* 3.139–40, 385–86, 6.680–82, 720; 10.65–67.

ously, a person's love for himself, explaining that "sincere love is never mercenary; it does not seek a reward for its labors, nor expect one . . . you do not love yourself in order to benefit yourself, but you benefit yourself because you love yourself."[70] That is, self-love has no trace of ulteriority; we do not love ourselves for any particular reason or reward, but unconditionally for our own sake. We love ourselves as an end, not a means.

For Vives, the structure of self-love is identical to parental and divine love, precisely because these latter two are variants of self-love. But for this very reason, the love of a parent or God is not selfish but genuinely directed toward the other. Vives continues, "a person loves his child or wife, whom he nevertheless well enough sees to be deformed or dull or slow; nevertheless because love (*caritas*) does not pertain to this, but to the person (*persona*) of the wife or son, love (*amor*) does not grow cold."[71] Self-love mutates into commitment to another person because the other is perceived as an image of the self. Thus, in the passage we have already cited on several occasions, Vives argues that "the benefactor loves the one he benefits as his own handiwork; so a father [loves] his son and a teacher his student. . . . Although love has the nature of fire, yet it descends rather than ascends. A parent loves his child more . . . than the reverse; and the greatest and most ardent of all loves is that of God toward us."[72] Love descends to the other as the image and handiwork of the self. But his self-love is not narcissism because it is not a self-absorbed desire to possess oneself either as a quasi-erotic object or as an Ideal-I. It is not desire at all, since desire is the product of lack or insufficiency on the part of the lover, whereas the love Vives describes constitutes its object from its own fullness. This self-love creates and nurtures the other—God and parents bring forth their image and cherish this reflection of their plentitude. The child who kisses himself in the mirror does not, like Narcissus, love himself as an other, but rather loves the other as himself. The mirror of participation thus allows parental affection to flow downward to the child precisely because it is a bond not based on merit, advantage, or erotic cupidity but on what Andrewes calls an

70. Vives, *De anima*, p. 173.
71. Vives, *De anima*, pp. 169–70. Note that here *persona* is used in its modern sense.
72. Vives, *De anima*, p. 159; compare *Nicomachean Ethics* 9:7.1167b–68a.

"act of nature" that is "ever determined in the identity" of the begetter and the begotten.[73]

PATRIARCHY AND THE WOLF-PACK

Patriarchal idealism seems partly a reaction against absolutist theology, isolating political structures of domination and submission from the divine and domestic workings of natural affection. Yet *storge* also suffuses the analysis of political relations in the Renaissance. Kings and fathers are at least as often equated as contrasted. So James, as mentioned above, describes the king as a "loving nourish-father." In the same vein, Hooker speaks of the first Christian rulers as "nursing Fathers" and Andrewes, of magistrates as "right nursing fathers and mothers," all drawing on Isaiah 49:23: "And kings shall be thy nursing fathers, and their queens thy nursing mothers."[74] The confusion about the relation of patriarchy to politics results from the double meaning of "political." On the one hand, it may signify anything that pertains to public government, on the other, to Hobbes's "perpetual and restless desire of power after power that ceases only in death."[75] It is in this latter sense that politics can be contrasted to patriarchy. For patriarchy obviously pertains to government, as well as to family and divinity. The royalist justification of kingship rests on the identification of king and father; like fathers, rulers cherish, love, and care for those placed in their charge. Thus Hooker describes the king as a "common parent, whose care is presumed to extend most indifferently over all."[76] An-

73. Andrewes, *Works,* 1:291. This analysis of self-love may elucidate the troublesome passage in book 4 of *Paradise Lost* where Eve, immediately after awakening, becomes entranced by her reflection in the lake (4.449–92). As critics have noted, this looks like an allusion to Narcissus and thus implies that even before the Fall woman was a vain and problematic creature. But if the love of one's own image is not evil but the ground of all love, then Eve's action need have no negative moral import. To love the reflected image is not wrong; it is just that to love a watery reflection is somewhat less satisfying than to love a human one. So God tells her not that she should not love her image, but that He will bring her to one "Whose image thou art" and "to him shalt [thou] bear / Multitudes like thy self" (4.472–74). Marital and parental love are both loves of one's own image; that is how God describes them.

74. Hooker, *Works,* 3:319; Andrewes, *Works,* 6:199.

75. Thomas Hobbes, *Leviathan,* ed. Herbert Schneider, The Library of Liberal Arts (Indianapolis, 1958), p. 86.

76. Hooker, *Works,* 3:405.

drewes similarly notes that God has given rulers the "names of father and mother . . . which are names of nature, full of love."[77] This analogy appears repeatedly in King James's own political treatises and speeches. In *Basilikon Doron* the king is referred to as a "naturall father" of his people; in *The Trew Law of Free Monarchies* as "a loving Father . . . caring for [his subjects] more then for himselfe," as "our god in earth, and loving Father."[78] The point of the analogy is always the same: the king is like a father—and like the Father—because he loves and cares for his subjects. Even in the speech of 1609 where James does associate the father with the *potestas vitae et necis,* the power to kill one's children, he immediately points out that fathers do not generally exercise this authority because they generally have no desire to hurt their offspring.[79]

The concept of paternal government implies rule without coercion. The Renaissance found the use of force within a Christian society deeply problematic, although only the Anabaptists denied its necessity.[80] In *Religion, Order, and Law,* David Little observes that Calvin and his successors attempted to resolve "the dilemma of earthly power" by setting it within an evolutionary theological scheme. For Calvin "nothing is surer than that the Kingdom of God, toward which all things move, includes overcoming the engines of coercion in favor of voluntary obedience to the will of God. . . . the entire movement of history [is] . . . a movement from political-legal regulation and coercion toward the self-determining, self-integrating freedom of the conscience."[81] The Puritan communities established in England were an endeavor to found just such a consensual order within the coercive frame of the Tudor state. Patriarchy, likewise, belongs to the struggle

77. Andrewes, *Works,* 6:179.

78. James I, *Political Works,* pp. 18, 55, 70.

79. James I, *Political Works,* pp. 308–9.

80. Both conciliar and Jesuit political theorists distinguish paternal from political government on the ground that *only* the latter involves coercion. Political government is furthermore the result of the Fall and hence not part of the original divine gift to Adam, who had only paternal (and therefore not coercive) powers. See Quentin Skinner, *The Foundations of Modern Political Thought,* 2 vols. (Cambridge, 1978), 2:116–18, 156. Bynum associates the medieval image of the nurturing, "maternal" male with problems of authority in a Christian society (*Jesus as Mother,* pp. 146, 154–58). In both cases, images of parenthood are used to project an alternative to political rule.

81. David Little, *Religion, Order, and Law: A Study in Pre-Revolutionary England* (Oxford, 1970), pp. 53–56.

to conceive how voluntary obedience might replace force as the cement of social organization. This is true in both divinity and politics. Thus Hooker writes that insofar as God is considered as the "Creator or Father," He orders all things "in power . . . but yet with gentleness: mightily, but yet in amiable manner. So that under him they feel no unpleasant constraint . . . such [is] his wisdom to overrule forcibly without force."[82] Tyndale repeatedly makes the same point. Christ "came to overcome thee with kindness; and to make thee do, of very love, the thing which the law compelleth thee to do." Likewise, husbands should strive to "overcome" their wives "with kindness, that of love they may obey"; and a master should "nurture" his servants "as thy own sons . . . that they may see in Christ a cause why they ought lovingly to obey"; and a father "loveth his son first, and studieth . . . to overcome his child with love and with kindness, to make him do that which is comely, honest, and good for itself."[83]

The same belief (or wish) that love has the power to overcome the beloved and hence to instill uncoerced obedience reappears in patriarchal politics. The ruler should care for the subject and the subject cheerfully, willingly, and lovingly obey the ruler.[84] So James explains to Prince Henry that the husband should command and the wife obey, "but yet with such a sweet harmonie, as shee shold be as ready to obey, as ye to command; as willing to follow, as ye to go before; your love being wholly knit unto her, and all her affections lovingly bent to follow your will." *The Trew Law* ends with the wish that England's king will be "as our God in earth, and loving Father," and therefore that his "deare countreymen" will strive

> by all means to procure the prosperitie and welfare of your King; that as hee must on the one part thinke all his earthly felicitie and happinesse grounded upon your weale . . . thinking himselfe onely ordained for your weale; such holy and happy emulation may arise betwixt him and you, as his care for your quietnes, and your care for his honour and

82. Hooker, *Works,* 2:565–66.

83. Tyndale, *Obedience,* in *Doctrinal Treatises,* pp. 170–71, 200–201; *The Wicked Mammon,* in *Doctrinal Treatises,* p. 107.

84. John C. Bean, "Comic Structure and the Humanizing of Kate in *The Taming of the Shrew,*" in *The Woman's Part: Feminist Criticism of Shakespeare,* ed. Carolyn Ruth Swift Lenz, Gayle Greene, and Carol Thomas Neely (Urbana, 1980), p. 70; Frank Whigham, *Ambition and Privilege: The Social Tropes of Elizabethan Courtesy Theory* (Berkeley, 1984), pp. 66–67.

> preservation, may in all your actions daily strive together, that the Land may thinke themselves blessed with such a King, and the king may thinke himselfe most happy in ruling over so loving and obedient subjects.[85]

As in *Paradise Lost,* but now transferred to the civil sphere, the relations between superior and inferior spring from a mutual *storge.* The coercive state becomes the loving family—withers away, one might say, for like Marxism, this patriarchal ideology evolves from the struggle to conceive of a social order not based on force and constraint. It differs, however, from Marxism and related theories (for example, More's *Utopia*) by grounding the possibility of transformation on psychodynamics rather than on economics. That is, it presupposes that love in fact descends, those in power being therefore apt to care for those beneath them, and that those on whom it descends can indeed be "overcome" with kindness. Patriarchy thus does not depend on structural transformation but, like Donne's theology, on mystification: on the king's perceiving himself as a father and the subject's perceiving himself as the son of a loving parent.

And, of course, this "holy and happy emulation" seems like a fiction. English history during the late Renaissance presents us with considerable evidence of rulers who did not govern for the sake of their subjects and subjects who were less than cheerfully obedient. We are back to the problem we started out with: how to construe patriarchalism as anything besides a rhetorical mask of interest and oppression. But in fact the representation of king as father never masked anything. The same texts that ground civil order in *storge* also affirm that power is likely to be coercive, unpleasant, and predatory—and that people are generally driven by the "Hobbesian" *libido dominandi* rather than by childlike reverence for superiors. Andrewes thus agrees with Hobbes that civil government is necessary because "*praestat timere unum quam multos,* ' 'tis better to fear one than many;' better one wolf than a great many."[86] Tyndale says the same thing: "It is better to suffer one tyrant than many," remarking elsewhere with Morean disillusion, "the great keep the small under, for their own profit, with the violence of the

85. James I, *Political Works,* p. 70.
86. Andrewes, *Works,* 6:198.

law."[87] If rulers are likely to be wolves, their subjects are rarely innocent as lambs; so Hooker advises that

> laws politic, ordained for external order and regiment amongst men, are never framed as they should be, unless presuming the will of man to be inwardly obstinate, rebellious, and averse from all obedience unto the sacred laws of his nature; in a word, unless presuming man to be in regard of his depraved mind little better than a wild beast, they do accordingly provide notwithstanding so to frame his outward actions, that they be no hindrance unto the common good for which societies are instituted.[88]

Again Tyndale describes the feelings of those below for those above with rather disarming bluntness: "There is no king in christendom so well beloved, but he hath enow of his own evil subjects (if God kept them not down with fear) that would at one hour rise upon him and slay him, to make havoc of all he hath."[89] Fear, apparently, as well as kindness, is necessary to "overcome" men and make them obedient. Renaissance Protestantism, in fact, agrees with a good deal of contemporary theory that, in Calvin's words, "the nature of man is such that every man would be lord and master over his neighbours, and no man by good will [*sic*] be subject."[90] Goneril and Regan are, in one sense, unnatural daughters, but in another, very natural indeed.

So the problem is not one of masking but of contradiction. Renaissance thinkers seem to hold two opposite views of the relation between ruler and ruled, one based on mutual love, one on "appetite, an universal wolf."[91] This contradiction is not an inexplicable mental lapse but the outcome of a centuries-long struggle to understand the relation between existing sociopolitical arrangements and Christian values—a struggle, once again, to connect institutions and holiness. We can perhaps best see this by looking at St. Augustine's distinction between the city of man and the city of God. According to Augustine,

87. Tyndale, *Obedience,* in *Doctrinal Treatises,* p. 180; *The Wicked Mammon,* in *Doctrinal Treatises,* p. 114.

88. Hooker, *Works,* 1:239–40.

89. Tyndale, *Exposition on Matthew,* in *Expositions and Notes,* p. 117.

90. Quoted in Christopher Hill, "Sin and Society," in *The Collected Essays of Christopher Hill: Religion and Politics in Seventeenth-Century England* (Amherst, 1986), p. 123.

91. William Shakespeare, *Troilus and Cressida,* ed. Jackson Campbell, The Yale Shakespeare (New Haven, 1965), 1.3.121.

"two cities have been formed by two loves: the earthly by the love of self, even to the contempt of God; the heavenly by the love of God, even to the contempt of self. . . . In the one, the princes and the nations it subdues are ruled by the love of ruling; in the other, the princes and subjects serve one another in love, the latter obeying, while the former take thought for all."[92] Augustine's two cities clearly correspond to the distinction we have been making between the political (in the Hobbesian sense) and the patriarchal. But in Augustine, the two cities are sharply separated; all temporal regimes belong to the earthly city, while the city of God is the transnational, invisible congregation of the faithful. Augustine never supposes that there could be a temporal regime where "princes and subjects serve one another in love," where the church would be coextensive with the state. But that is exactly what happens in the English Reformation. In Hooker's words, "we hold, that . . . there is not any man of the Church of England but the same man is also a member of the commonwealth; nor any man a member of the commonwealth, which is not also of the Church of England."[93] The king was likewise both head of the state and the church. The result was a conflation of Augustine's two cities and the analyses appropriate to each.[94] This conflation did not originate in the Renaissance; Yates traces it back to Leo III's coronation of Charlemagne, which symbolically transformed the Empire from the "*civitas terrena* in opposition to the *civitas Dei*" into "a city representing the earthly portion of the church, the kingdom of eternal peace in this world, as Alcuin said."[95] As imperial ideology migrates to the new nation-states of the Renaissance, the king ends up being both loving father of loving subjects and a wolf among wolves.[96] English political

92. St. Augustine, *The City of God,* trans. Marcus Dods, *The Works of Aurelius Augustine* (Edinburgh, 1871–72), 14.28.

93. Hooker, *Works,* 3:330.

94. For the notion of Tudor and Stuart England as a "quasi-Church" and "mystical monarchy" see Ernst H. Kantorowicz, "Mysteries of State, An Absolutist Concept and Its Late Medieval Origins," in Ernst H. Kantorowicz, *Selected Studies* (Locust Valley, N.Y., 1965), p. 382.

95. Frances A. Yates, *Astrea: The Imperial Theme in the Sixteenth Century* (London, 1975), p. 3.

96. This conflation resembles the confusion of Enlightenment morality described by Alasdair MacIntyre in *After Virtue: A Study in Moral Theory* (Notre Dame, 1981), pp. 49–59. In both cases, the original opposition between human nature-as-it-is and human nature-as-it-might-become collapses. In ethics, the result is a paradoxical and doomed attempt to find a basis for traditional ethics in untutored human nature when such ethics

thought during the Renaissance is incoherent because the notion of a monarchal state-church, like that of a Christian empire, is, in terms of classical Augustinian theology, contradictory.

And this contradiction between the political and patriarchal generates tragedy. In *Mustapha,* the sultan's vivid awareness that love descends, that fathers love their children more than the reverse, breeds suspicion of his son's intentions, encourages his fear that his son plans to betray him. Thus his paternal love drives him toward the violence of politics. Conversely, in *King Lear, Macbeth,* and *Paradise Lost,* descending paternal love occasions resentment, ambition, and treachery.[97] Instead of voluntary obedience, patriarchy here creates the *libido dominandi*—the response of inferiors to a love that, by descending, marks its objects as inferiors, burdened with "the debt immense of endless gratitude."[98] As one of Herbert's *Outlandish Proverbs* puts it with a faintly bitter irony, "God, and Parents, and our Master, can never be requited."[99] Goneril, Edmund, Macbeth, or Satan cannot be overcome with kindness because the very kindness shown to them instills a restless impatience with being on the receiving end; it instills political consciousness, the consciousness of power relations of superiority and subordination.[100] So Wyatt writes, "all is turned thorough my gentleness / Into a strange fashion of forsaking." In these works, the loving father breeds wolves, and fear of potential wolves turns the loving father into a wolf. Within hierarchically structured relations—

had been "expressly designed to be discrepant with" such nature. In Renaissance political thought the result is to apply the analysis of social relations in the heavenly city to the city of man, when such an analysis had been expressly designed to be discrepant with the standards and practices of this earthly city.

97. The same motif of the rebellious son and suspicious father occurs in Shakespeare's Henry IV plays, but there tragedy is averted.

98. Milton, *Paradise Lost,* 4.52.

99. *The Works of George Herbert,* ed. F. E. Hutchinson (Oxford, 1945), p. 348; quoted in Michael Schoenfeldt, "Standing on Ceremony: The Comedy of Manners in Herbert's 'Love (III),'" in *"Bright Shootes of Everlastingnesse": The Seventeenth-Century Religious Lyric,* ed. Claude J. Summers and Ted-Larry Pebworth (Columbia, Mo., 1987), p. 122n.

100. Ben Jonson's analysis of the meaning of the benevolence of superiors to those beneath them is instructive: "I have discovered, that a fain'd familiarity in great ones, is a note of certaine usurpation on the lesse. For great and popular men, faine themselves to bee servants to others, to make those slaves to them" (*Discoveries,* in *Ben Jonson,* ed. C. H. Herford, Percy Simpson, and Evelyn Simpson, 11 vols. [Oxford, 1925–52], 8:597–98).

whether regal, domestic, or supernatural—where love implies inferiors, the submerged interdependence of politics and patriarchy reveals itself. And it reveals itself as tragedy, as the failure of divine and human love to avert politics—as the complicity of divine and human love in creating politics.

Renaissance patriarchy was not without its contradictions, yet this does not mean that it should be construed as what it explicitly was not: a justification of male despotism. This seems far more characteristic of absolutist theology, which treats fathers as domestic monarchs rather than monarchs as national fathers—although in the writings of King James this may be a distinction without a difference. While no one would deny the existence of oppressive male power in English Renaissance society or that the father's power over his children *was* sometimes used to justify marital and political autocracy, in its most characteristic form patriarchalism is not concerned with legitimating such power. Rather, it provides a model for sacred and social relations based on the mutual love (*storge*) of parents and children, a love frequently defined in contrast to political relations of domination and oppression. In some texts, this contrast suggests the nascent separation of family from the public realm; in others, however, a conception of that realm as a family. But almost always, patriarchalism expresses two things: a longing for the gentle and forgiving intimacy of parental love and a deep anxiety about subordination and hierarchy. It seems related to the early separation of children from their parents, a separation breeding nostalgia and thus the retrospective idealization of familial tenderness that allowed parent/child relations to become paradigmatic for divine, marital, and social *caritas*. Of course, the *need* for parental love and cherishing does not entail that such love was *in fact* unavailable, from either earthly or heavenly fathers. Indeed, Renaissance texts assume that fathers do love their children intensely. But this need—so similar to that visible in Donne's otherwise radically different absolutist theology—leads one to hypothesize the prevalence of a psychological formation characterized by a longing for personal contact of a basically nonsexual variety: a longing for the kindness and encircling protection of the father's bosom rather than for the passionate ecstasy of sexual embrace. Patriarchy, however, expresses social as well as private needs. It is an attempt to conceive of inequalities that are not coercive, not exploitative and unjust (even if necessary to avoid anarchy) because based on the paternal affection of the ruler for the ruled. But at this point the firm outlines of settled ideological discourse begin to lose their clarity. In some works, political relations, now understood in a Hobbesian sense, begin to precipitate out of the bonds of *storge,* with a concomitant intensifying of the connection between domestic and sacred patriarchy. Yet this is not invariably the case, for other texts, most notably those by King James, repeatedly assert the analogic compactness of king, father, and God. But often the same works that affirm this compactness also present an incompatible view of social relations as permeated by ambition, aggression, and hostility. And this self-contradiction indicates considerable uncertainty about the relation between the social order and the sacred: is society the temporal reflection of sacred patriarchy or the *civitas terrena?* does it function (can it function) according to what Tyndale called the "law of love" or is it basically governed by the reciprocal principles of big-fish-eat-little-fish and two-little-fishes-eat-big-fish?[101] Finally, especially in tragedy and epic, the contradiction between patriarchy and politics discloses the implication of the former in the generation of the latter, for every hierarchical structure breeds resentment and fear, and love (*storge*) operates hierarchically.

Mustapha begins with Solyman speaking to his wife: "*Rossa!* Th' eternall wisdome doth not covet / Of man, his strength, or reason, but his love." But not only does God the Father need to be loved, but the sultan needs it too, for after a few more lines of such theological musings, he concludes, "I speake by *Mustapha.*" He then turns from his need for love to declare his love for his son, and the recognition of his own desires frightens him into the half-rhetorical question: "But is contempt the fruit of Parents care? / Doth kindnesse lessen Kings authority" (1.1.1–12). He tries to shake off "this frailty" of loving and needing love but the desires return:

> For Power may be fear'd; Empire ador'd;
> Rewards may make knees bow; and selfe-love humble:
> *But love is onely that which Princes covet;*
> *And for they have it least, they must doe love it.*
> (1.1.73–76)

101. On Tyndale's "law of love," see W. D. J. Cargill Thompson, "The Two Regiments: The Continental Setting of William Tyndale's Political Thought," in *Reform and Reformation: England and the Continent, c. 1500–c. 1750*, ed. Derek Baker (Oxford, 1979), pp. 23, 25, 30.

The old king's love makes him vulnerable, and his fear of such weakness leads him from patriarchy to political analysis. He sees his own affection for Mustapha making him prey to the operations of the *libido dominandi:*

> And shall Love be a chaine, tyed to my Crowne,
> Either to helpe him up, or pull me downe?
> No, No: This *Father*-language fits not Kings.
> (2.2.36–38)

The need to love and be loved becomes tangled in darker psychological terrain where love breeds contempt, threatening to destroy the loving father, making him destroy his beloved son. Solyman kills his son because he loves him.

Neither Solyman nor James nor Lear could figure out how to make their children and subjects return their love. Parents, Tyndale remarks, "promise more gifts still without ceasing" to make their children love them,[102] but the consequences of such patriarchal kindness can be unpredictable. As Lear finds out, give your daughters each half your kingdom, and they will hate you. If the language of patriarchy resonates with the child's need for security, warmth, and parental tenderness, it is also shaped by the pathos of the parents' need for gratitude, the king's need for his subjects' affection. Even Milton's God seems extraordinarily happy that His Son loves Him:

> O Son, in whom my Soul hath chief delight,
> Son of my bosom
> . . . .
> O thou
> My sole complacence!
> (3.168–69, 275–76)

But except for offspring like Christ and Cordelia, the only way to make one's child love back is to hide one's love and use parental power—to deprive the child of the mother's breast and hence create the guilty confusions of desire, aggression, and dependence that lie at the center of absolutist theology. Or at least Tyndale suggests as much in a little allegory about the meaning of suffering, remarkable not only for its intertwinings of love and manipulation but also for its acute

102. Tyndale, *Exposition on Matthew,* in *Expositions and Notes,* p. 74.

awareness of how much the patriarch (or matriarch, in this case) needs the child's love, how desperately and problematically downward love flows:

> A loving mother, to make her child to perceive and feel her kindness, to love her again and be thankful, letteth it hunger in a morning; and when it calleth for his breakfast, maketh as she heard it not, till for pain and impatience it beginneth to cry agood: and then she stilleth it, and giveth it all it asketh, and more too, to please it; and when it is peaced and beginneth to eat, and rejoiceth and is glad and fain, she asketh, "Who gave thee that, thy mother?" and it saith, "Yea." Then saith she, "Am not I a good mother, that give thee all things?" And it answereth, "Yea." And she asketh, "Wilt thou love thy mother?" &c. And it saith, "Yea." And so cometh it to the knowledge of his mother's kindness, and is thankful. Such is the temptation of Christ's elect, and otherwise not.[103]

The manipulations of pain and deprivation here point to an underlying resemblance between the parent's love and the tactics of Donne's fearsome *rex*. And curiously in this passage the parent is the mother, suggesting the vertiginous possibility that the infantile separation from the mother's breast is somehow implicated in the production of theological politics—a symbolic inversion parallel to that of the nursing father. The psychogenetic basis of such supernatural cross-dressing would not be easily demonstrable, although it might help to account for the strange absence of mothers in Renaissance literature. What the passage more evidently implies is that patriarchal discourse cannot be strictly separated from political, that the theological model of the loving family is shot through with strategies based on guilt and suffering. And these discourses cannot be separated, because the need to be loved entails the need for power. It is only in the drama, however, that the contradictions between these two needs surface.

103. Tyndale, *Exposition on Matthew,* in *Expositions and Notes,* pp. 110–11.

Conclusion

> La modernité de l'ouvrage tient essentiellement à la redistribution du matériau historique, au nouveau découpage.
>
> François Laplanche,
> "A Propos d'Isaac Casaubon"

"In Bakhtin the 'classical body' "—elevated, asexual, static, closed—"denotes the inherent *form* of the high official culture," the domain of rationality, repression, and neoclassical correctness.[1] But when Francis Bacon saw the earl of Arundel's gallery of ancient statuary, the first collection of classical nudes in England, he raised his hands, started back, and burst out, "The Resurrection!"[2] In the early seventeenth century, the body of faith persists as the form of the high official culture, and the domain of that culture and that body has been the subject of this book.

Its premise has been the continued centrality of religion in the high culture of the Elizabethan and Jacobean eras—that whatever the orthodoxies or dominant ideologies of the period might be, they could not be divorced from theocentric concerns. But granted the centrality of religion, one might still argue that such professed concerns in fact conceal the actual underlying structures, and that these are only disclosed by theory, whether psychoanalytic, Foucauldian, Marxist, or whatever else. One might thus protest that the pneumatic self, for example, should not be treated as if it were a real entity but rather be exposed as a fictive offspring of early capitalist individualism or as a strategy for appropriating the female (the anima) and thus allowing the

1. Peter Stallybrass and Allon White, *The Politics and Poetics of Transgression* (Ithaca, 1986), pp. 21–22.
2. G. P. V. Akrigg, *Jacobean Pageant or the Court of King James* (Cambridge, Mass., 1963), p. 276.

devaluation of actual women. But this response confuses the object of investigation. To elucidate the subterranean mechanisms determining individual or collective behavior is a rather different project from that which seeks to examine how individuals (and collectivities) experience and interpret their world. The distinction between the objects of theory and experience can be elucidated by the parallel distinction between scientific and subjective realism. The scientific realist describes, let us say a table, as mostly empty space intersected by the paths of whirling electrons, protons, and other subatomic bits; the subjective realist describes the same table as solid, motionless, teak, and rococo. One table is the object of theory, the other of experience (including historically informed experience), and it seems rather pointless to declare one real and the other an illusion. But insofar as a culture differs from an economic or social *system* by being inseparable from the beliefs, attitudes, assumptions, values, and representations of persons, then this experiential aggregate—whether true or false from the perspective of a given theory—is the primary object of cultural analysis. In studying high culture, that is, the relevant tables are the inlaid marble ones, not the colorless vibrations of particles.

But if a culture should not be confused with its hypothesized material substrate, neither is it identical to some collection of beliefs. Since Reformation Christianity descends to us as a body of dogmatic texts, there always exists the temptation to consider it as a disembodied credal system. Since, however, that system often seems less real (that is, relevant) to us than the more tangible systems of social status, economic distribution, and political power, there is also the temptation to regard it simply as a function—whether reflection or obfuscation—of these secular structures. But these temptations toward idealism or materialism both oversimplify the relation between the conceptual and the empirical in the culture of the English Renaissance, for "ideas" have no determinate meaning apart from their *use* within a given historical milieu, but milieux, in turn, do not *cause* ideas.[3] If the conceptual only exists in a historical and material context, it is likewise true that economic, political, and social institutions are not prior to and independent of the conceptual. Or, to put it in Aristo-

3. Quentin Skinner, "Meaning and Understanding in the History of Ideas," *History and Theory* 8 (1969): 3–53.

telian terms, the universal only exists in matter, but such matter becomes a "this" only through being informed by the universal—in this case, through being interpreted, for "cultural universals" are the interpretive categories the mind imposes. The conceptual may be said to shape cultural matter—economic, political, and social organization; events and practices; all that can be seen, touched, and quantified—both actively and reflexively. That is, beliefs, values, and so forth can give rise to certain events or institutions—so anti-Catholicism influenced Elizabethan foreign policy—but the relation may be less linearly causal insofar as the conceptual attributes meaning to already extant sociopolitical practices. Thus, for example, the notion of sacred kingship did not cause the consolidation of royal power in the late Renaissance, but by interpreting it, gave that particular attempt at absolutism its specific historical character—made it a "this" instead of a "that." Yet if the conceptual shapes the material, the converse also holds, since events and practices element ideas and attitudes. So the Gunpowder Plot occasioned the Oath of Allegiance, which led to the controversies between Andrewes and Bellarmine, which insinuated the notion of a secular state into the heart of Jacobean theological absolutism.

To speak, however, of the interactions of the material and conceptual lands one in the Cartesian dilemma: how, precisely, can the immaterial impinge on the physical and vice versa; what is the pineal gland in this process? This problem is compounded by the fact that both conceptual structures and material ones are abstractions and, therefore, cannot, properly speaking, act at all. The only way, in fact, that ideas and events can touch each other or that structures can be said to do anything is through the mediation of individual psyches. Thus, to take a famous example, Calvinist views of sanctification cannot facilitate capitalism except by engendering in individuals certain expectations, attitudes, and values. The modern tendency to think in terms of systems tends to obscure the obvious truth that, however much conditioned by events and ideology, only people can be historical agents. But this truth complicates any binary analysis of culture in terms of sub- and superstructures, for the mind does not simply take a passive impression from its surroundings and dutifully reflect it in belief systems nor does it directly instantiate its dogmas in praxis. It seems to me plausible, for instance, that the ambitious jockeying for status and power that suffused the Elizabethan and Jacobean court may have simultaneously heightened and repressed feelings of neediness, passivity, powerlessness, and dependency, and that these feelings in turn suffered a theological displacement, surfacing in the religious constructions of the pneumatic self.

But this notion of the psyche as the *tertium quid* between material and conceptual structures is further complicated by the fact that the psyche is not invariant, an ahistorical given. Rather, inwardness is itself shaped by culture, so that all experience has already been filtered through culturally based interpretive categories. The public character of language guarantees that the relation between "inside" and "outside" more resembles a Möbius strip than nesting boxes. This is why one cannot translate something like Donne's valorization of guilt as masochism; the experience qua experience has already been interpreted, so that to alter its name is to alter its essence. We might postulate a primal feeling—the need to be punished—but the nature of the experience depends on whether that feeling is interpreted as redemptive or pathological. The phrase "habits of thought" coined at the beginning of this study was an attempt precisely to denote this indissoluble mixture of feeling and ideation that constitutes experience—where "experience" is not simply elemental feeling but feeling that has become meaningful by being interpreted. Indeed, the function of habits of thought seems less to make sense of (naturalize) sociopolitical orderings than to make sense of feeling, to construct meaning out of the raw materials of needs, desires, expectations (both frustrated and fulfilled), fears, and anxieties. These, however, are not mutually exclusive functions, since social structures frequently give rise to feelings; the Renaissance system of patronage, for example, may have occasioned both resentment and gratitude. But I have chosen to examine certain texts rather than others, because in order to "get at" the habits of thought of a given period, it seemed necessary to explore works that conveyed the affective, felt quality of existence rather than either works of pure dogma, like Perkins's *Golden Chain* and the Book of Homilies, or those of pure data, like parish registers and exchequer rolls.

To ask about the habits of thought characteristic of the high culture of the Renaissance (or of texts written by Renaissance authors who have a fair claim to belong to the center rather than the margins of society) is to ask about the "point" of the dominant ideology: what are the questions to which these texts are answers? what are the emotional, religious, and social needs to which they are responses? how do their strategies—analogy, mystification, etymologizing—construct those meanings or "cultural universals" by which the mind categorizes and interprets the world we half-perceive and half-create. This is not to discount the hegemonic function of the dominant ideology—a function so overt in many of these texts as to be not worth arguing for—nor to deny that the elements of this ideology have their own histories as "ideas." But the focus on habits of thought stresses the mediating role of the psyche in all cultural production: that ideology is not simply a function or an entity but the creation of people feeling, thinking, interpreting, persuading, and struggling for meaning.

"Meaning" here, of course, does not refer to systematic theorizing; we are not talking about Hegel but about habits of thought that are frequently diverse, discrepant, and incompatible—as anything grounded in either feeling or history is likely to be. High culture therefore cannot be identified with any single monological worldview. Moreover, as Malcolm Smuts has pointed out, ideological conflict during this period "was frequently fought out within the minds of individuals" rather than between classes, camps, or parties.[4] The meanings constructed even by single persons display at least as much discontinuity as coherence. In this respect, "Renaissance orthodoxy" has no more precise signification than "the Renaissance" itself—the dream of Bacon, Hobbes, and their successors to confine language to unequivocal referents having awakened to the ambiguous light of history.

Yet some sort of deep structure or inner logic does seem discernible in the diversity and contradictions of the dominant culture. Tillyard was perhaps on the right track in emphasizing the centrality of analogy to the Elizabethan world-picture, although he gave his data too static and Neoplatonic a frame. For analogy concerns the boundaries between categories: how, for example, domestic, political, and sacred hierarchies mirror and participate in one another. And the persistent questions threading through the texts of the high official culture of the English Renaissance have to do with boundaries, not, to be sure, of the

4. R. Malcolm Smuts, *Court Culture and the Origins of a Royalist Tradition in Early Stuart England* (Philadelphia, 1987), p. 75.

Platonic great-chain-of-being variety, but the cultural boundaries marking the relations between the self, God, history, kings, language, church, and so forth. These questions cannot be stabilized into a coherent doctrine of order, as Tillyard attempted to do; rather, they tend to suggest a crisis of order—one that seems to center on the social boundaries of the holy. Greenblatt thus rightly calls attention to the "intense and sustained struggle in late sixteenth- and early seventeenth-century England to redefine the central values of society . . . [which entailed] rethinking the conceptual categories by which the ruling elites constructed their world. . . . At the heart of this struggle . . . was the definition of the sacred."[5] On the one hand, there remains the archaic compactness of the political and supernatural orders visible in theological absolutism and absolutist theology as well as the equally archaic participations of the word in its referent and the mind in its objects characteristic of Andrewes's sermons. On the other hand, one notes various attempts to pull apart these analogic ties. Luther's *Zwei-Regimente-Lehre,* which opposes the sphere of sociopolitical activity to that of private spirituality; Perkins's distinction between a person in respect of others and a person of one's own self under Christ; Hooker's division of the church into the national institution and the mystical body of Christ, as well as his distinction between certainty of evidence and certainty of adherence; Herbert's division between "The Church Porch" and "The Church" all tend to remove the locus of the sacred from its temporal lodgings in institutions, social forms, and public rationality. But neither can one divide orthodoxy into two groups—the "mystifiers" and the "privatizers"—since both parties betray a significant uncertainty over precisely these boundaries. Thus Andrewes, at different moments, asserts the sanctity of the king and the secularity of the state, while Perkins, after separating sociopolitical roles from the private, religious self, introduces the notion of vocation, which is premised on the sacredness of social roles.

The "rethinking of conceptual categories" was less a matter of factions and theories than of assumptions, desires, fears, and expectations, as these were shaped by the cataclysmic effects of the Reforma-

5. Stephen Greenblatt, *Shakespearean Negotiations: The Circulation of Social Energy in Renaissance England,* New Historicism: Studies in Cultural Poetics (Berkeley, 1988), p. 95.

tion on ecclesiastical, political, and psychological organization as well as by the new methodologies of the new learning and the old needs still persisting in an old faith. In attempting to summarize this process of rethinking, one always runs the risk of overschematizing, but in order to pull together the threads of the previous chapters we can provisionally distinguish four conceptual territories—psychological, epistemic, hermeneutic, and institutional—as the primary loci in these disputes over boundaries.

In general, the texts discussed in this study evince a tendency to isolate inwardness—the pneumatic self—from social roles and social behavior in order to obtain a depoliticized space of mystical participation. This is the private space of the certainty of adherence, eucharistic indwelling, and the mystical body of Christ; the inner voice heard in lyric and prosopopoeia. Except in Donne, there is little sense of inwardness as conscience, a juridical inhabitation that implicitly denies the bifurcation of the sacred and the sociopolitical, since the voice of conscience is the voice of *law,* both statute and sacred. But to the extent that the social environment becomes merely secular, the domain of ambition, power, status anxieties, and repressive control, the psyche becomes the primary locus of the sacred, the place where God comes, the "paradise within . . . happier far." This pneumatic self, characteristic of Andrewes, Hooker, and Herbert, is experienced as desire rather than law. It is permeable, hollow, not a "thing" but an emptiness needing to be filled from without—a representation of the self evocative (to the contemporary reader, at least) of the female body. Its lack of sufficiency leaves the pneumatic self open to the crisis of desolation; in turn, this crisis differentiates the self as desire for the absent Other, which desire, by a piece of transcendental logic, is interpreted as evidence of presence.

The distinction between the public/social and private/sacred self is neatly set forth in Perkins's notion of a *duplex persona,* a distinction deriving from Luther's *Zwei-Regimente-Lehre* and thus possessing political as well as anthropological implications. However, the boundaries between these two selves or persons tend themselves to be unstable or permeable. As noted in chapter 3, Herbert cannot finally keep the motives of the social self analyzed in "The Church Porch" out of the lyrics of "The Church." The pneumatic self uses the same social gestures of submission, ingratiation, self-deprecation, and petition to "flatter power" that the social self employs for similar, although secularized, ends. In like fashion, the intimate, domestic bonds of *storge* are both contrasted to political relations of coercion and interest and yet not finally separable from them, since both share a common hierarchical structure where, again, one can either "flatter power" by gratitude and obedience or resentfully rebel against it. The instability of the division between pneumatic and political relations appears in its most problematic form in Donne's sermons, where images of God as terrible king threatening to break heart or neck of the vulnerable self are juxtaposed to images of longing to be covered by God, to touch His hand, embrace Him mouth to mouth, to suck His wounds. Here the psychological dynamics of political relations are not segregated from theocentric emotionality but coupled to expose their essential likeness, a likeness more often concealed by the various strategies of privatization.

The placement of epistemic boundaries overlaps that of psychological ones, partly because the desire that striates the pneumatic self also has an epistemological component. The central problematic of knowledge for the English Renaissance concerns the relationship between desire and truth: to what extent is the desire for something evidence for its existence? to what extent is it the only evidence? Hooker, Andrewes, Herbert, and Perkins all assert, in one form or another, that the longing for God guarantees its own fulfillment—a view premised on the participation of the mind in the objective order of things, yet half-admitting the epistemic fragility of that relation, since desire is always for that which is *not* present. This fragility is strained almost to the breaking point in Hooker, whose consciousness of how desire distorts its objects throws in question his assertion that natural desire can never be deceived; the boundaries between mind and world thus seem thickened and yet somehow still permeable.

The connection between desire and knowledge also appears in the handling of noetic participation. As the desires of the pneumatic self and the object of its desire are substantially identical, so for Andrewes the light of the intellect remains consubstantial with its luminous object. The knower participates in the known, and one knows by being inhabited. But the notion of participated knowledge appears less frequently than that of participated desire; only Andrewes consistently maintains it, at least in the sermons. Writers like King James or Herbert can scarcely be said to have an epistemological position; it was not a principal concern of the period.

One finds, instead of a theorized epistemology, that the pressures of the controversy between the presbyterian Puritans of the late sixteenth century and the defenders of the Church of England encouraged the development of both rationalism and historicism. This controversy drives the argument of *The Laws of Ecclesiastical Polity*. To counter the Puritan claim that they possessed, via the illumination of the Holy Spirit, a privileged access to the meaning of Holy Scripture and that Holy Scripture so interpreted provides an exact model for all subsequent Christian societies, Hooker insists that the only sociopolitically relevant knowledge rests on rational evidence, including the evidence of historical context. This maneuver effectively pushes apart the mind and its objects, setting up the twin concepts of reason and evidence to mediate the space they create. Similarly, by locating statements and practices along a historical perspective, it conceptualizes "the pastness of the past."[6] Only Hooker's notorious judiciousness prevents these strategies from subverting his affirmation of tradition, authority, and sacramental presence. Andrewes's *Discourse on Ceremonies* suggests how easily, in the hands of a less sophisticated historicist, the idea of the contingent origins of religious practice could slip into the assertion of the contingent (and therefore political) substance of such practice.

As mentioned above, *The Laws* implicitly relates the epistemic status of desire to hermeneutic questions by bringing up the role of desire in ideological production and the interpretation of texts. Hooker's sensitivity to how the mind projects what it wishes to believe into the text and then "discovers" there its own preconceits seems akin to both Calvin's notion of "idolatry" and Bacon's Idols. One senses behind all three formulations an emerging anxiety, perhaps generated by the need to account for the religious pluralism of post-Reformation Europe, about self-deception and ideological manipulation. With Greville, these anxieties shade into an unsettling perception of how the central virtues of Jacobean Christianity—humility, obedience, passive suffering—serve the interests of the ruling elite. Whereas the more conventional doctrines of *recta ratio* and conscience hold that

6. Erwin Panofsky, *Renaissance and Renascences in Western Art* (New York, 1972), pp. 108–13.

objective ethical intuitions are "prescribed" onto the mind, Greville suggests the social and hegemonic function of such axioms: the ruling elite produces sacred value to authorize its oppression.

The role of the mind in producing meaning also glimmers somewhat problematically around the edges of far more orthodox texts. In Donne's sermons one thus notes a hermeneutic of suffering, an awareness that pain becomes theologically comprehensible only by means of a deliberate interpretive act and therefore that the mind, in some sense, constructs its own consolations. In these sermons, the hermeneutic role of desire problematizes theodicy by stressing the disjunction between experience and doctrine, between, that is, human suffering and divine goodness; by insisting on the need for interpretation they imply that on the surface of things experience does *not* confirm dogma. Some of the same ambivalence appears in the political mystifications of patriarchal discourse. The need to read power as love, the king as father, suggests a certain nervousness about the actual workings of absolutism. As before, one senses the need to avoid the conclusion that power might in fact be hostile or interested.

The problem of hermeneutic boundaries in the Renaissance concerns not only what we may call the psychogenesis of meaning—the extent to which the needs and desires of the mind shape its constructions—but also the related questions of exegesis and analogy. Chapter 1 differentiated the two poles of exegetic practice coexisting within the dominant culture, one based on participation, the other on rational method. The former, characteristic of Andrewes, does not sharply distinguish between sign and signified; all things are signs, yet the sign contains its signified, so that the etymon of the word discloses the true nature of its referent, and the sequence of signs reveals the interconnections of history. The latter, characteristic of Hooker, tends to divorce words from things. In place of the mystic depths of the word participating in its own meaning, Hooker argues that meaning and truth are subject to rational procedure, including the determination of historical context, intention of the speaker, and the rules of logic and evidence. The differences between participatory and rational exegesis reemerge in Renaissance uses of analogy, for analogy would seem to be one of the primary interpretive strategies of participatory consciousness. That is, although the characteristic metaphor of analogy is reflection rather than inhabitation, both analogy and participation affirm some sort of mystic ties interconnecting categories, events, or things. Andrewes's exegetic practice relies upon these interconnections, while Hooker's does not, instead structuring relations by means of secular connectives like causality, sequence, and logic.

Analogy in the Renaissance is more a problematic than a doctrine. It is a useful term because it locates a crucially contested procedure rather than a stable interpretive frame. Analogy itself has both a diachronic and synchronic aspect. Diachronic analogy—the *analogia temporum*—perceives temporal sequence as patterned repetition, later events mirroring prior ones in an atemporal design. So, for Andrewes, the Davidic kingship repeats itself in the Stuart, and the coming of the Magi provides the pattern for all comings to Christ. Such diachronic analogy seems inconsistent with historical consciousness, which, as mentioned above, is committed to the pastness of the past. It is rather easy to order this opposition between diachronic analogy and historicism as a disagreement between different authors; Andrewes and Hooker come to mind at once. But it is also a tension within individuals. Hooker's traditionalism, for example, rests on the continuity between past and present—on the availability of the past to the present—and is thus fundamentally at odds with his sense of change and discontinuity. Hooker needs to distance the past in order to authorize the English church's right to alter ritual and polity, but he equally needs an analogous past in order to validate the same church's traditionalism. The instability of diachronic analogy in such a text derives partly from its specific polemical context. But it also derives from the contradictions implicit in the humanist enterprise. As Anthony Grafton has shown, such "interpretive schizophrenia" pervades humanist methodology, where from Politian to Bacon allegoresis, which presupposes the relevance of earlier works to present concerns, mingles awkwardly with historical philology in text after text.[7] Beginning with Petrarch, the belief in a reusable, and therefore potentially analogous, past inspired the exacting study of antiquity, but the historically self-conscious philology developed for such study both presupposed and disclosed the radical distance between past and present.

A second sort of instability occurs in Renaissance handling of syn-

7. Anthony Grafton, "Renaissance Readers and Ancient Texts: Comments on Some Commentaries," *Renaissance Quarterly* 38 (1985): 615–49.

chronic analogy. This sort of analogy, familiarized by the works of Lovejoy and Tillyard, asserts the vertical correspondence of equivalent roles or the *analogia personarum* down different "levels of being." In Renaissance England the central axis of such analogy describes the structure of patriarchy: father, husband, king, God. The texts examined here suggest that these analogies should not be construed as a doctrine, Neoplatonic or otherwise, but as a language for examining the relation between the sociopolitical, domestic, and supernatural orders. It is the language of boundary disputes rather than fixed hierarchies. The analogies have neither a preassigned metaphysic nor sociology but rather provide a means for exploring, among other things, the social constructions of divinity: what does it mean to say God is like a king or a father? Alternatively, what does it mean to say the king is like God? What is the relation between divinity and politics? One thinks of Hooker's deconstruction of the parallel between liturgy and a royal audience or Donne's deliberately unsettling correspondences between political absolutism and divine power.

Synchronic analogy may therefore be termed the hermeneutic aspect of the problem of institutional boundaries, that is, the boundaries between sociopolitical institutions and the sacred. This problem was not new in post-Reformation England, having dominated a good deal of European ecclesiopolitical conflict since the twelfth century, but both the Erasmianism and Erastianism of the Elizabethan Settlement gave it peculiar force, the one by draining away the sacrality of rite, sacrament, and tradition, the other by draining away the sacrality of the church in subordinating it to the needs and conveniences of the state. The secular state, in this sense as in others, was expanding its boundaries. But, as anti-court satires were often written by courtiers, so both secularization and religious recuperation proceeded from the same milieu. This recuperation generally moved along two divergent paths of cosmology and privatization, the one sanctifying the state and so rather drastically reversing (or attempting to reverse) the process of *Entzauberung,* the other relocating the sacred in inner regions fortified against political annexation. This relocation of sacred presence to incorporeal regions—the soul, the mystical body of Christ, and the sacraments—split apart areas of experience, yielding the dual structure of the *Zwei-Regimente-Lehre* and the related notion of a *duplex persona,* dualities visible in Tyndale, Whitgift, Perkins, and Hooker; it informs the tripartite divisions of Herbert's *Temple* and the contrast of father and king in patriarchal discourse.

Neither path, it should be noted, required any actual institutional changes—a significant difference between the recuperations of the dominant ideology and that attempted by presbyterian Puritanism. In part, this requires no explanation; dominant ideologies are not, by definition, subversive of their own institutional bases. But since the prevailing assumption of recent scholarship seems to be that one ought *not* support the status quo and that those who do so have been either seduced by interest or blinded by pageantry, and since this assumption leads naturally to the inference that men like Hooker, Donne, and Andrewes were either dishonest or unintelligent, we might press this issue a bit further.

The sociologist Edward Shils has defined the intellectual as a person unusually sensitive to the sacred or the ideal.[8] The difference between these two sensitivities is significant. An ideal is an abstraction. In the Judeo-Christian tradition, the sacred is a person. And while one may attempt to embody an abstraction in the actual workings of the social order—let us say by struggling for justice, equality, freedom—one can only seek (or avoid) relationship with a person. The habits of thought in the high culture of the English Renaissance remain personalist. What is desired is neither justice nor liberty but contact with the sacred Other, contact described in the intractably personal images of being touched and held, of tasting, indwelling, nursing, and covering. One even desires the agonizing contact with divine power—the battering, imprisonment, and ravishing of Donne's Holy Sonnet—because it establishes at least some sort of relationship. The structures of desire orient themselves toward union with the Father/Lover/King, not transformation of the social environment. Hooker, for example, simply cannot understand Cartwright's ecclesiastical idealism as anything but frustrated ambition combined with vanity. Like his contemporaries, he is as aware as modern Renaissance historians of political interest, of the workings of ambition, emulation, and status. But that perception of how a person acts with respect to others is not set against a sociopolitical ideal, either hierarchical or egalitarian, but against the

8. Edward Shils, *The Intellectuals and the Powers and Other Essays* (Chicago, 1972), pp. 3–17.

person of one's own self under Christ. Even political thought tends to take the form of devotion to the person of the monarch rather than attachment to platforms (except religious platforms).[9] One might, in fact, argue that the official Christian ideologies of the West have generally expressed a psychological formation oriented toward the sacred rather than the ideal, which is why most modern revolutionary movements, from the French to the Chinese, were hostile to religion and also why, in order to supplant it, they were led to develop personality cults.

The last boundary is between an author and her subject. The knower must participate the known, and so we finally can only see what we are. We bring to bear our own categories, formed by our own language, culture, experiences, onto the printed surface of the text and read back our selves to ourselves. This little circle is especially vicious when one attempts to analyze emotional resonances, psychological nuance, and all the mental life going on behind the lines. But if my reading of these texts has been contaminated by autobiography, then, here, autobiography has already been shaped by the same texts. I began reading seventeenth-century prose the summer I graduated from college—for an independent study that never materialized. And now, when over a decade later I have come to study the same books in a more systematic fashion, I find that the self projected onto the past has in part been formed by that past. And so, even if there is no invariant human nature that would allow us intuitive access to other cultures, the transmission of texts molds the present in the image of the past (and even girl-children can look like their fathers). Those old books gave me my desires and thoughts and beliefs, at least gave me the words to name them with. And so, the known is in fact in the knower, in the historicized and textualized participations of the subject.

9. On James's failure to become a focus of patriotic devotion as Elizabeth had been, see Smuts, *Court Culture,* pp. 26–27.

Bibliography

PRIMARY SOURCES

Andrewes, Lancelot. *The Works of Lancelot Andrewes.* 11 vols. Library of Anglo-Catholic Theology. Oxford, 1854.

Aquinas, Thomas. *Commentum in quatour libros sententiarum Magistri Petri Lombardi. Opera omnia.* 25 vols. Parma, 1852–73. Reprint. New York, 1948.

———. *Summa Theologiae.* 60 vols. New York, 1963.

Aristotle. *The Complete Works of Aristotle.* 2 vols. Edited by Jonathan Barnes. Princeton, 1984.

Augustine, Aurelius. *The City of God.* In *The Works of Aurelius Augustine.* Translated by Marcus Dods. Edinburgh, 1871–72.

———. *On Christian Doctrine.* Translated by D. W. Robertson. Indianapolis, 1958.

———. *On the Two Cities: Selections from "The City of God."* Edited by F. W. Strothman. New York, 1957.

Bacon, Francis. *The Refutation of Philosophies.* In *The Philosophy of Francis Bacon.* Edited and translated by Benjamin Farrington. Chicago, 1964.

Bancroft, Richard. *Tracts Ascribed to Richard Bancroft.* Edited by Albert Peel. Cambridge, 1953.

Calvin, John. *The Gospel according to St. John 11–21 and The First Epistle of John.* Translated by T. H. L. Parker. Calvin's Commentaries. Edinburgh, 1961.

———. *Institutes of the Christian Religion.* 2 vols. Edited by John T. McNeill. Translated by Ford Lewis Battles. The Library of Christian Classics. Philadelphia, 1960.

———. *John Calvin: Selections from His Writings.* Edited by John Dillenberger. Missoula, Mont., 1971.

Castellio, Sebastian. *De arte dubitandi et confidendi, ignorandi et sciendi (1563).* Edited by Elisabeth Feist Hirsch. Studies in Medieval and Reformation Thought. Leiden, 1981.

Donne, John. *The Sermons of John Donne.* 10 vols. Edited by George Potter and Evelyn Simpson. Berkeley, 1953–62.

Downame, John. *The Christian Warfare.* London, 1604. Reprint. Amsterdam, 1974.

Fortescue, Sir John. *The Governance of England (ca. 1471–1476).* Edited by Charles Plummer. Oxford, 1885.

Greville, Fulke. *Poems and Dramas of Fulke Greville, First Lord Brooke.* 2 vols. Edited by Geoffrey Bullough. Edinburgh, 1939.

Herbert, George. *George Herbert and Henry Vaughan.* Edited by Louis L. Martz. Oxford, 1986.

———. *The Works of George Herbert.* Edited by F. E. Hutchinson. Oxford, 1945.

Hobbes, Thomas. *Leviathan.* Edited by Herbert Schneider. The Library of Liberal Arts. Indianapolis, 1958.

Hooker, Richard. *The Folger Edition of the Works of Richard Hooker.* 4 vols. General ed. W. Speed Hill. Cambridge, Mass., 1977–81.

———. *The Works of that Learned and Judicious Divine, Mr. Richard Hooker.* 3 vols. Edited by Rev. John Keble. Revised by R. W. Church and F. Paget. 7th ed. Oxford, 1888. Reprint. New York, 1970.

Hugh of St. Victor. *On the Sacraments of the Christian Faith (De sacramentis).* Translated by Roy Deferrari. Cambridge, Mass., 1951.

James I (James Stuart). *The Political Works of James I.* Introduction by Charles McIlwain. Cambridge, Mass., 1918. Reprint. New York, 1965.

Jewel, John. *An Apology of the Church of England.* Edited by John E. Booty. Folger Documents of Tudor and Stuart Civilization. Charlottesville, Va., 1963.

Jonson, Ben. *Discoveries.* In *Ben Jonson.* 11 vols. Edited by C. H. Herford, Percy Simpson, and Evelyn Simpson. Oxford, 1925–52.

Lapide, Cornelius a. *The Great Commentary.* 8 vols. Translated by Thomas Mossman. 5th ed. London, 1893.

Machiavelli, Niccolò. *The Prince and the Discourses.* Introduction by Max Lerner. New York, 1950.

Melanchthon, Philip. *Liber de anima.* Vol. 13 of *Opera quae supersunt omnia.* 28 vols. Edited by Carolus Gottlieb Bretschneider. Corpus Reformatorum. Brunswick and Halle, 1834–60.

Milton, John. *Paradise Lost.* In *John Milton: Complete Poetry and Major Prose.* Edited by Merritt Y. Hughes. New York, 1957.

———. *Prose Selections.* Edited by Merritt Y. Hughes. New York, 1947.

Montaigne, Michel de. *The Complete Essays of Montaigne.* Translated by Donald M. Frame. Stanford, 1958.

Otto von Freising. *The Two Cities: A Chronicle of Universal History to the Year 1146 A.D.* Edited by Austin P. Evans and Charles Knapp. Translated by Charles C. Mierow. New York, 1928. Reprint. New York, 1966.

Perkins, William. *The Work of William Perkins.* Edited by Ian Breward. The Courtenay Library of Reformation Classics. Appleford, Eng., 1970.

Plato. *The Collected Dialogues of Plato.* Edited by Edith Hamilton and Huntington Cairns. Princeton, 1961.

Roper, William. *The Lyfe of Sir Thomas Moore, Knighte.* Edited by Elsie V. Hitchcock. Early English Texts Society. London, 1935.

Smith, Sir Thomas. *De republica Anglorum.* Edited by Mary Dewar. Cambridge Studies in the History and Theory of Politics. Cambridge, 1982.

Tyndale, William. *Doctrinal Treatises and Introductions to Different Portions of The Holy Scriptures.* Edited by Rev. Henry Walter. The Parker Society. Cambridge, 1848.

———. *Expositions and Notes on Sundry Portions of The Holy Scriptures.* Edited by Rev. Henry Walter. The Parker Society. Cambridge, 1849.

Valla, Laurentius (Lorenzo). *Elegantiarum libri sex.* In *Opera omnia.* 2 vols. Introduction by Eugenio Garin. Turin, 1962.

Vives, Juan Luis. *De anima et vita.* Basel, 1538. Reprint. Turin, 1959.

Whitgift, John. *Works.* 3 vols. Edited by Rev. John Ayre. The Parker Society. Cambridge, 1852.

SECONDARY SOURCES

Akrigg, G. P. V. *Jacobean Pageant or the Court of King James.* Cambridge, Mass., 1963.

Allen, Don Cameron. "Dean Donne Sets His Text." *English Literary History* 10 (1943): 208–29.

Allen, J. W. *English Political Thought, 1603–1660.* 2 vols. London, 1938.

———. *A History of Political Thought in the Sixteenth Century.* London, 1928.

Allison, C. F. *The Rise of Moralism: The Proclamation of the Gospel from Hooker to Baxter.* New York, 1966.

Archer, Stanley. *Richard Hooker.* Boston, 1983.

Armstrong, Brian G. *Calvinism and the Amyraut Heresy: Protestant Scholasticism and Humanism in Seventeenth-Century France.* Madison, 1969.

Baker, Derek, ed. *Reform and Reformation: England and the Continent, c. 1500–c. 1750.* Oxford, 1979.

———. *Sanctity and Secularity: The Church and the World.* Studies in Church History. Oxford, 1973.

Barbu, Zevedei. *Problems of Historical Psychology.* International Library of Sociology and Social Reconstruction. London, 1960.

Barfield, Owen. *Saving the Appearances: A Study in Idolatry.* New York, n.d.

Barker, Francis, et al., eds. *Literature, Politics, and Theory.* New Accents. London, 1986.

Battenhouse, Roy W. "The Grounds of Religious Toleration in the Thought of John Donne." *Church History* 11 (1942): 217–48.

Bauckham, Richard. "Hooker, Travers, and the Church of Rome in the 1580s." *Journal of Ecclesiastical History* 29 (1978): 37–50.

Bean, John C. "Comic Structure and the Humanizing of Kate in *The Taming of the Shrew.*" In *The Woman's Part: Feminist Criticism of Shakespeare.* Edited by Carolyn Ruth Swift Lenz, Gayle Greene, and Carol Thomas Neely, 65–78. Urbana, 1980.

Beilin, Elaine V. *Redeeming Eve: Women Writers of the English Renaissance.* Princeton, 1987.

Berman, Harold J. *Law and Revolution: The Formation of the Western Legal Tradition.* Cambridge, Mass., 1983.

Berry, Boyd M. *Process of Speech: Puritan Religious Writing and "Paradise Lost."* Baltimore, 1976.

Bethell, Samuel L. *The Cultural Revolution of the Seventeenth Century*. London, 1951.

Bloch, Chana. *Spelling the Word: George Herbert and the Bible*. Berkeley, 1985.

Bloch, Marc. *The Royal Touch: Sacred Monarchy and Scrofula in England and France*. Translated by J. E. Anderson. London, 1973.

Blumenberg, Hans. *The Legitimacy of the Modern Age*. Translated by Robert M. Wallace. Studies in Contemporary German Social Thought. Cambridge, Mass., 1983.

Booty, John E. "Hooker and Anglicanism." In *Studies in Richard Hooker: Essays Preliminary to an Edition of His Works,* edited by W. Speed Hill, 207–39. Cleveland, 1972.

———. "Hooker's Understanding of the Presence of Christ in the Eucharist." In *The Divine Drama in History and Liturgy*. Edited by John E. Booty, 131–48. Pittsburgh Theological Monographs. Allison Park, Penn., 1984.

Booty, John E., ed. *The Divine Drama in History and Liturgy*. Pittsburgh Theological Monographs. Allison Park, Penn., 1984.

Bossy, John. "Blood and Baptism: Kinship, Community, and Christianity in Western Europe from the Fourteenth to the Seventeenth Centuries." In *Sanctity and Secularity: The Church and the World*. Edited by Derek Baker, 129–43. Studies in Church History. Oxford, 1973.

———. *Christianity in the West, 1400–1700*. Oxford, 1985.

Bouwsma, William J. *John Calvin: A Sixteenth-Century Portrait*. Oxford, 1988.

———. "The Two Faces of Renaissance Humanism: Stoicism and Augustinianism in Renaissance Thought." In *Itinerarium Italicum: The Profile of the Italian Renaissance in the Mirror of Its European Transformations*. Edited by Heiko A. Oberman with Thomas Brady, Jr., 3–60. Leiden, 1975.

Bredvold, Louis I. "The Religious Thought of Donne in Relation to Medieval and Later Traditions." In *Studies in Shakespeare, Milton, and Donne*. New York, 1925.

Brown, Paul. "'This Thing of Darkness I Acknowledge Mine': *The Tempest* and the Discourse of Colonialism." In *Political Shakespeare: New Essays in Cultural Materialism*. Edited by Jonathan Dollimore and Alan Sinfield, 48–71. Ithaca, 1985.

Brown, Peter. *Society and the Holy in Late Antiquity*. Berkeley, 1982.

Burtt, Edwin Arthur. *The Metaphysical Foundations of Modern Physical Science: A Historical and Critical Essay*. 2d ed. London, 1932.

Bynum, Caroline Walker. "The Body of Christ in the Later Middle Ages: A Reply to Leo Steinberg." *Renaissance Quarterly* 39 (1986): 399–439.

———. *Jesus as Mother: Studies in the Spirituality of the High Middle Ages*. Berkeley, 1982.

Carey, John. *John Donne: Life, Mind, and Art*. New York, 1981.

Cargill Thompson, W. D. J. "The Philosopher of the 'Politic Society': Richard Hooker as a Political Thinker." In *Studies in Richard Hooker: Essays Preliminary to an Edition of His Works*. Edited by W. Speed Hill, 3–76. Cleveland, 1972.

———. *Studies in the Reformation: Luther to Hooker.* Edited by C. W. Dugmore. London, 1980.

———. "The Two Regiments: The Continental Setting of William Tyndale's Political Thought." In *Reform and Reformation: England and the Continent, c. 1500–c. 1750.* Edited by Derek Baker, 17–33. Oxford, 1979.

Chadwick, Owen. *The Secularization of the European Mind in the Nineteenth Century.* Cambridge, 1975.

Chamberlin, John. *Increase and Multiply: Arts-of-Discourse Procedure in the Preaching of Donne.* Chapel Hill, 1976.

Collinson, Patrick. *The Religion of Protestants: The Church in English Society, 1559–1625.* Oxford, 1982.

Coolidge, John S. *The Pauline Renaissance in England: Puritanism and the Bible.* Oxford, 1970.

Courtney, William. "Nominalism and Late Medieval Religion." In *The Pursuit of Holiness in Late Medieval and Renaissance Religion.* Edited by Charles Trinkaus with Heiko A. Oberman, 37–43. Leiden, 1974.

Crewe, Jonathan V. "The *'Encomium Moriae'* of William Roper." *English Literary History* 55 (1988): 287–307.

Cross, Claire. "Churchmen and the Royal Supremacy." In *Church and Society in England: Henry VIII to James I.* Edited by Felicity Heal and Rosemary O'Day, 15–34. London, 1977.

Davies, Stevie. *Images of Kingship in "Paradise Lost": Milton's Politics and Christian Liberty.* Columbia, Mo., 1983.

Delumeau, Jean. *Catholicism between Luther and Voltaire: A New View of the Counter-Reformation.* Translated by Jeremy Moiser. London, 1977.

Dollimore, Jonathan. *Radical Tragedy: Religion, Ideology, and Power in the Drama of Shakespeare and His Contemporaries.* Chicago, 1984.

Dollimore, Jonathan, and Alan Sinfield, eds. *Political Shakespeare: New Essays in Cultural Materialism.* Ithaca, 1985.

Dubrow, Heather, and Richard Strier, eds. *The Historical Renaissance: New Essays on Tudor and Stuart Literature and Culture.* Chicago, 1988.

Dugmore, C. W., ed. *Studies in the Reformation: Luther to Hooker.* London, 1980.

Durkheim, Emile. *The Elementary Forms of the Religious Life.* Translated by Joseph Swain. New York, 1915.

Elton, Geoffrey R. *Studies in Tudor and Stuart Politics and Government.* 2 vols. Cambridge, 1974.

Endicott [Patterson], Annabel. "The Structure of George Herbert's *Temple:* A Reconsideration." *University of Toronto Quarterly* 34 (1965): 226–37.

Evans-Pritchard, E. E. *Theories of Primitive Religion.* Oxford, 1965.

Ezell, Margaret J. M. *The Patriarch's Wife: Literary Evidence and the History of the Family.* Chapel Hill, 1987.

Febvre, Lucien. *The Problem of Unbelief in the Sixteenth Century: The Religion of Rabelais.* Translated by Beatrice Gottlieb. Cambridge, Mass., 1982.

Ferguson, Arthur B. *Clio Unbound: Perception of the Social and Cultural Past in*

Renaissance England. Duke Monographs in Medieval and Renaissance Studies. Durham, 1979.

Ferguson, Margaret W., with Maureen Quilligan and Nancy J. Vickers. "Introduction." In *Rewriting the Renaissance: The Discourses of Sexual Difference in Early Modern Europe*. Edited by Margaret W. Ferguson, Maureen Quilligan, and Nancy J. Vickers, xv–xxxi. Chicago, 1986.

Ferguson, Margaret W., Maureen Quilligan, and Nancy J. Vickers, eds. *Rewriting the Renaissance: The Discourses of Sexual Difference in Early Modern Europe*. Chicago, 1986.

Ferry, Anne. *The "Inward" Language: Sonnets of Wyatt, Sidney, Shakespeare, Donne*. Chicago, 1983.

Figgis, John N. *The Divine Right of Kings*. 2d. ed. Cambridge, 1922.

Fish, Stanley. *The Living Temple: George Herbert and Catechizing*. Berkeley, 1978.

———. "Sequence and Meaning in Seventeenth-Century Narrative." In *To Tell a Story: Narrative Theory and Practice*, 59–76. Los Angeles, 1973.

Fish, Stanley, ed. *Seventeenth-Century Prose: Modern Essays in Criticism*. New York, 1971.

Foucault, Michel. *Discipline and Punish: The Birth of the Prison*. Translated by Alan Sheridan. New York, 1977.

———. *The Order of Things: An Archaeology of the Human Sciences*. New York, 1970.

French, Marilyn. *Shakespeare's Division of Experience*. New York, 1981.

Funkenstein, Amos. *Theology and the Scientific Imagination from the Middle Ages to the Seventeeth Century*. Princeton, 1986.

Fussner, F. Smith. *The Historical Revolution: English Historical Writing and Thought*. New York, 1962.

Gane, Erwin R. "The Exegetical Methods of Some Sixteenth-Century Anglican Preachers: Latimer, Jewel, Hooker, and Andrewes." *Andrews University Seminary Studies* 17 (1979): 23–38, 169–88.

Geertz, Clifford. *The Interpretation of Cultures*. New York, 1973.

———. *Local Knowledge: Further Essays in Interpretive Anthropology*. New York, 1983.

Gerrish, B. A. "The Lord's Supper in the Reformed Confessions." *Theology Today* 23 (1966): 224–43.

Gilbert, Sandra. "Patriarchal Poetry and Woman Readers: Reflections on Milton's Bogey." *Publications of the Modern Language Association* 93 (1978): 368–82.

Goez, Werner. *Translatio Imperii: Ein Beitrag zur Geschichte des Geschichtsdenkens und der politischen Theorien im Mittelalter und in der frühen Neuzeit*. Tübingen, 1958.

Goldberg, Jonathan. "Fatherly Authority: The Politics of Stuart Family Images." In *Rewriting the Renaissance: The Discourses of Sexual Difference in Early Modern Europe*. Edited by Margaret W. Ferguson, Maureen Quilligan, and Nancy J. Vickers, 3–32. Chicago, 1986.

———. *James I and the Politics of Literature: Jonson, Shakespeare, Donne, and Their Contemporaries.* Baltimore, 1983.

Grafton, Anthony. "Renaissance Readers and Ancient Texts: Comments on Some Commentaries." *Renaissance Quarterly* 38 (1985): 615–49.

Grant, Patrick. *The Transformation of Sin: Studies in Donne, Herbert, Vaughan, and Traherne.* Montreal, 1974.

Greenblatt, Stephen. "Invisible Bullets: Renaissance Authority and Its Subversion, *Henry IV* and *Henry V.*" In *Political Shakespeare: New Essays in Cultural Materialism.* Edited by Jonathan Dollimore and Alan Sinfield, 18–47. Ithaca, 1985.

———. "Psychoanalysis and Renaissance Culture." In *Literary Theory/Renaissance Texts.* Edited by Patricia Parker and David Quint, 210–24. Baltimore, 1986.

———. *Renaissance Self-Fashioning from More to Shakespeare.* Chicago, 1980.

———. *Shakespearean Negotiations: The Circulation of Social Energy in Renaissance England.* New Historicism: Studies in Cultural Poetics. Berkeley, 1988.

Greenblatt, Stephen, ed. *The Forms of Power and the Power of Forms in the Renaissance.* Genre Special Topics 7. Norman, Okla., 1982.

Greenleaf, W. H. *Order, Empiricism, and Politics: Two Traditions of English Political Thought, 1500–1700.* London, 1964.

Grislis, Egil. "The Hermeneutical Problem of Richard Hooker." In *Studies in Richard Hooker: Essays Preliminary to an Edition of His Works.* Edited by W. Speed Hill, 159–206. Cleveland, 1972.

Harris, Victor. "Allegory to Analogy in the Interpretation of Scriptures." *Philological Quarterly* 45 (1966): 1–23.

Heal, Felicity. "Economic Problems of the Clergy." In *Church and Society in England: Henry VIII to James I.* Edited by Felicity Heal and Rosemary O'Day, 99–118. London, 1977.

Heal, Felicity, and Rosemary O'Day, eds. *Church and Society in England: Henry VIII to James I.* London, 1977.

Hill, Christopher. *The Collected Essays of Christopher Hill: Religion and Politics in Seventeenth-Century England.* Amherst, 1986.

———. *Economic Problems of the Church from Archbishop Whitgift to the Long Parliament.* Oxford, 1956.

———. *Intellectual Origins of the English Revolution.* Oxford, 1965.

Hill, W. Speed. "The Evolution of Hooker's *Laws of Ecclesiastical Polity.*" In *Studies in Richard Hooker: Essays Preliminary to an Edition of His Works.* Edited by W. Speed Hill, 117–58. Cleveland, 1972.

Hill, W. Speed, ed. *Studies in Richard Hooker: Essays Preliminary to an Edition of His Works.* Cleveland, 1972.

Hillerdal, Gunnar. *Reason and Revelation in Richard Hooker.* Acta Universitatis Lundensis, new series, 54 (1959–61): 1–150.

Horton, Robin. "African Traditional Thought and Western Science." In *Rationality.* Edited by Bryan R. Wilson, 131–71. Evanston, 1970.

Hovey, Kenneth Alan. "Church History in 'The Church.'" *George Herbert Journal* 6 (1982): 1–14.

———. "'Wheel'd about . . . into Amen': 'The Church Militant' on Its Own Terms." *George Herbert Journal* 10 (1986): 71–84.

Howard, Jean. "The New Historicism in Renaissance Studies." *English Literary Renaissance* 16 (1986): 13–43.

Howard, Jean, and Marion O'Connor, eds. *Shakespeare Reproduced: the Text in History and Ideology*. New York, 1987.

Jameson, Fredric. "Religion and Ideology: A Political Reading of *Paradise Lost*." In *Literature, Politics and Theory*. Edited by Francis Barker et al., 35–56. New Accents. London, 1986.

Jessopp, Augustus. *John Donne, Sometime Dean of St. Paul's, A.D. 1621–31*. New York, 1972.

Johnson, A. R. "Hebrew Conceptions of Kingship." In *Myth, Ritual, and Kingship: Essays on the Theory and Practice of Kingship in the Ancient Near East and in Israel*. Edited by S. H. Hooke, 204–35. Oxford, 1958.

Johnson, Lee Ann. "The Relationship of 'The Church Militant' to *The Temple*." *Studies in Philology* 68 (1971): 200–206.

Kahn, Coppélia. "The Absent Mother in *King Lear*." In *Rewriting the Renaissance: The Discourses of Sexual Difference in Early Modern Europe*. Edited by Margaret W. Ferguson, Maureen Quilligan, and Nancy J. Vickers, 33–49. Chicago, 1986.

———. *Man's Estate: Masculine Identity in Shakespeare*. Berkeley, 1981.

Kantorowicz, Ernst H. *The King's Two Bodies: A Study in Mediaeval Political Theology*. Princeton, 1957.

———. "*Deus per Naturam, Deus per Gratiam:* A Note on Medieval Political Theology," 121–37; "Kingship under the Impact of Scientific Jurisprudence," 151–66; and "Mysteries of State: An Absolutist Concept and Its Late Medieval Origins," 381–98. In *Selected Studies*. Locust Valley, N.Y., 1965.

Kelley, Donald R. *The Beginning of Ideology: Consciousness and Society in the French Reformation*. Cambridge, 1981.

———. *Foundations of Modern Historical Scholarship: Language, Law, and History in the French Renaissance*. New York, 1970.

Kelso, Ruth. *Doctrine for the Lady of the Renaissance*. Urbana, 1956.

Kendall, R. T. *Calvin and English Calvinism to 1649*. Oxford Theological Monographs. Oxford, 1979.

Kingdon, Robert M., ed. *Transition and Revolution: Problems and Issues of European Renaissance and Reformation History*. Minneapolis, 1974.

Knott, John, Jr. *The Sword of the Spirit: Puritan Responses to the Bible*. Chicago, 1980.

Lake, Peter G. *Anglicans and Puritans? Presbyterianism and English Conformist Thought from Whitgift to Hooker*. London, 1988.

———. "Calvinism and the English Church, 1570–1635." *Past and Present* 114 (1987): 32–76.

———. *Moderate Puritans and the Elizabethan Church*. Cambridge, 1982.

Lamont, William, and Sybil Oldfield, eds. *Politics, Religion, and Literature in the Seventeenth Century*. London, 1975.

Laslett, Peter. *The World We Have Lost: Further Explored*. 3d ed. London, 1983.

Leeuw, G. van der. *Religion in Essence and Manifestation*. 2 vols. Translated by J. E. Turner. London, 1938. Reprint. New York, 1963.

Lenz, Carolyn Ruth Swift, Gayle Greene, and Carol Thomas Neely, eds. *The Woman's Part: Feminist Criticism of Shakespeare*. Urbana, 1980.

Leverenz, David. "The Woman in *Hamlet:* An Interpersonal View." In *Representing Shakespeare: New Psychoanalytic Essays*. Edited by Murray M. Schwartz and Coppélia Kahn, 110–28. Baltimore, 1980.

Levy-Bruhl, Lucien. *How Natives Think*. Translated by Lilian A. Clare. New York, 1979.

———. *The "Soul" of the Primitive*. Translated by Lilian A. Clare. New York, 1966.

Lewalski, Barbara. "Milton on Women—Yet Once More." *Milton Studies* 6 (1974): 4–20.

Little, David. *Protestant Poetics and the Seventeenth-Century Religious Lyric*. Princeton, 1979.

———. *Religion, Order, and Law: A Study in Pre-Revolutionary England*. Oxford, 1970.

Lloyd, G. E. R. *Magic, Reason, and Experience: Studies in the Origin and Development of Greek Science*. Cambridge, 1979.

Long, Charles H. *Significations: Signs, Symbols, and Images in the Interpretation of Religion*. Philadelphia, 1986.

Lubac, Henri de, S.J. *Exégèse médiévale: les quatre sens de l'écriture*. 4 vols. N.p., 1964.

Luoma, John K. "Who Owns the Fathers? Hooker and Cartwright on the Authority of the Primitive Church." *Sixteenth-Century Journal* 8 (1977): 45–59.

McColley, Diane. *Milton's Eve*. Urbana, 1983.

Macfarlane, Alan. *Marriage and Love in England: Modes of Reproduction, 1300–1840*. Oxford, 1986.

McGee, James S. *The Godly Man in Stuart England: Anglicans, Puritans, and the Two Tables, 1620–1670*. New Haven, 1976.

MacIntyre, Alasdair. *After Virtue: A Study in Moral Theory*. Notre Dame, 1981.

McKenzie, John. *Guilt: Its Meaning and Significance*. New York, 1962.

Maclean, Ian. "The Interpretation of Natural Signs: Cardano's *De subtilitate* versus Scaliger's *Exercitationes*." In *Occult and Scientific Mentalities in the Renaissance*. Edited and introduction by Brian Vickers, 231–52. Cambridge, 1984.

Macleane, Douglas. *Lancelot Andrewes and the Reaction*. London, 1910.

McLuskie, Kathleen. "The Patriarchal Bard: Feminist Criticism and Shakespeare: *King Lear* and *Measure for Measure*." In *Political Shakespeare: New Essays in Cultural Materialism*. Edited by Jonathan Dollimore and Alan Sinfield, 88–108. Ithaca, 1985.

Madsen, William G. *From Shadowy Types to Truth: Studies in Milton's Symbolism*. New Haven, 1968.

Malament, Barbara, ed. *After the Reformation: Essays in Honor of J.H. Hexter*. Manchester, 1980.

Marcus, Leah S. *Childhood and Cultural Despair: A Theme and Variations in Seventeenth-Century Literature*. Pittsburgh, 1978.

Miller, Perry. *The New England Mind: The Seventeenth Century*. New York, 1939. Reprint. Boston, 1961.

Minogue, Kenneth. *Alien Powers: The Pure Theory of Ideology*. New York, 1985.

Mueller, William R. *John Donne: Preacher*. Princeton, 1962.

Mulligan, Lotte. "'Reason,' 'Right Reason,' and 'Revelation' in Mid-Seventeenth-Century England." In *Occult and Scientific Mentalities in the Renaissance*. Edited and introduction by Brian Vickers, 375–401. Cambridge, 1984.

Munz, Peter. *The Place of Hooker in the History of Thought*. London, 1952.

Nijenhuis, Willem. *Adrianus Saravia (c. 1532–1613)*. Studies in the History of Christian Thought. Leiden, 1980.

Norbrook, David. *Poetry and Politics in the English Renaissance*. London, 1984.

Novy, Marianne. *Love's Argument: Gender Relations in Shakespeare*. Chapel Hill, 1984.

Nygren, Anders. *Agape and Eros: The History of the Christian Idea of Love*. 2 vols. Translated by Philip Watson. London, 1939.

Oakley, Francis. *Omnipotence, Covenant, and Order: An Excursion in the History of Ideas from Abelard to Leibniz*. Ithaca, 1984.

Oberman, Heiko A. "The Shape of Late Medieval Thought: The Birthpangs of the Modern Era." In *The Pursuit of Holiness in Late Medieval and Renaissance Religion*. Edited by Charles Trinkaus with Heiko A. Oberman, 12–13. Leiden, 1974.

———. "*Via antiqua* and *Via moderna:* Late Medieval Prolegomena to Early Reformation Thought." *Journal of the History of Ideas* 48 (1987): 23–40.

Oberman, Heiko A., with Thomas Brady, Jr., eds. *Itinerarium Italicum: The Profile of the Italian Renaissance in the Mirror of Its European Transformations*. Leiden, 1975.

Orgel, Stephen. "Making Greatness Familiar." In *The Forms of Power and the Power of Forms*. Edited by Stephen Greenblatt. Genre Special Topics 7, 41–48. Norman, Okla., 1982.

———. "Prospero's Wife." In *Rewriting the Renaissance: The Discourses of Sexual Difference in Early Modern Europe*. Edited by Margaret W. Ferguson, Maureen Quilligan, Nancy J. Vickers, 50–64. Chicago, 1986.

———. "The Spectacles of State." In *Persons in Groups: Social Behavior as Identity Formation in Medieval and Renaissance Europe*. Edited by Richard Trexler. Medieval and Renaissance Texts and Studies, 101–21. Binghamton, N.Y., 1985.

Otto, Rudolph. *The Idea of the Holy*. Translated by John W. Harvey. New York, 1958.

Owen, Trevor A. *Lancelot Andrewes*. Boston, 1981.

Ozment, Steven. "Luther and the Late Middle Ages: The Formation of Reformation Thought." In *Transition and Revolution: Problems and Issues of European Renaissance and Reformation History*. Edited by Robert M. Kingdon, 109–52. Minneapolis, 1974.

———. *When Fathers Ruled: Family Life in Reformation Europe*. Cambridge, Mass., 1983.

Painter, Borden W. "Anglican Terminology in Recent Tudor and Stuart Historiography." *Anglican and Episcopal History* 56 (1987): 237–49.

Panofsky, Erwin. *Renaissance and Renascences in Western Art*. New York, 1972.

Parker, Patricia, and David Quint, eds. *Literary Theory/Renaissance Texts*. Baltimore, 1986.

Parker, T. H. L. *Calvin's New Testament Commentaries*. Grand Rapids, Mich., 1971.

Pattison, Mark. *Isaac Casaubon, 1559–1614*. London, 1875.

Pearlman, E. "George Herbert's God." *English Literary Renaissance* 13 (1983): 88–112.

Pechter, Edward. "The New Historicism and Its Discontents: Politicizing Renaissance Drama." *Publications of the Modern Language Association* 102 (1987): 292–303.

Pelikan, Jaroslav. *The Christian Tradition: A History of the Development of Doctrine*. 5 vols. Vol. 4, *Reformation of Church and Dogma, 1300–1700*. Chicago, 1984.

Pocock, J. G. A. "The Origins of the Study of the Past: A Comparative Approach." *Comparative Studies in Society and History* 4 (1961–62): 209–46.

Pollock, Linda A. *Forgotten Children: Parent-Child Relations from 1500 to 1900*. Cambridge, 1983.

Preus, James Samuel. *From Shadow to Promise: Old Testament Interpretation from Augustine to the Young Luther*. Cambridge, Mass., 1969.

Quinn, Dennis. "John Donne's Principles of Biblical Exegesis." *Journal of English and Germanic Philology* 61 (1962): 313–29.

Rebholz, Ronald. *The Life of Fulke Greville, First Lord Brooke*. Oxford, 1971.

Reidy, Maurice F., S.J. *Bishop Lancelot Andrewes, Jacobean Court Preacher: A Study in Early-Seventeenth-Century Religious Thought*. Chicago, 1955.

Reiss, Timothy J. *The Discourse of Modernism*. Ithaca, 1982.

Riviere, Joan, and Melanie Klein. *Love, Hate, and Reparation*. New York, 1964.

Russell, Conrad, ed. *The Origins of the English Civil War*. New York, 1973.

Schochet, Gordon J. *Patriarchalism in Political Thought: The Authoritarian Family and Political Speculation and Attitudes Especially in Seventeenth-Century England*. Oxford, 1975.

Schoenfeldt, Michael. "Standing on Ceremony: The Comedy of Manners in Herbert's 'Love (III).' " In "*Bright Shootes of Everlastingnesse*": *The Seventeenth-Century Religious Lyric*. Edited by Claude J. Summers and Ted-Larry Pebworth, 116–33. Columbia, Mo., 1987.

———. "'Subject to Ev'ry Mounters Bended Knee': Herbert and Authority." In *The Historical Renaissance: New Essays on Tudor and Stuart Literature and*

Culture. Edited by Heather Dubrow and Richard Strier, 242–69. Chicago, 1988.

———. "Submission and Assertion: The 'Double Motion' of Herbert's 'Dedication.'" *John Donne Journal* 2 (1983): 39–47.

Schwartz, Murray M., and Coppélia Kahn, eds. *Representing Shakespeare: New Psychoanalytic Essays*. Baltimore, 1980.

Sessions, William A. "Abandonment and the English Religious Lyric in the Seventeenth Century." In *"Bright Shootes of Everlastingnesse": The Seventeenth-Century Religious Lyric*. Edited by Claude J. Summers and Ted-Larry Pebworth, 1–19. Columbia, Mo., 1987.

Shils, Edward. *The Intellectuals and the Powers and Other Essays*. Chicago, 1972.

Shuger, Debora. *Sacred Rhetoric: The Christian Grand Style in the English Renaissance*. Princeton, 1988.

Singleton, Marion White. *God's Courtier: Configuring a Different Grace in George Herbert's "Temple."* Cambridge, 1987.

Sisson, C. J. *The Judicious Marriage of Mr. Hooker and the Birth of "The Laws of Ecclesiastical Polity."* Cambridge, 1940. Reprint. New York, 1974.

Skinner, Quentin. *The Foundations of Modern Political Thought*. 2 vols. Cambridge, 1978.

———. "Meaning and Understanding in the History of Ideas." *History and Theory* 8 (1969): 3–53.

———. "The Origins of the Calvinist Theory of Revolution." In *After the Reformation: Essays in Honour of J.H. Hexter*. Edited by Barbara Malament, 309–30. Manchester, Eng., 1980.

Smalley, Beryl. *The Study of the Bible in the Middle Ages*. Oxford, 1941.

Smuts, R. Malcolm. *Court Culture and the Origins of a Royalist Tradition in Early Stuart England*. Philadelphia, 1987.

Snell, Bruno. *The Discovery of the Mind in Greek Philosophy and Literature*. Translated by T. G. Rosenmeyer. New York, 1982.

Sommerville, J. P. *Politics and Ideology in England, 1603–1640*. London, 1986.

Sorge, Thomas. "The Failure of Orthodoxy in *Coriolanus*." In *Shakespeare Reproduced: The Text in History and Ideology*. Edited by Jean Howard and Marion O'Connor, 225–39. New York, 1987.

Stachniewski, John. "The Despair of Donne's Holy Sonnets." *English Literary History* 48 (1981): 677–705.

Stallybrass, Peter. "Patriarchal Territories: The Body Enclosed." In *Rewriting the Renaissance: The Discourses of Sexual Difference in Early Modern Europe*. Edited by Margaret W. Ferguson, Maureen Quilligan, Nancy J. Vickers, 123–42. Chicago, 1986.

Stallybrass, Peter, and Allon White. *The Politics and Poetics of Transgression*. Ithaca, 1986.

Stone, Lawrence. *The Causes of the English Revolution, 1629–1642*. New York, 1972.

———. *The Crisis of the Aristocracy, 1558–1641*. Abridged ed. London, 1967.

———. *The Family, Sex, and Marriage in England, 1500–1800*. Abridged ed. New York, 1977.

Strier, Richard. *Love Known: Theology and Experience in George Herbert's Poetry*. Chicago, 1983.

———. "Sanctifying the Aristocracy: 'Devout Humanism' in François de Sales, John Donne, and George Herbert." *Journal of Religion* 69 (1989): 36–58.

Summers, Claude J., and Ted-Larry Pebworth, eds. *"Bright Shootes of Everlastingnesse": The Seventeenth-Century Religious Lyric*. Columbia, Mo., 1987.

Summers, Joseph H. *George Herbert: His Religion and Art*. Cambridge, Mass., 1954.

———. *The Muse's Method: An Introduction to "Paradise Lost."* Cambridge, Mass., 1962.

Tennenhouse, Leonard. "Strategies of State and Political Plays: *A Mid-Summer Night's Dream, Henry IV, Henry V, Henry VIII*." In *Political Shakespeare: New Essays in Cultural Materialism*. Edited by Jonathan Dollimore and Alan Sinfield, 109–28. Ithaca, 1985.

Thickstun, Margaret Olofson. *Fictions of the Feminine: Puritan Doctrine and the Representation of Women*. Ithaca, 1988.

Thomas, Keith. *Religion and the Decline of Magic: Studies in Popular Beliefs in Sixteenth- and Seventeenth-Century England*. London, 1971.

Tierney, Brian. *Religion, Law, and the Growth of Constitutional Thought, 1150–1650*. Cambridge, 1982.

Tillich, Paul. *A History of Christian Thought from Its Judaic and Hellenistic Origins to Existentialism*. Edited by Carl Braaten. New York, 1967.

Trexler, Richard, ed. *Persons in Groups: Social Behavior as Identity Formation in Medieval and Renaissance Europe*. Medieval and Renaissance Texts and Studies. Binghamton, N.Y., 1985.

Trinkaus, Charles. *The Scope of Renaissance Humanism*. Ann Arbor, 1983.

Trinkaus, Charles, with Heiko A. Oberman, eds. *The Pursuit of Holiness in Late Medieval and Renaissance Religion*. Leiden, 1974.

Tulloch, John. *Rational Theology and Christian Philosophy in England in the Seventeenth Century*. 2 vols. Edinburgh, 1872.

Turner, Bryan S. *The Body and Society: Explorations in Social Theory*. Oxford, 1984.

Tyacke, Nicholas. *Anti-Calvinists: The Rise of English Arminianism, c. 1590–1640*. Oxford Historical Monographs. Oxford, 1987.

———. "Puritanism, Arminianism, and Counter-Revolution." In *The Origins of the English Civil War*. Edited by Conrad Russell, 119–43. New York, 1973.

———. "The Rise of Arminianism Reconsidered." *Past and Present* 115 (1987): 201–16.

Veith, Gene Edward, Jr. *Reformation Spirituality: The Religion of George Herbert*. London, 1985.

Vergote, Antoine, and Alvaro Tamayo. *The Parental Figures and the Representation of God: A Psychological and Cross-Cultural Study*. Religion and Society. The Hague, 1981.

Vickers, Brian. "Analogy versus Identity: The Rejection of Occult Symbolism, 1580–1680." In *Occult and Scientific Mentalities in the Renaissance*. Edited and introduction by Brian Vickers, 95–163. Cambridge, 1984.

Vickers, Brian, ed. *Occult and Scientific Mentalities in the Renaissance*. Cambridge, 1984.

Voegelin, Eric. *Order and History*. 5 vols. Vol. 1, *Israel and Revelation*. Baton Rouge, 1956.

Waswo, Richard. *Language and Meaning in the Renaissance*. Princeton, 1987.

Webber, Joan. "Celebration of Word and World in Lancelot Andrewes's Style." In *Seventeenth-Century Prose: Modern Essays in Criticism*. Edited by Stanley Fish, 336–52. New York, 1971.

———. *The Eloquent "I": Style and Self in Seventeenth-Century Prose*. Madison, 1968.

———. "The Politics of Poetry: Feminism and *Paradise Lost*." *Milton Studies* 14 (1980): 3–24.

Weinberg, Bernard. *A History of Literary Criticism in the Italian Renaissance*. 2 vols. Chicago, 1963.

Welsby, Paul A. *Lancelot Andrewes, 1555–1626*. London, 1958.

Whigham, Frank. *Ambition and Privilege: The Social Tropes of Elizabethan Courtesy Theory*. Berkeley, 1984.

White, Peter. "A Rejoinder." *Past and Present* 115 (1987): 217–29.

Williams, Raymond. *Marxism and Literature*. Marxist Introductions. Oxford, 1977.

Wilson, Bryan R., ed. *Rationality*. Evanston, 1970.

Wolfson, Harry A. *The Philosophy of the Church Fathers*. 3d rev. ed. Cambridge, Mass., 1970.

Yates, Frances A. *Astrea: The Imperial Theme in the Sixteenth Century*. London, 1975.

———. *The Rosicrucian Enlightenment*. London, 1972.

Index

Compositor: Interactive Composition Corporation
Text: 10/13 Bembo
Display: Bembo
Printer: Edwards Brothers, Inc.
Binder: Edwards Brothers, Inc.